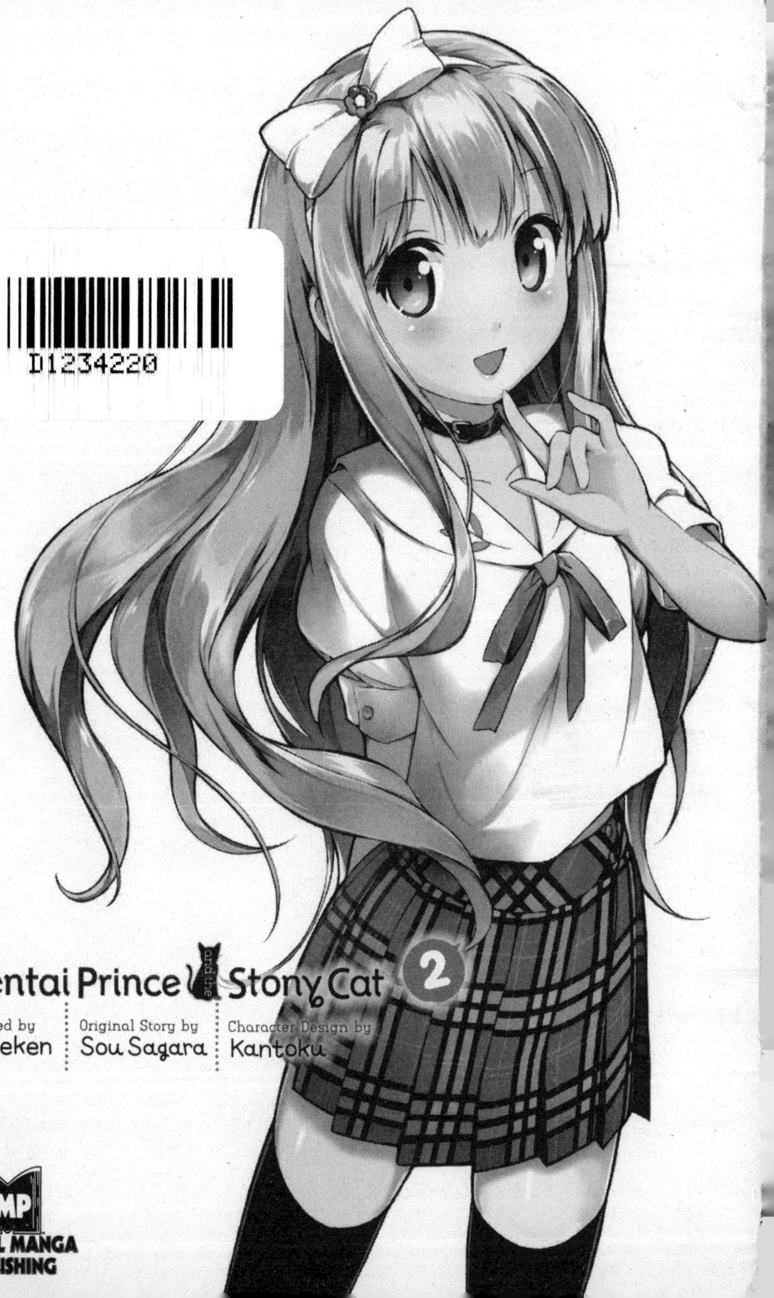

The Hentai Prince and the Stony Cat 2

Illustrated by
Okomeken

Original Story by
Sou Sagara

Character Design by
Kantoku

DMP
DIGITAL MANGA
PUBLISHING

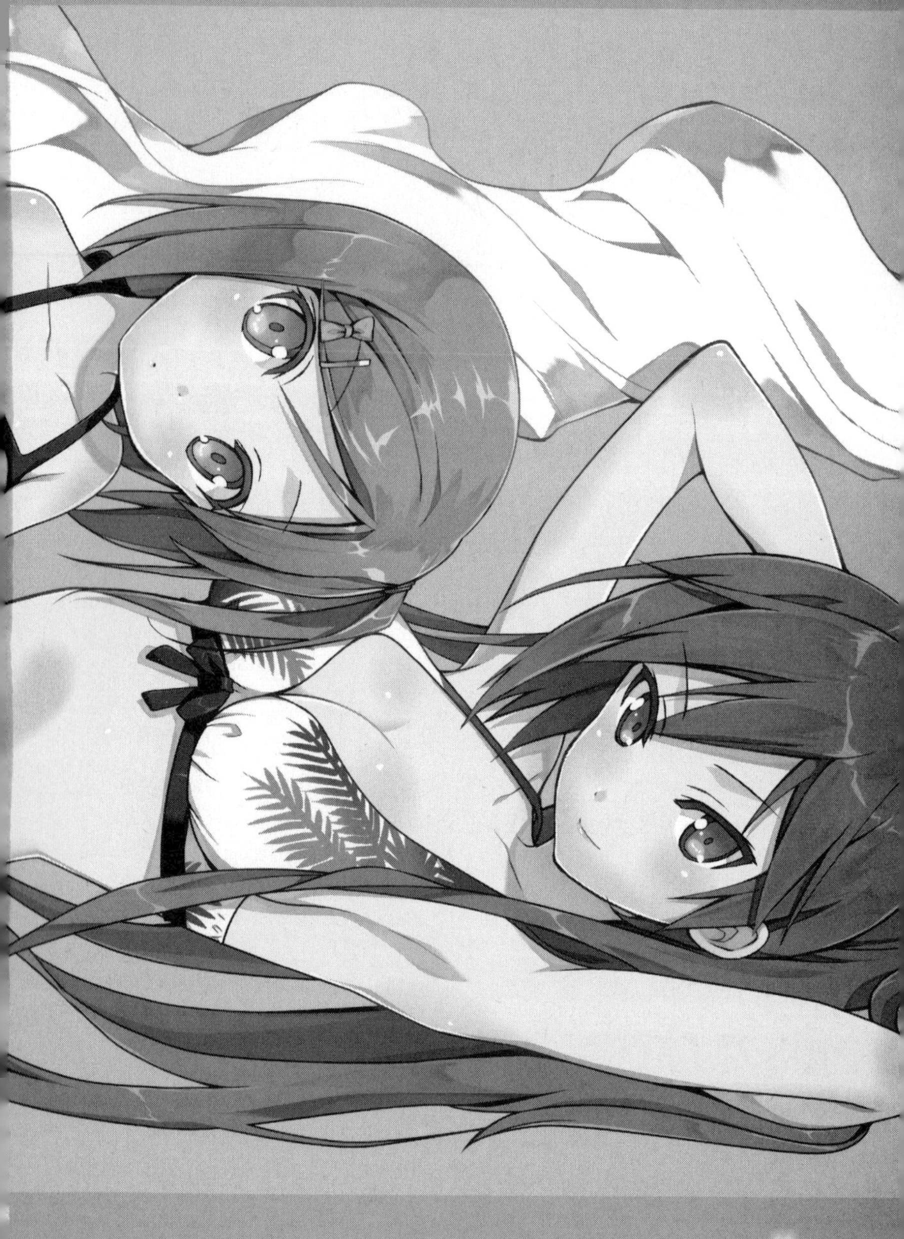

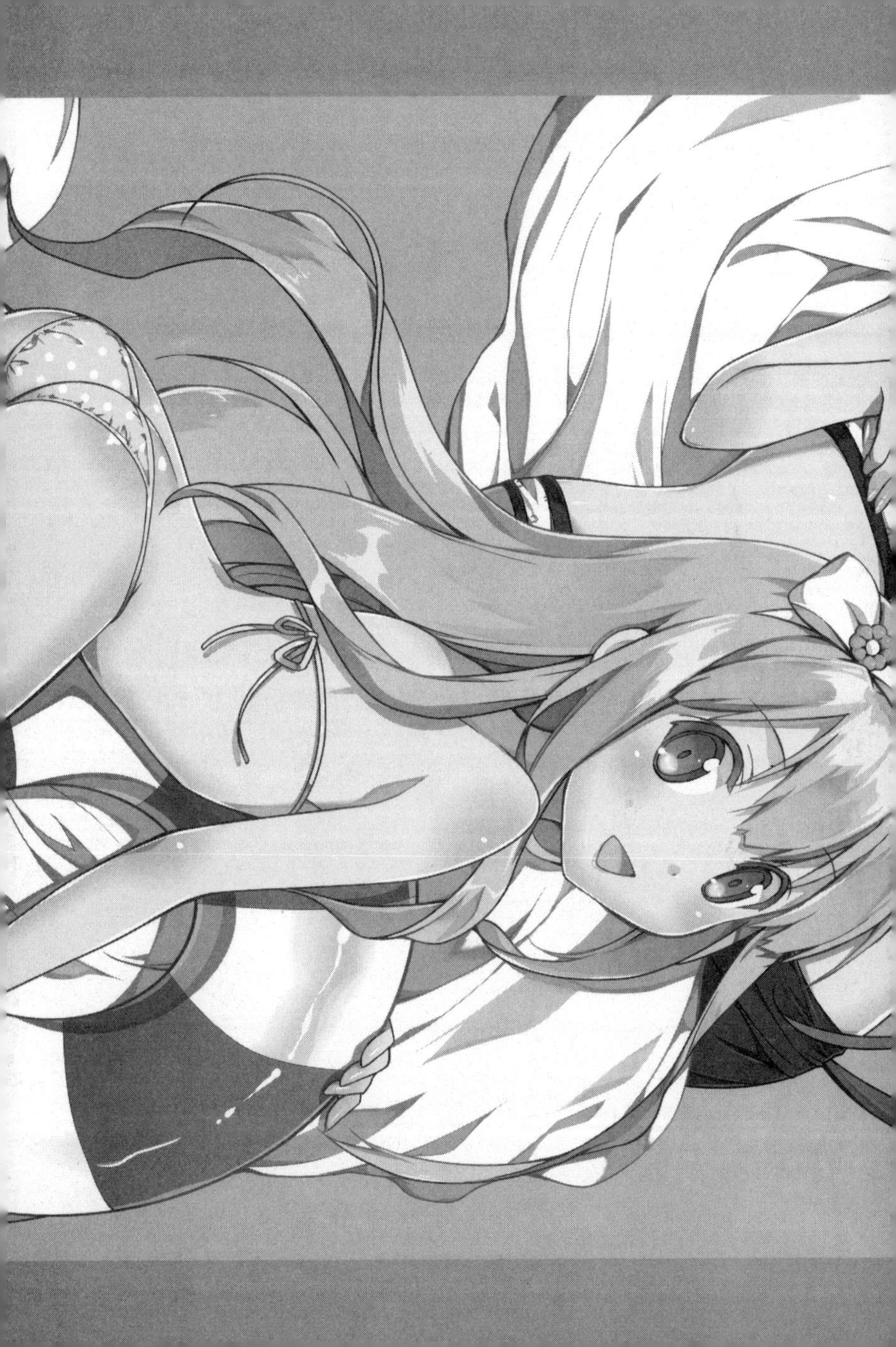

The Hentai Prince and the Stony Cat 2

Illustrated by
Okomeken

Original Story by
Sou Sagara

Character Design by
Kantoku

Contents

Translation:	Lea Hisatake	Japan Relations:	Yoshio Ogura
Lettering:	April Brown	Licensing / Sales & Distribution:	Yoko Tanigaki
Editing:	Stephanie Donnelly	Editor in Chief:	Fred Lui
Graphic Design:	Stephanie Han	Publisher:	Hikaru Sasahara

English Edition Published by
DIGITAL MANGA PUBLISHING
A division of DIGITAL MANGA, Inc.
1487 W 178th Street, Suite 300
Gardena, CA 90248

www.dmpbooks.com

First Edition: June 2014
ISBN-10: 1-56970-328-0
ISBN-13: 978-1-56970-328-1
1 3 5 7 9 10 8 6 4 2

Printed in Canada

Read digital titles at
www.emanga.com

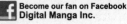
More print titles at
www.akadot.com

Become our fan on Facebook
Digital Manga Inc.

Follow us on Twitter
@DigitalManga

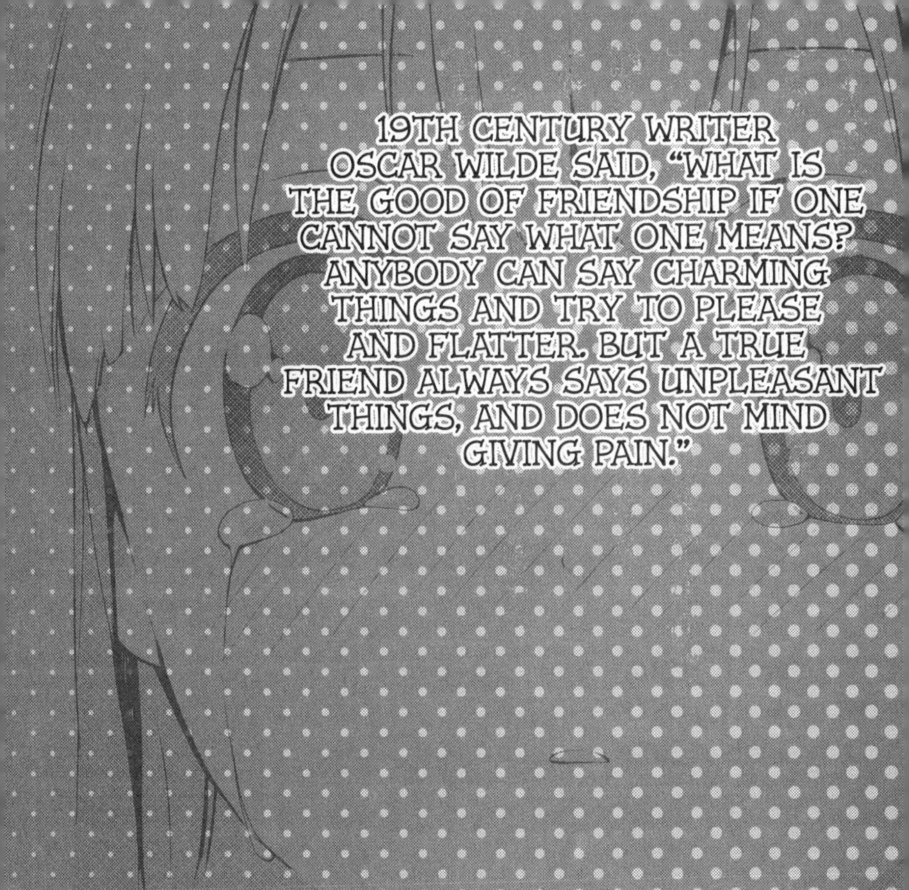
19TH CENTURY WRITER OSCAR WILDE SAID, "WHAT IS THE GOOD OF FRIENDSHIP IF ONE CANNOT SAY WHAT ONE MEANS? ANYBODY CAN SAY CHARMING THINGS AND TRY TO PLEASE AND FLATTER. BUT A TRUE FRIEND ALWAYS SAYS UNPLEASANT THINGS, AND DOES NOT MIND GIVING PAIN."

What is good of friendship if one cannot say what one means?

Anybody can say charming things

and try to pleasure and flatter,

but a true friend always says unpleasant things,

and does not mind giving pain.

The "HENTAI" prince and the stony cat. 2

The "HENTAI" prince and the stony cat.

変態王子と
笑わない猫。

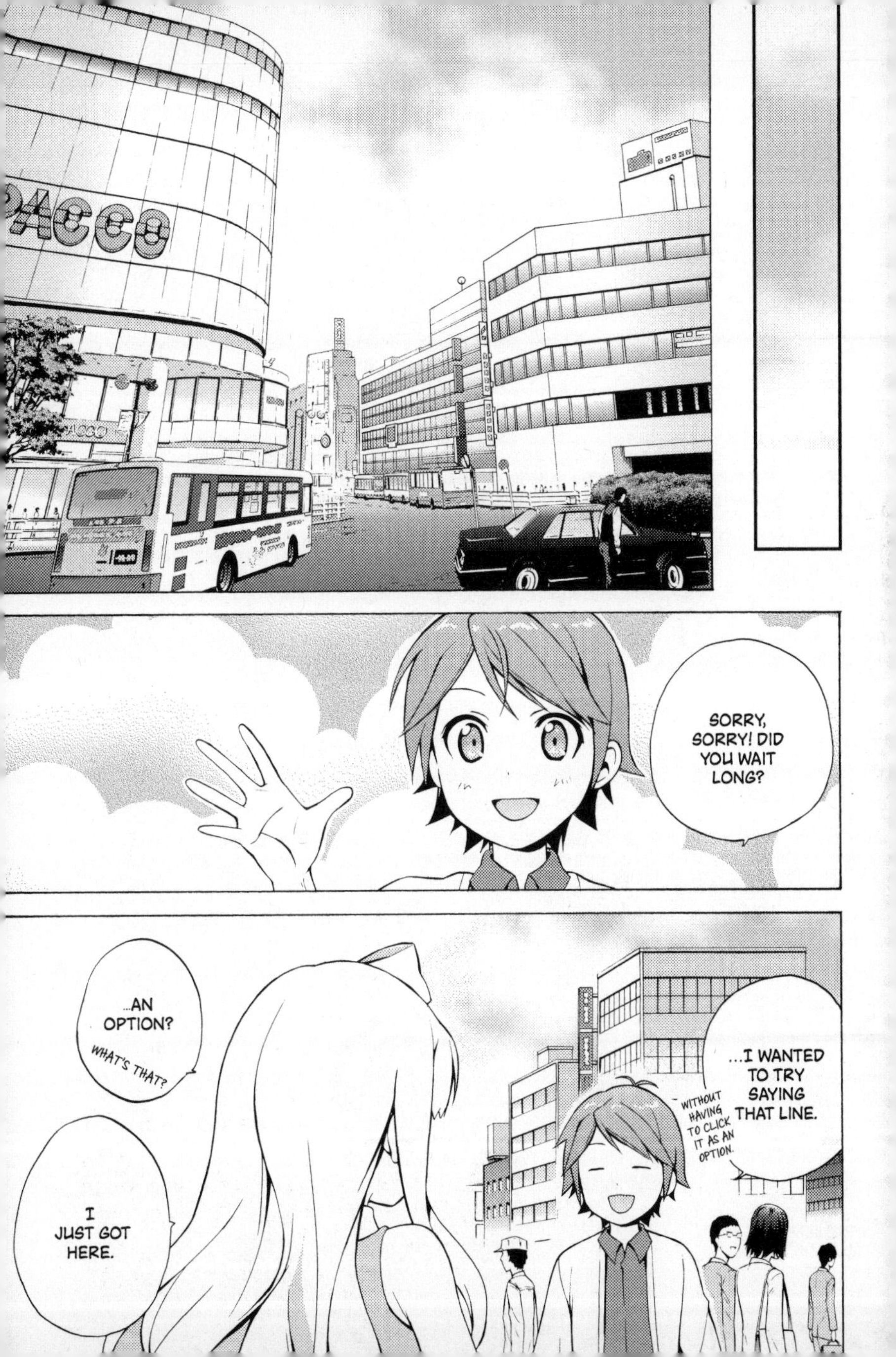
PACCO
SORRY, SORRY! DID YOU WAIT LONG?
...I WANTED TO TRY SAYING THAT LINE.
WITHOUT HAVING TO CLICK IT AS AN OPTION.
...AN OPTION?
WHAT'S THAT?
I JUST GOT HERE.

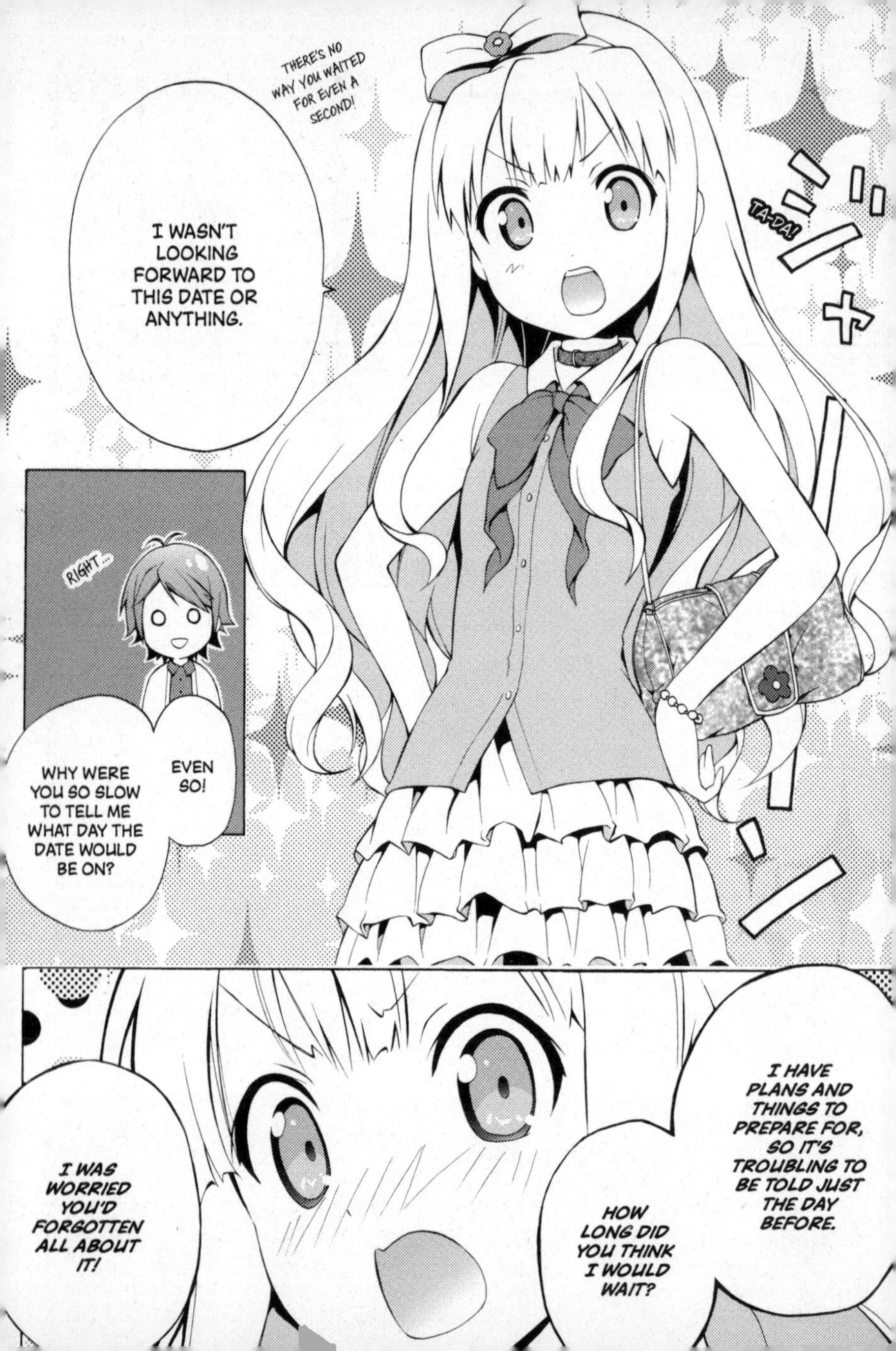
TA-DA!
THERE'S NO WAY YOU WAITED FOR EVEN A SECOND!
I WASN'T LOOKING FORWARD TO THIS DATE OR ANYTHING.
RIGHT...
EVEN SO!
WHY WERE YOU SO SLOW TO TELL ME WHAT DAY THE DATE WOULD BE ON?
I HAVE PLANS AND THINGS TO PREPARE FOR, SO IT'S TROUBLING TO BE TOLD JUST THE DAY BEFORE.
HOW LONG DID YOU THINK I WOULD WAIT?
I WAS WORRIED YOU'D FORGOTTEN ALL ABOUT IT!

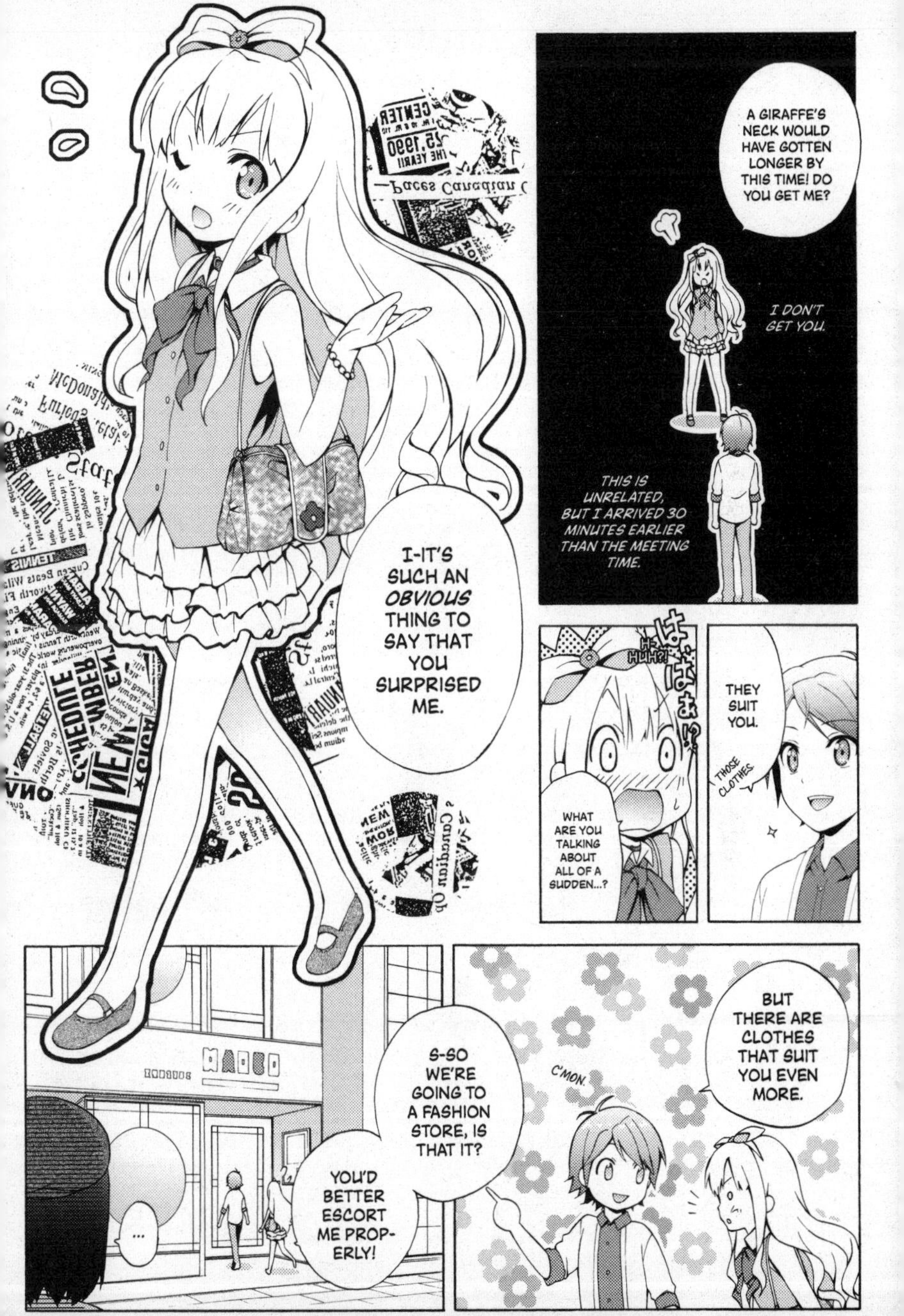
A GIRAFFE'S NECK WOULD HAVE GOTTEN LONGER BY THIS TIME! DO YOU GET ME?
I DON'T GET YOU.
THIS IS UNRELATED, BUT I ARRIVED 30 MINUTES EARLIER THAN THE MEETING TIME.
THEY SUIT YOU.
THOSE CLOTHES.
HUH?!
WHAT ARE YOU TALKING ABOUT ALL OF A SUDDEN...?
I-IT'S SUCH AN OBVIOUS THING TO SAY THAT YOU SURPRISED ME.
BUT THERE ARE CLOTHES THAT SUIT YOU EVEN MORE.
C'MON.
S-SO WE'RE GOING TO A FASHION STORE, IS THAT IT?
YOU'D BETTER ESCORT ME PROPERLY!
...

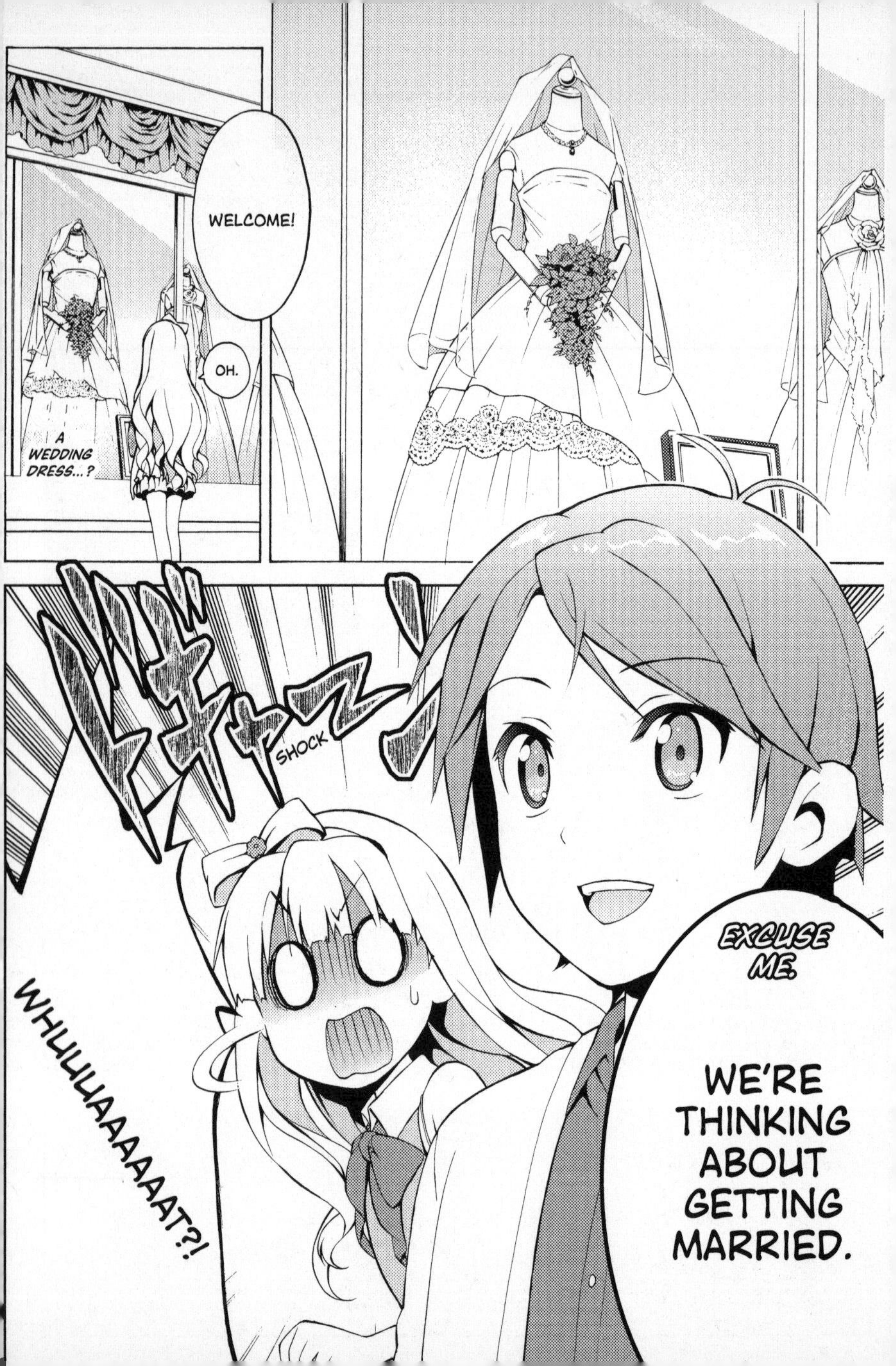

WELCOME!
OH.
A WEDDING DRESS...?
EXCUSE ME.
WE'RE THINKING ABOUT GETTING MARRIED.
SHOCK
WHUUUAAAAAAT?!

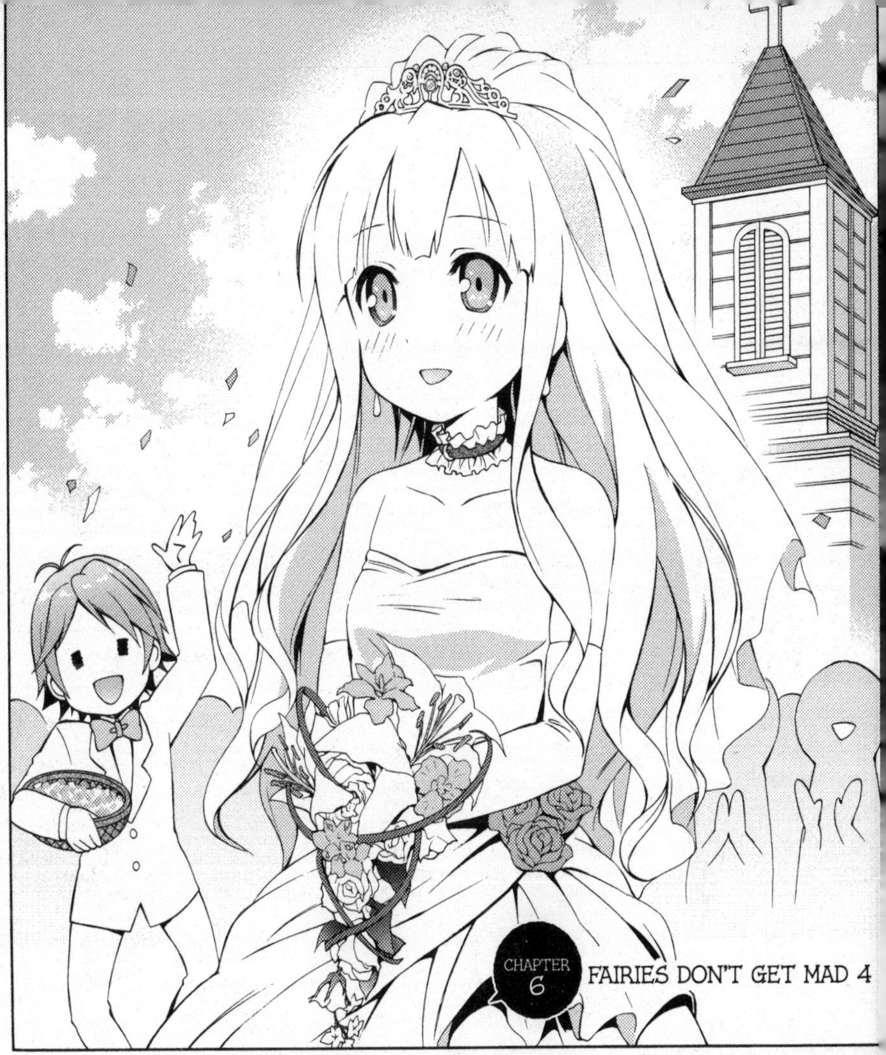
CHAPTER 6
FAIRIES DON'T GET MAD 4

I WANT TO TEACH AZUSA AZUKI...

IF SHE BECOMES A PRINCESS, PROBLEMS OF PEDIGREE AND POLITICS MIGHT COME OUT.

BUT IF SHE STAYS A COMMONER, SHE'LL HAVE THE JOY OF BEING ABLE TO MARRY THE PERSON SHE LIKES...

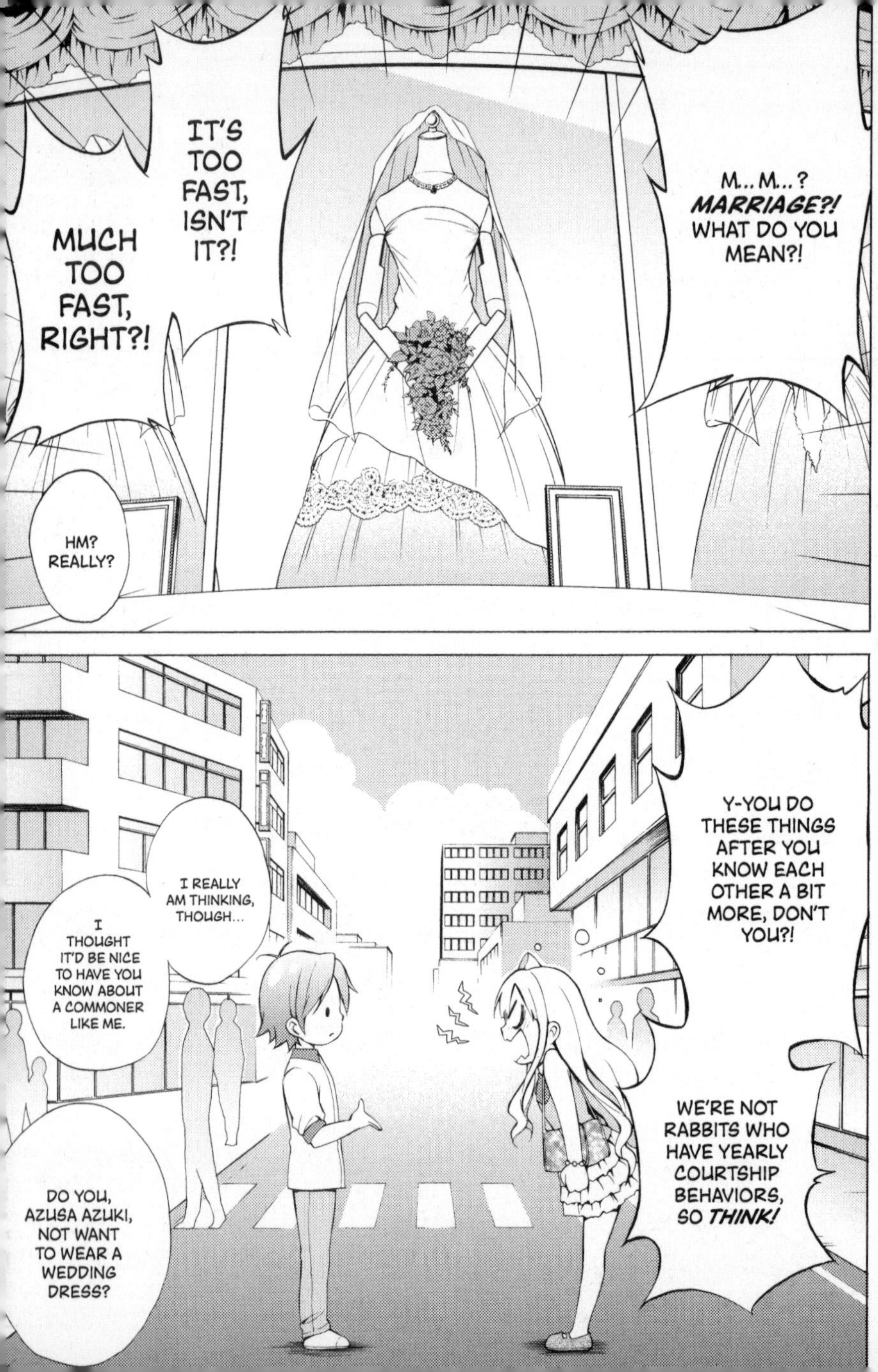
M...M...? *MARRIAGE?!* WHAT DO YOU MEAN?!
IT'S TOO FAST, ISN'T IT?!
MUCH TOO FAST, RIGHT?!
HM? REALLY?
Y-YOU DO THESE THINGS AFTER YOU KNOW EACH OTHER A BIT MORE, DON'T YOU?!
WE'RE NOT RABBITS WHO HAVE YEARLY COURTSHIP BEHAVIORS, SO *THINK!*
I REALLY AM THINKING, THOUGH...
I THOUGHT IT'D BE NICE TO HAVE YOU KNOW ABOUT A COMMONER LIKE ME.
DO YOU, AZUSA AZUKI, NOT WANT TO WEAR A WEDDING DRESS?

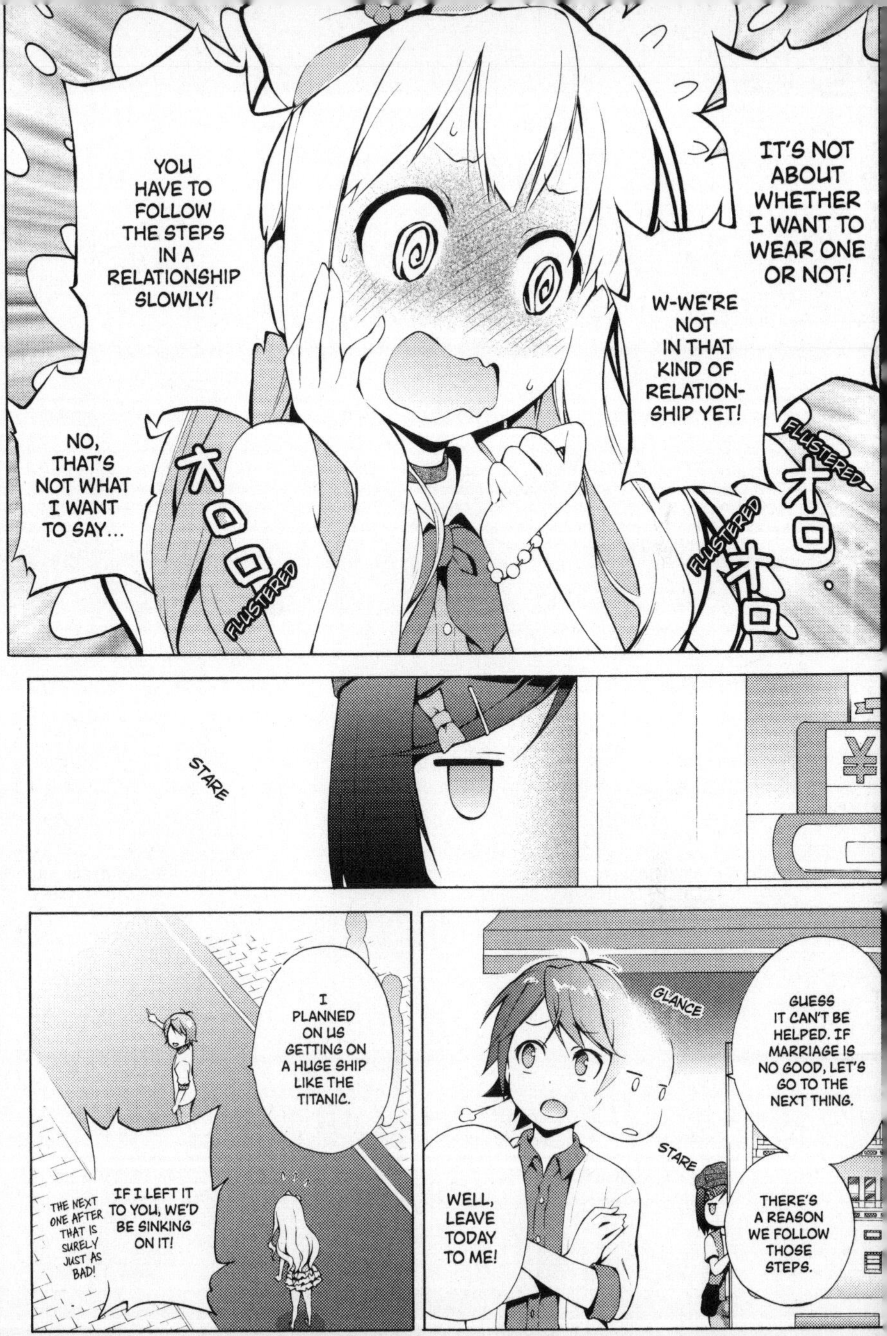
IT'S NOT ABOUT WHETHER I WANT TO WEAR ONE OR NOT!
W-WE'RE NOT IN THAT KIND OF RELATIONSHIP YET!
FLUSTERED
FLUSTERED
YOU HAVE TO FOLLOW THE STEPS IN A RELATIONSHIP SLOWLY!
NO, THAT'S NOT WHAT I WANT TO SAY...
FLUSTERED
STARE
GLANCE
GUESS IT CAN'T BE HELPED. IF MARRIAGE IS NO GOOD, LET'S GO TO THE NEXT THING.
STARE
THERE'S A REASON WE FOLLOW THOSE STEPS.
WELL, LEAVE TODAY TO ME!
I PLANNED ON US GETTING ON A HUGE SHIP LIKE THE TITANIC.
IF I LEFT IT TO YOU, WE'D BE SINKING ON IT!
THE NEXT ONE AFTER THAT IS SURELY JUST AS BAD!

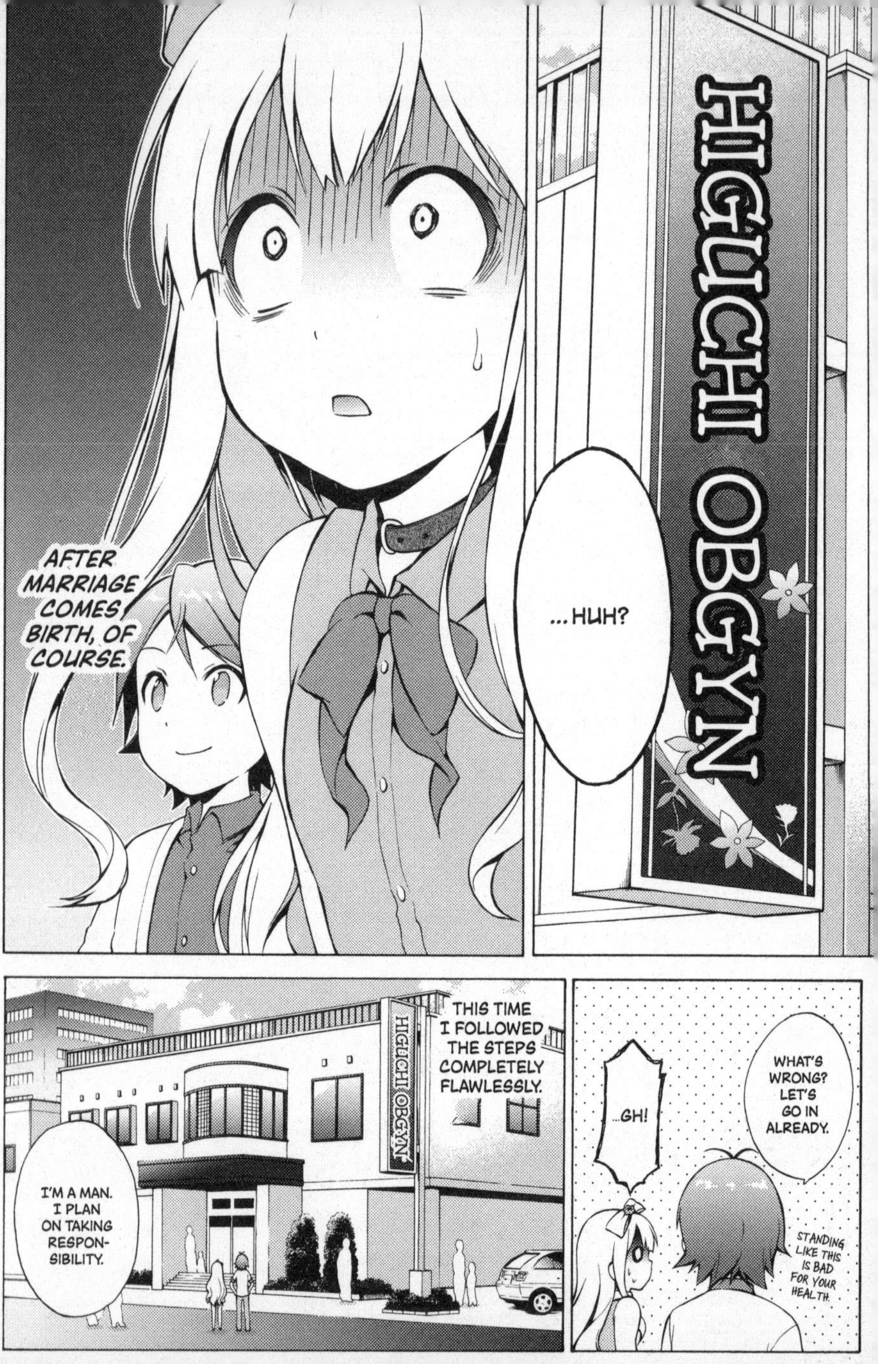
HIGUCHI OBGYN
...HUH?
AFTER MARRIAGE COMES BIRTH, OF COURSE.
WHAT'S WRONG? LET'S GO IN ALREADY.
...GH!
STANDING LIKE THIS IS BAD FOR YOUR HEALTH.
HIGUCHI OBGYN
THIS TIME I FOLLOWED THE STEPS COMPLETELY FLAWLESSLY.
I'M A MAN. I PLAN ON TAKING RESPONSIBILITY.

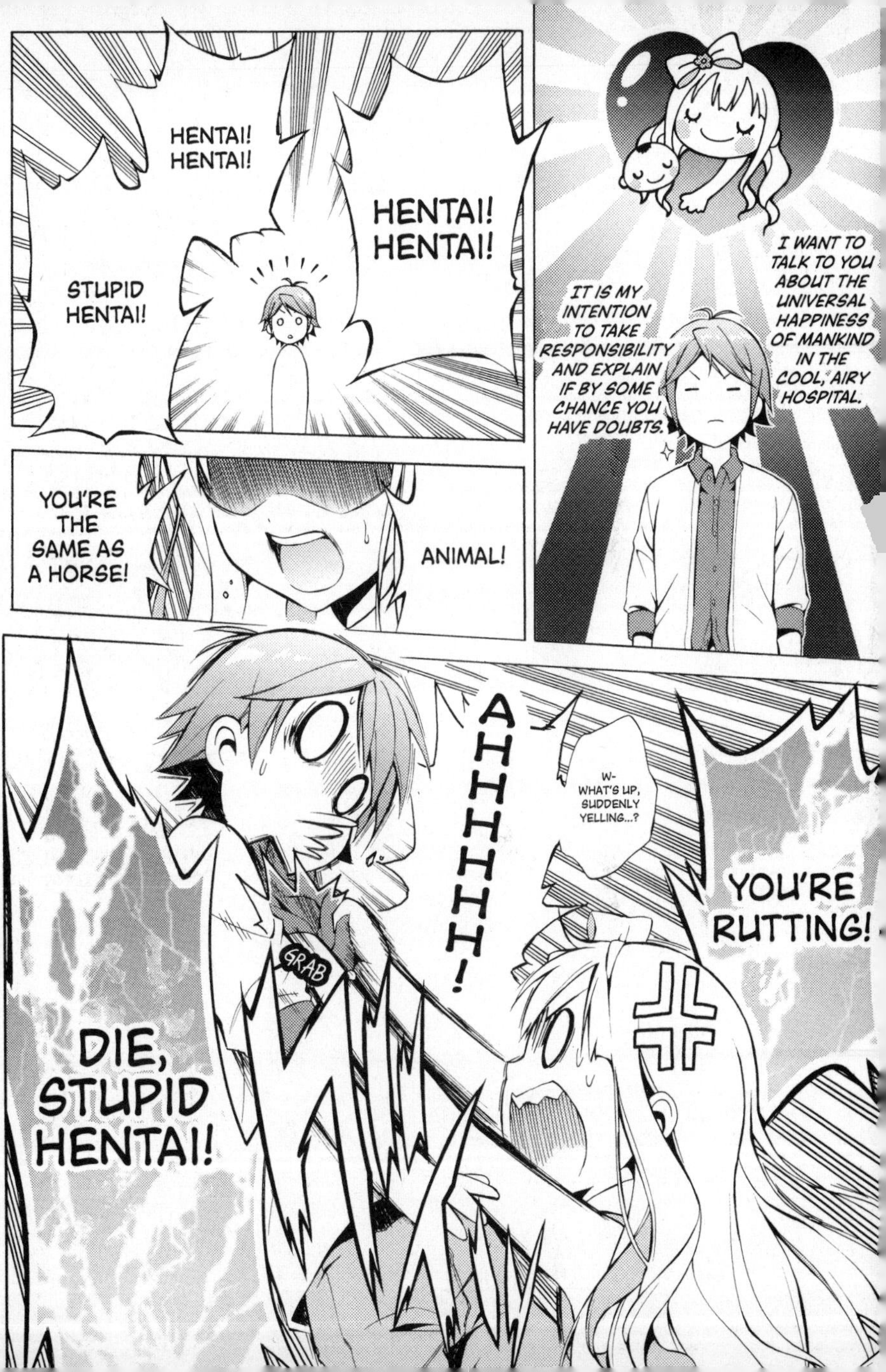
I WANT TO TALK TO YOU ABOUT THE UNIVERSAL HAPPINESS OF MANKIND IN THE COOL, AIRY HOSPITAL.
IT IS MY INTENTION TO TAKE RESPONSIBILITY AND EXPLAIN IF BY SOME CHANCE YOU HAVE DOUBTS.
HENTAI! HENTAI!
HENTAI! HENTAI!
STUPID HENTAI!
ANIMAL!
YOU'RE THE SAME AS A HORSE!
AHHHHHH!
W- WHAT'S UP, SUDDENLY YELLING...?
YOU'RE RUTTING!
GRAB
DIE, STUPID HENTAI!

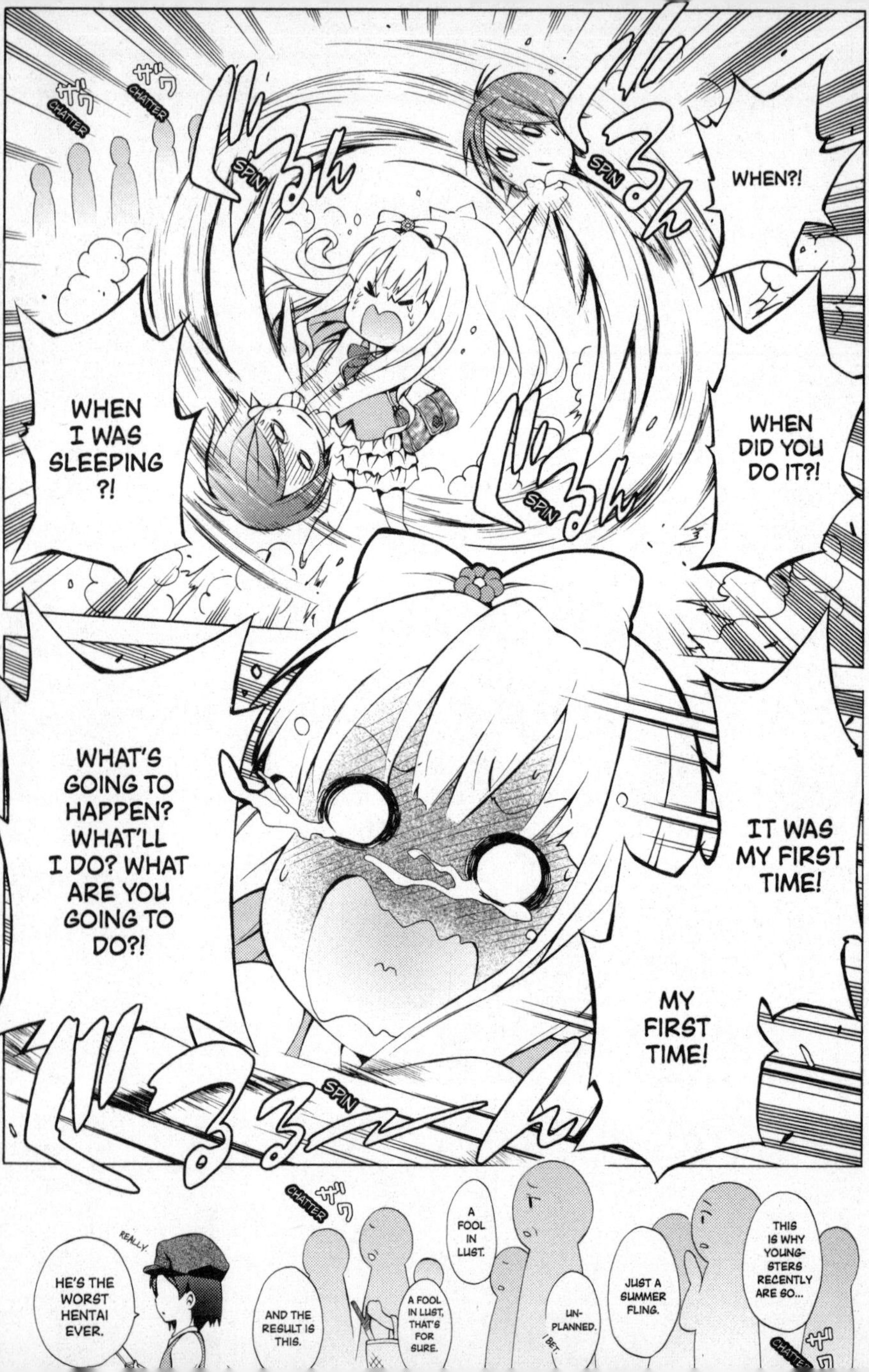

ザワ CHATTER
ザワ CHATTER
SPIN
SPIN
WHEN?!
WHEN DID YOU DO IT?!
WHEN I WAS SLEEPING ?!
SPIN
IT WAS MY FIRST TIME!
MY FIRST TIME!
WHAT'S GOING TO HAPPEN? WHAT'LL I DO? WHAT ARE YOU GOING TO DO?!
SPIN
ザワ CHATTER
THIS IS WHY YOUNG-STERS RECENTLY ARE SO...
JUST A SUMMER FLING.
UN-PLANNED.
I BET.
A FOOL IN LUST.
A FOOL IN LUST, THAT'S FOR SURE.
AND THE RESULT IS THIS.
ザワ CHATTER
REALLY.
HE'S THE WORST HENTAI EVER.

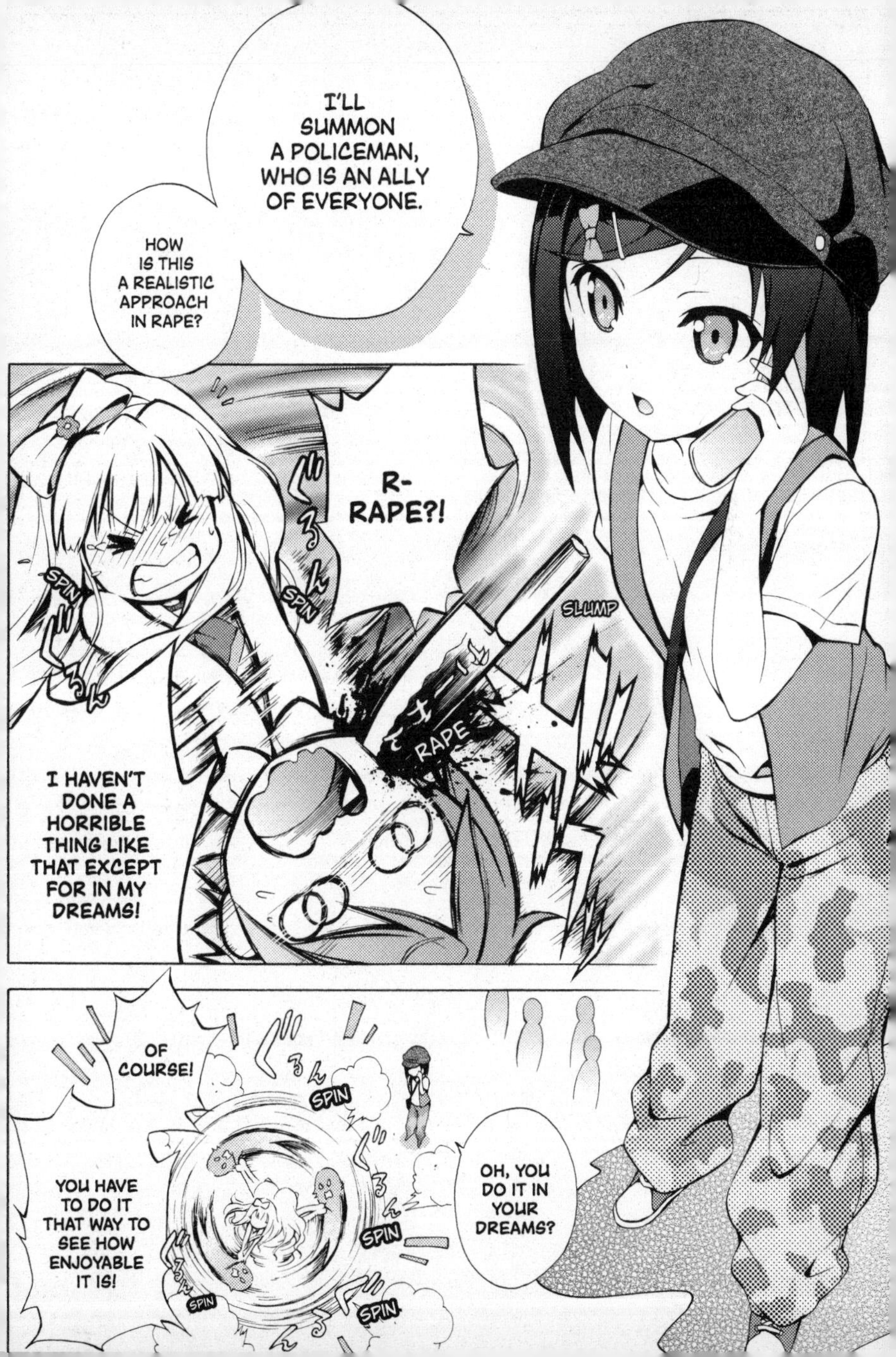
I'LL SUMMON A POLICEMAN, WHO IS AN ALLY OF EVERYONE.
HOW IS THIS A REALISTIC APPROACH IN RAPE?
R-RAPE?!
SLUMP
RAPE
SPIN
SPIN
I HAVEN'T DONE A HORRIBLE THING LIKE THAT EXCEPT FOR IN MY DREAMS!
OH, YOU DO IT IN YOUR DREAMS?
SPIN
OF COURSE!
SPIN
YOU HAVE TO DO IT THAT WAY TO SEE HOW ENJOYABLE IT IS!
SPIN
SPIN

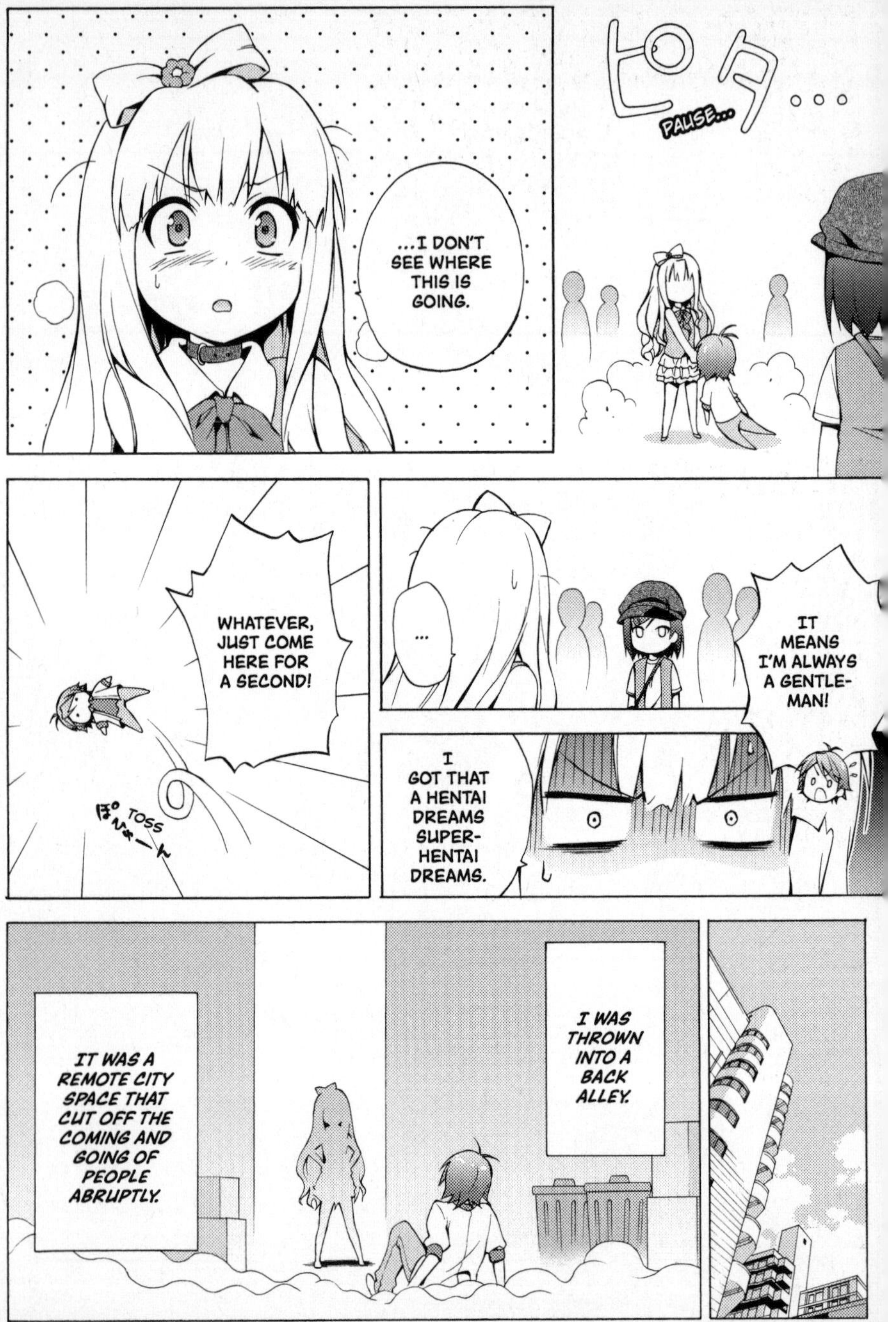
ピタ…
PAUSE...
...I DON'T SEE WHERE THIS IS GOING.
IT MEANS I'M ALWAYS A GENTLE-MAN!
...
I GOT THAT A HENTAI DREAMS SUPER-HENTAI DREAMS.
WHATEVER, JUST COME HERE FOR A SECOND!
ぽひゅーん
TOSS
I WAS THROWN INTO A BACK ALLEY.
IT WAS A REMOTE CITY SPACE THAT CUT OFF THE COMING AND GOING OF PEOPLE ABRUPTLY.

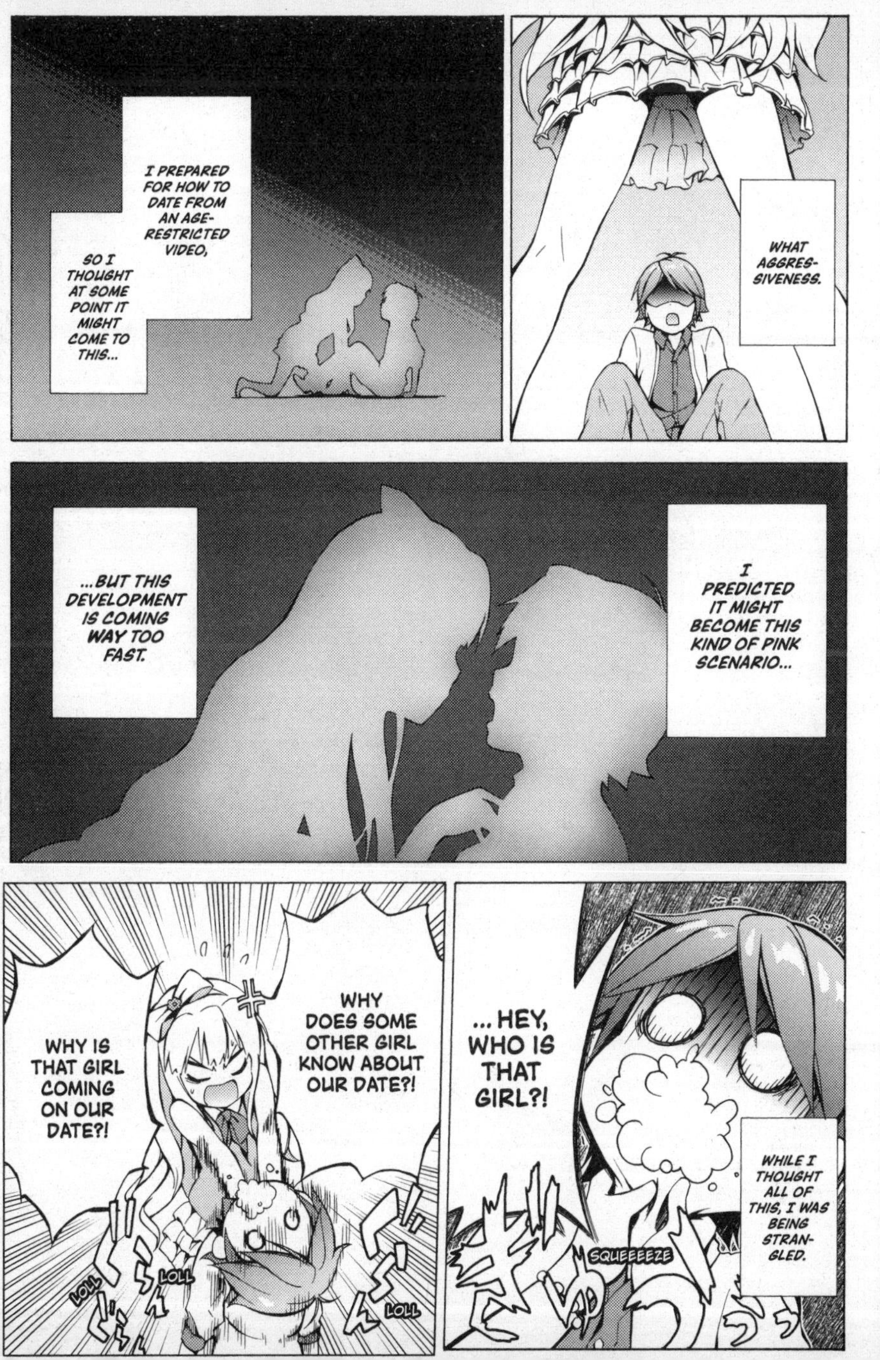
WHAT AGGRES-SIVENESS.
I PREPARED FOR HOW TO DATE FROM AN AGE-RESTRICTED VIDEO,
SO I THOUGHT AT SOME POINT IT MIGHT COME TO THIS...
I PREDICTED IT MIGHT BECOME THIS KIND OF PINK SCENARIO...
...BUT THIS DEVELOPMENT IS COMING WAY TOO FAST.
...HEY, WHO IS THAT GIRL?!
WHILE I THOUGHT ALL OF THIS, I WAS BEING STRANGLED.
SQUEEEEZE
WHY DOES SOME OTHER GIRL KNOW ABOUT OUR DATE?!
WHY IS THAT GIRL COMING ON OUR DATE?!
LOLL
LOLL
LOLL

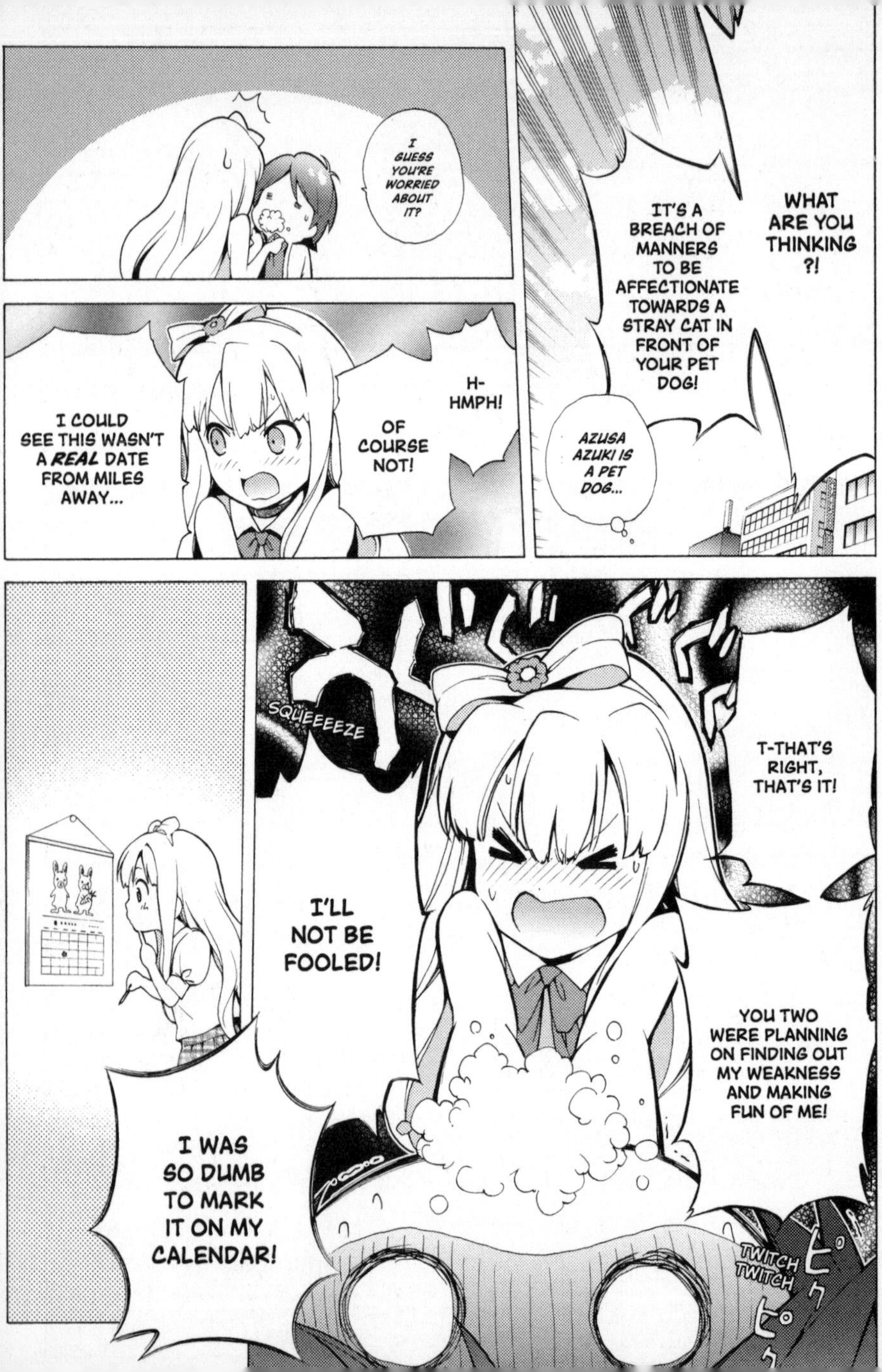
WHAT ARE YOU THINKING ?!
IT'S A BREACH OF MANNERS TO BE AFFECTIONATE TOWARDS A STRAY CAT IN FRONT OF YOUR PET DOG!
AZUSA AZUKI IS A PET DOG...
I GUESS YOU'RE WORRIED ABOUT IT?
H- HMPH!
OF COURSE NOT!
I COULD SEE THIS WASN'T A *REAL* DATE FROM MILES AWAY...
SQUEEEEEZE
T-THAT'S RIGHT, THAT'S IT!
YOU TWO WERE PLANNING ON FINDING OUT MY WEAKNESS AND MAKING FUN OF ME!
I'LL NOT BE FOOLED!
TWITCH TWITCH
I WAS SO DUMB TO MARK IT ON MY CALENDAR!

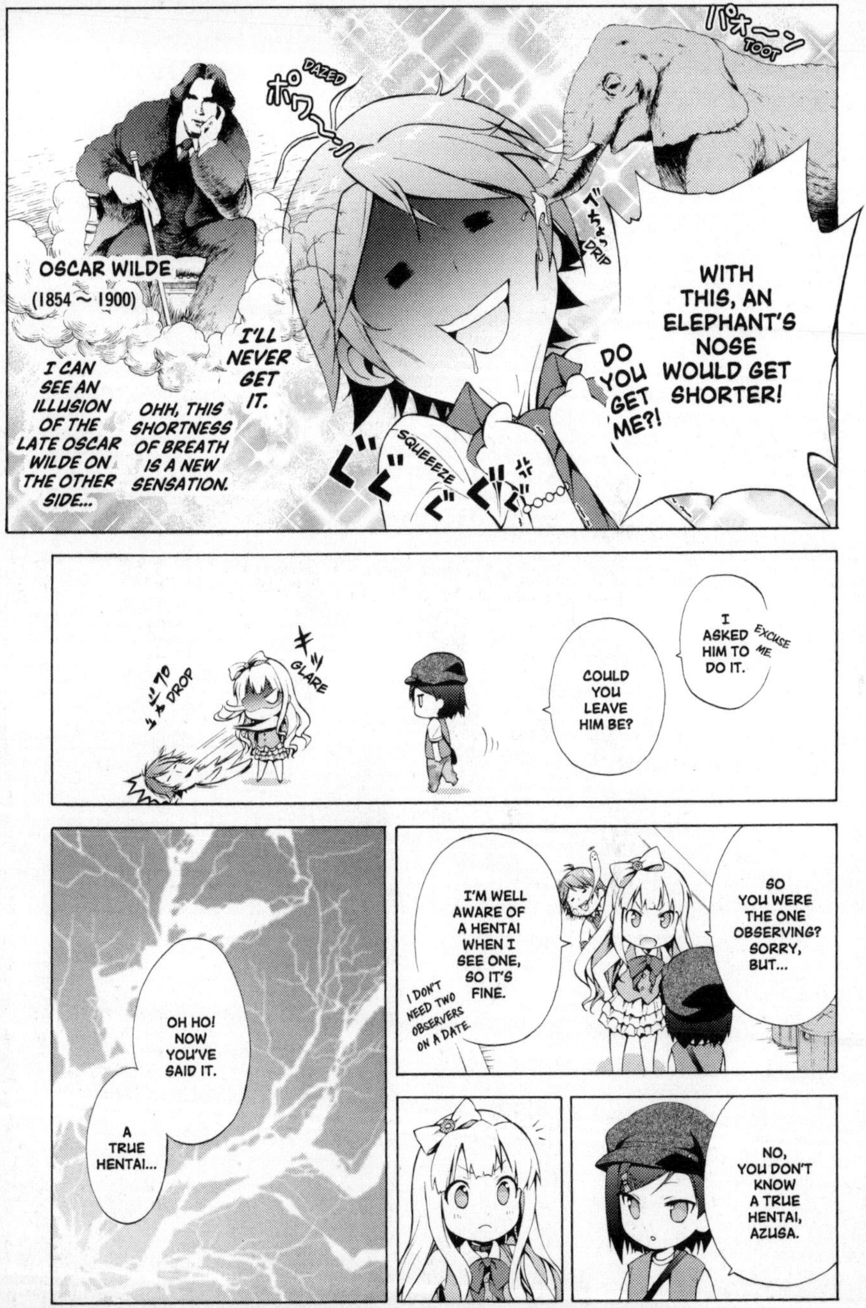
パオ～ン
TOOT
WITH THIS, AN ELEPHANT'S NOSE WOULD GET SHORTER!
DO YOU GET ME?!
DRIP
ポワ～～
DAZED
SQUEEZE
I'LL NEVER GET IT.
OHH, THIS SHORTNESS OF BREATH IS A NEW SENSATION.
I CAN SEE AN ILLUSION OF THE LATE OSCAR WILDE ON THE OTHER SIDE...
OSCAR WILDE
(1854～1900)
I ASKED HIM TO DO IT.
EXCUSE ME.
COULD YOU LEAVE HIM BE?
GLARE
DROP
SO YOU WERE THE ONE OBSERVING? SORRY, BUT...
I'M WELL AWARE OF A HENTAI WHEN I SEE ONE, SO IT'S FINE.
I DON'T NEED TWO OBSERVERS ON A DATE.
NO, YOU DON'T KNOW A TRUE HENTAI, AZUSA.
OH HO! NOW YOU'VE SAID IT.
A TRUE HENTAI...

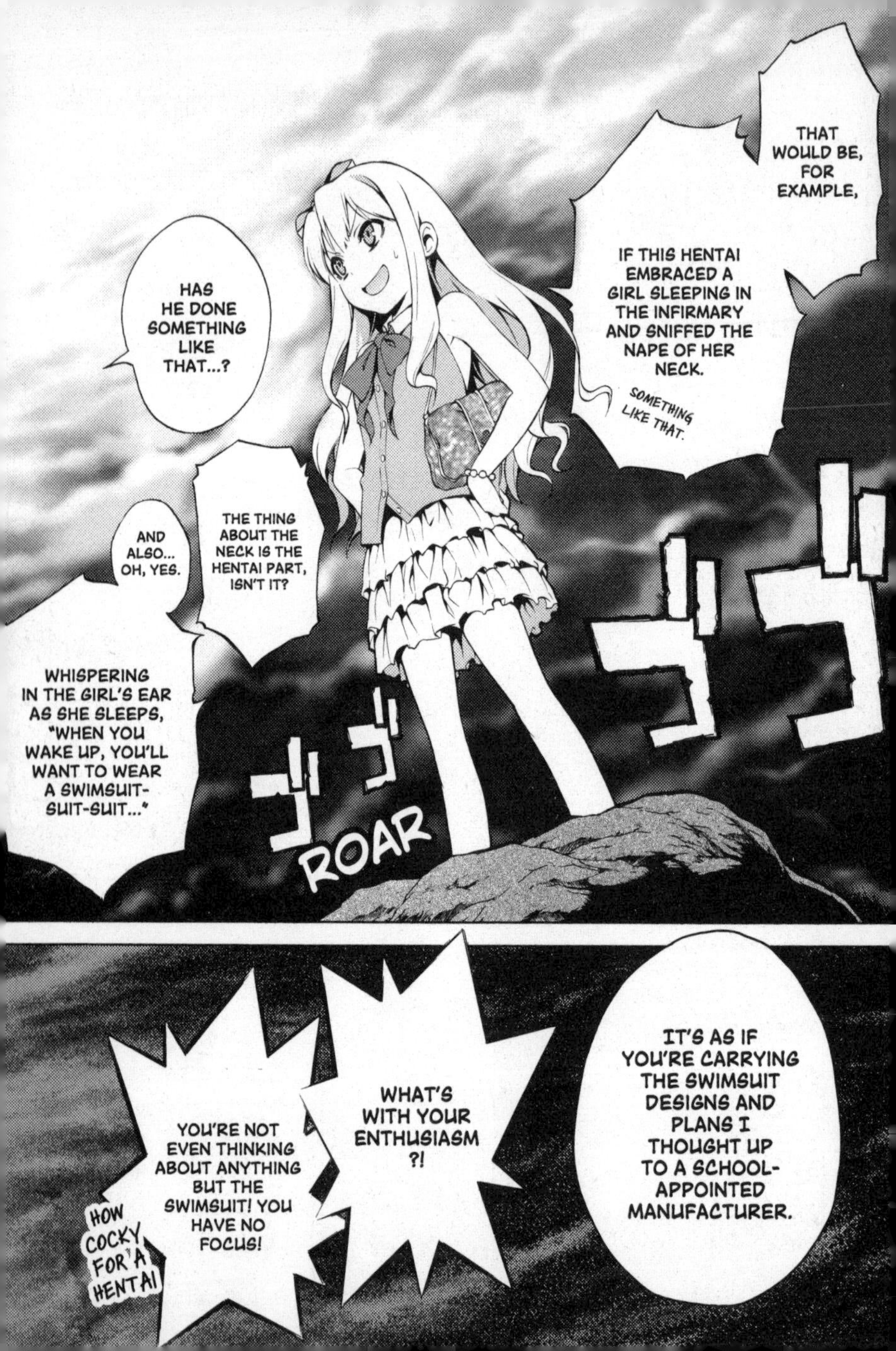

THAT WOULD BE, FOR EXAMPLE,
IF THIS HENTAI EMBRACED A GIRL SLEEPING IN THE INFIRMARY AND SNIFFED THE NAPE OF HER NECK.
SOMETHING LIKE THAT.
HAS HE DONE SOMETHING LIKE THAT...?
THE THING ABOUT THE NECK IS THE HENTAI PART, ISN'T IT?
AND ALSO... OH, YES.
WHISPERING IN THE GIRL'S EAR AS SHE SLEEPS, "WHEN YOU WAKE UP, YOU'LL WANT TO WEAR A SWIMSUIT-SUIT-SUIT..."
ROAR
IT'S AS IF YOU'RE CARRYING THE SWIMSUIT DESIGNS AND PLANS I THOUGHT UP TO A SCHOOL-APPOINTED MANUFACTURER.
WHAT'S WITH YOUR ENTHUSIASM ?!
YOU'RE NOT EVEN THINKING ABOUT ANYTHING BUT THE SWIMSUIT! YOU HAVE NO FOCUS!
HOW COCKY FOR A HENTAI

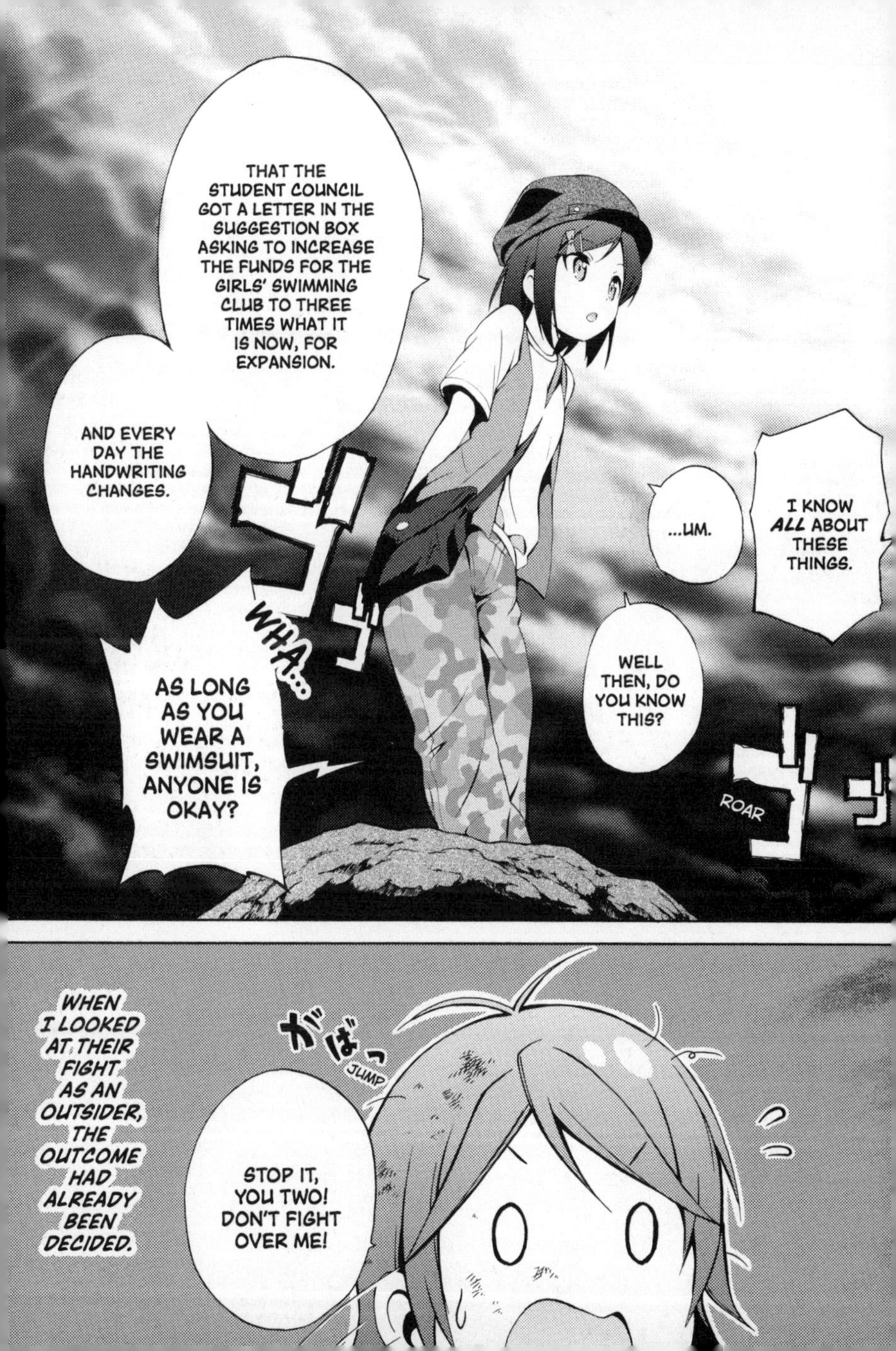

I KNOW ALL ABOUT THESE THINGS.
...UM.
WELL THEN, DO YOU KNOW THIS?
ROAR
THAT THE STUDENT COUNCIL GOT A LETTER IN THE SUGGESTION BOX ASKING TO INCREASE THE FUNDS FOR THE GIRLS' SWIMMING CLUB TO THREE TIMES WHAT IT IS NOW, FOR EXPANSION.
AND EVERY DAY THE HANDWRITING CHANGES.
WHA...
AS LONG AS YOU WEAR A SWIMSUIT, ANYONE IS OKAY?
がばっ
JUMP
STOP IT, YOU TWO! DON'T FIGHT OVER ME!
WHEN I LOOKED AT THEIR FIGHT AS AN OUTSIDER, THE OUTCOME HAD ALREADY BEEN DECIDED.

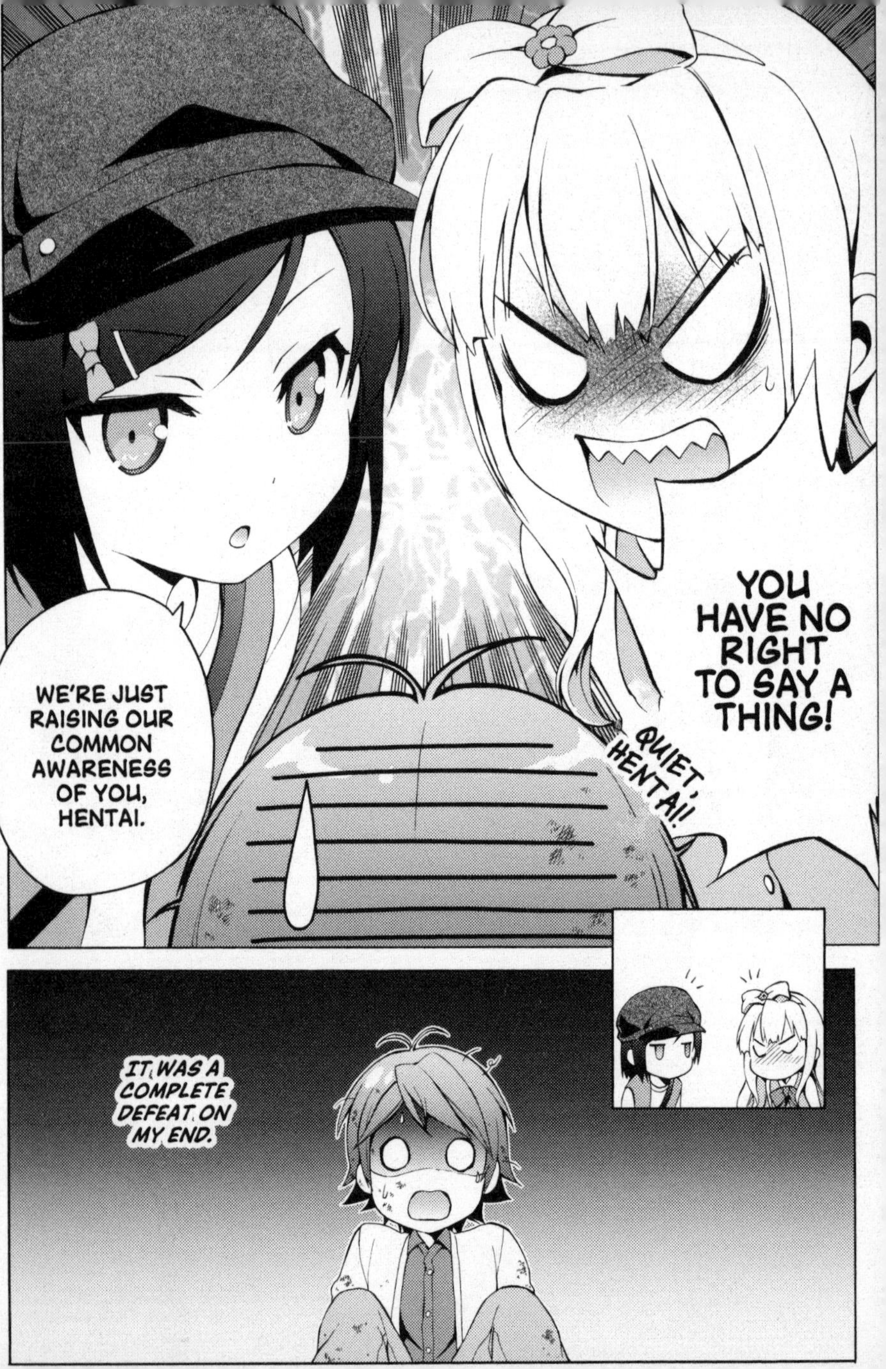
YOU HAVE NO RIGHT TO SAY A THING!
QUIET, HENTAI!!
WE'RE JUST RAISING OUR COMMON AWARENESS OF YOU, HENTAI.
IT WAS A COMPLETE DEFEAT ON MY END.

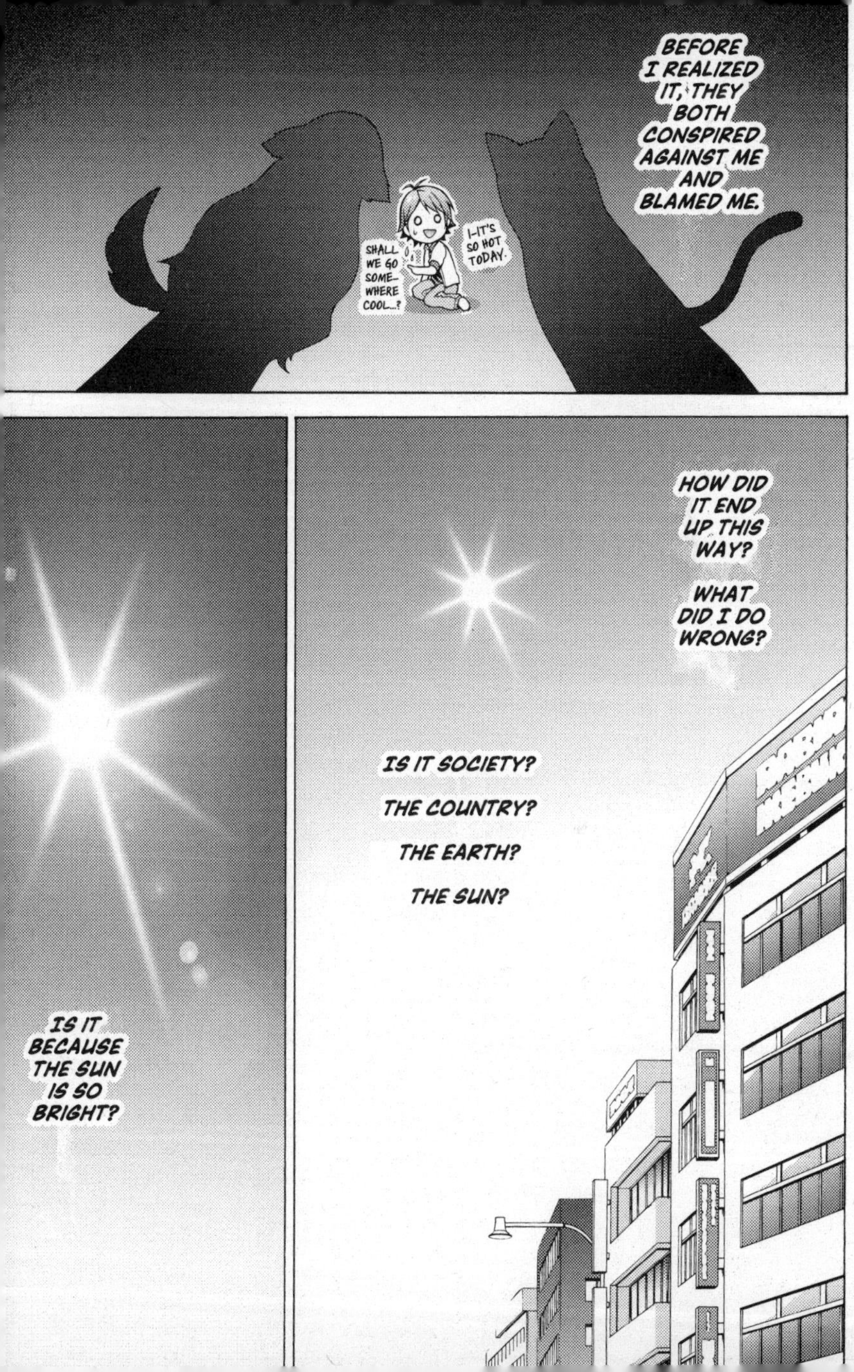
BEFORE I REALIZED IT, THEY BOTH CONSPIRED AGAINST ME AND BLAMED ME.
I-IT'S SO HOT TODAY.
SHALL WE GO SOME-WHERE COOL...?
HOW DID IT END UP THIS WAY?
WHAT DID I DO WRONG?
IS IT SOCIETY?
THE COUNTRY?
THE EARTH?
THE SUN?
IS IT BECAUSE THE SUN IS SO BRIGHT?

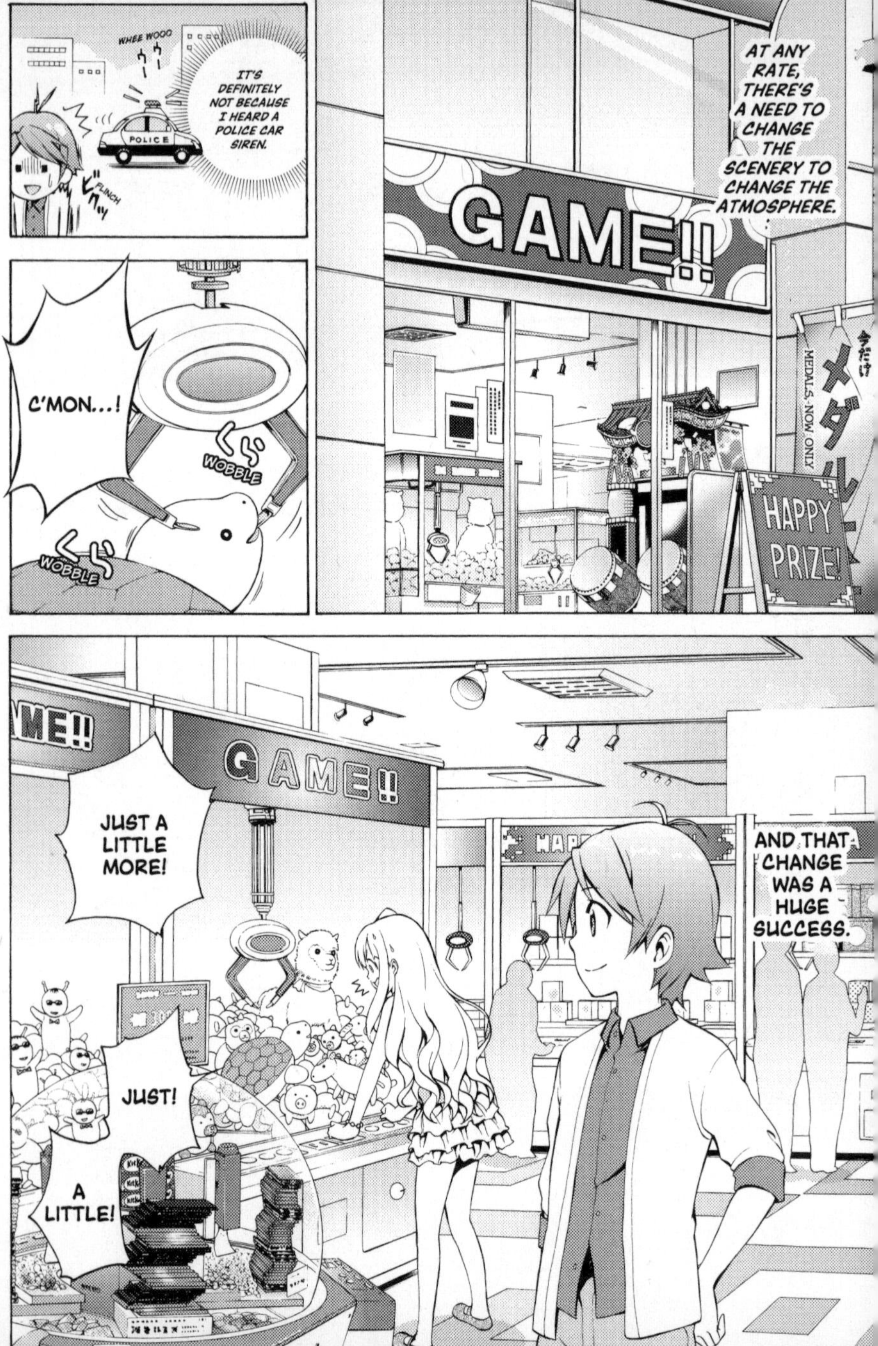
AT ANY RATE, THERE'S A NEED TO CHANGE THE SCENERY TO CHANGE THE ATMOSPHERE.
GAME!!
MEDALS, NOW ONLY
HAPPY PRIZE!
WHEE WOOO
POLICE
IT'S DEFINITELY NOT BECAUSE I HEARD A POLICE CAR SIREN.
FLINCH
C'MON...!
WOBBLE
WOBBLE
AND THAT CHANGE WAS A HUGE SUCCESS.
GAME!!
JUST A LITTLE MORE!
JUST!
A LITTLE!

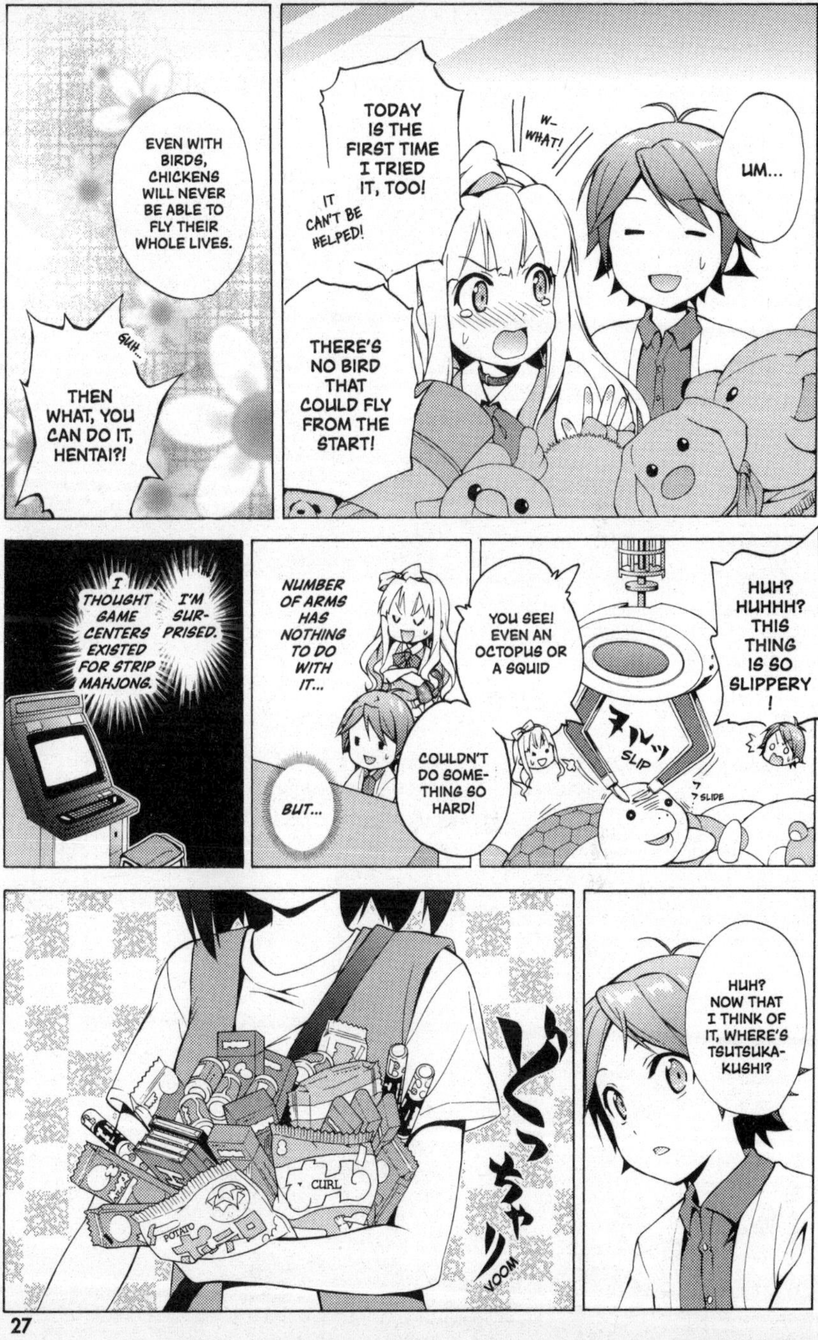
UM...
W-WHAT!
TODAY IS THE FIRST TIME I TRIED IT, TOO!
IT CAN'T BE HELPED!
THERE'S NO BIRD THAT COULD FLY FROM THE START!
EVEN WITH BIRDS, CHICKENS WILL NEVER BE ABLE TO FLY THEIR WHOLE LIVES.
GUH...
THEN WHAT, YOU CAN DO IT, HENTAI?!
HUH? HUHHH? THIS THING IS SO SLIPPERY!
SLIP
SLIDE
YOU SEE! EVEN AN OCTOPUS OR A SQUID
COULDN'T DO SOMETHING SO HARD!
NUMBER OF ARMS HAS NOTHING TO DO WITH IT...
BUT...
I'M SURPRISED.
I THOUGHT GAME CENTERS EXISTED FOR STRIP MAHJONG.
HUH? NOW THAT I THINK OF IT, WHERE'S TSUTSUKAKUSHI?
VOOM
CURL
POTATO

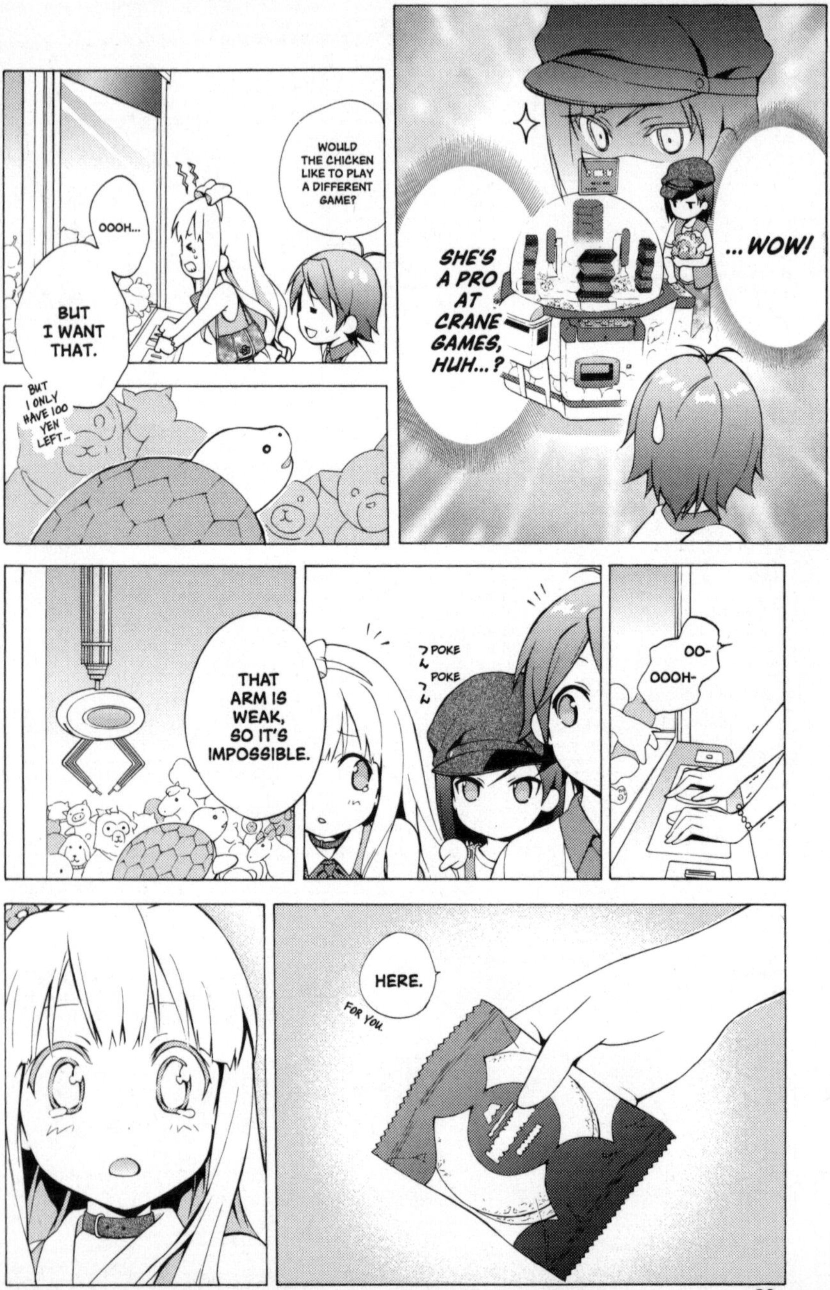
...WOW!
SHE'S A PRO AT CRANE GAMES, HUH...?
WOULD THE CHICKEN LIKE TO PLAY A DIFFERENT GAME?
OOOH...
BUT I WANT THAT.
BUT I ONLY HAVE 100 YEN LEFT...
OO- OOOH-
POKE POKE
THAT ARM IS WEAK, SO IT'S IMPOSSIBLE.
HERE.
FOR YOU.

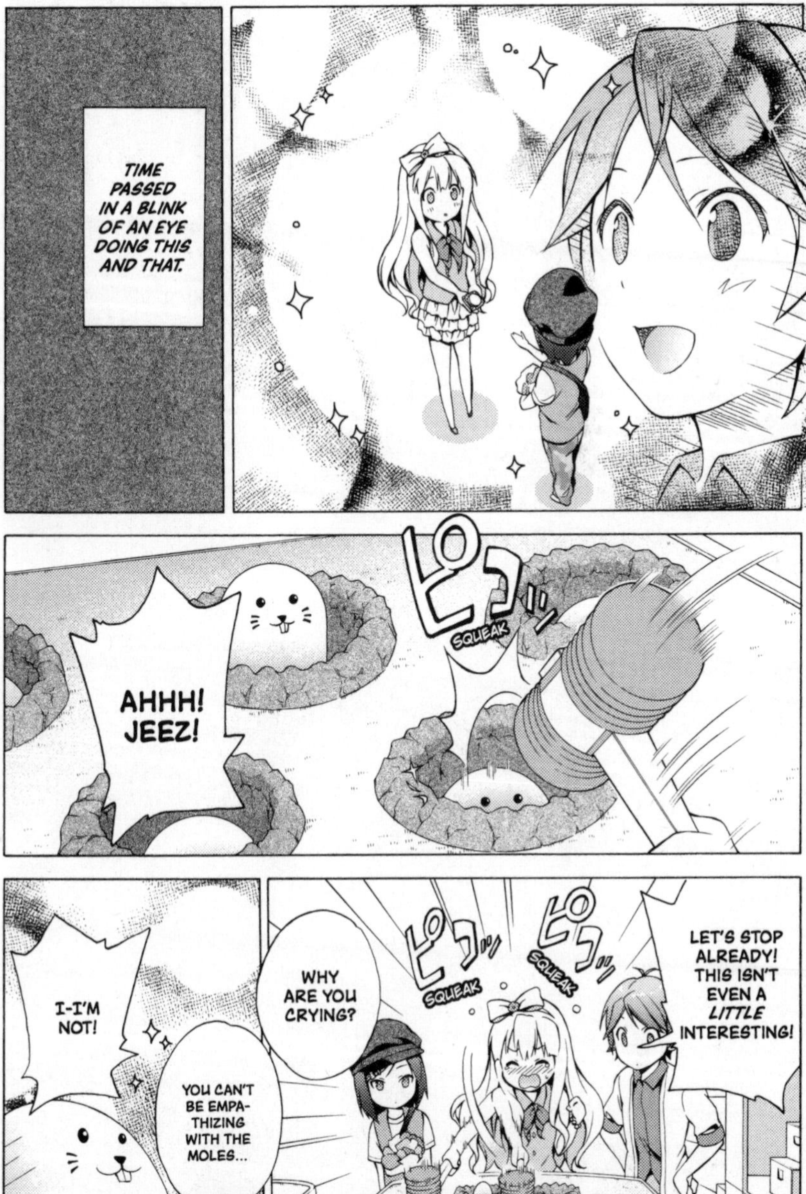
TIME PASSED IN A BLINK OF AN EYE DOING THIS AND THAT.
ピコッ
SQUEAK
AHHH! JEEZ!
LET'S STOP ALREADY! THIS ISN'T EVEN A *LITTLE* INTERESTING!
ピコッ
SQUEAK
ピコッ
SQUEAK
WHY ARE YOU CRYING?
YOU CAN'T BE EMPA-THIZING WITH THE MOLES...
I-I'M NOT!

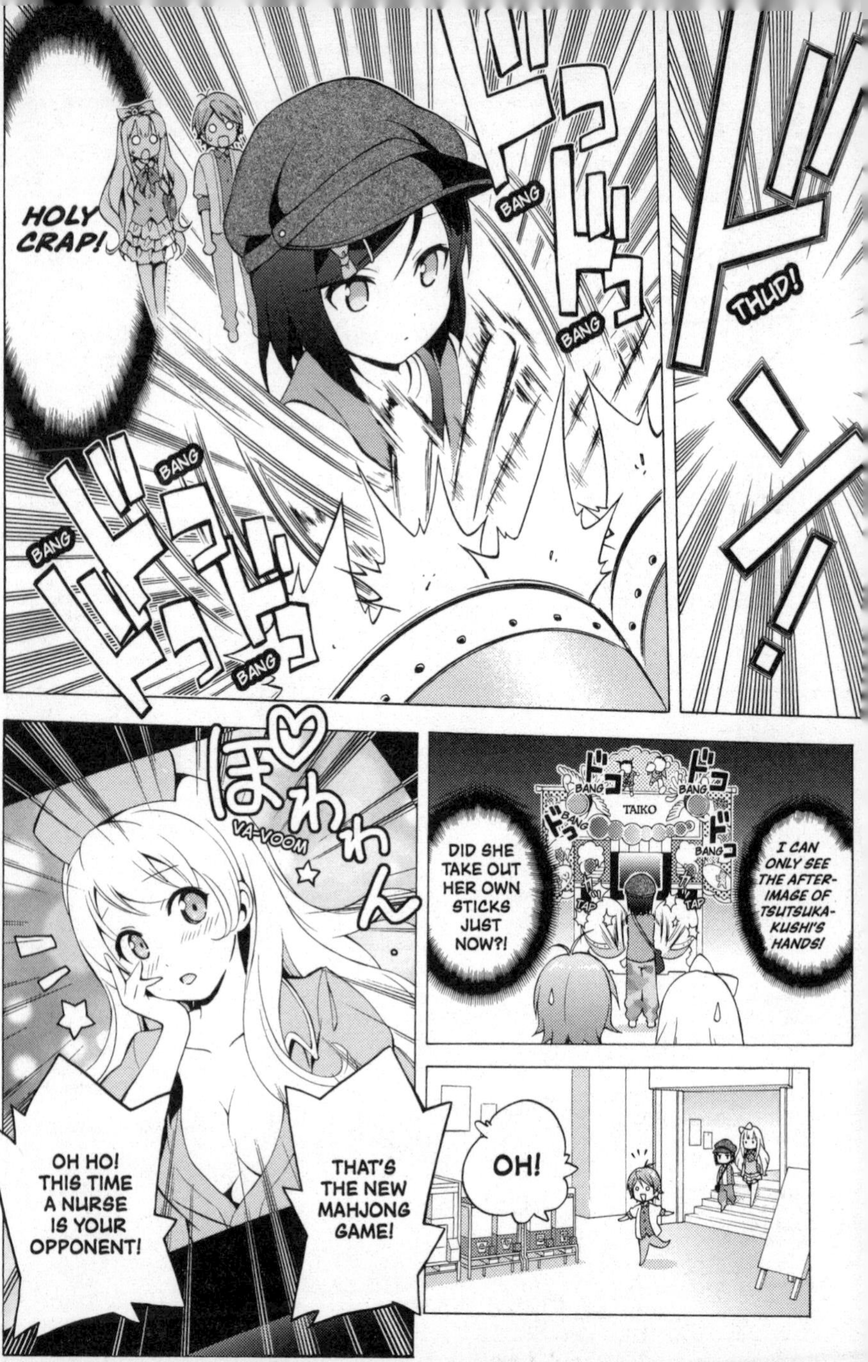

THUD!
BANG
BANG
HOLY CRAP!
BANG
BANG
BANG
TAIKO
BANG
BANG
BANG
BANG
TAP
TAP
I CAN ONLY SEE THE AFTER-IMAGE OF TSUTSUKA-KUSHI'S HANDS!
DID SHE TAKE OUT HER OWN STICKS JUST NOW?!
OH!
ぽわわん
VA-VOOM
THAT'S THE NEW MAHJONG GAME!
OH HO! THIS TIME A NURSE IS YOUR OPPONENT!

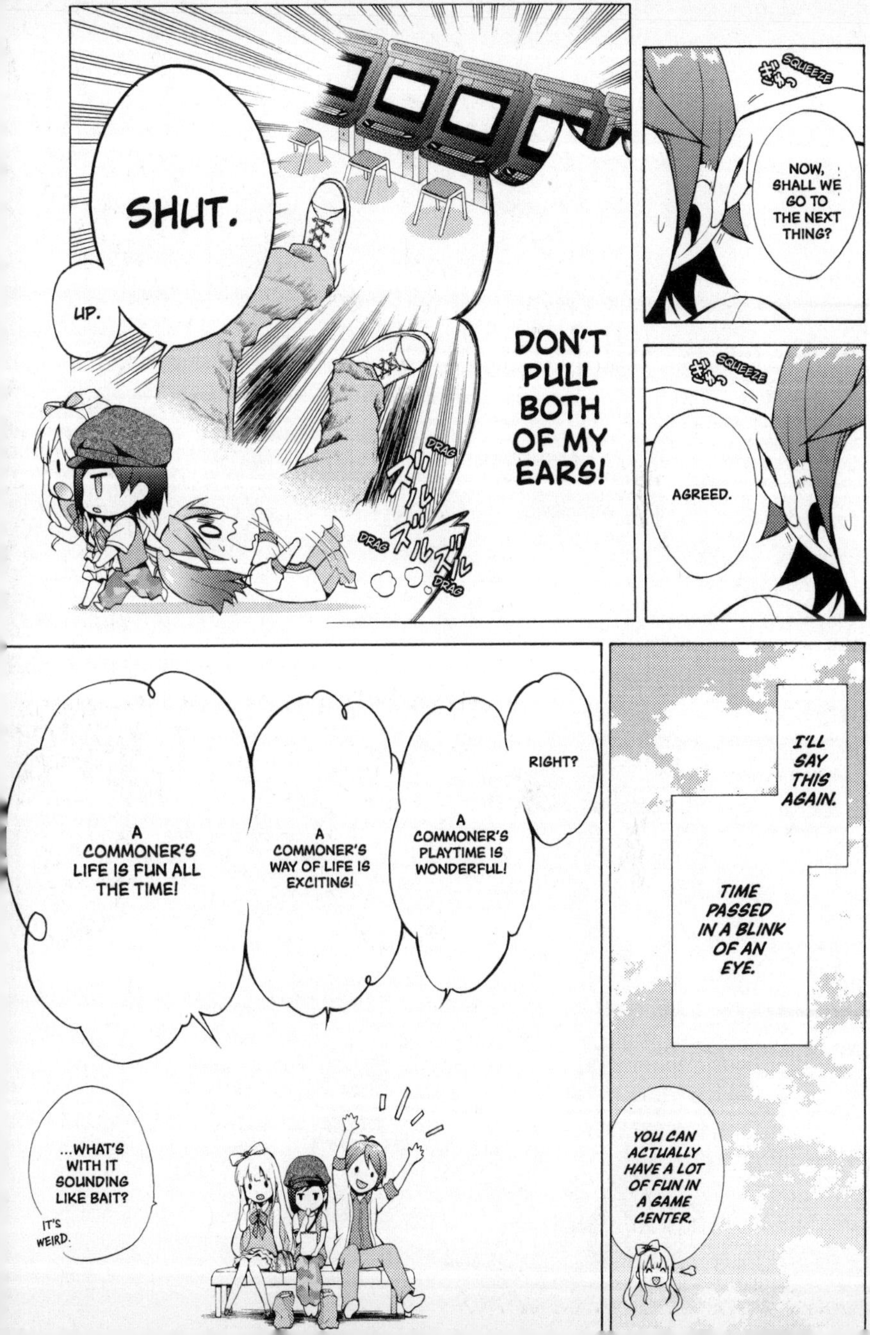
SQUEEZE
ぎゅっ
NOW, SHALL WE GO TO THE NEXT THING?
SQUEEZE
ぎゅっ
AGREED.
SHUT.
UP.
DRAG
DRAG
DRAG
DON'T PULL BOTH OF MY EARS!
I'LL SAY THIS AGAIN.
TIME PASSED IN A BLINK OF AN EYE.
YOU CAN ACTUALLY HAVE A LOT OF FUN IN A GAME CENTER.
RIGHT?
A COMMONER'S PLAYTIME IS WONDERFUL!
A COMMONER'S WAY OF LIFE IS EXCITING!
A COMMONER'S LIFE IS FUN ALL THE TIME!
...WHAT'S WITH IT SOUNDING LIKE BAIT?
IT'S WEIRD.

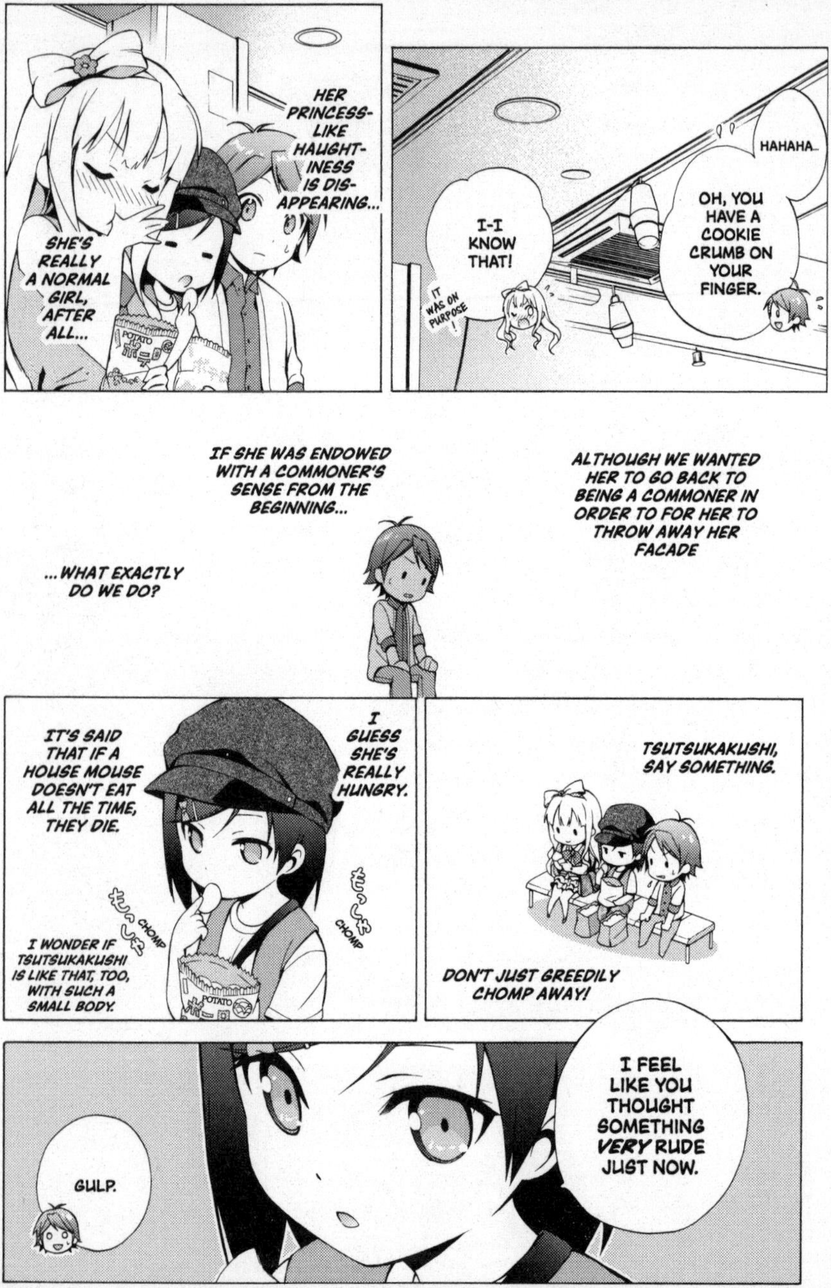
HAHAHA...
OH, YOU HAVE A COOKIE CRUMB ON YOUR FINGER.
I-I KNOW THAT!
IT WAS ON PURPOSE!
HER PRINCESS-LIKE HAUGHTINESS IS DISAPPEARING...
SHE'S REALLY A NORMAL GIRL, AFTER ALL...
POTATO
ALTHOUGH WE WANTED HER TO GO BACK TO BEING A COMMONER IN ORDER TO FOR HER TO THROW AWAY HER FACADE
IF SHE WAS ENDOWED WITH A COMMONER'S SENSE FROM THE BEGINNING...
...WHAT EXACTLY DO WE DO?
TSUTSUKAKUSHI, SAY SOMETHING.
DON'T JUST GREEDILY CHOMP AWAY!
I GUESS SHE'S REALLY HUNGRY.
IT'S SAID THAT IF A HOUSE MOUSE DOESN'T EAT ALL THE TIME, THEY DIE.
CHOMP
CHOMP
I WONDER IF TSUTSUKAKUSHI IS LIKE THAT, TOO, WITH SUCH A SMALL BODY.
POTATO
I FEEL LIKE YOU THOUGHT SOMETHING VERY RUDE JUST NOW.
GULP.

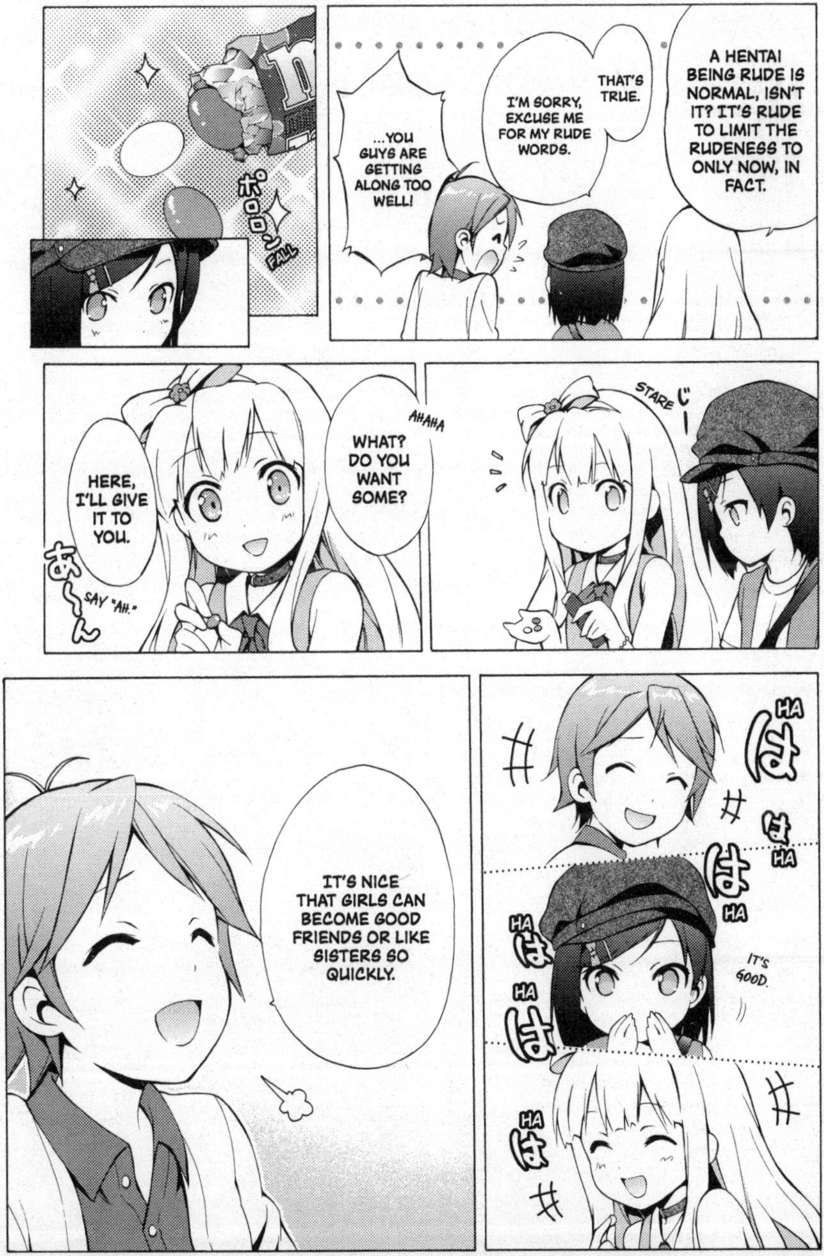

A HENTAI BEING RUDE IS NORMAL, ISN'T IT? IT'S RUDE TO LIMIT THE RUDENESS TO ONLY NOW, IN FACT.
THAT'S TRUE.
I'M SORRY, EXCUSE ME FOR MY RUDE WORDS.
...YOU GUYS ARE GETTING ALONG TOO WELL!
ポロロン
FALL
じー
STARE
AHAHA
WHAT? DO YOU WANT SOME?
HERE, I'LL GIVE IT TO YOU.
あ～ん
SAY "AH."
HA
は
は
HA
は
HA
HA
は
HA
は
IT'S GOOD.
HA
は
IT'S NICE THAT GIRLS CAN BECOME GOOD FRIENDS OR LIKE SISTERS SO QUICKLY.

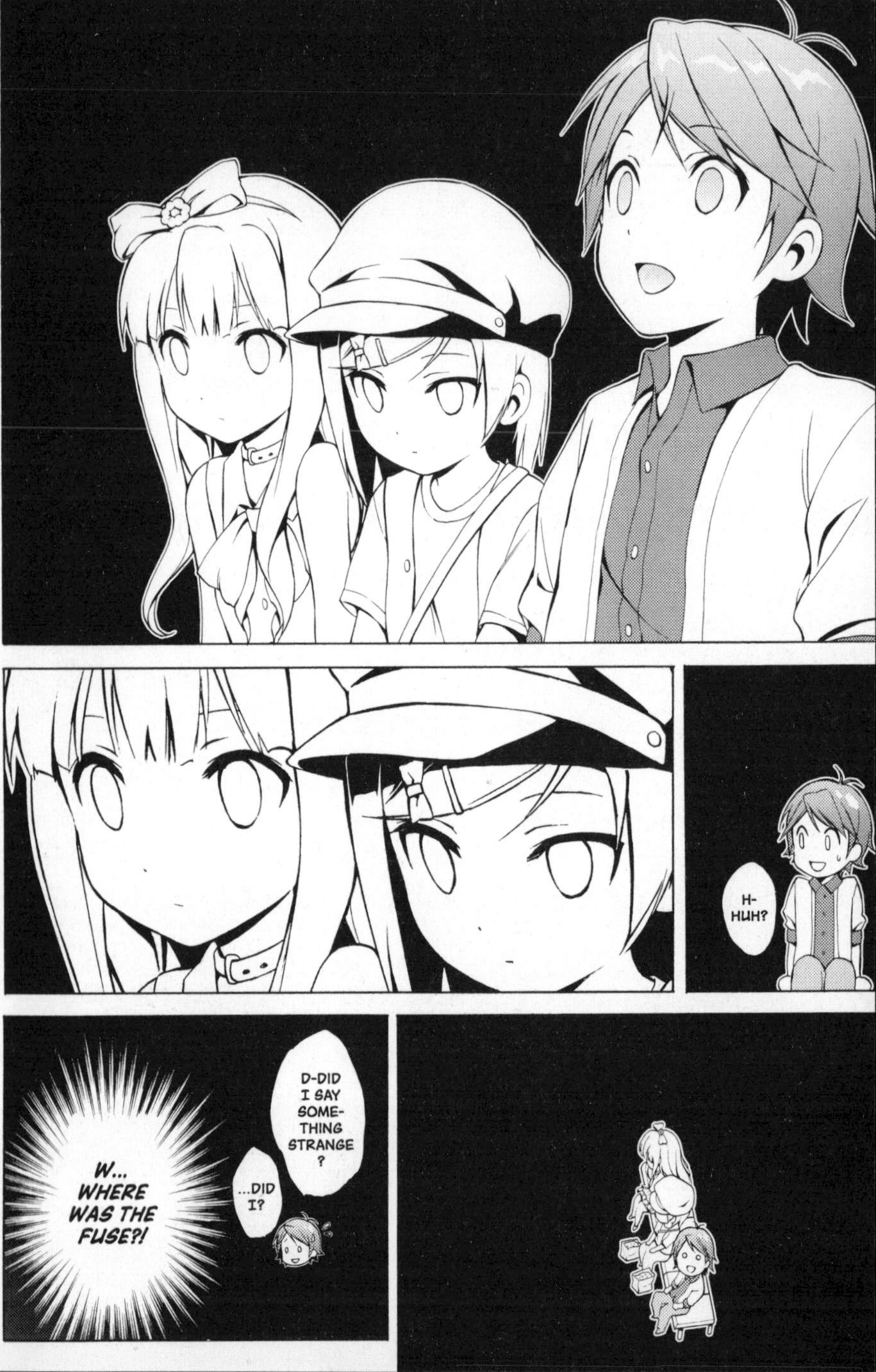
H-HUH?
D-DID I SAY SOME-THING STRANGE?
...DID I?
W... WHERE WAS THE FUSE?!

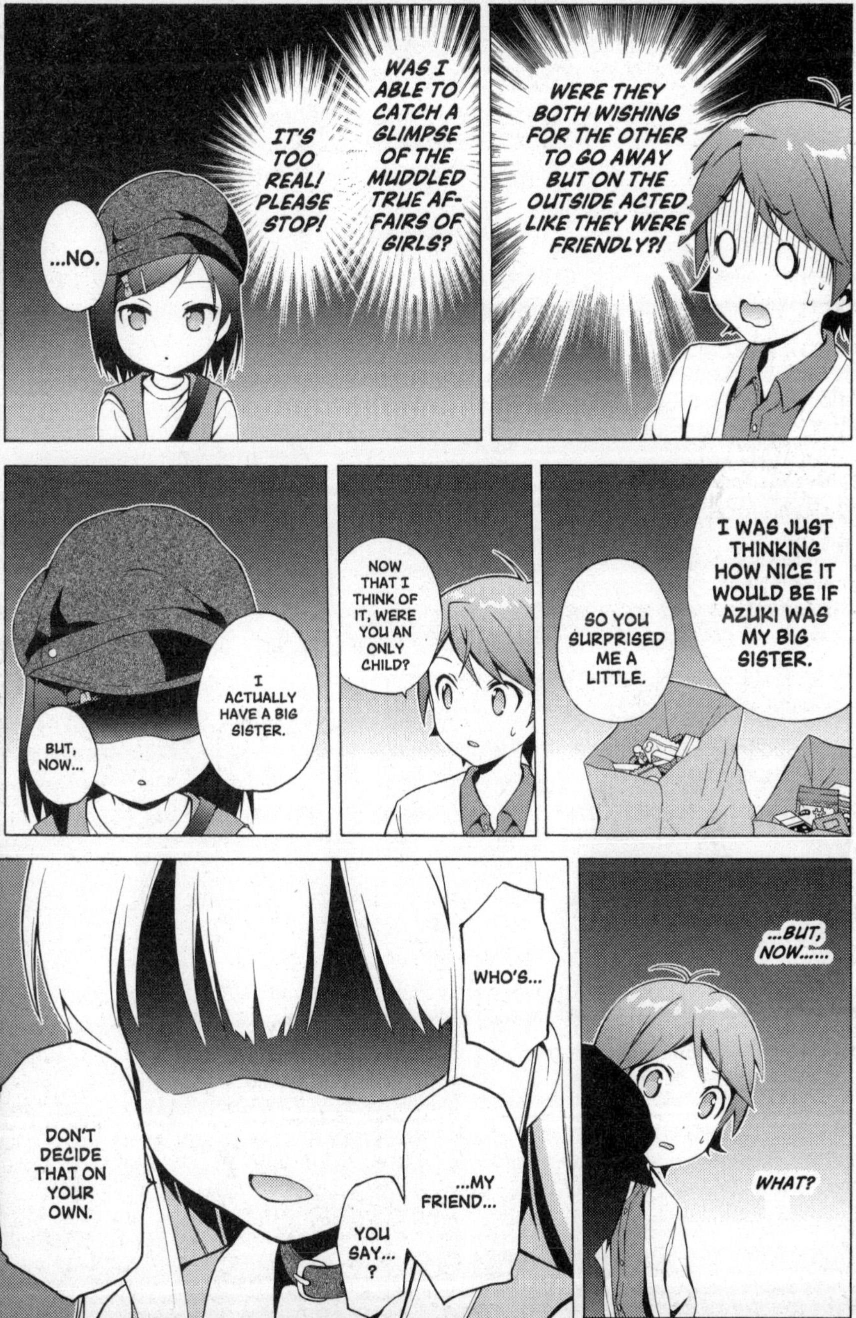
WERE THEY BOTH WISHING FOR THE OTHER TO GO AWAY BUT ON THE OUTSIDE ACTED LIKE THEY WERE FRIENDLY?!
WAS I ABLE TO CATCH A GLIMPSE OF THE MUDDLED TRUE AF- FAIRS OF GIRLS?
IT'S TOO REAL! PLEASE STOP!
...NO.
I WAS JUST THINKING HOW NICE IT WOULD BE IF AZUKI WAS MY BIG SISTER.
SO YOU SURPRISED ME A LITTLE.
NOW THAT I THINK OF IT, WERE YOU AN ONLY CHILD?
I ACTUALLY HAVE A BIG SISTER.
BUT, NOW...
...BUT, NOW......
WHAT?
WHO'S...
...MY FRIEND...
YOU SAY... ?
DON'T DECIDE THAT ON YOUR OWN.

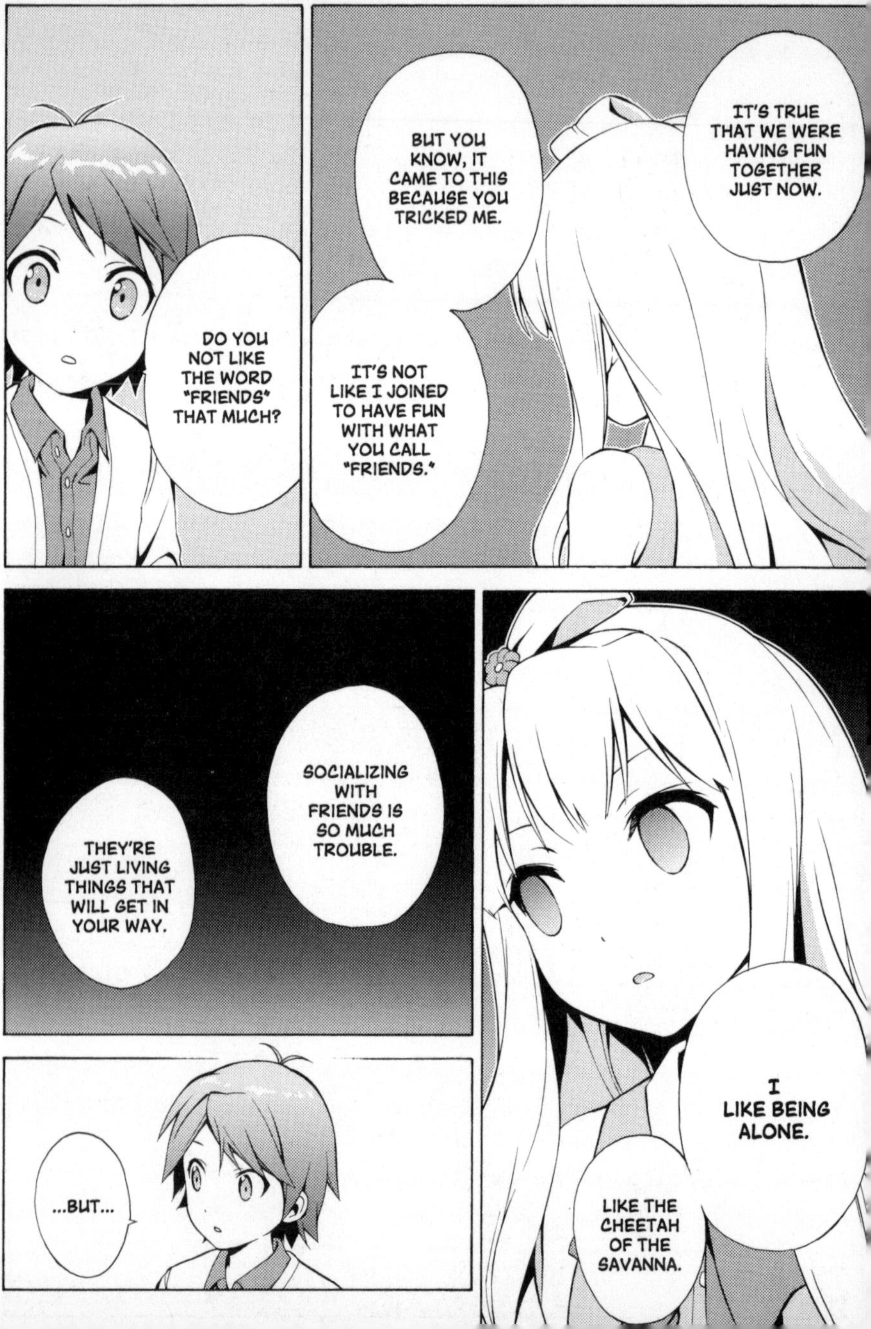
IT'S TRUE THAT WE WERE HAVING FUN TOGETHER JUST NOW.
BUT YOU KNOW, IT CAME TO THIS BECAUSE YOU TRICKED ME.
IT'S NOT LIKE I JOINED TO HAVE FUN WITH WHAT YOU CALL "FRIENDS."
DO YOU NOT LIKE THE WORD "FRIENDS" THAT MUCH?
I LIKE BEING ALONE.
LIKE THE CHEETAH OF THE SAVANNA.
SOCIALIZING WITH FRIENDS IS SO MUCH TROUBLE.
THEY'RE JUST LIVING THINGS THAT WILL GET IN YOUR WAY.
...BUT...

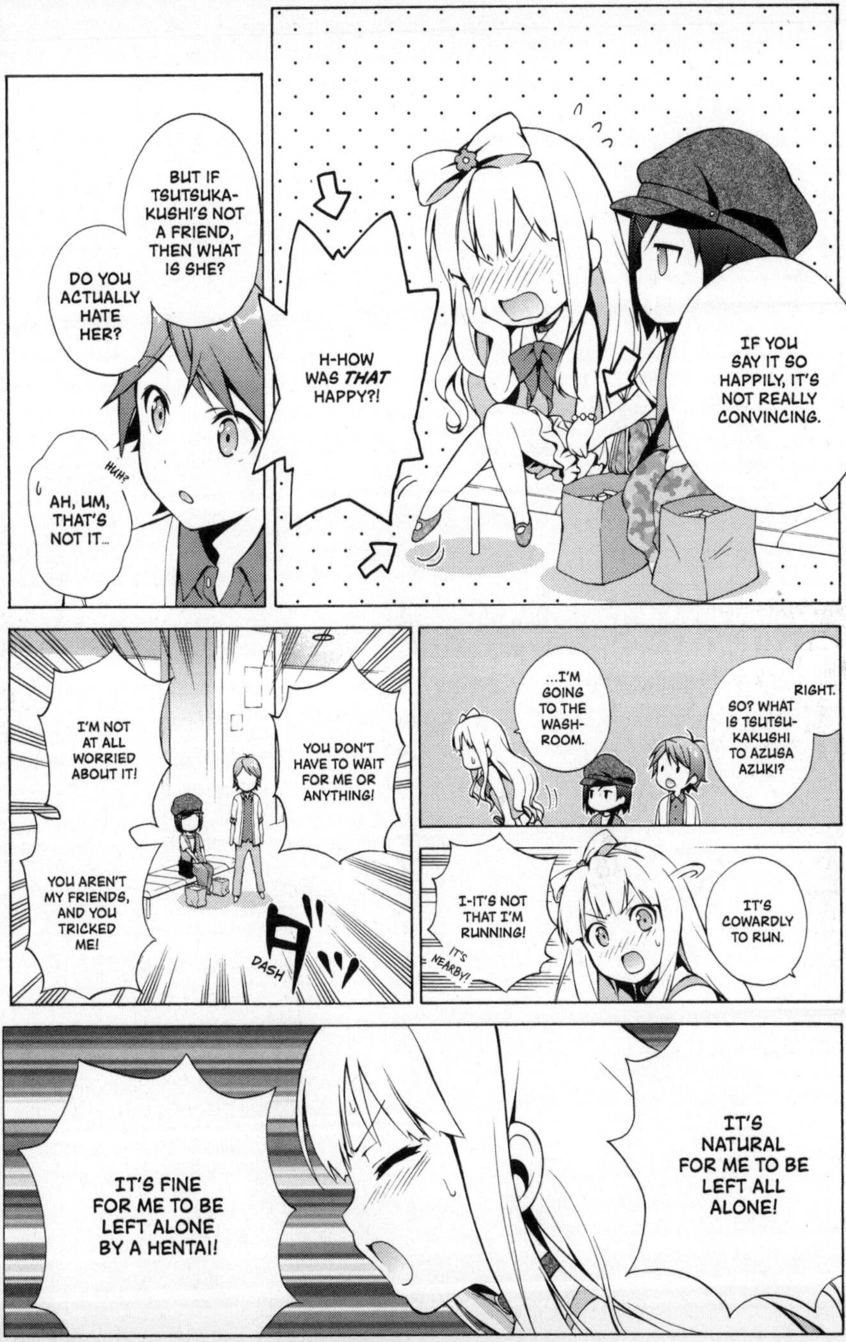
IF YOU SAY IT SO HAPPILY, IT'S NOT REALLY CONVINCING.
H-HOW WAS *THAT* HAPPY?!
BUT IF TSUTSUKAKUSHI'S NOT A FRIEND, THEN WHAT IS SHE?
DO YOU ACTUALLY HATE HER?
HUH?
AH, UM, THAT'S NOT IT...
RIGHT.
SO? WHAT IS TSUTSUKAKUSHI TO AZUSA AZUKI?
...I'M GOING TO THE WASHROOM.
IT'S COWARDLY TO RUN.
I-IT'S NOT THAT I'M RUNNING!
IT'S NEARBY!
YOU DON'T HAVE TO WAIT FOR ME OR ANYTHING!
I'M NOT AT ALL WORRIED ABOUT IT!
YOU AREN'T MY FRIENDS, AND YOU TRICKED ME!
ダッ
DASH
IT'S NATURAL FOR ME TO BE LEFT ALL ALONE!
IT'S FINE FOR ME TO BE LEFT ALONE BY A HENTAI!

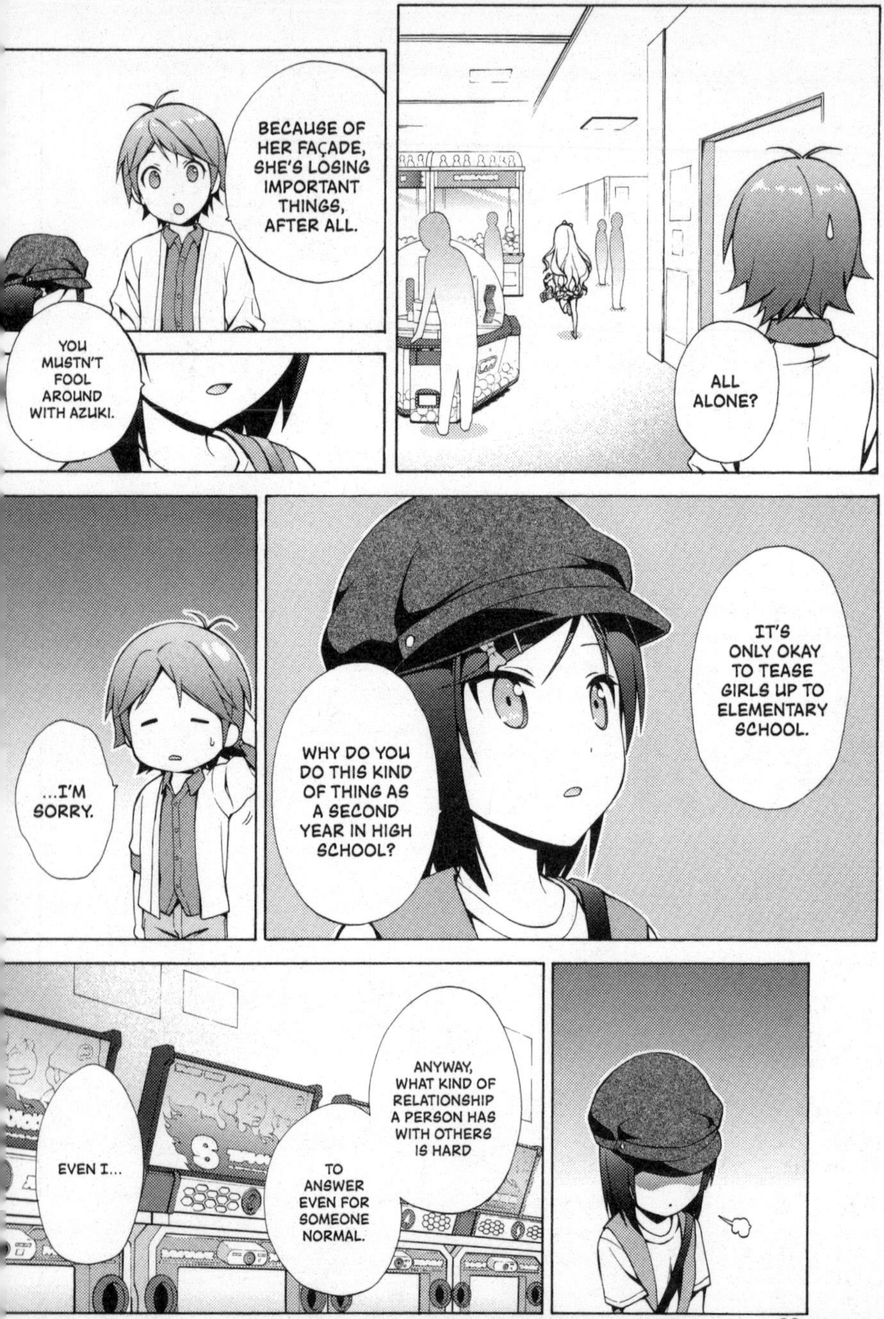
ALL ALONE?
BECAUSE OF HER FAÇADE, SHE'S LOSING IMPORTANT THINGS, AFTER ALL.
YOU MUSTN'T FOOL AROUND WITH AZUKI.
IT'S ONLY OKAY TO TEASE GIRLS UP TO ELEMENTARY SCHOOL.
WHY DO YOU DO THIS KIND OF THING AS A SECOND YEAR IN HIGH SCHOOL?
...I'M SORRY.
ANYWAY, WHAT KIND OF RELATIONSHIP A PERSON HAS WITH OTHERS IS HARD
TO ANSWER EVEN FOR SOMEONE NORMAL.
EVEN I...

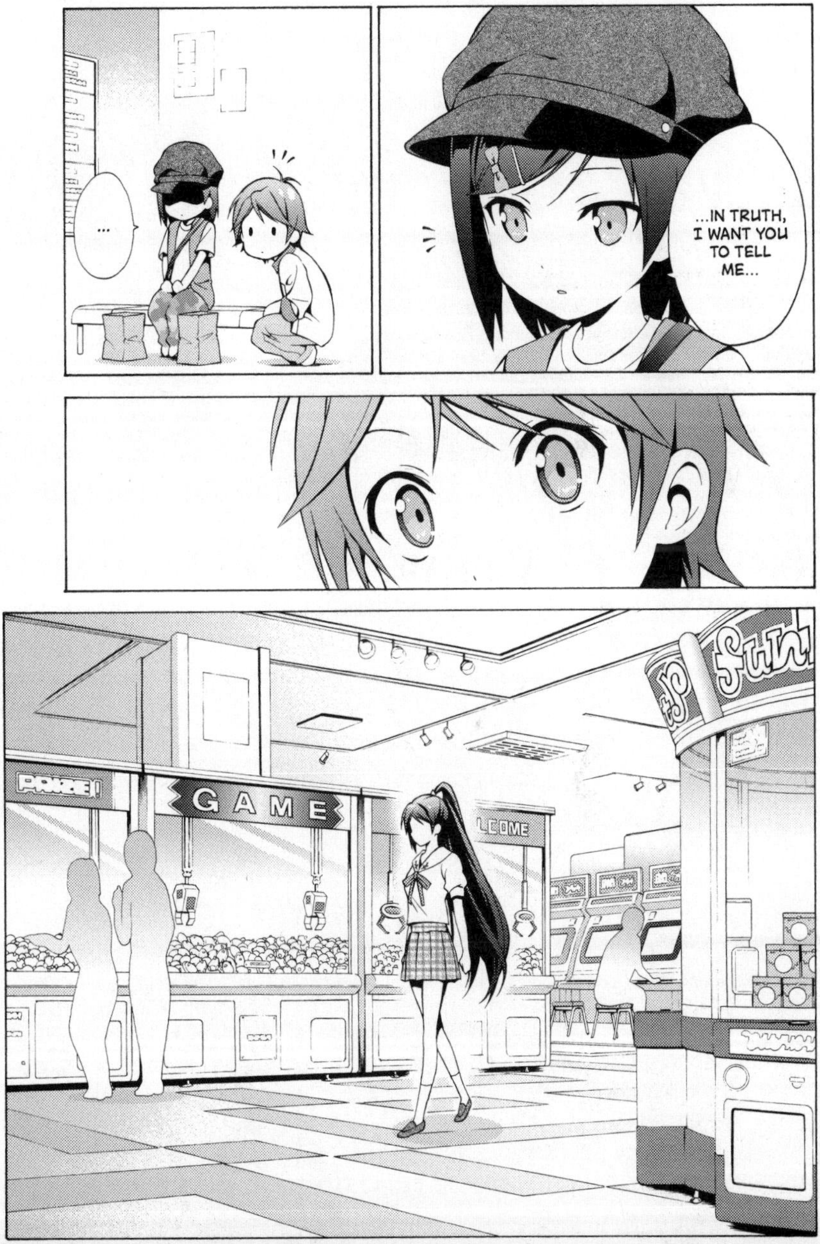
...IN TRUTH, I WANT YOU TO TELL ME...
...
GAME

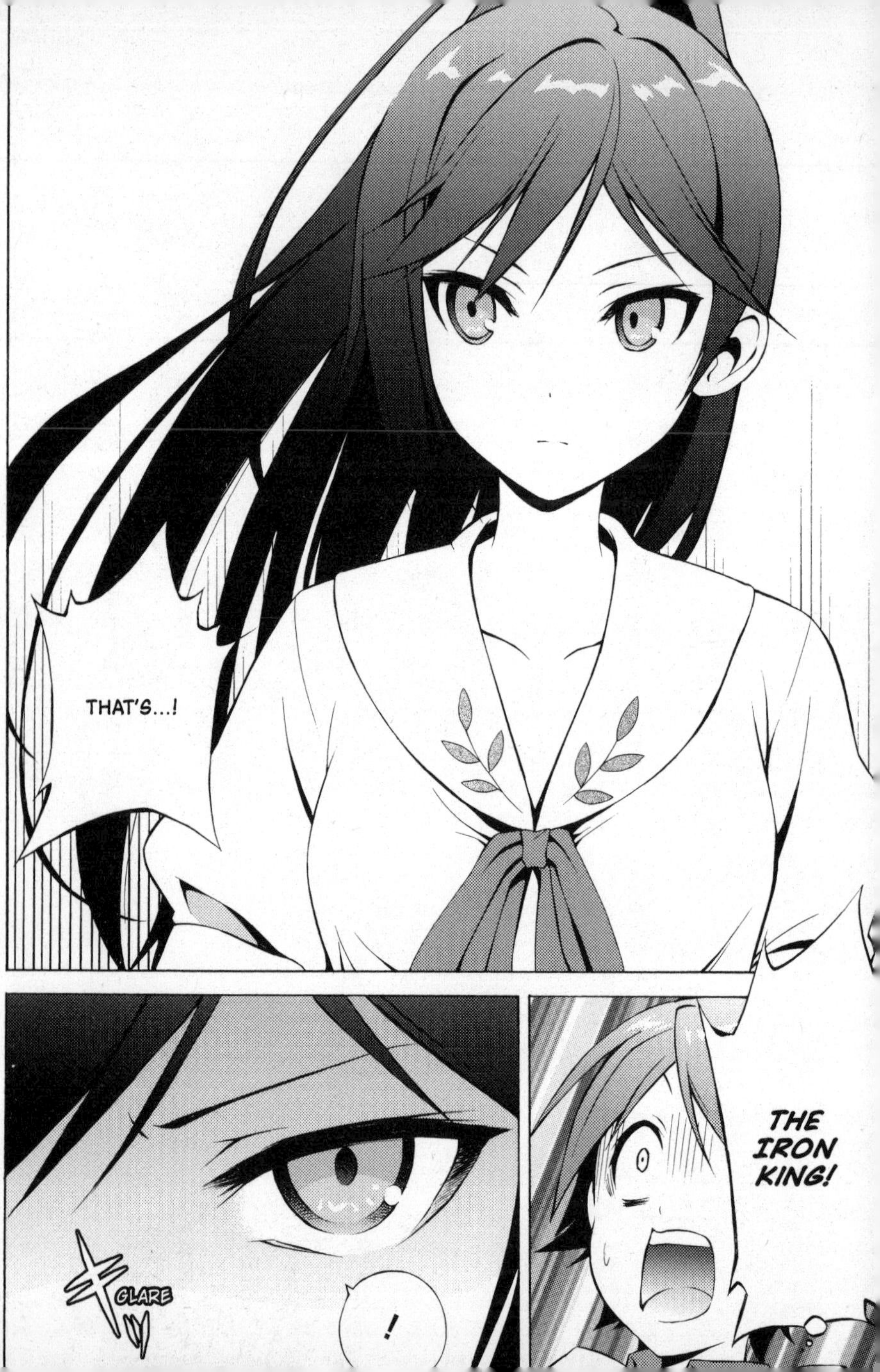
THAT'S...!
THE IRON KING!
GLARE
!

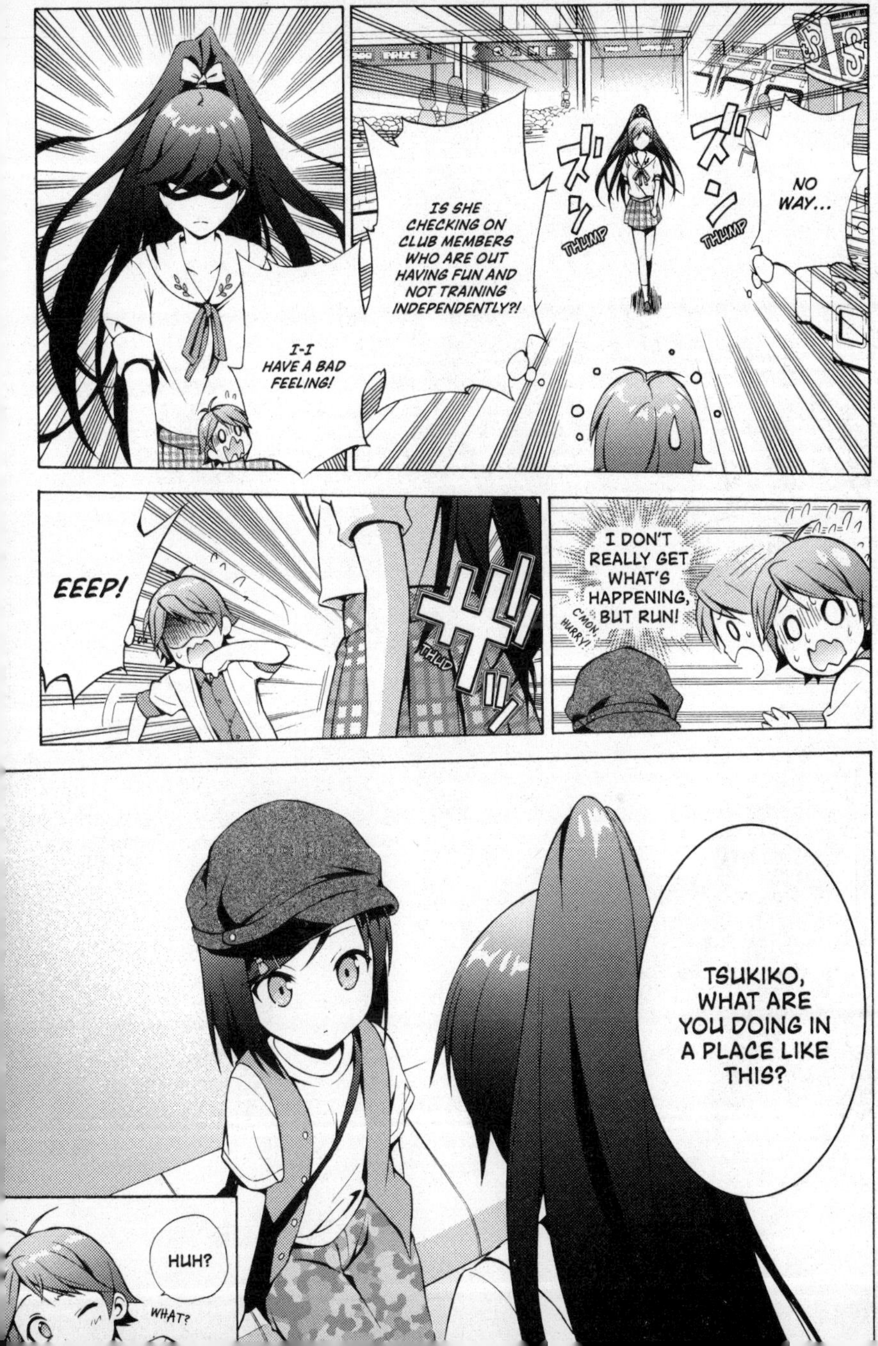
NO WAY...
THUMP
THUMP
IS SHE CHECKING ON CLUB MEMBERS WHO ARE OUT HAVING FUN AND NOT TRAINING INDEPENDENTLY?!
I-I HAVE A BAD FEELING!
I DON'T REALLY GET WHAT'S HAPPENING, BUT RUN!
C'MON, HURRY!
THUD
EEEP!
TSUKIKO, WHAT ARE YOU DOING IN A PLACE LIKE THIS?
HUH?
WHAT?

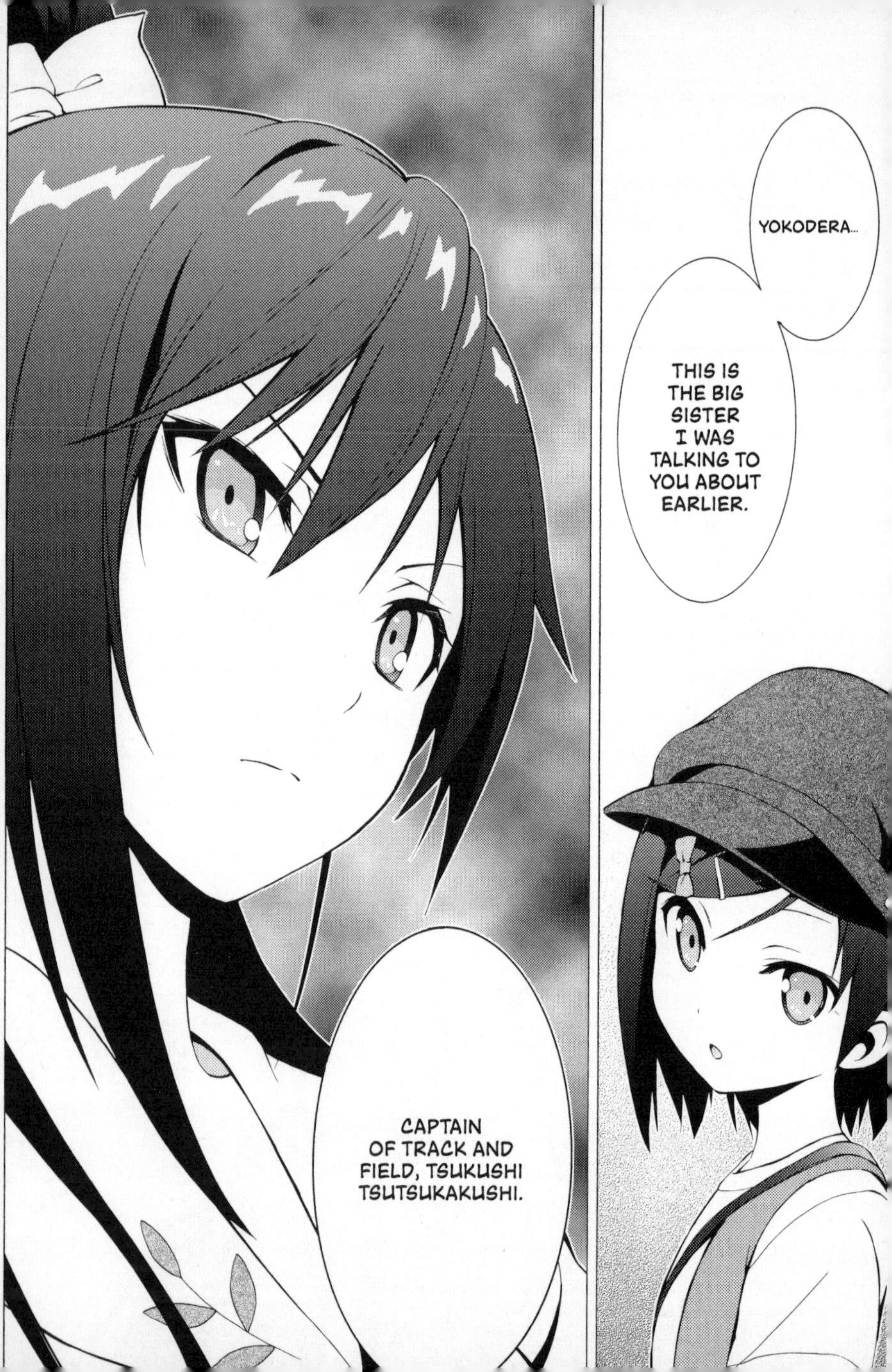
YOKODERA...
THIS IS THE BIG SISTER I WAS TALKING TO YOU ABOUT EARLIER.
CAPTAIN OF TRACK AND FIELD, TSUKUSHI TSUTSUKAKUSHI.

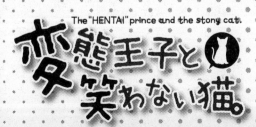

The "HENTAI" prince and the stony cat.

変態王子と
笑わない猫。

ILLUSTRATED CATS OF THE WORLD

SIAMESE

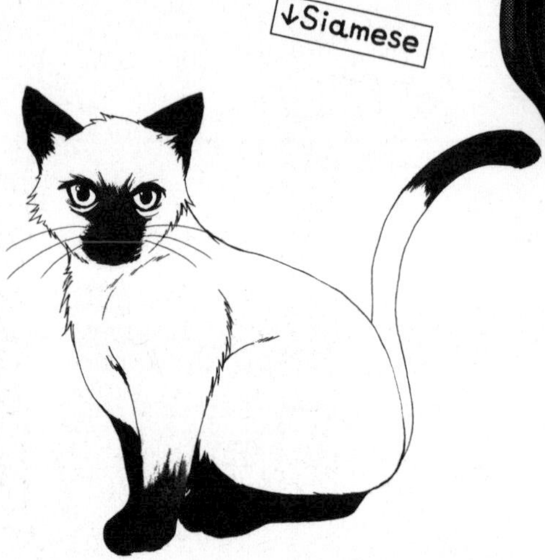
↓Siamese

THEY ARE SHORT-HAIRED CATS ORIGINATING FROM THE KINGDOM OF THAILAND, AND THEIR MAIN CHARACTERISTICS ARE HAVING LONG AND NARROW NECKS, LIMBS, AND TAILS. STARTING WITH THE MODEL CERULEAN, BLUE, CHOCOLATE AND LILAC, THESE 4 ARE THE RECOGNIZED FUR COLORS, AND MANY TIMES, NEAR THE MOUTH AND EARS, AND ALSO THE LIMBS AND TAIL ARE SEEN AS HAVING POINT COLORS. HOWEVER, NEWLY BORN KITTENS ARE WHITE. THEY ARE GOOD AT BEING SPOILED AND LOVE PLAYING WITH THEIR MASTERS. EVEN NOW, THEY ARE A VERY POPULAR BREED IN CAT SHOWS.

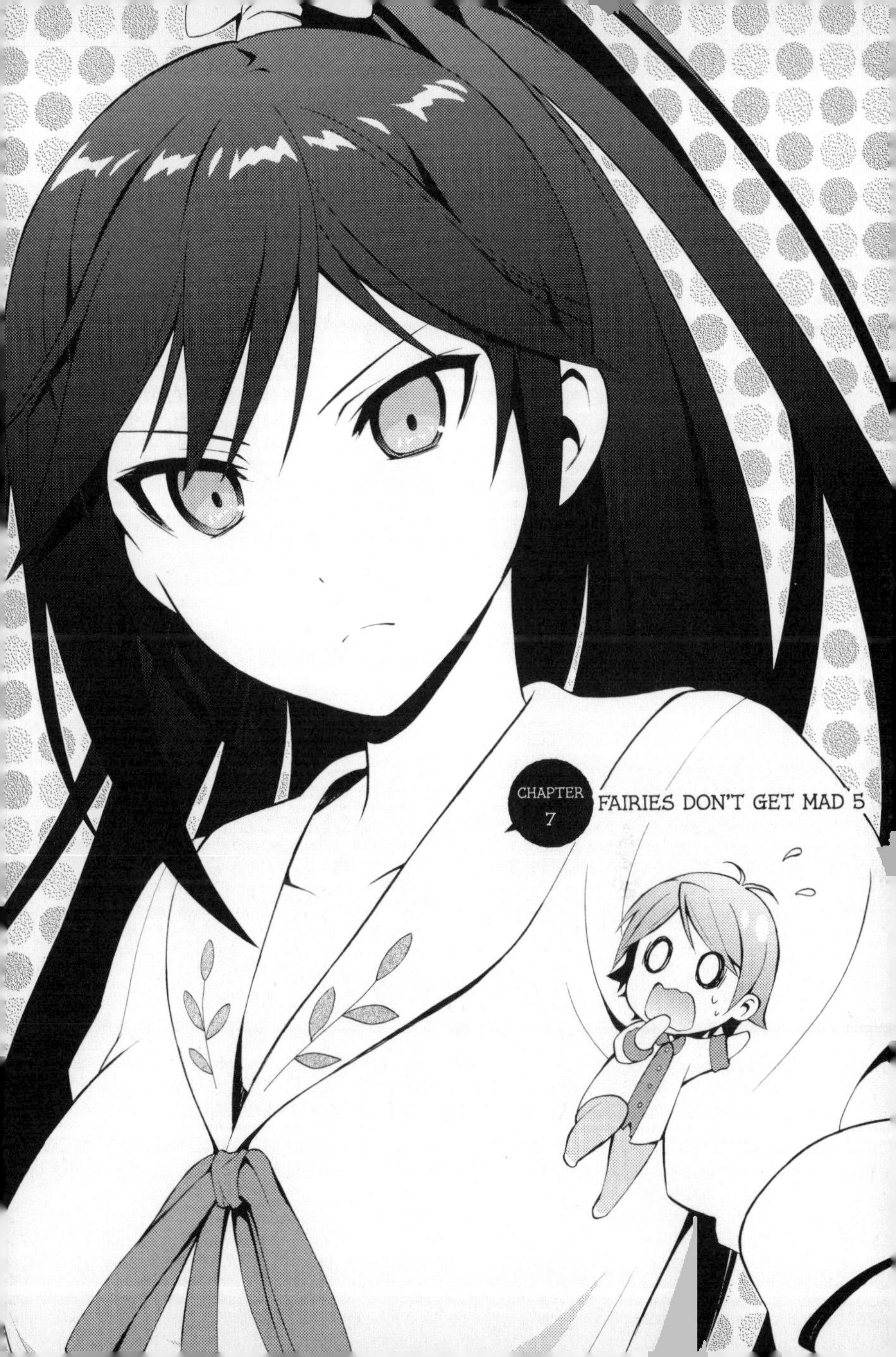

CHAPTER 7 FAIRIES DON'T GET MAD 5

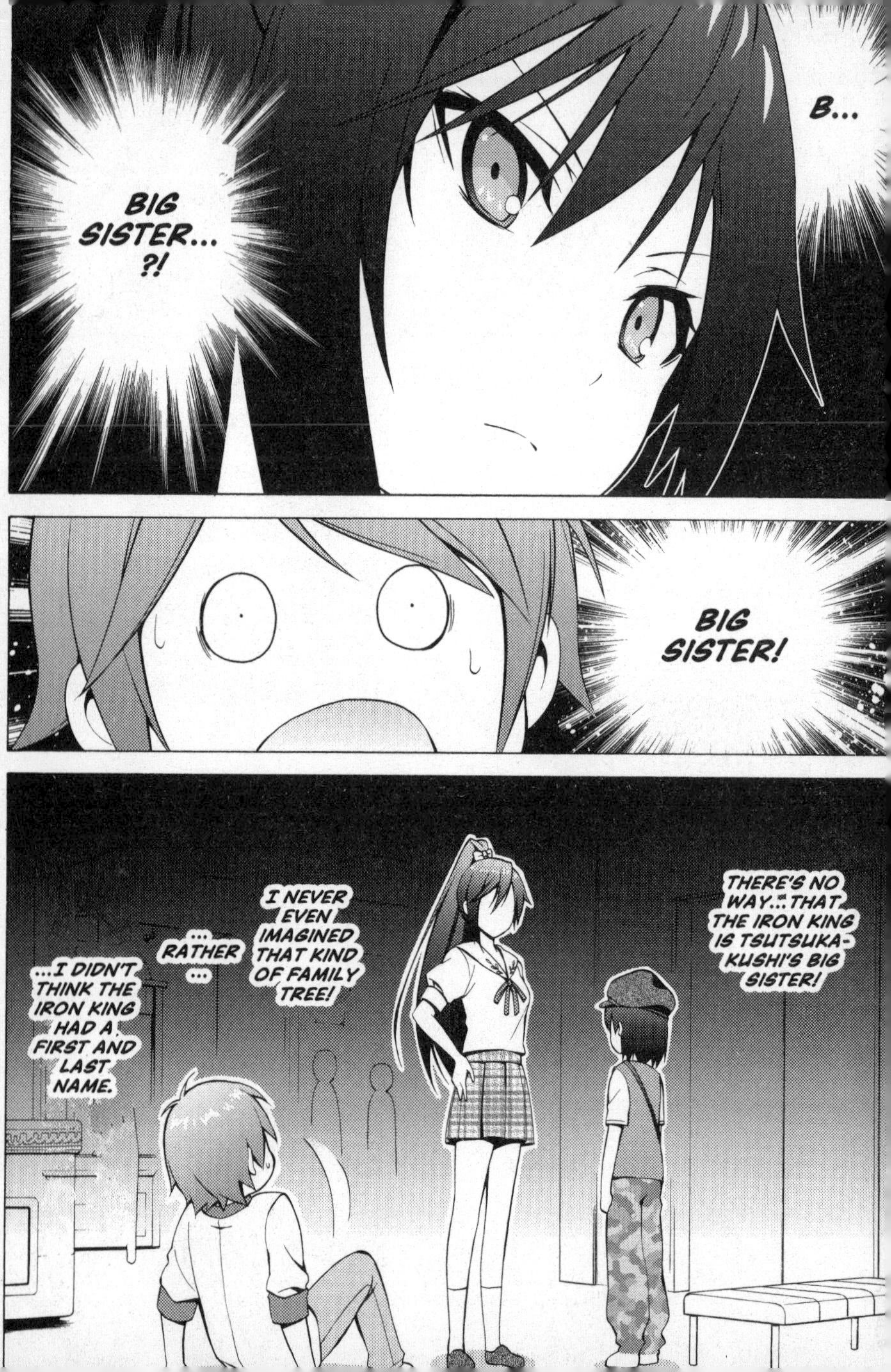
B...
BIG SISTER...?!
BIG SISTER!
THERE'S NO WAY... THAT THE IRON KING IS TSUTSUKA-KUSHI'S BIG SISTER!
I NEVER EVEN IMAGINED THAT KIND OF FAMILY TREE!
...RATHER...
...I DIDN'T THINK THE IRON KING HAD A FIRST AND LAST NAME.

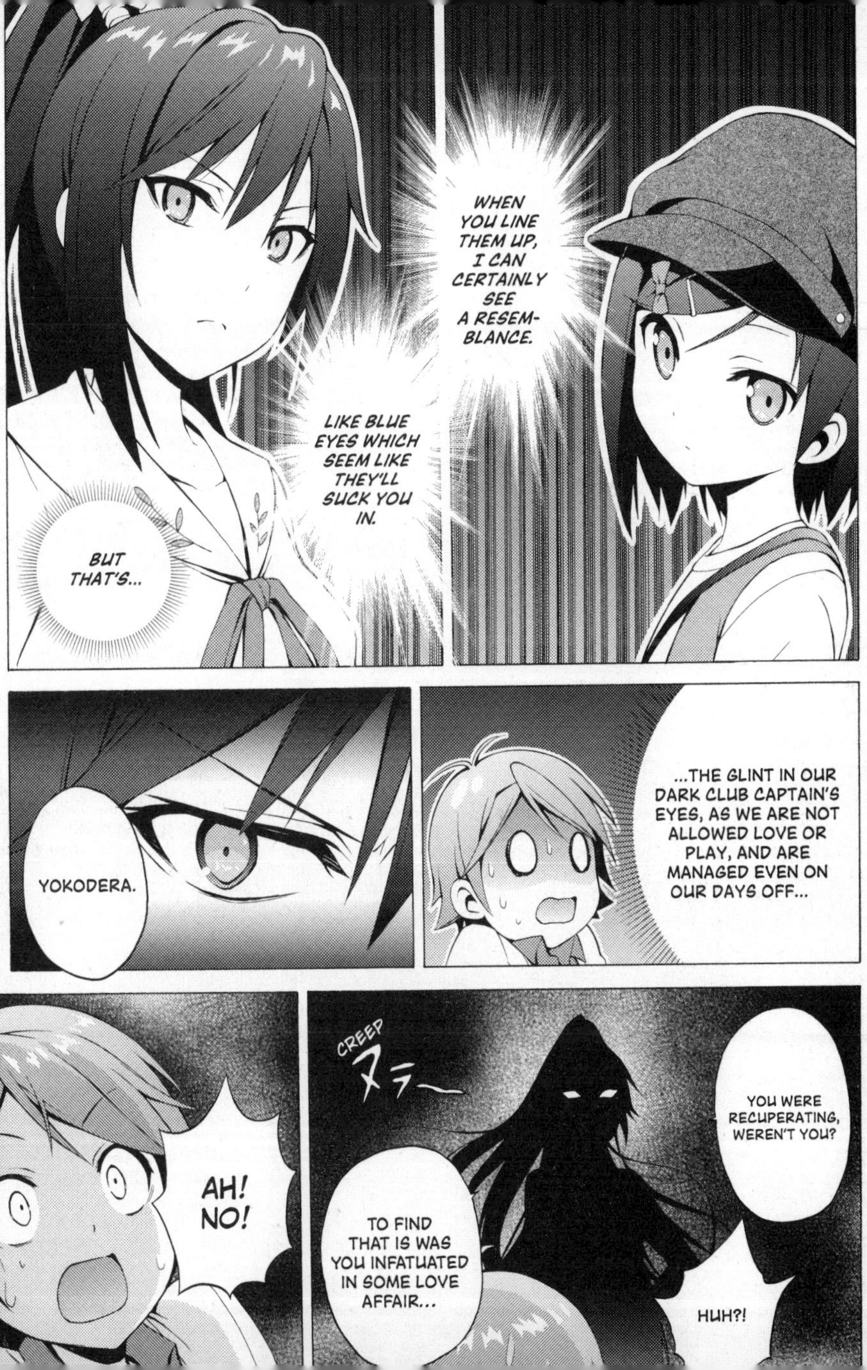
WHEN YOU LINE THEM UP, I CAN CERTAINLY SEE A RESEM-BLANCE.
LIKE BLUE EYES WHICH SEEM LIKE THEY'LL SUCK YOU IN.
BUT THAT'S...
...THE GLINT IN OUR DARK CLUB CAPTAIN'S EYES, AS WE ARE NOT ALLOWED LOVE OR PLAY, AND ARE MANAGED EVEN ON OUR DAYS OFF...
YOKODERA.
CREEP
YOU WERE RECUPERATING, WEREN'T YOU?
TO FIND THAT IS WAS YOU INFATUATED IN SOME LOVE AFFAIR...
HUH?!
AH! NO!

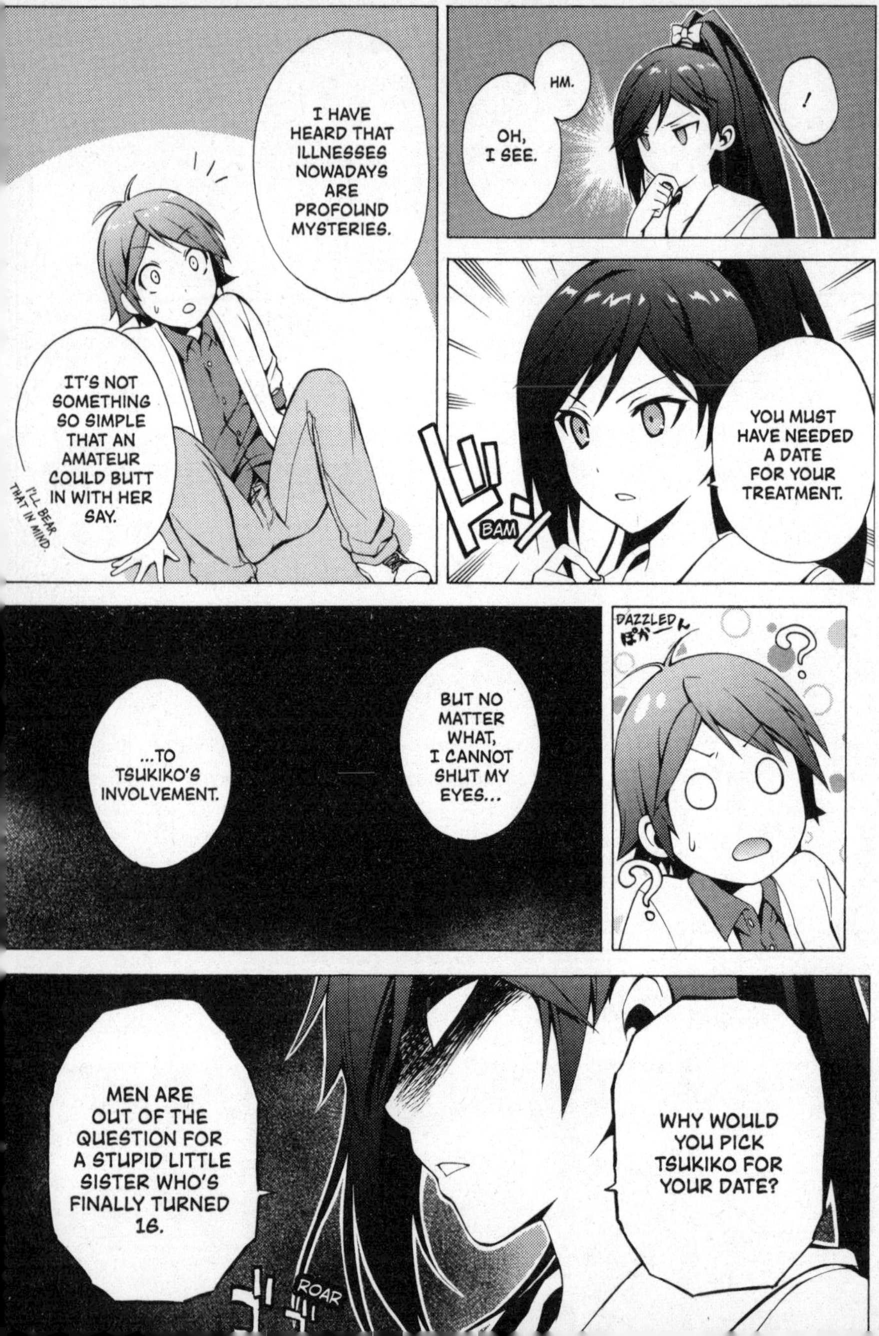
!
HM.
OH, I SEE.
YOU MUST HAVE NEEDED A DATE FOR YOUR TREATMENT.
BAM
I HAVE HEARD THAT ILLNESSES NOWADAYS ARE PROFOUND MYSTERIES.
IT'S NOT SOMETHING SO SIMPLE THAT AN AMATEUR COULD BUTT IN WITH HER SAY.
I'LL BEAR THAT IN MIND.
DAZZLED
ぽかーん
BUT NO MATTER WHAT, I CANNOT SHUT MY EYES...
...TO TSUKIKO'S INVOLVEMENT.
WHY WOULD YOU PICK TSUKIKO FOR YOUR DATE?
MEN ARE OUT OF THE QUESTION FOR A STUPID LITTLE SISTER WHO'S FINALLY TURNED 16.
ROAR

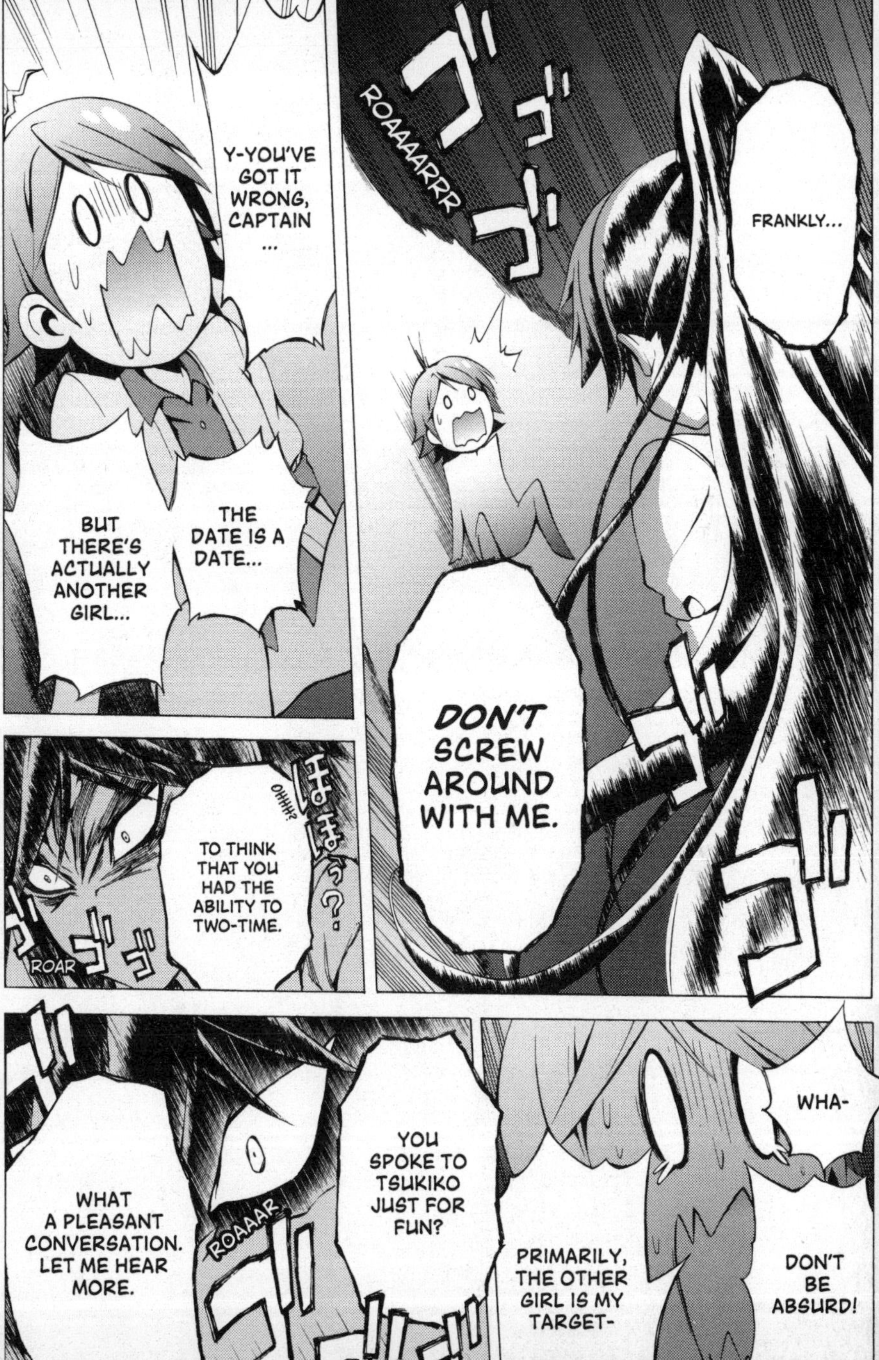

FRANKLY...
ROAAAARRR
DON'T SCREW AROUND WITH ME.
Y-YOU'VE GOT IT WRONG, CAPTAIN ...
THE DATE IS A DATE...
BUT THERE'S ACTUALLY ANOTHER GIRL...
OHHH?
TO THINK THAT YOU HAD THE ABILITY TO TWO-TIME.
ROAR
WHA-
DON'T BE ABSURD!
PRIMARILY, THE OTHER GIRL IS MY TARGET-
YOU SPOKE TO TSUKIKO JUST FOR FUN?
ROAAAR
WHAT A PLEASANT CONVERSATION. LET ME HEAR MORE.

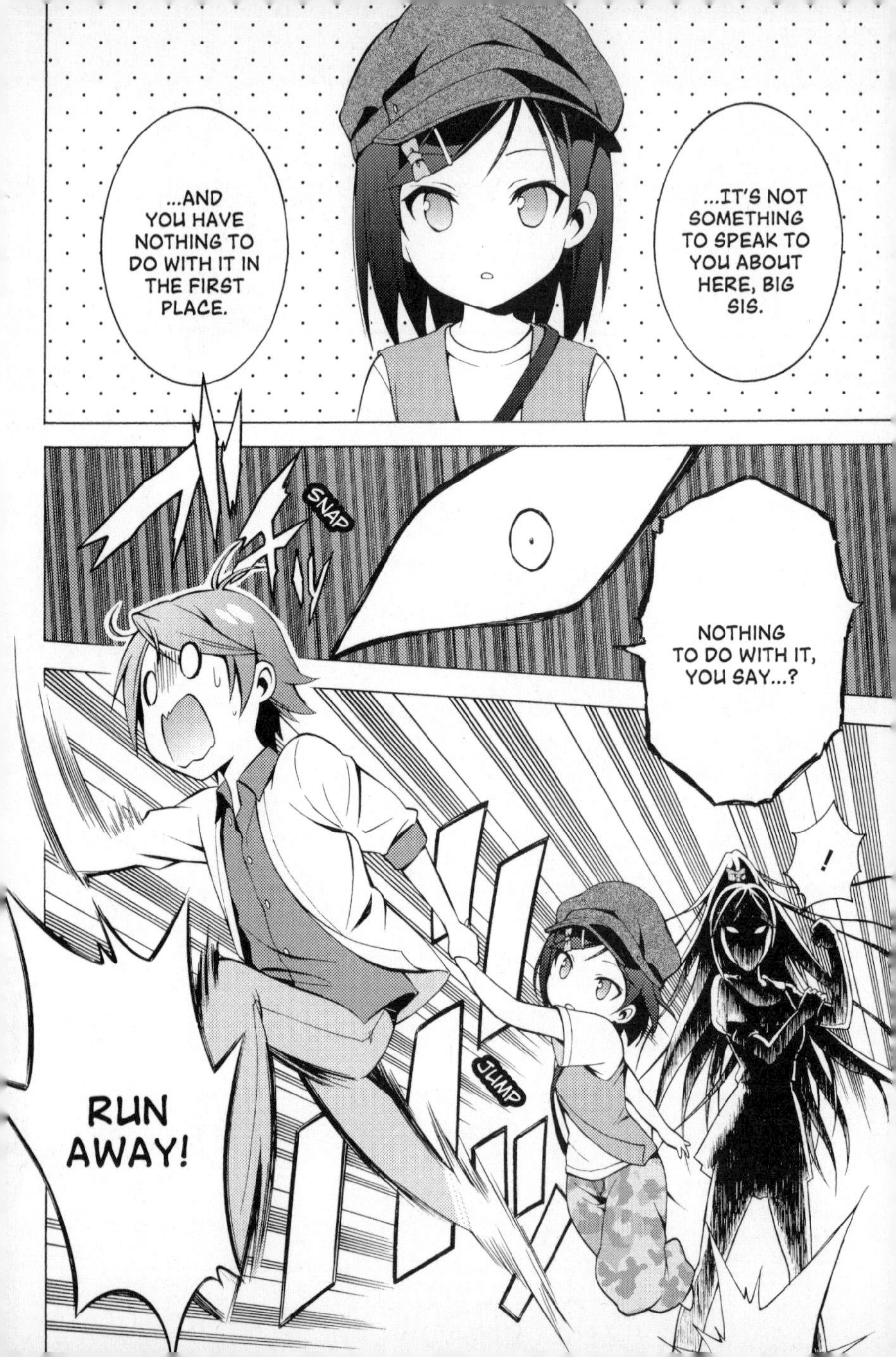
...IT'S NOT SOMETHING TO SPEAK TO YOU ABOUT HERE, BIG SIS.
...AND YOU HAVE NOTHING TO DO WITH IT IN THE FIRST PLACE.
NOTHING TO DO WITH IT, YOU SAY...?
SNAP
!
JUMP
RUN AWAY!

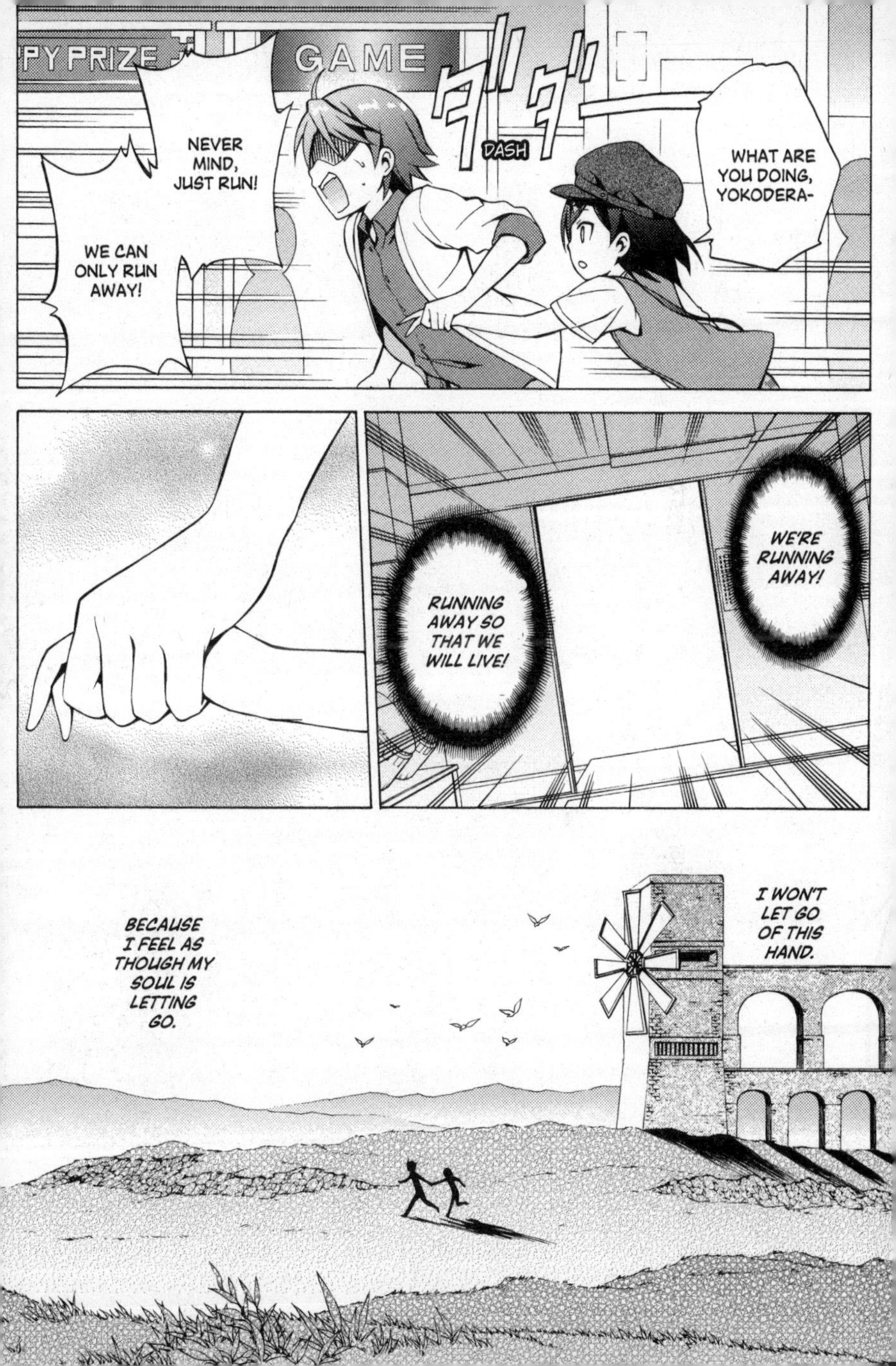

PY PRIZE
GAME
WHAT ARE YOU DOING, YOKODERA-
DASH
NEVER MIND, JUST RUN!
WE CAN ONLY RUN AWAY!
WE'RE RUNNING AWAY!
RUNNING AWAY SO THAT WE WILL LIVE!
I WON'T LET GO OF THIS HAND.
BECAUSE I FEEL AS THOUGH MY SOUL IS LETTING GO.

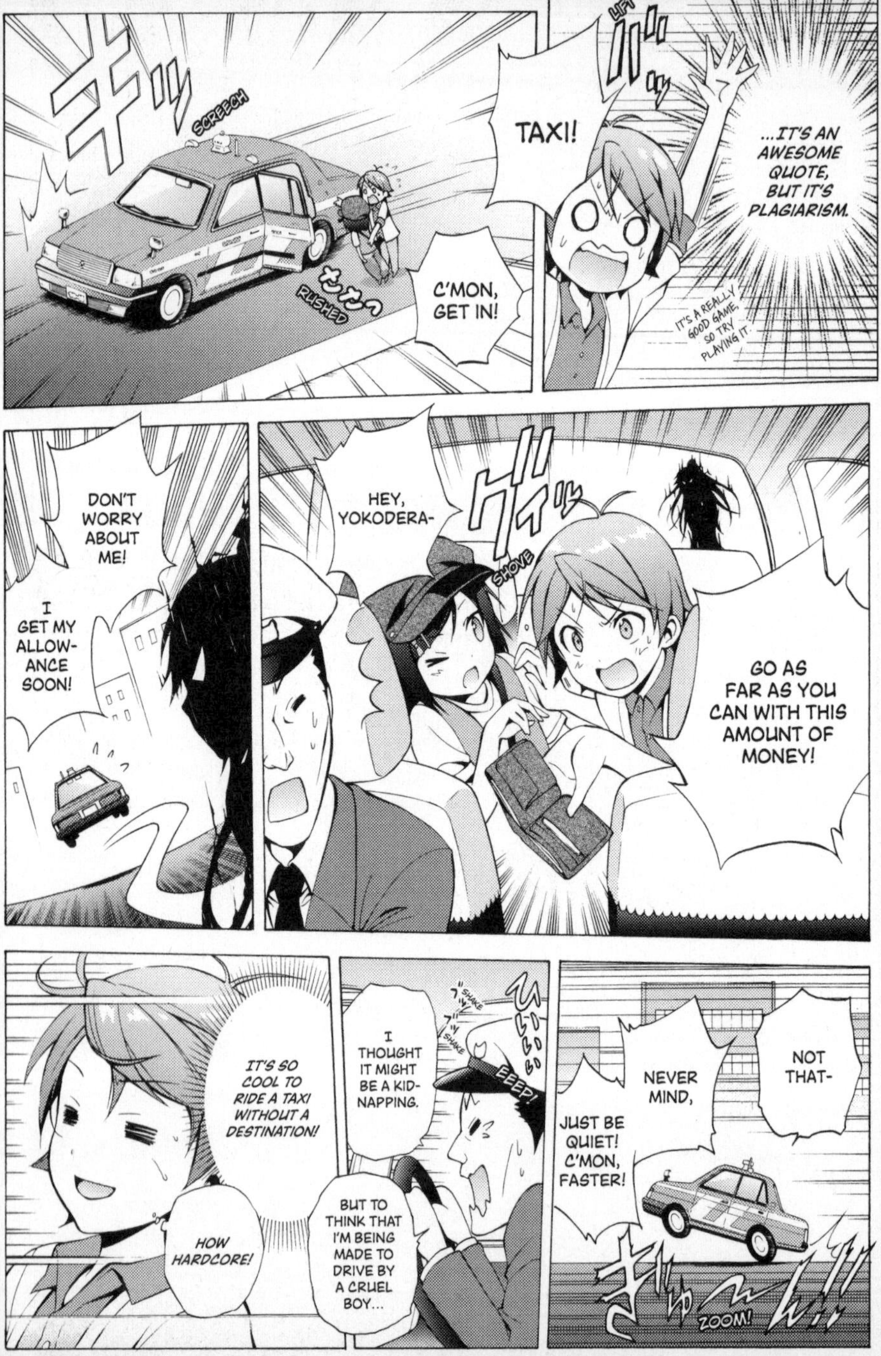
LIFT
...IT'S AN AWESOME QUOTE, BUT IT'S PLAGIARISM.
TAXI!
IT'S A REALLY GOOD GAME, SO TRY PLAYING IT.
SCREECH
C'MON, GET IN!
RUSHED
HEY, YOKODERA-
SHOVE
GO AS FAR AS YOU CAN WITH THIS AMOUNT OF MONEY!
DON'T WORRY ABOUT ME!
I GET MY ALLOW-ANCE SOON!
NOT THAT-
NEVER MIND,
JUST BE QUIET! C'MON, FASTER!
ZOOM!
SHAKE
SHAKE
EEEP!
I THOUGHT IT MIGHT BE A KID-NAPPING.
BUT TO THINK THAT I'M BEING MADE TO DRIVE BY A CRUEL BOY...
IT'S SO COOL TO RIDE A TAXI WITHOUT A DESTINATION!
HOW HARDCORE!

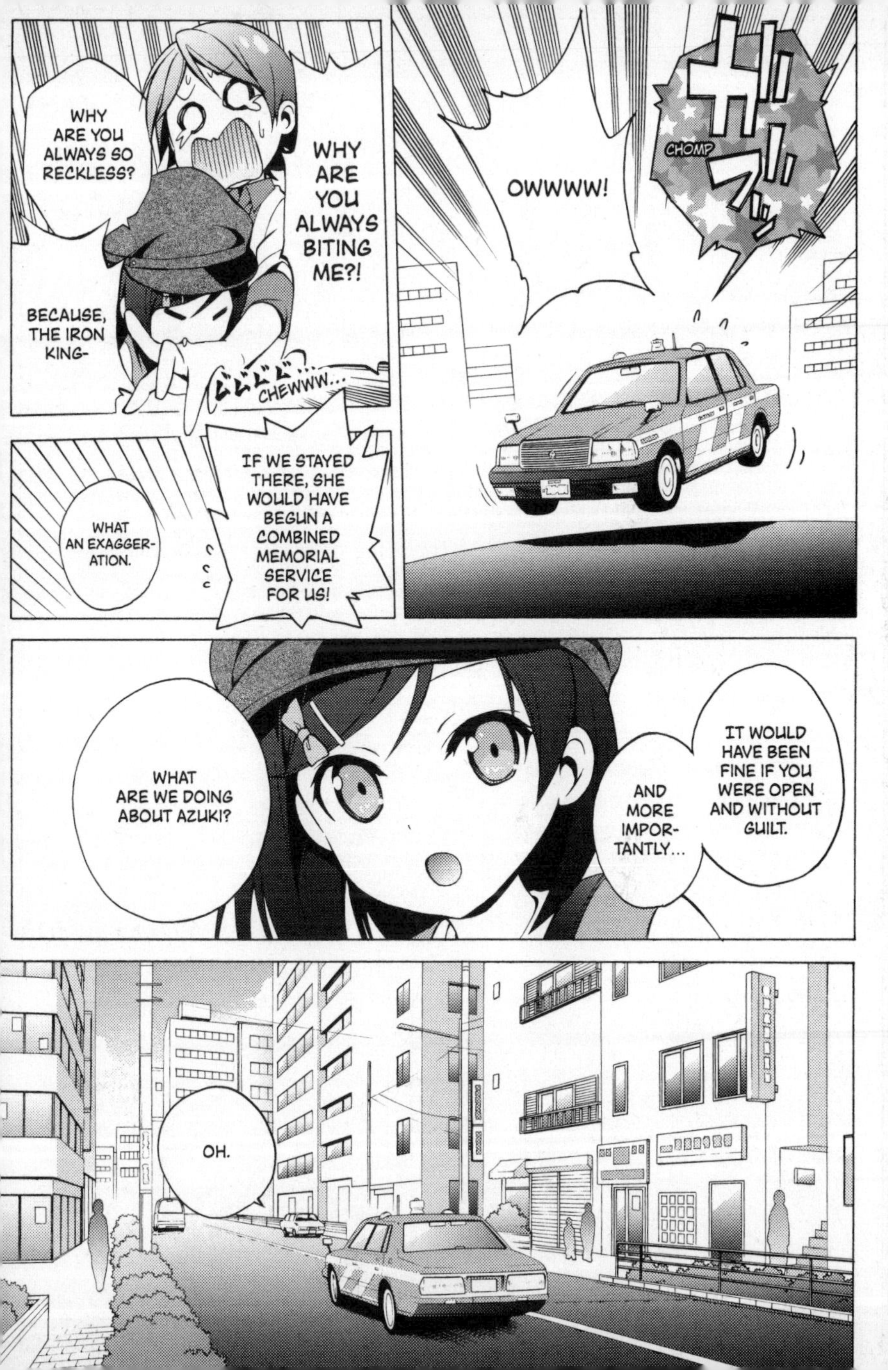
CHOMP
OWWWW!
WHY ARE YOU ALWAYS BITING ME?!
WHY ARE YOU ALWAYS SO RECKLESS?
BECAUSE, THE IRON KING-
CHEWWW...
IF WE STAYED THERE, SHE WOULD HAVE BEGUN A COMBINED MEMORIAL SERVICE FOR US!
WHAT AN EXAGGER-ATION.
IT WOULD HAVE BEEN FINE IF YOU WERE OPEN AND WITHOUT GUILT.
AND MORE IMPOR-TANTLY...
WHAT ARE WE DOING ABOUT AZUKI?
OH.

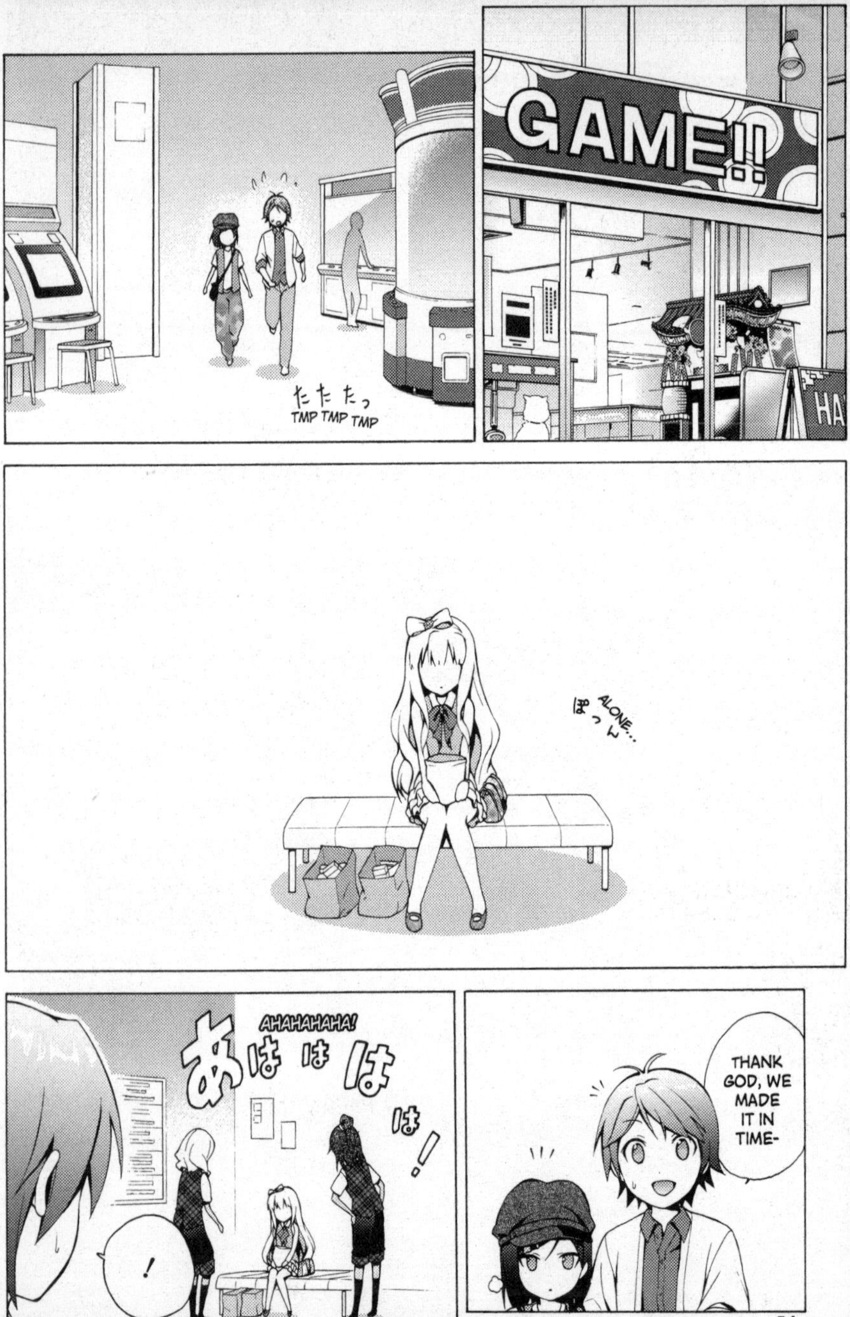
GAME!!
HA
たたたっ
TMP TMP TMP
ALONE...
ぽっん
THANK GOD, WE MADE IT IN TIME-
あははは
は!
AHAHAHAHA!
!

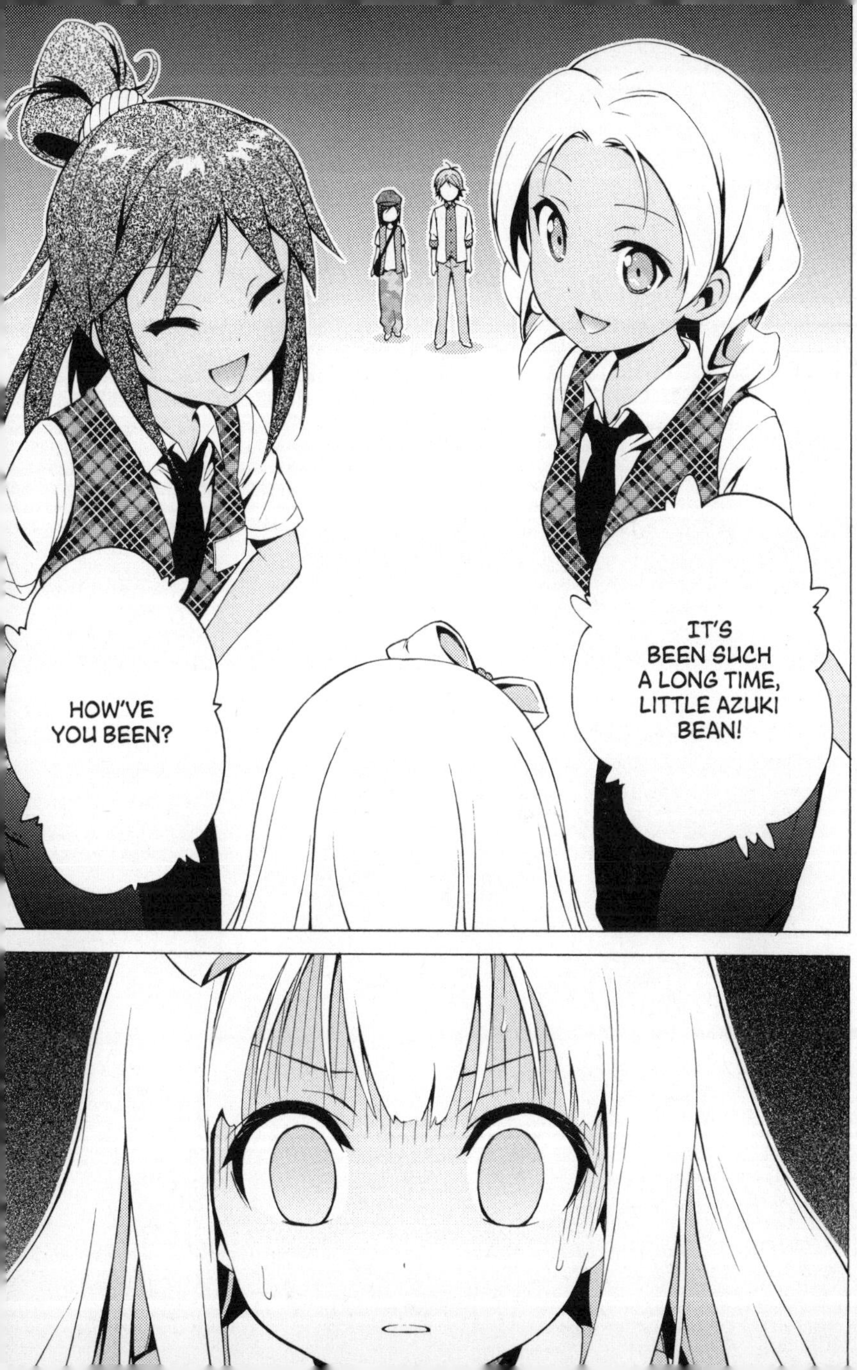
IT'S BEEN SUCH A LONG TIME, LITTLE AZUKI BEAN!
HOW'VE YOU BEEN?

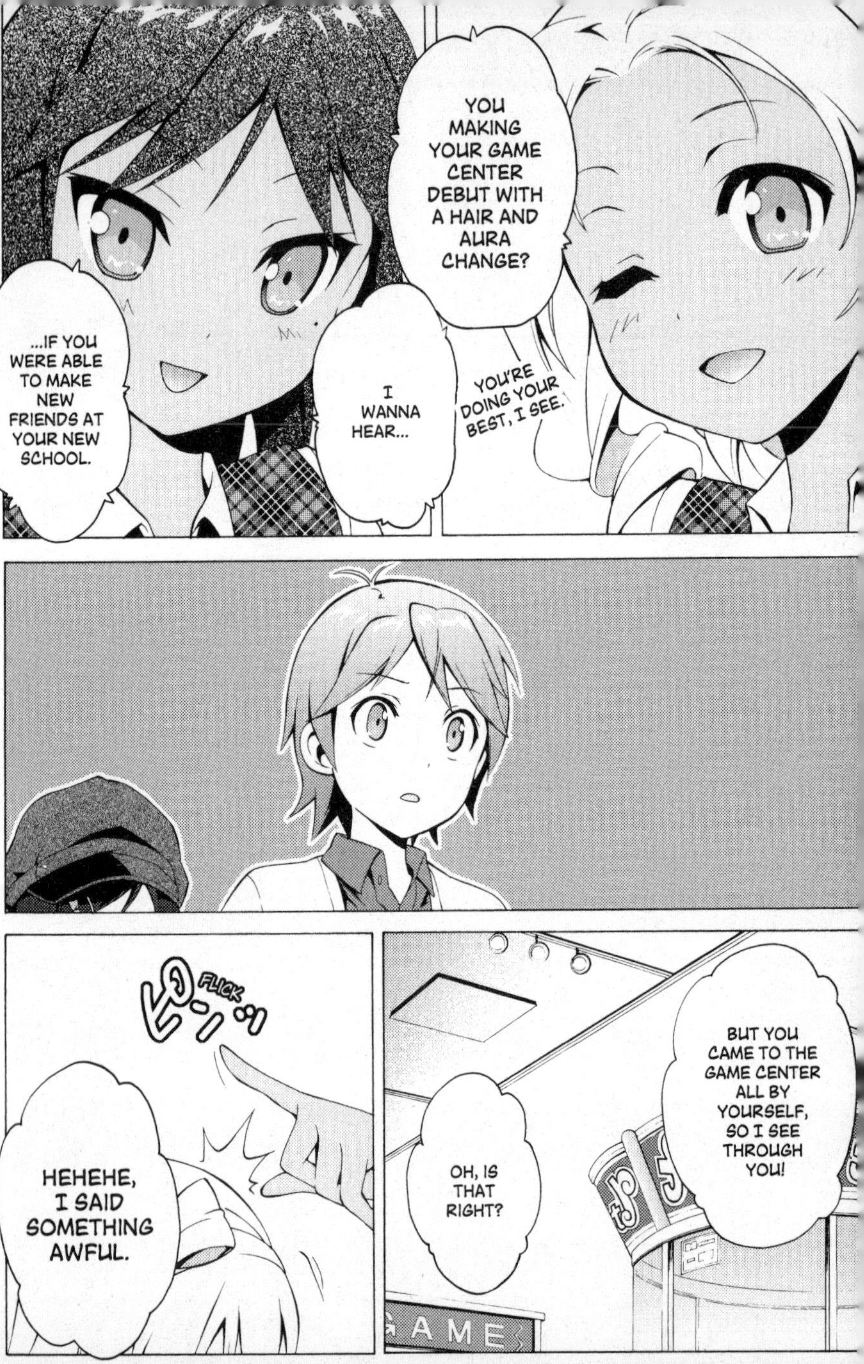
YOU MAKING YOUR GAME CENTER DEBUT WITH A HAIR AND AURA CHANGE?
YOU'RE DOING YOUR BEST, I SEE.
I WANNA HEAR...
...IF YOU WERE ABLE TO MAKE NEW FRIENDS AT YOUR NEW SCHOOL.
BUT YOU CAME TO THE GAME CENTER ALL BY YOURSELF, SO I SEE THROUGH YOU!
OH, IS THAT RIGHT?
GAME
FLICK
HEHEHE, I SAID SOMETHING AWFUL.

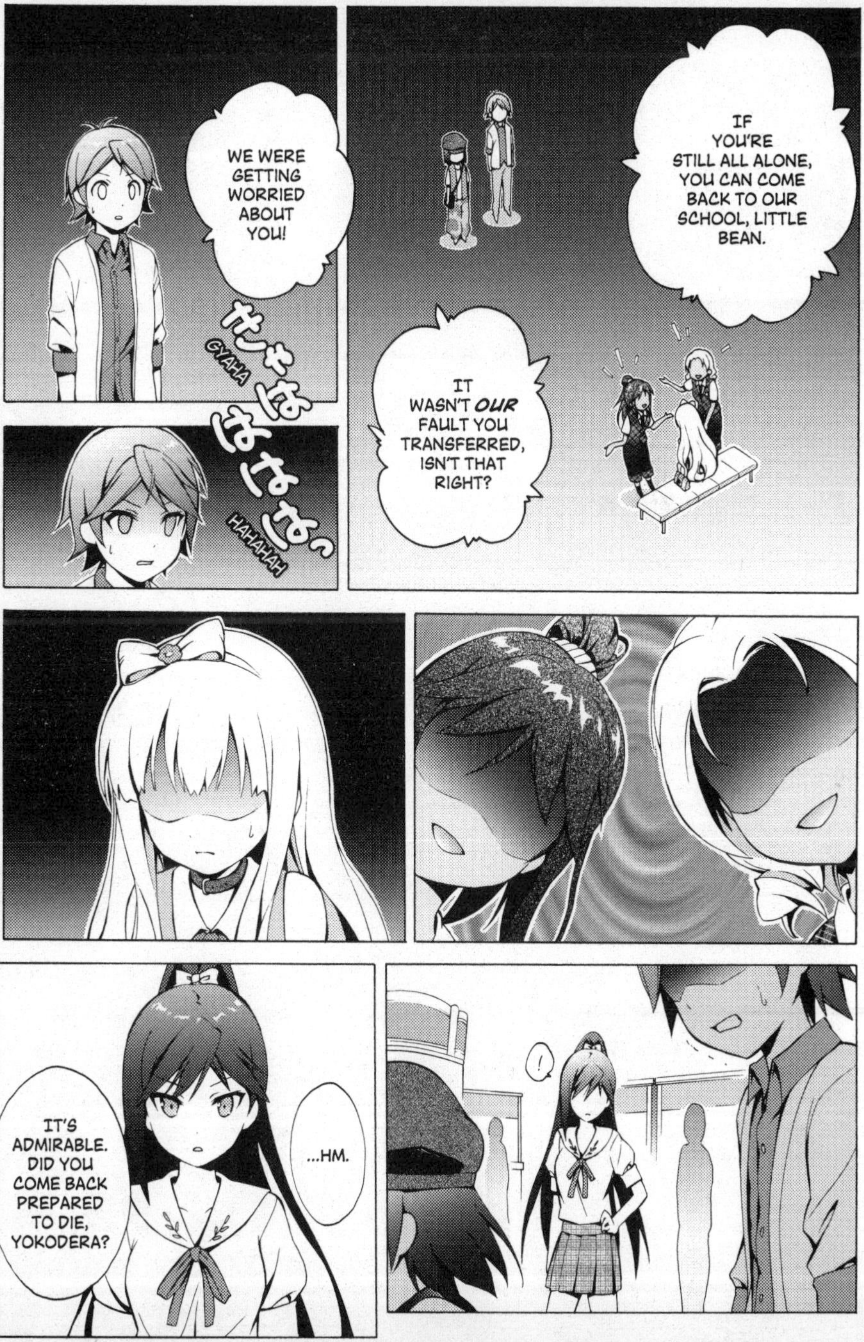
IF YOU'RE STILL ALL ALONE, YOU CAN COME BACK TO OUR SCHOOL, LITTLE BEAN.
IT WASN'T *OUR* FAULT YOU TRANSFERRED, ISN'T THAT RIGHT?
WE WERE GETTING WORRIED ABOUT YOU!
きゃははははっ
GYAHA HAHAHAH
!
...HM.
IT'S ADMIRABLE. DID YOU COME BACK PREPARED TO DIE, YOKODERA?

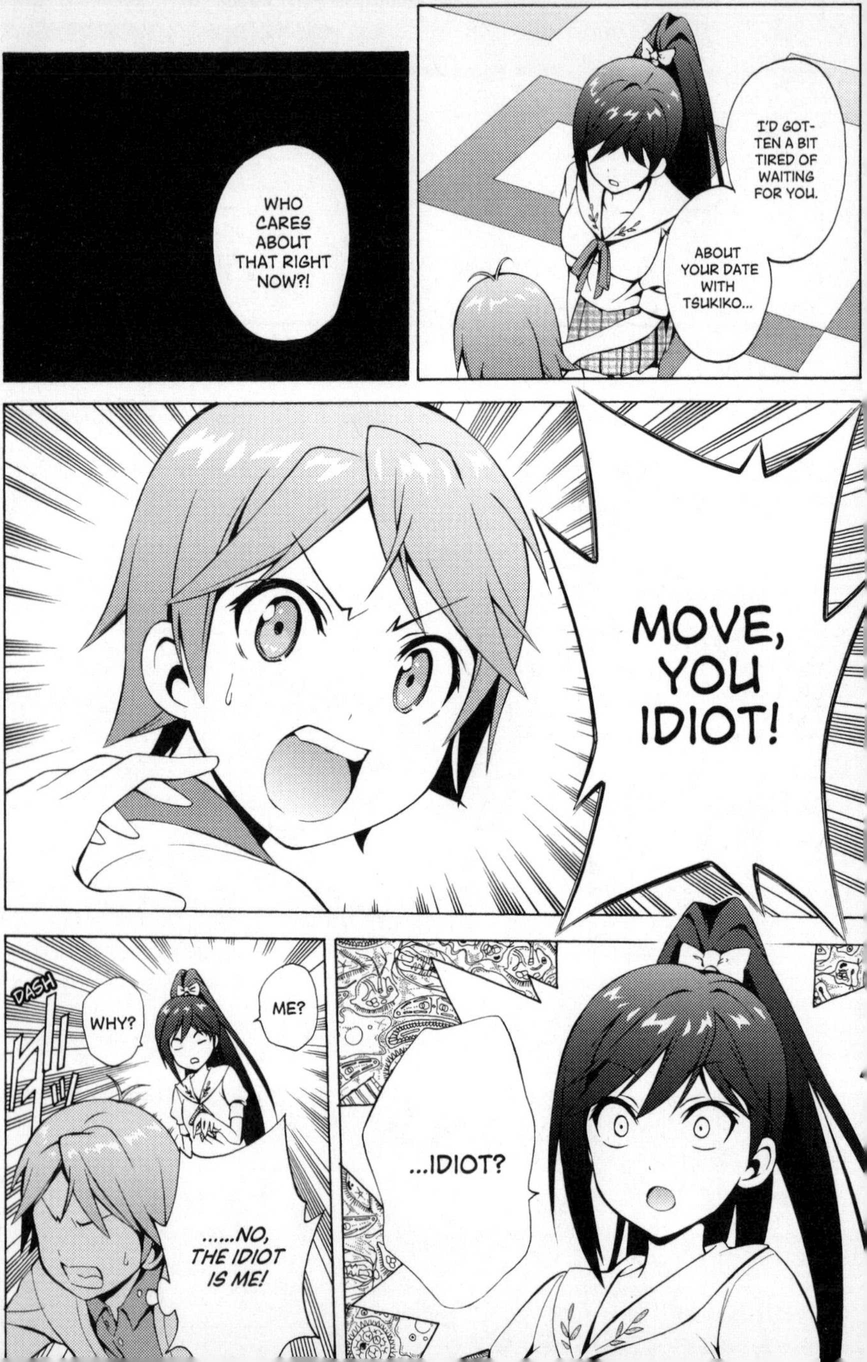
I'D GOT-TEN A BIT TIRED OF WAITING FOR YOU.
ABOUT YOUR DATE WITH TSUKIKO...
WHO CARES ABOUT THAT RIGHT NOW?!
MOVE, YOU IDIOT!
...IDIOT?
ME?
WHY?
DASH
......NO, THE IDIOT IS ME!

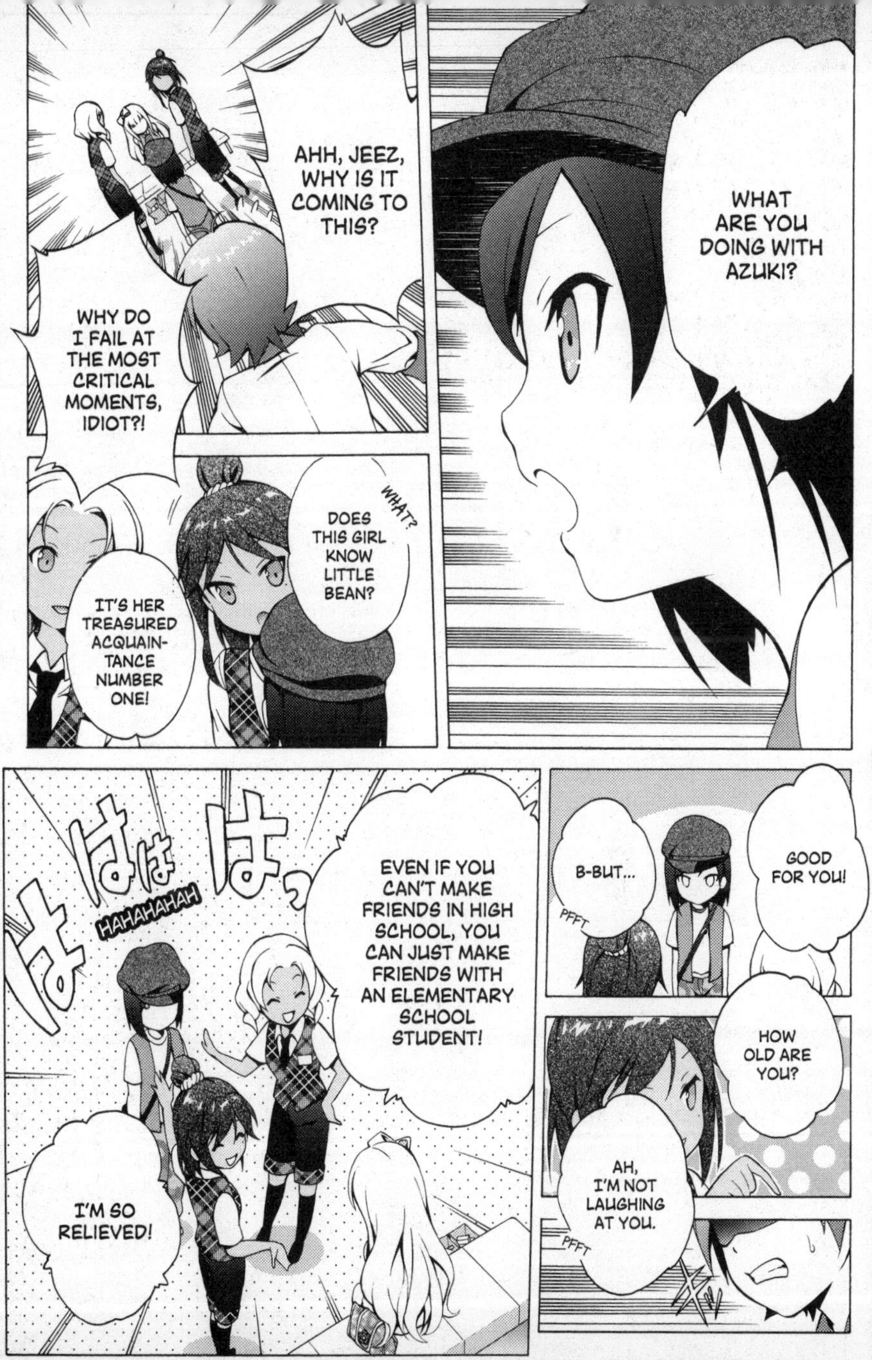
WHAT ARE YOU DOING WITH AZUKI?
AHH, JEEZ, WHY IS IT COMING TO THIS?
WHY DO I FAIL AT THE MOST CRITICAL MOMENTS, IDIOT?!
WHAT?
DOES THIS GIRL KNOW LITTLE BEAN?
IT'S HER TREASURED ACQUAIN-TANCE NUMBER ONE!
GOOD FOR YOU!
B-BUT...
PFFT
HOW OLD ARE YOU?
AH, I'M NOT LAUGHING AT YOU.
PFFT
ははははっ
HAHAHAHAH
EVEN IF YOU CAN'T MAKE FRIENDS IN HIGH SCHOOL, YOU CAN JUST MAKE FRIENDS WITH AN ELEMENTARY SCHOOL STUDENT!
I'M SO RELIEVED!

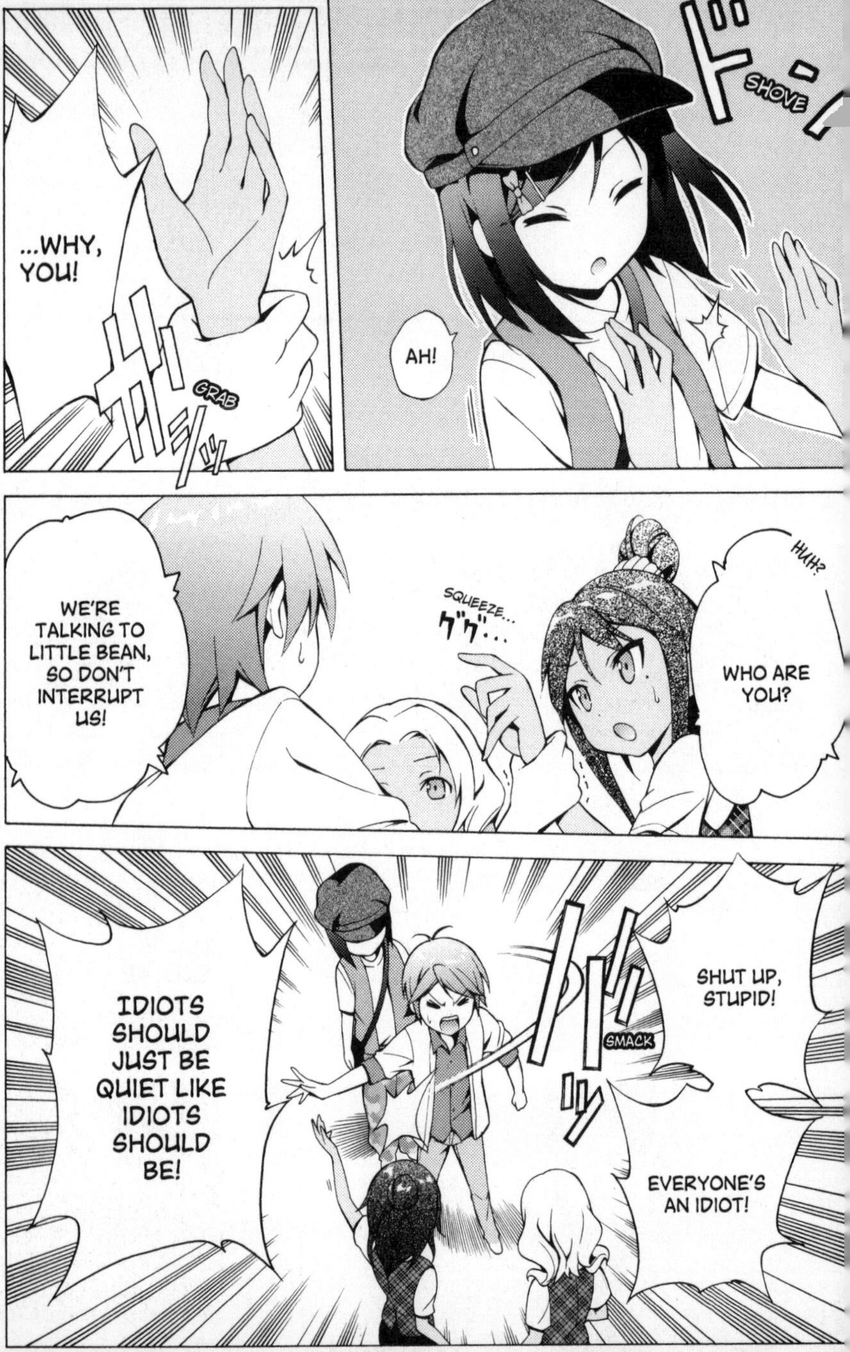
SHOVE
AH!
...WHY, YOU!
GRAB
HUH?
WHO ARE YOU?
SQUEEZE...
ググ…
WE'RE TALKING TO LITTLE BEAN, SO DON'T INTERRUPT US!
SHUT UP, STUPID!
SMACK
EVERYONE'S AN IDIOT!
IDIOTS SHOULD JUST BE QUIET LIKE IDIOTS SHOULD BE!

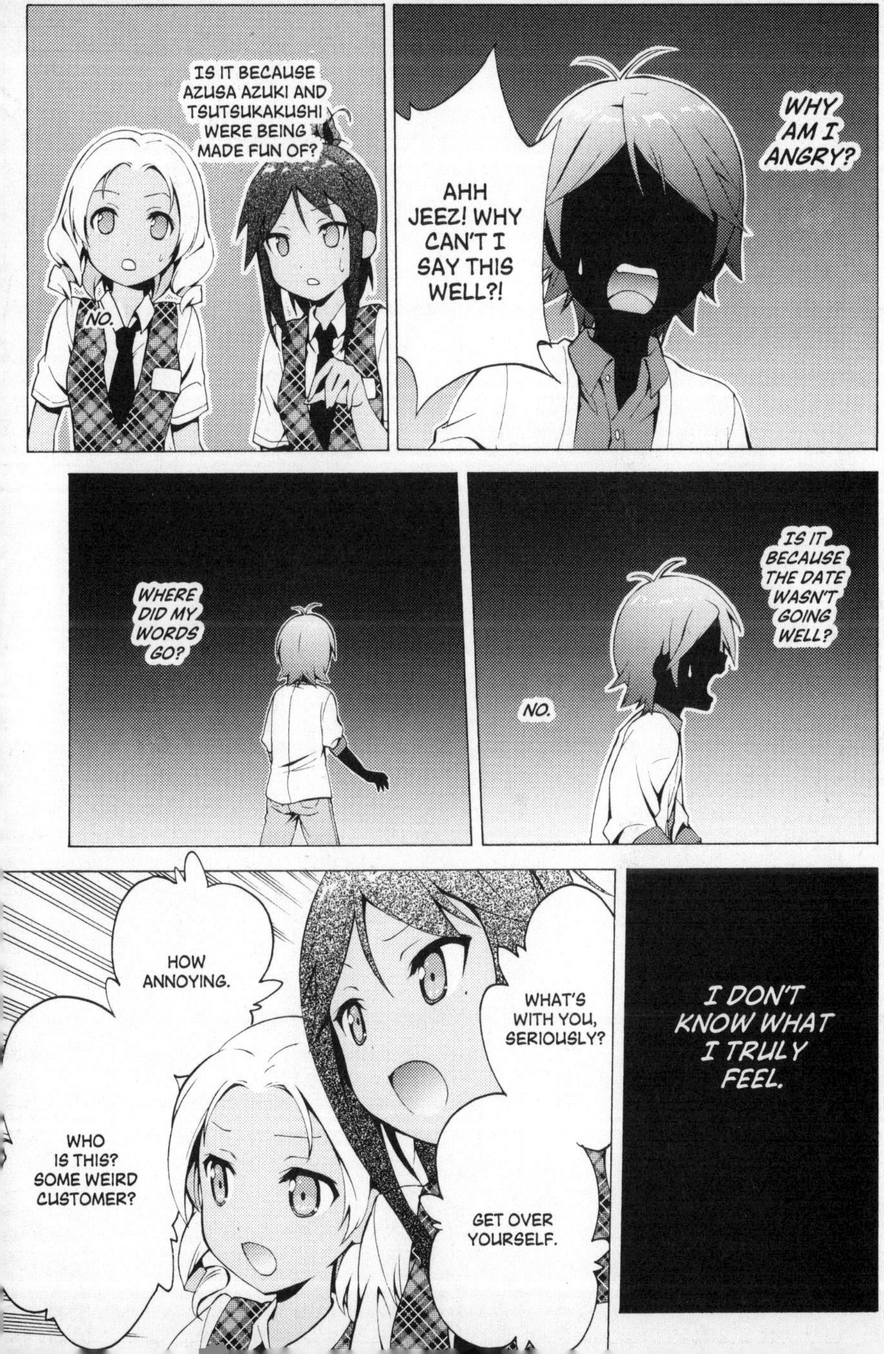
WHY AM I ANGRY?
AHH JEEZ! WHY CAN'T I SAY THIS WELL?!
IS IT BECAUSE AZUSA AZUKI AND TSUTSUKAKUSHI WERE BEING MADE FUN OF?
NO.
IS IT BECAUSE THE DATE WASN'T GOING WELL?
NO.
WHERE DID MY WORDS GO?
I DON'T KNOW WHAT I TRULY FEEL.
WHAT'S WITH YOU, SERIOUSLY?
HOW ANNOYING.
GET OVER YOURSELF.
WHO IS THIS? SOME WEIRD CUSTOMER?

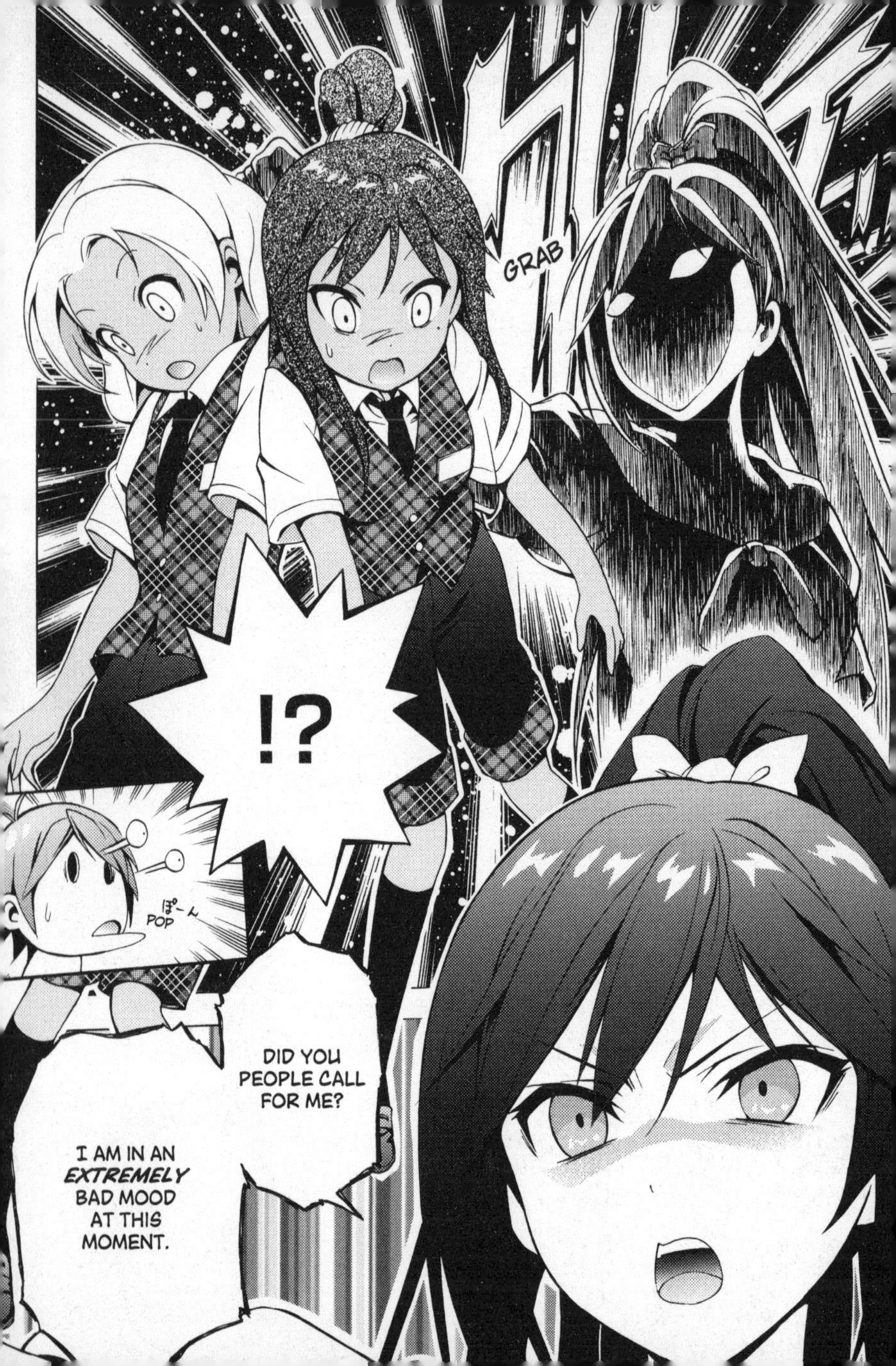
GRAB
!?
DID YOU PEOPLE CALL FOR ME?
I AM IN AN *EXTREMELY* BAD MOOD AT THIS MOMENT.
ぽーん
POP

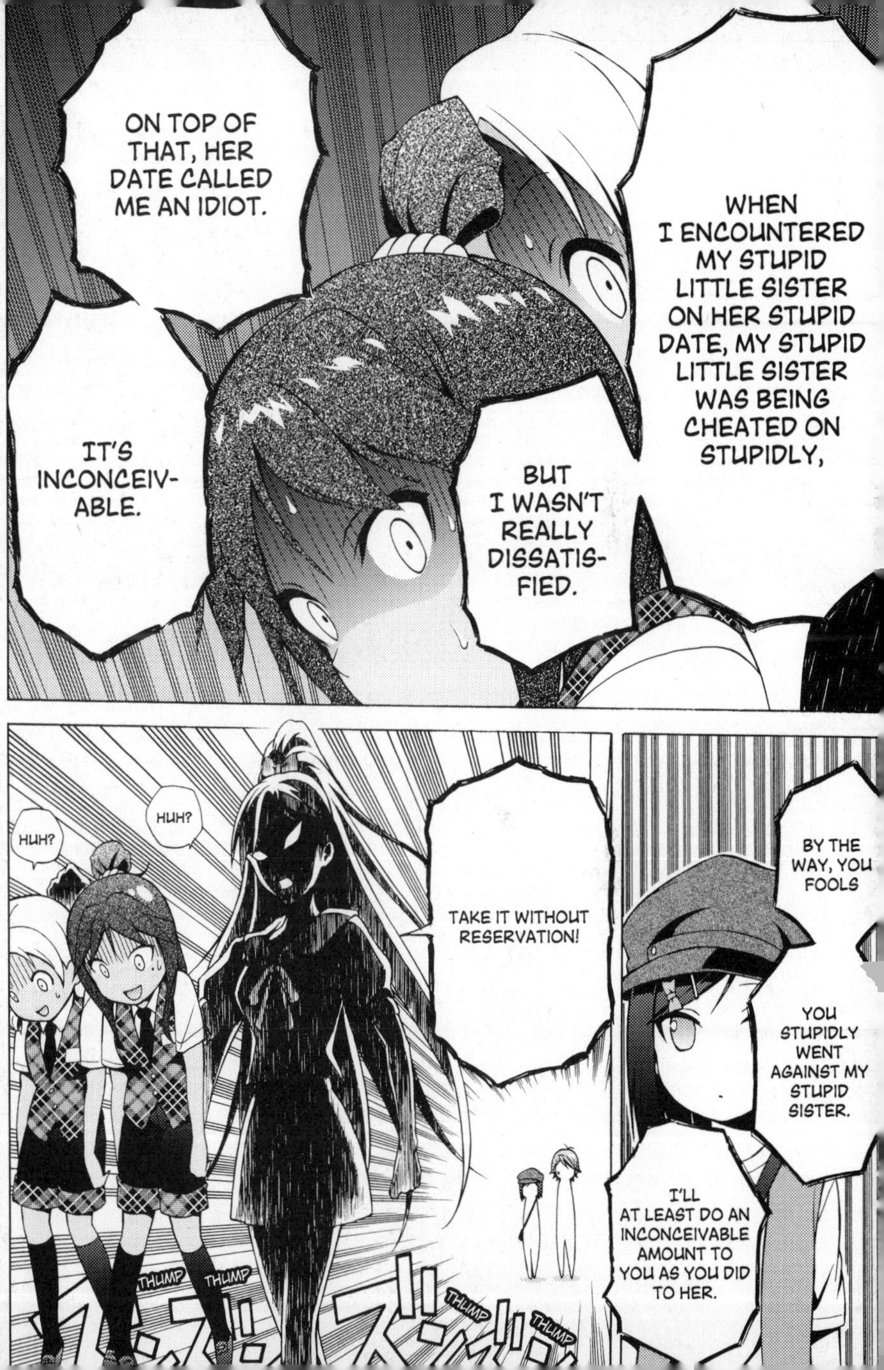
WHEN I ENCOUNTERED MY STUPID LITTLE SISTER ON HER STUPID DATE, MY STUPID LITTLE SISTER WAS BEING CHEATED ON STUPIDLY,
BUT I WASN'T REALLY DISSATIS-FIED.
ON TOP OF THAT, HER DATE CALLED ME AN IDIOT.
IT'S INCONCEIV-ABLE.
BY THE WAY, YOU FOOLS
YOU STUPIDLY WENT AGAINST MY STUPID SISTER.
I'LL AT LEAST DO AN INCONCEIVABLE AMOUNT TO YOU AS YOU DID TO HER.
THUMP
THUMP
TAKE IT WITHOUT RESERVATION!
HUH?
HUH?
THUMP
THUMP

...

GYAAAHHHHH

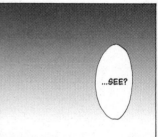

...SEE?

WE'RE NOT FRIENDS.

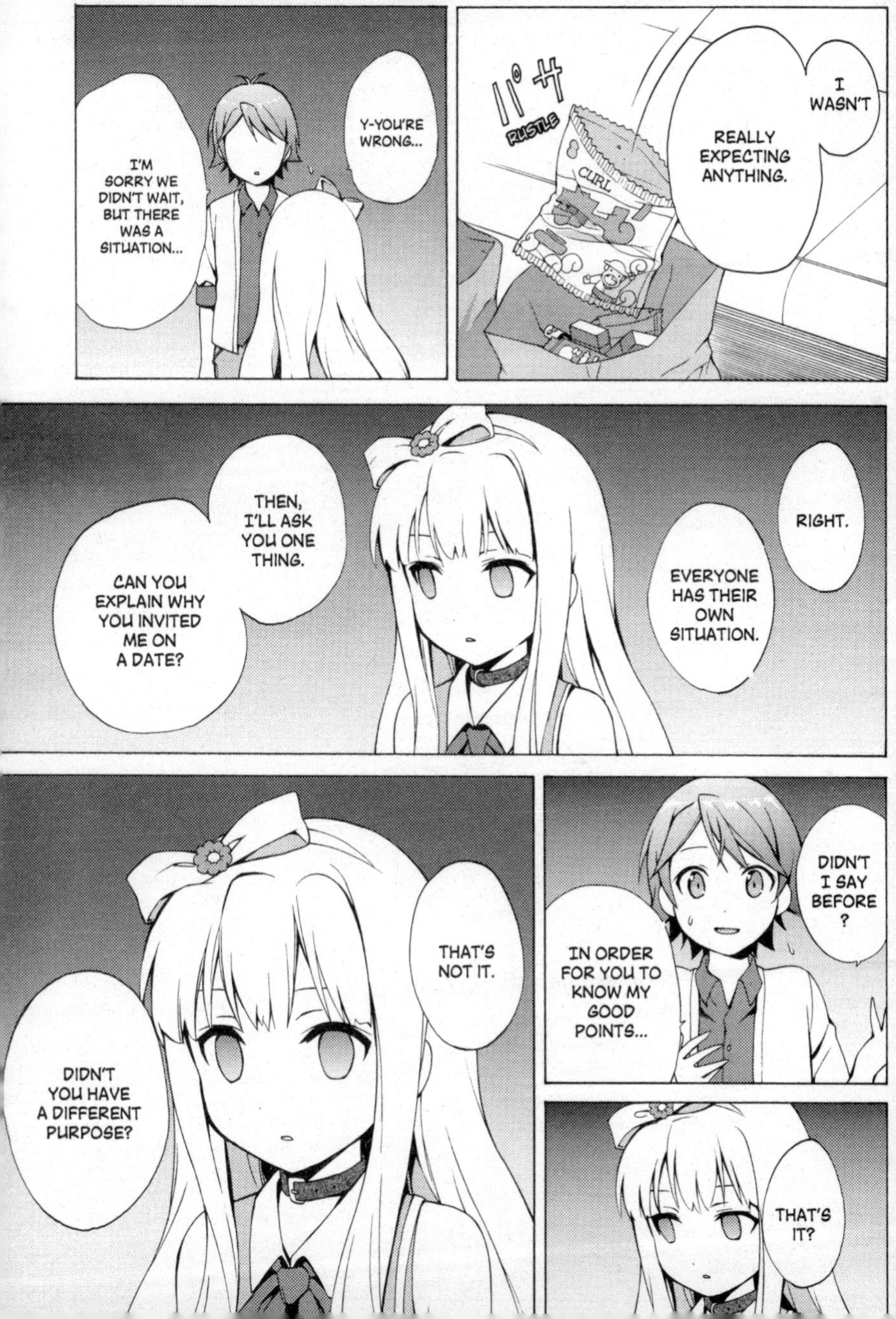
パサ
RUSTLE
CURL
I WASN'T REALLY EXPECTING ANYTHING.
Y-YOU'RE WRONG...
I'M SORRY WE DIDN'T WAIT, BUT THERE WAS A SITUATION...
RIGHT.
EVERYONE HAS THEIR OWN SITUATION.
THEN, I'LL ASK YOU ONE THING.
CAN YOU EXPLAIN WHY YOU INVITED ME ON A DATE?
DIDN'T I SAY BEFORE?
IN ORDER FOR YOU TO KNOW MY GOOD POINTS...
THAT'S IT?
THAT'S NOT IT.
DIDN'T YOU HAVE A DIFFERENT PURPOSE?

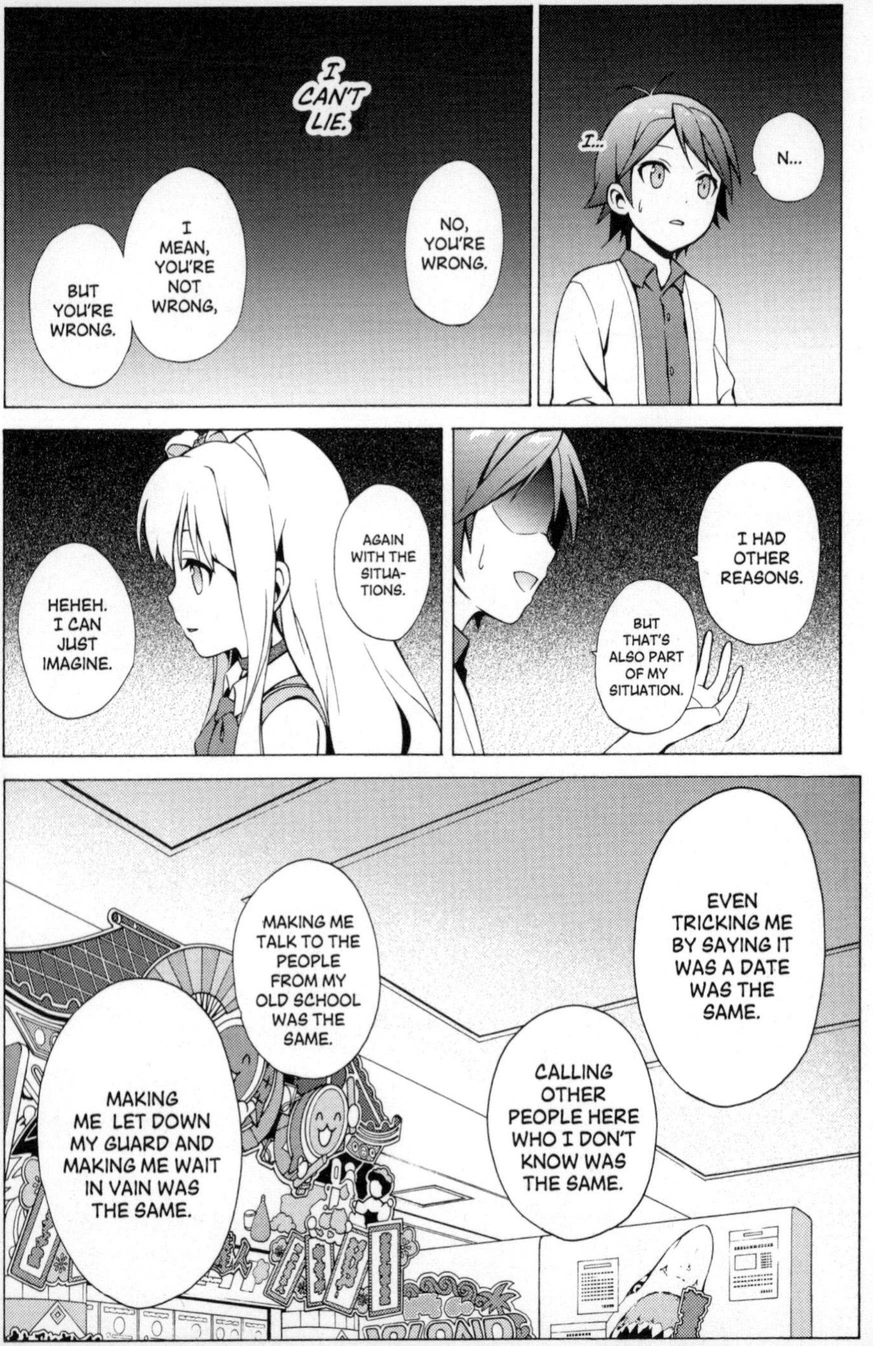
N...
I...
I CAN'T LIE.
NO, YOU'RE WRONG.
I MEAN, YOU'RE NOT WRONG,
BUT YOU'RE WRONG.
I HAD OTHER REASONS.
BUT THAT'S ALSO PART OF MY SITUATION.
AGAIN WITH THE SITUATIONS.
HEHEH. I CAN JUST IMAGINE.
EVEN TRICKING ME BY SAYING IT WAS A DATE WAS THE SAME.
CALLING OTHER PEOPLE HERE WHO I DON'T KNOW WAS THE SAME.
MAKING ME TALK TO THE PEOPLE FROM MY OLD SCHOOL WAS THE SAME.
MAKING ME LET DOWN MY GUARD AND MAKING ME WAIT IN VAIN WAS THE SAME.

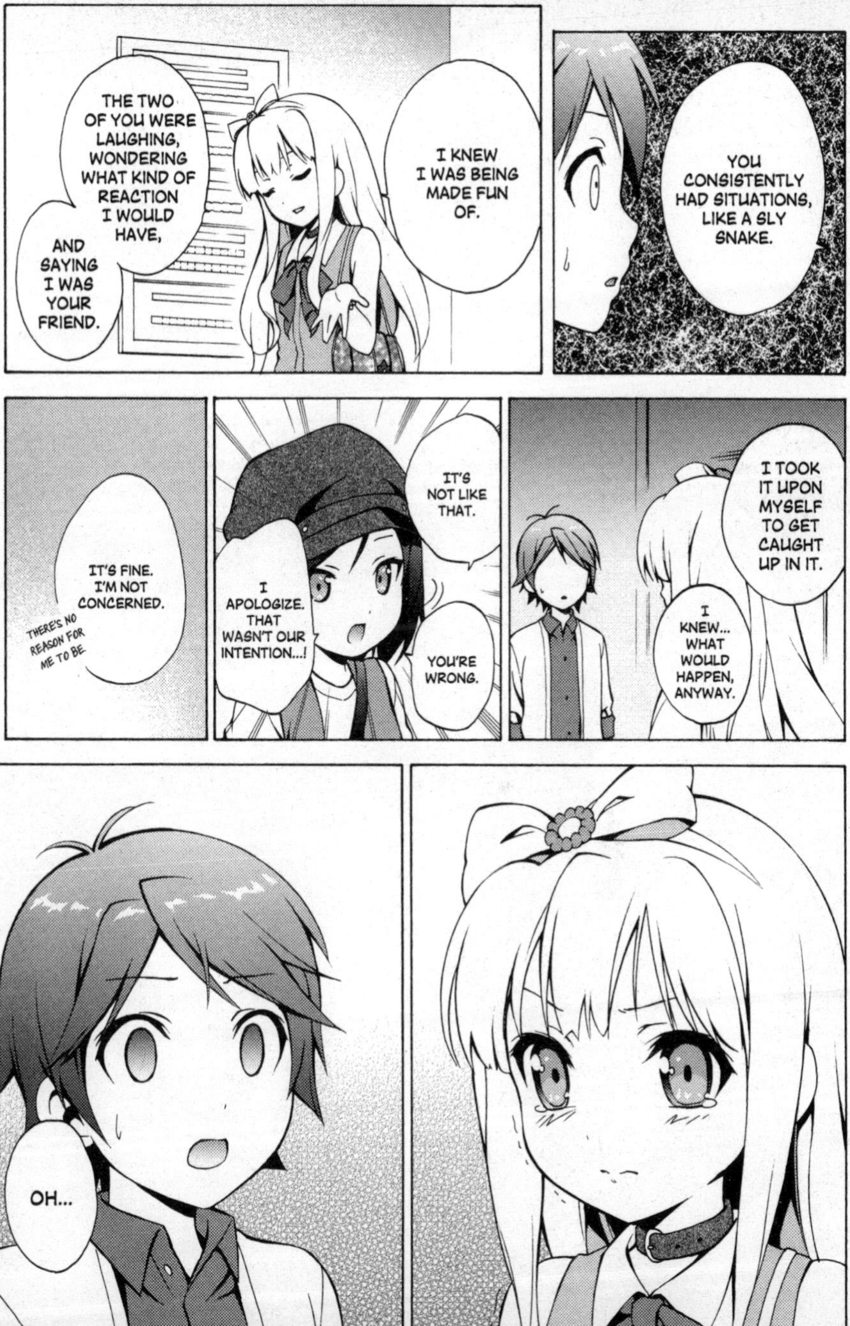
YOU CONSISTENTLY HAD SITUATIONS, LIKE A SLY SNAKE.
I KNEW I WAS BEING MADE FUN OF.
THE TWO OF YOU WERE LAUGHING, WONDERING WHAT KIND OF REACTION I WOULD HAVE,
AND SAYING I WAS YOUR FRIEND.
I TOOK IT UPON MYSELF TO GET CAUGHT UP IN IT.
I KNEW... WHAT WOULD HAPPEN, ANYWAY.
IT'S NOT LIKE THAT.
YOU'RE WRONG.
I APOLOGIZE. THAT WASN'T OUR INTENTION...!
IT'S FINE. I'M NOT CONCERNED.
THERE'S NO REASON FOR ME TO BE.
OH...

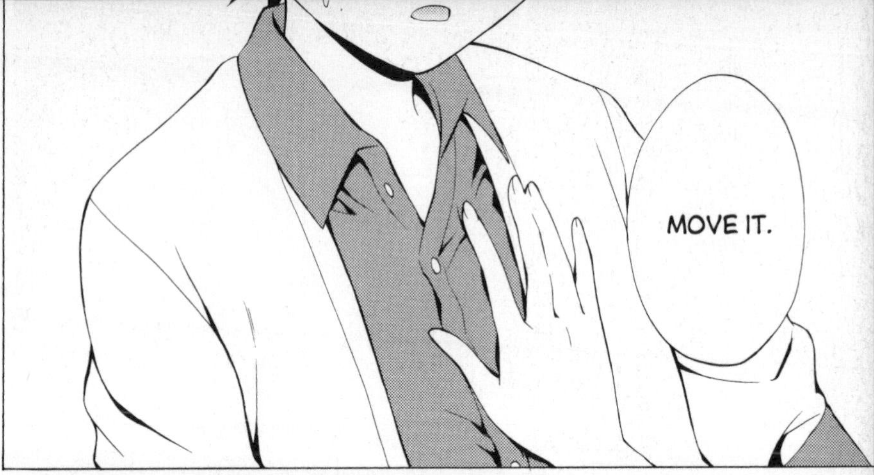
MOVE IT.

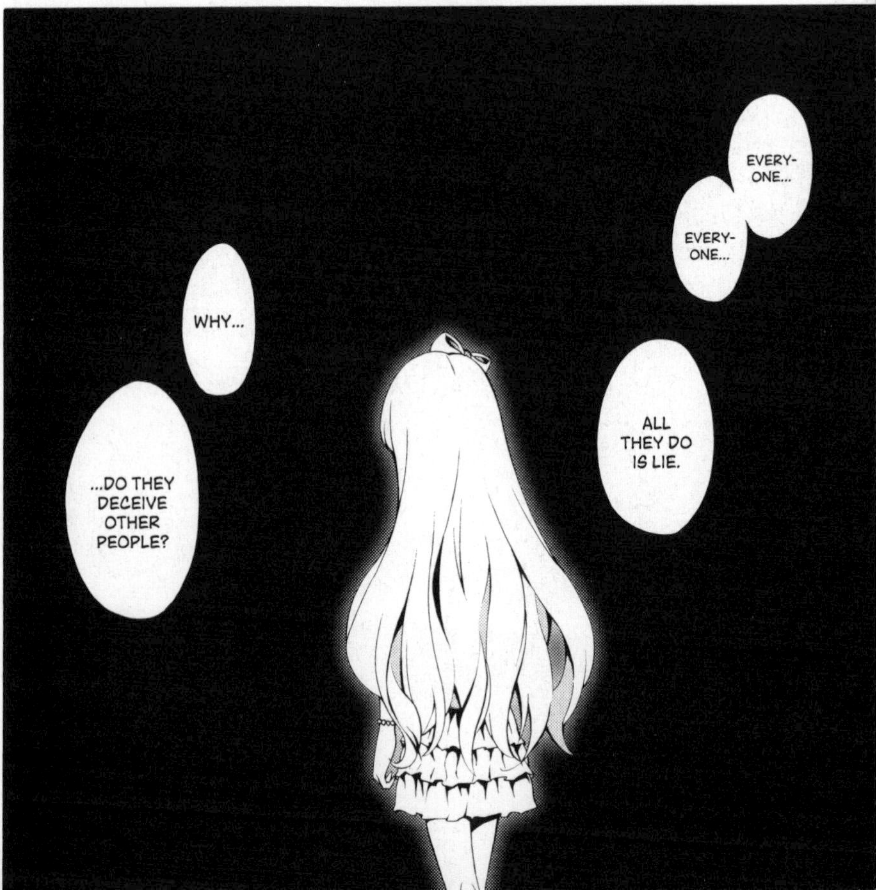
EVERY-
ONE...
EVERY-
ONE...
ALL THEY DO IS LIE.
WHY...
...DO THEY DECEIVE OTHER PEOPLE?

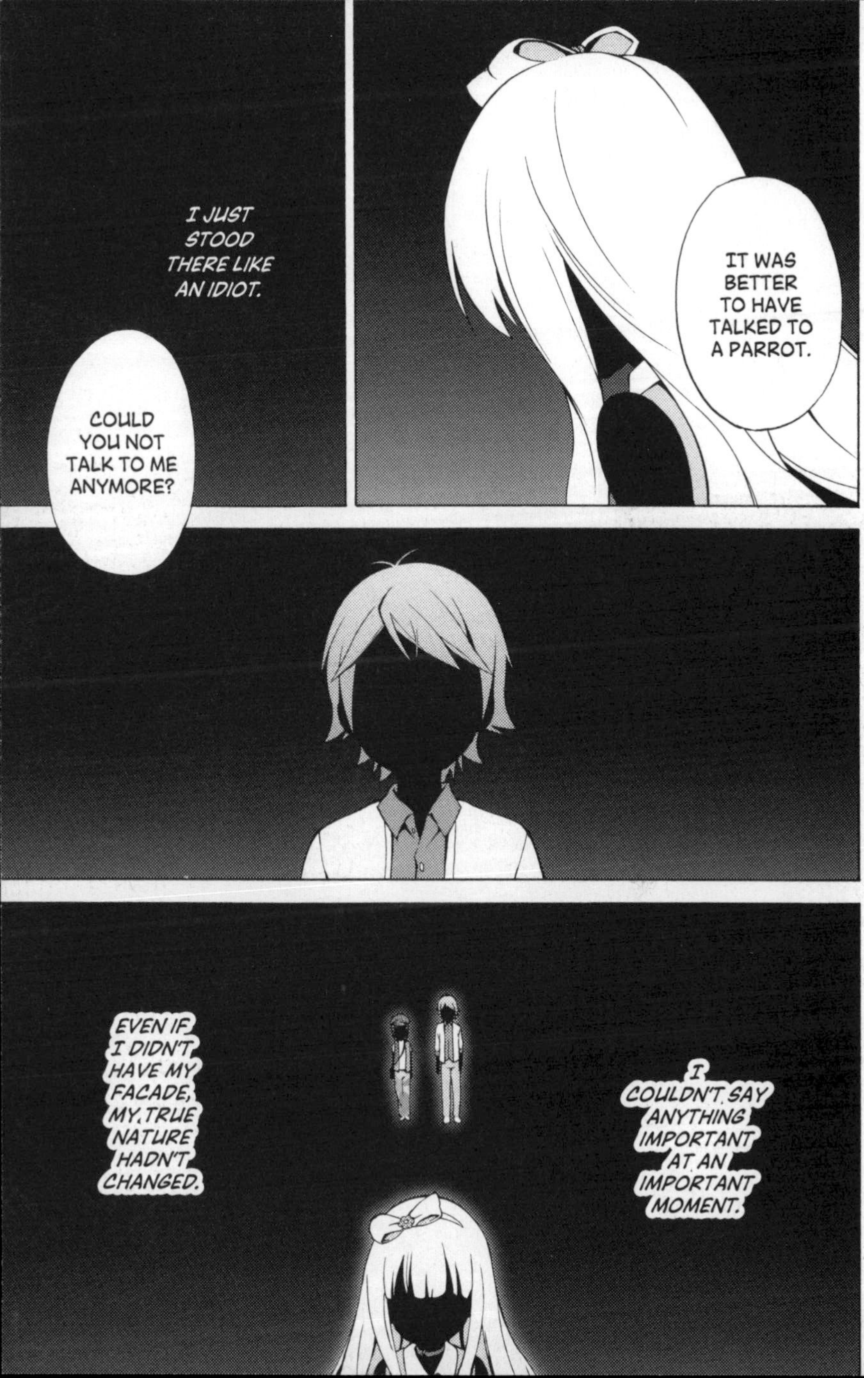
IT WAS BETTER TO HAVE TALKED TO A PARROT.
I JUST STOOD THERE LIKE AN IDIOT.
COULD YOU NOT TALK TO ME ANYMORE?
I COULDN'T SAY ANYTHING IMPORTANT AT AN IMPORTANT MOMENT.
EVEN IF I DIDN'T HAVE MY FACADE, MY TRUE NATURE HADN'T CHANGED.

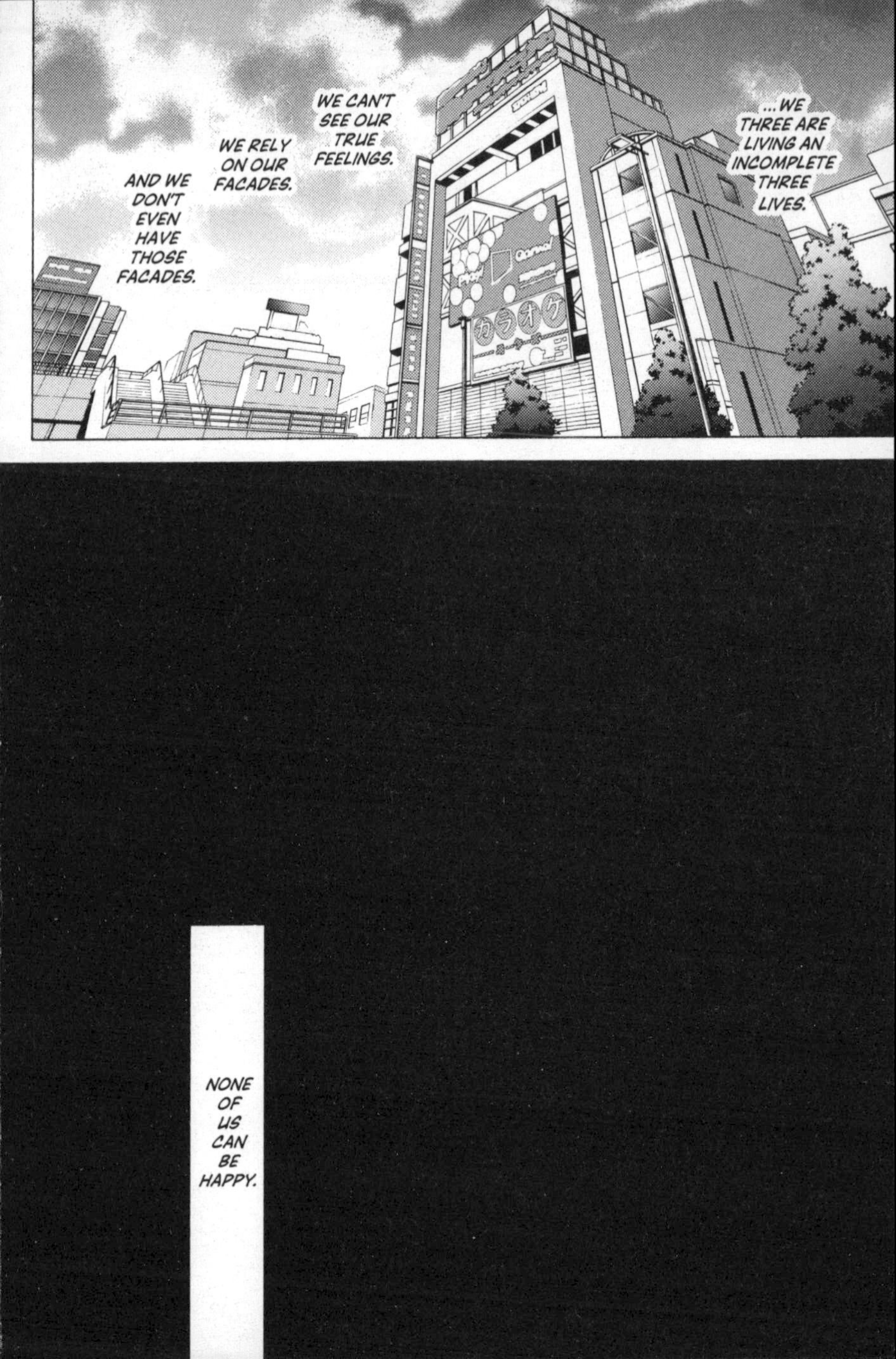
...WE THREE ARE LIVING AN INCOMPLETE THREE LIVES.
WE CAN'T SEE OUR TRUE FEELINGS.
WE RELY ON OUR FACADES.
AND WE DON'T EVEN HAVE THOSE FACADES.
カラオケ
NONE OF US CAN BE HAPPY.

The "HENTAI" prince and the stony cat.

変態王子と①
笑わない猫。

↓Scottish Fold

ILLUSTRATED
CATS OF THE
WORLD
....
SCOTTISH
FOLD

THEY ARE A SUDDEN VARIATION BREED THAT WAS
FOUND IN SCOTLAND, AND THEIR NAME IS DERIVED FROM
THE ENGLISH "FOLD." THEY HAVE MUSCULAR BODIES,
AND THEIR PERSONALITIES ARE MAINLY VERY KIND
AND GENTLE. THE FREQUENCY OF HAVING THEIR
CHARACTERISTIC FOLDED EARS IS 30%, WHICH IS NOT
THAT HIGH. AROUND 2-3 WEEKS AFTER BIRTH, THEIR
EARS START TO DROOP, AND DEPENDING ON THEIR
CONDITION, THERE ARE CASES IN WHICH THEIR EARS GO
BACK TO HOW IT WAS BEFORE, TOO. ALSO, THERE ARE
MANY THAT DO THE POSITION KNOWN AS " BUDDHA
POSITION," WHERE THE LEGS, ATTACHED TO THE
BOTTOM, ARE SPREAD OUT, AND THERE AREN'T A FEW
BREEDERS WHO LIKE THAT OLD MAN WAY OF SITTING.

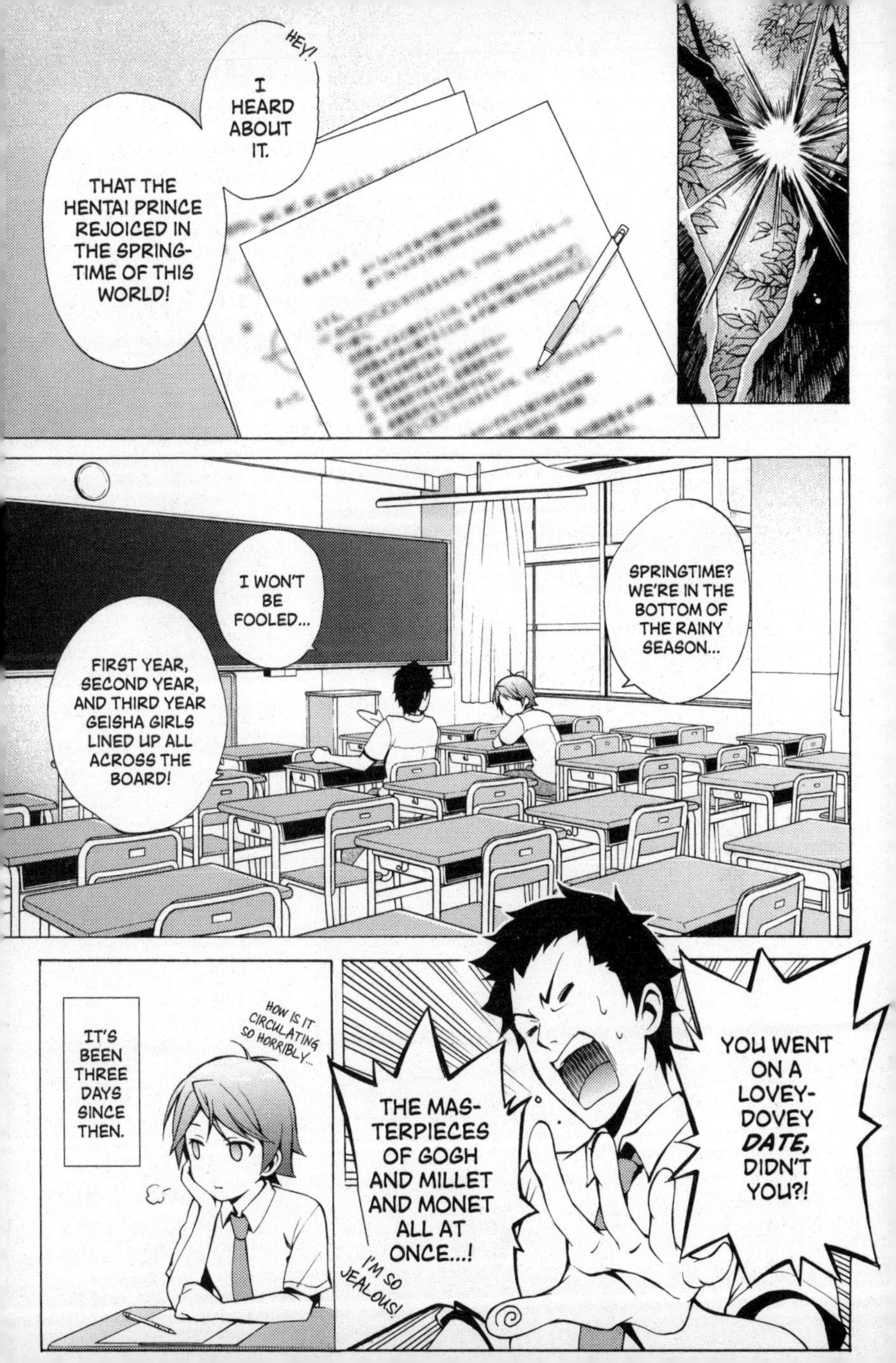
HEY!
I HEARD ABOUT IT.
THAT THE HENTAI PRINCE REJOICED IN THE SPRING-TIME OF THIS WORLD!
SPRINGTIME? WE'RE IN THE BOTTOM OF THE RAINY SEASON...
I WON'T BE FOOLED...
FIRST YEAR, SECOND YEAR, AND THIRD YEAR GEISHA GIRLS LINED UP ALL ACROSS THE BOARD!
YOU WENT ON A LOVEY-DOVEY *DATE,* DIDN'T YOU?!
THE MAS-TERPIECES OF GOGH AND MILLET AND MONET ALL AT ONCE...!
I'M SO JEALOUS!
IT'S BEEN THREE DAYS SINCE THEN.
HOW IS IT CIRCULATING SO HORRIBLY...

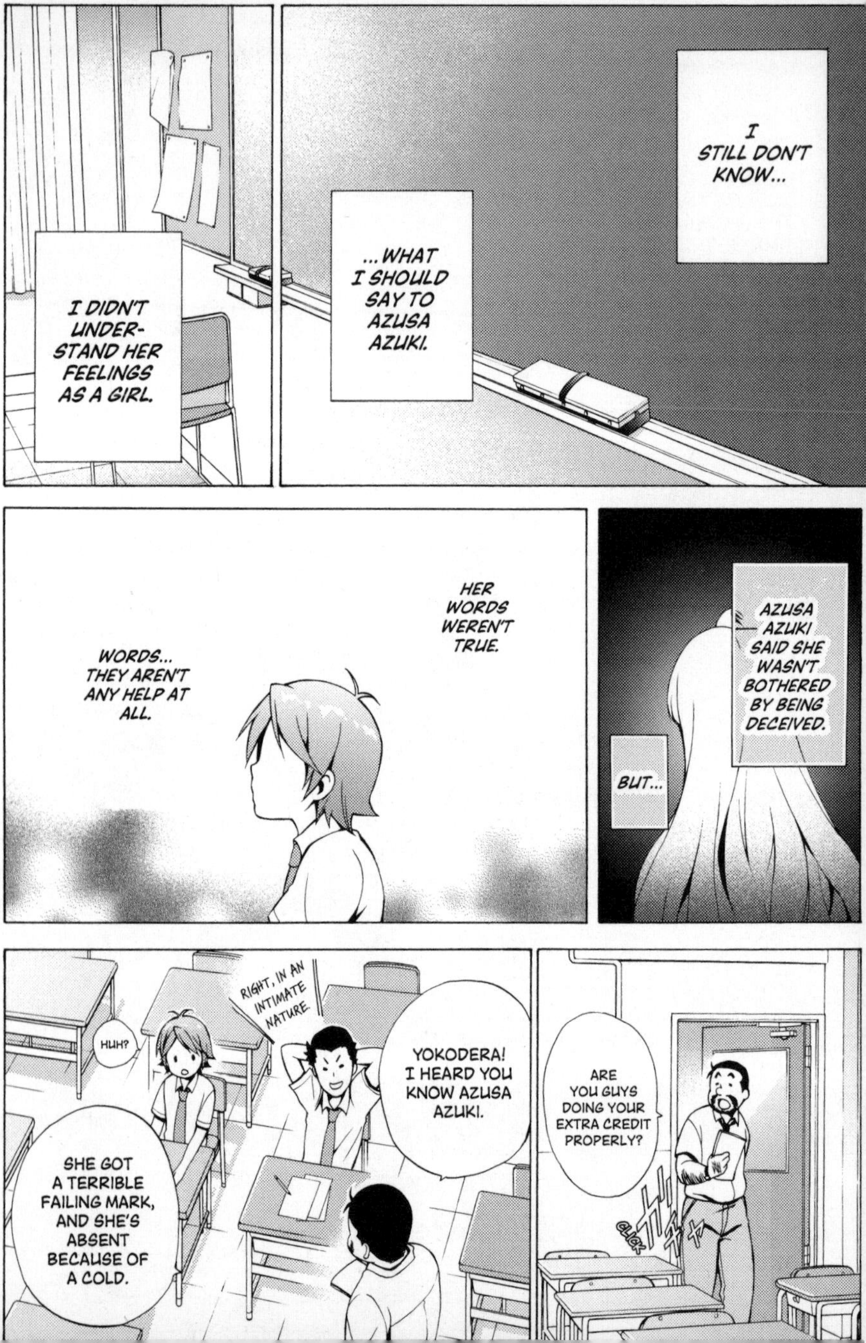
I STILL DON'T KNOW...
...WHAT I SHOULD SAY TO AZUSA AZUKI.
I DIDN'T UNDER-STAND HER FEELINGS AS A GIRL.
AZUSA AZUKI SAID SHE WASN'T BOTHERED BY BEING DECEIVED.
BUT...
HER WORDS WEREN'T TRUE.
WORDS... THEY AREN'T ANY HELP AT ALL.
ARE YOU GUYS DOING YOUR EXTRA CREDIT PROPERLY?
CLICK
YOKODERA! I HEARD YOU KNOW AZUSA AZUKI.
RIGHT, IN AN INTIMATE NATURE.
HUH?
SHE GOT A TERRIBLE FAILING MARK, AND SHE'S ABSENT BECAUSE OF A COLD.

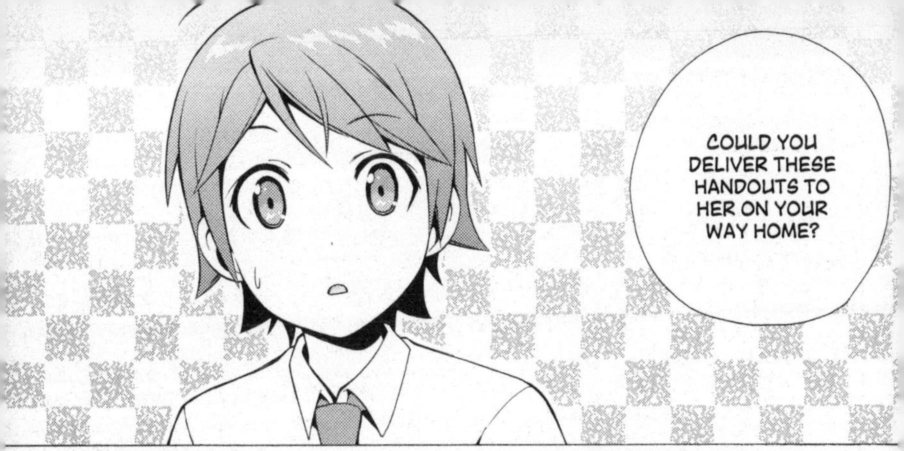
COULD YOU DELIVER THESE HANDOUTS TO HER ON YOUR WAY HOME?

CHAPTER 8 SAY SO BEFORE YOU GET SAD

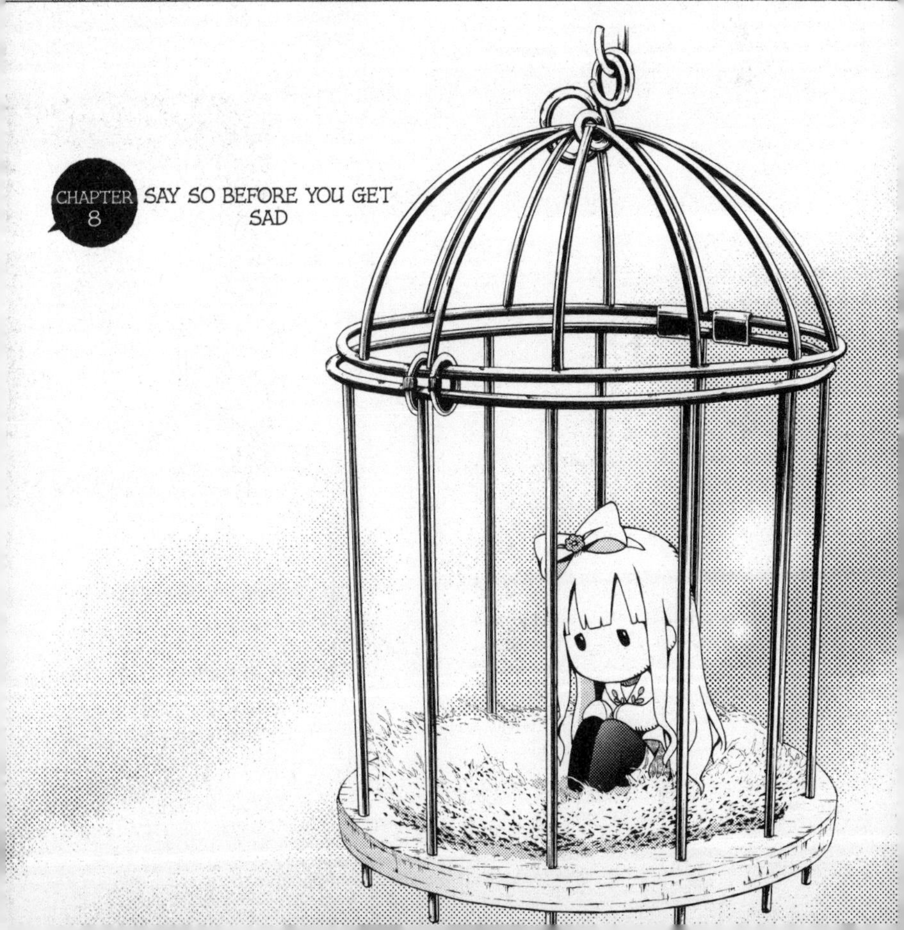

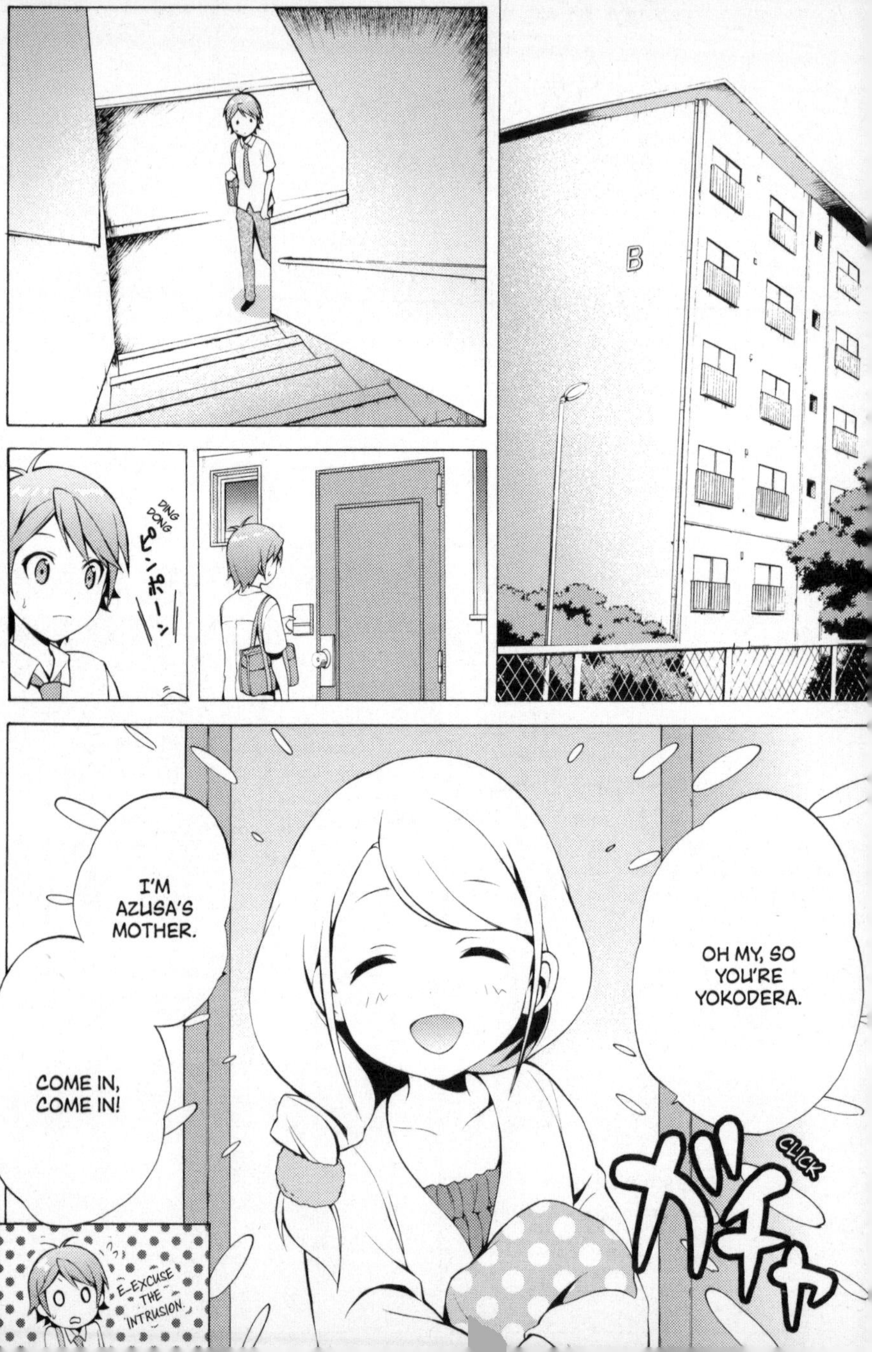
DING DONG
ピンポーン
OH MY, SO YOU'RE YOKODERA.
CLICK
ガチャ
I'M AZUSA'S MOTHER.
COME IN, COME IN!
E-EXCUSE THE INTRUSION.

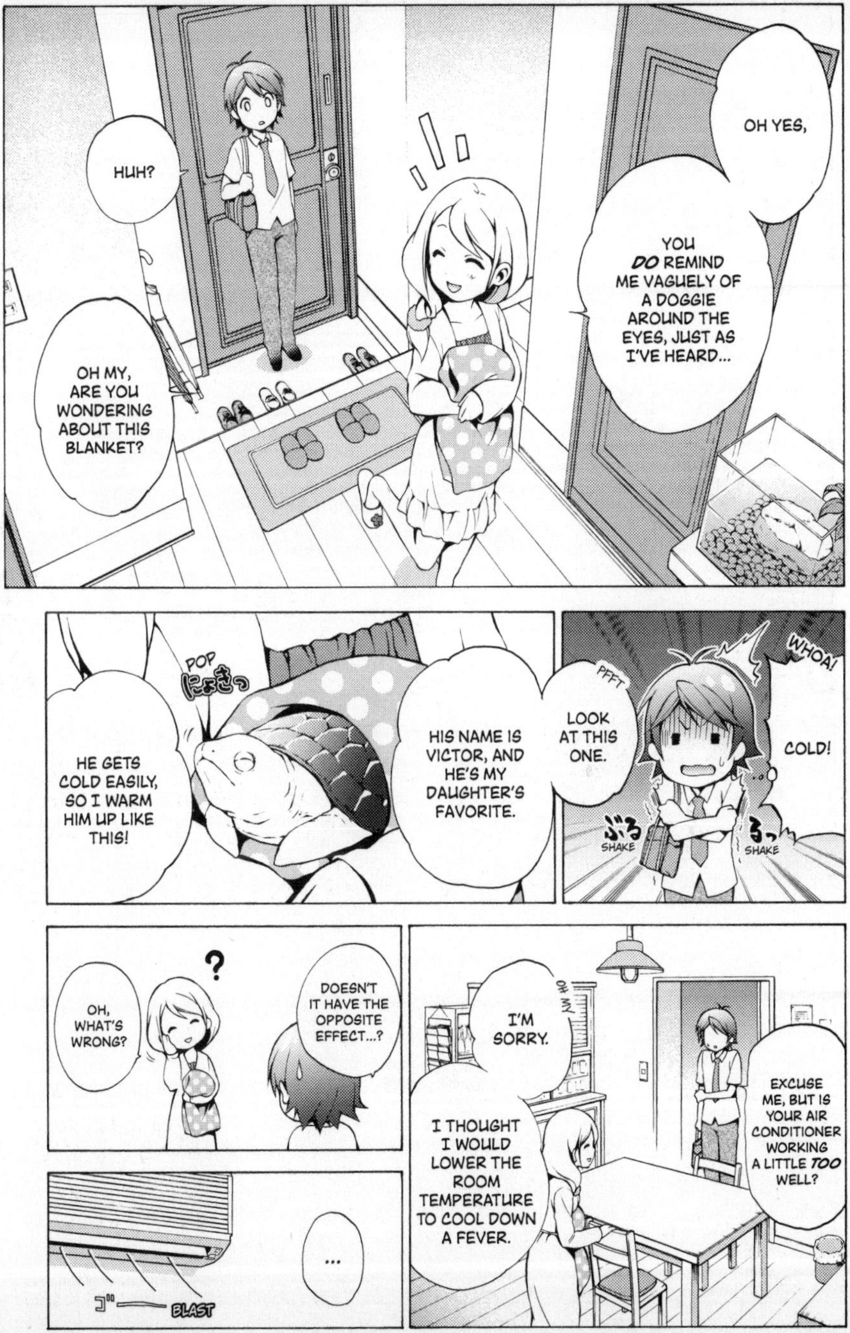
OH YES,
YOU *DO* REMIND ME VAGUELY OF A DOGGIE AROUND THE EYES, JUST AS I'VE HEARD...
HUH?
OH MY, ARE YOU WONDERING ABOUT THIS BLANKET?
WHOA!
COLD!
ぶる SHAKE
るっ SHAKE
PFFT
LOOK AT THIS ONE.
HIS NAME IS VICTOR, AND HE'S MY DAUGHTER'S FAVORITE.
POP にょきっ
HE GETS COLD EASILY, SO I WARM HIM UP LIKE THIS!
EXCUSE ME, BUT IS YOUR AIR CONDITIONER WORKING A LITTLE *TOO* WELL?
OH MY
I'M SORRY.
I THOUGHT I WOULD LOWER THE ROOM TEMPERATURE TO COOL DOWN A FEVER.
DOESN'T IT HAVE THE OPPOSITE EFFECT...?
?
OH, WHAT'S WRONG?
...
ゴー BLAST

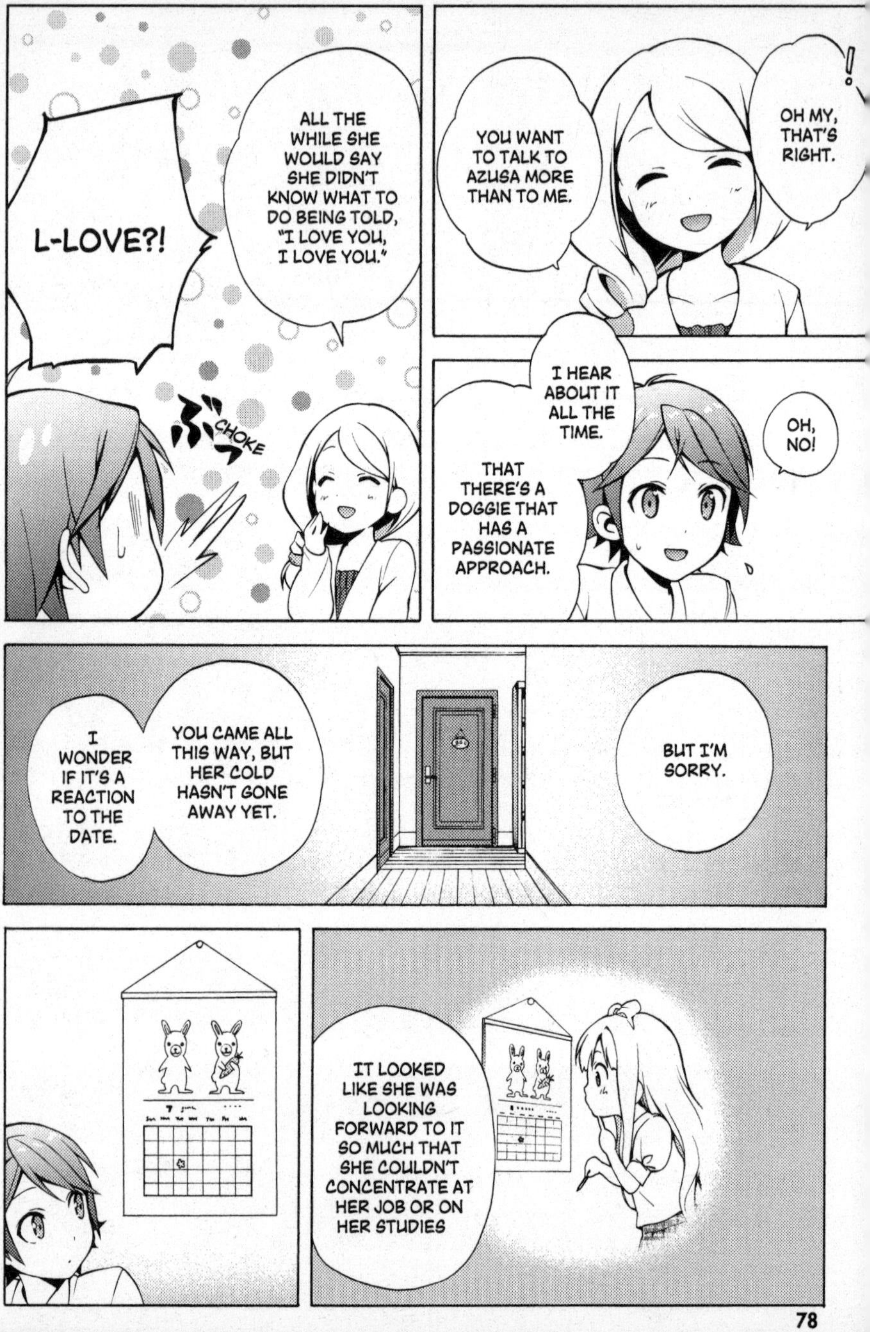
!
OH MY, THAT'S RIGHT.
YOU WANT TO TALK TO AZUSA MORE THAN TO ME.
OH, NO!
I HEAR ABOUT IT ALL THE TIME.
THAT THERE'S A DOGGIE THAT HAS A PASSIONATE APPROACH.
ALL THE WHILE SHE WOULD SAY SHE DIDN'T KNOW WHAT TO DO BEING TOLD, "I LOVE YOU, I LOVE YOU."
L-LOVE?!
CHOKE
BUT I'M SORRY.
YOU CAME ALL THIS WAY, BUT HER COLD HASN'T GONE AWAY YET.
I WONDER IF IT'S A REACTION TO THE DATE.
IT LOOKED LIKE SHE WAS LOOKING FORWARD TO IT SO MUCH THAT SHE COULDN'T CONCENTRATE AT HER JOB OR ON HER STUDIES

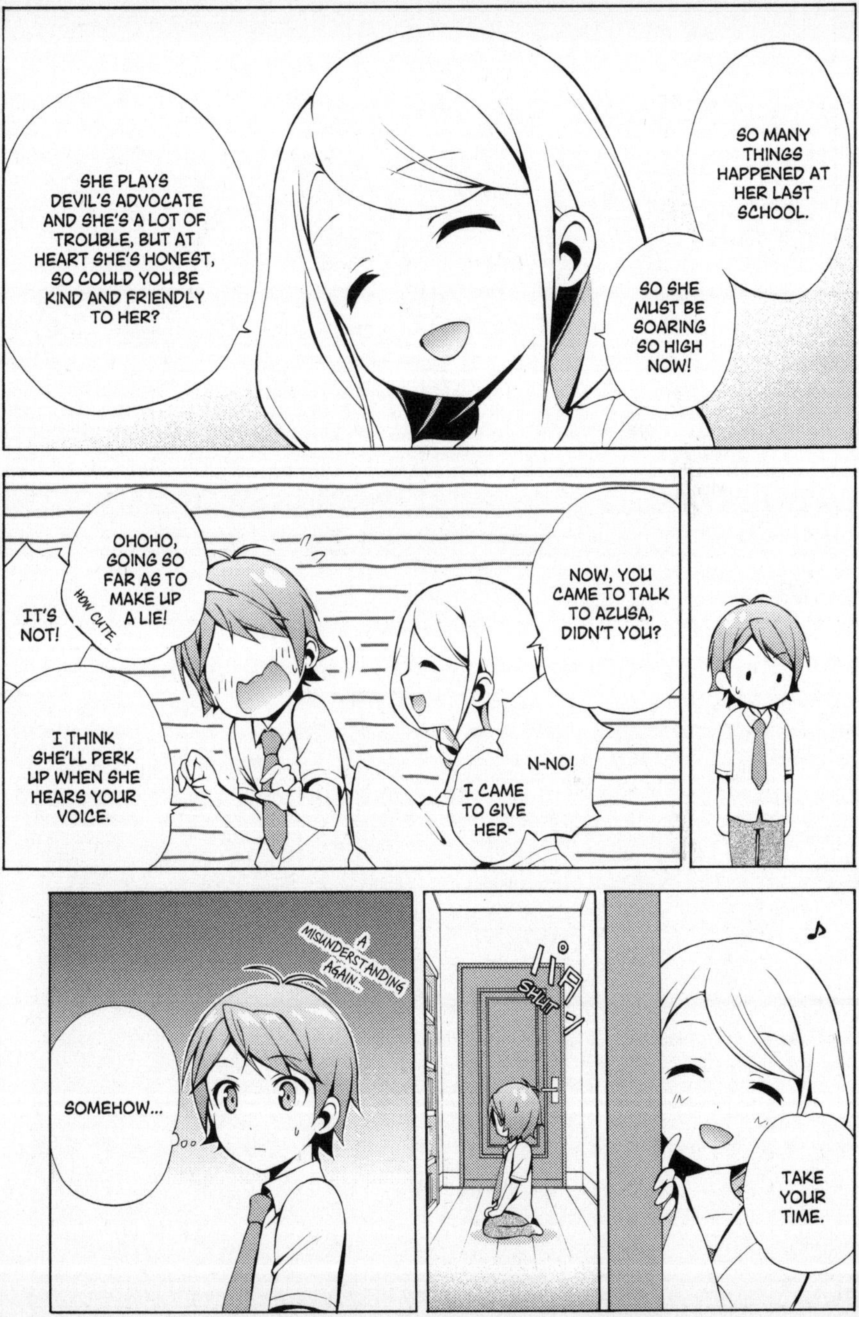
SO MANY THINGS HAPPENED AT HER LAST SCHOOL.
SO SHE MUST BE SOARING SO HIGH NOW!
SHE PLAYS DEVIL'S ADVOCATE AND SHE'S A LOT OF TROUBLE, BUT AT HEART SHE'S HONEST, SO COULD YOU BE KIND AND FRIENDLY TO HER?
NOW, YOU CAME TO TALK TO AZUSA, DIDN'T YOU?
N-NO!
I CAME TO GIVE HER-
OHOHO, GOING SO FAR AS TO MAKE UP A LIE!
HOW CUTE.
IT'S NOT!
I THINK SHE'LL PERK UP WHEN SHE HEARS YOUR VOICE.
♪
TAKE YOUR TIME.
SHUT
A MISUNDERSTANDING AGAIN...
SOMEHOW...

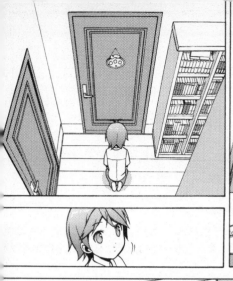

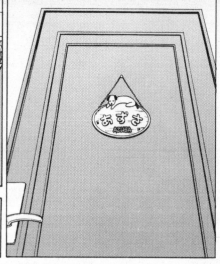

あずさ
AZUSA
"ZODIAC BASKETBALL"
"THE MOUSE"
"THE GREAT LION"
"PARASITIC DOGS"...
THEY'RE ALL ANIMAL MANGA...
...

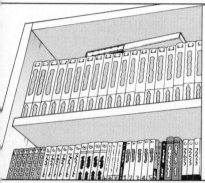

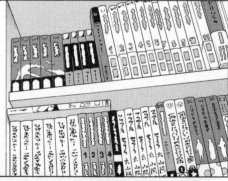

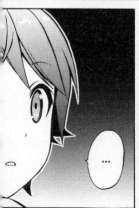

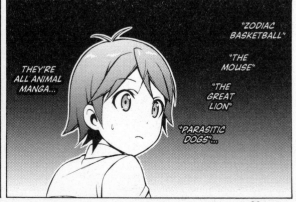

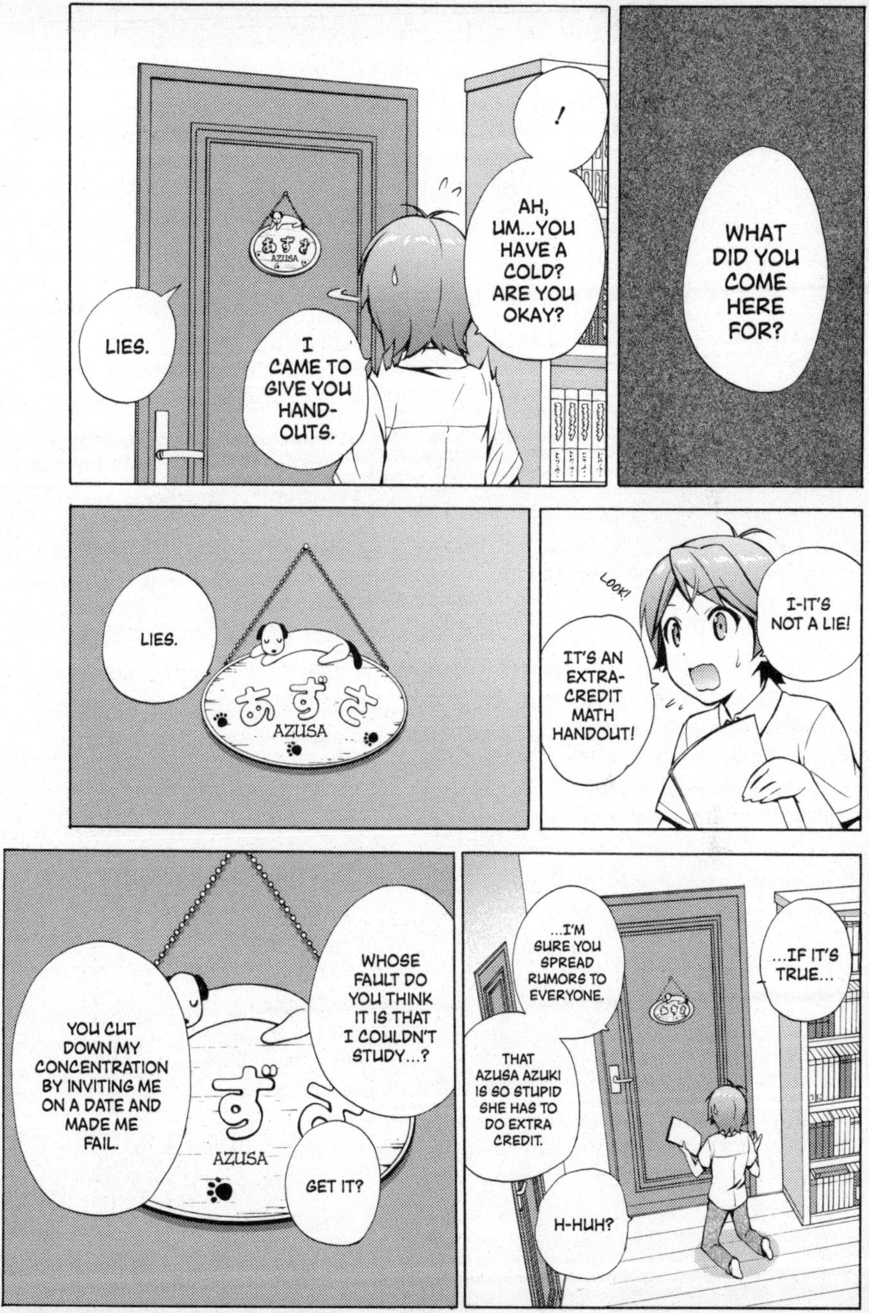
WHAT DID YOU COME HERE FOR?
!
AH, UM...YOU HAVE A COLD? ARE YOU OKAY?
あずさ AZUSA
I CAME TO GIVE YOU HAND-OUTS.
LIES.
I-IT'S NOT A LIE!
LOOK!
IT'S AN EXTRA-CREDIT MATH HANDOUT!
LIES.
あずさ AZUSA
...IF IT'S TRUE...
...I'M SURE YOU SPREAD RUMORS TO EVERYONE.
THAT AZUSA AZUKI IS SO STUPID SHE HAS TO DO EXTRA CREDIT.
H-HUH?
WHOSE FAULT DO YOU THINK IT IS THAT I COULDN'T STUDY...?
YOU CUT DOWN MY CONCENTRATION BY INVITING ME ON A DATE AND MADE ME FAIL.
AZUSA
GET IT?

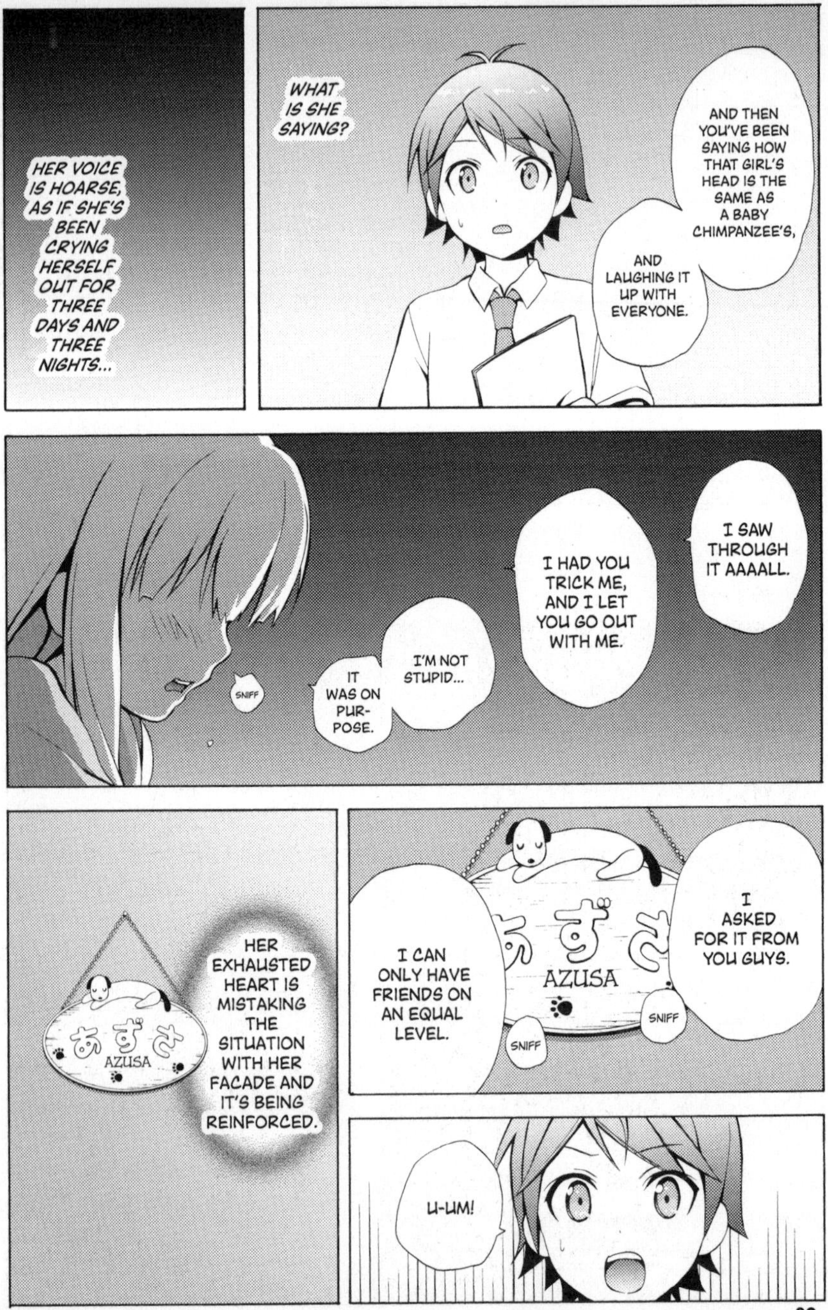
AND THEN YOU'VE BEEN SAYING HOW THAT GIRL'S HEAD IS THE SAME AS A BABY CHIMPANZEE'S,
AND LAUGHING IT UP WITH EVERYONE.
WHAT IS SHE SAYING?
HER VOICE IS HOARSE, AS IF SHE'S BEEN CRYING HERSELF OUT FOR THREE DAYS AND THREE NIGHTS...
I SAW THROUGH IT AAAALL.
I HAD YOU TRICK ME, AND I LET YOU GO OUT WITH ME.
I'M NOT STUPID...
IT WAS ON PUR-POSE.
SNIFF
I ASKED FOR IT FROM YOU GUYS.
あずさ
AZUSA
SNIFF
SNIFF
I CAN ONLY HAVE FRIENDS ON AN EQUAL LEVEL.
U-UM!
あずさ
AZUSA
HER EXHAUSTED HEART IS MISTAKING THE SITUATION WITH HER FACADE AND IT'S BEING REINFORCED.

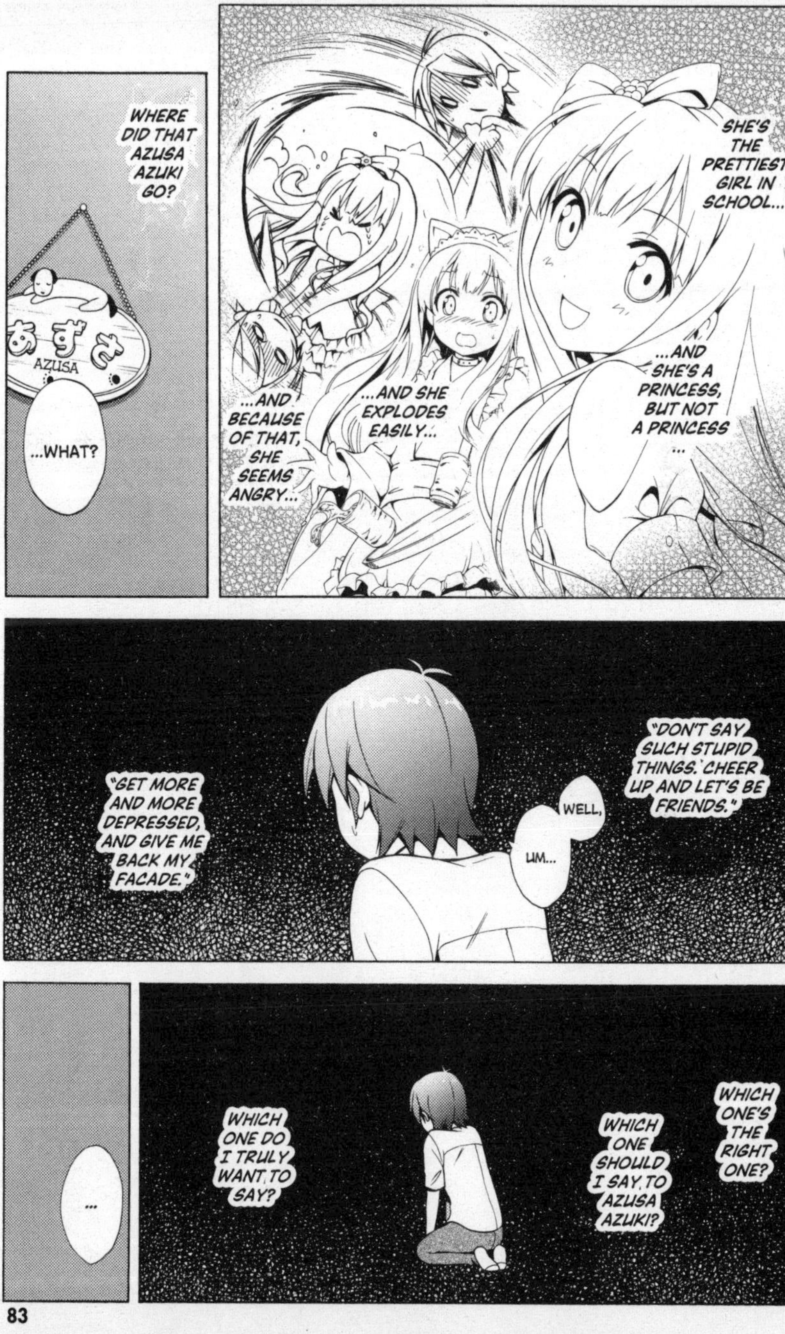
SHE'S THE PRETTIEST GIRL IN SCHOOL...
...AND SHE'S A PRINCESS, BUT NOT A PRINCESS ...
...AND SHE EXPLODES EASILY...
...AND BECAUSE OF THAT, SHE SEEMS ANGRY...
WHERE DID THAT AZUSA AZUKI GO?
あずさ
AZUSA
...WHAT?
"DON'T SAY SUCH STUPID THINGS. CHEER UP AND LET'S BE FRIENDS."
WELL,
UM...
"GET MORE AND MORE DEPRESSED, AND GIVE ME BACK MY FACADE."
WHICH ONE'S THE RIGHT ONE?
WHICH ONE SHOULD I SAY TO AZUSA AZUKI!?
WHICH ONE DO I TRULY WANT TO SAY?
...

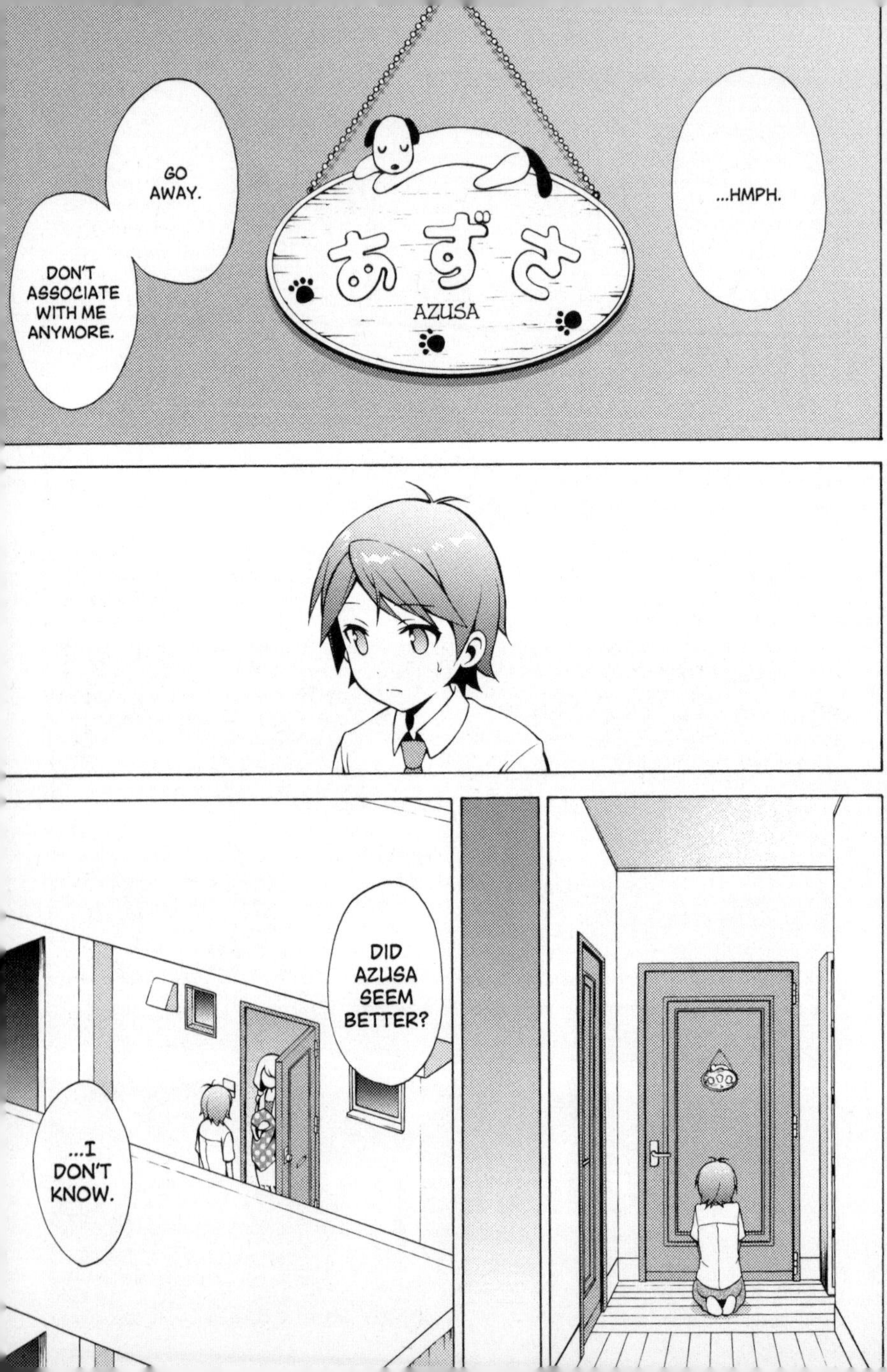
...HMPH.
あずさ
AZUSA
GO AWAY.
DON'T ASSOCIATE WITH ME ANYMORE.
DID AZUSA SEEM BETTER?
...I DON'T KNOW.

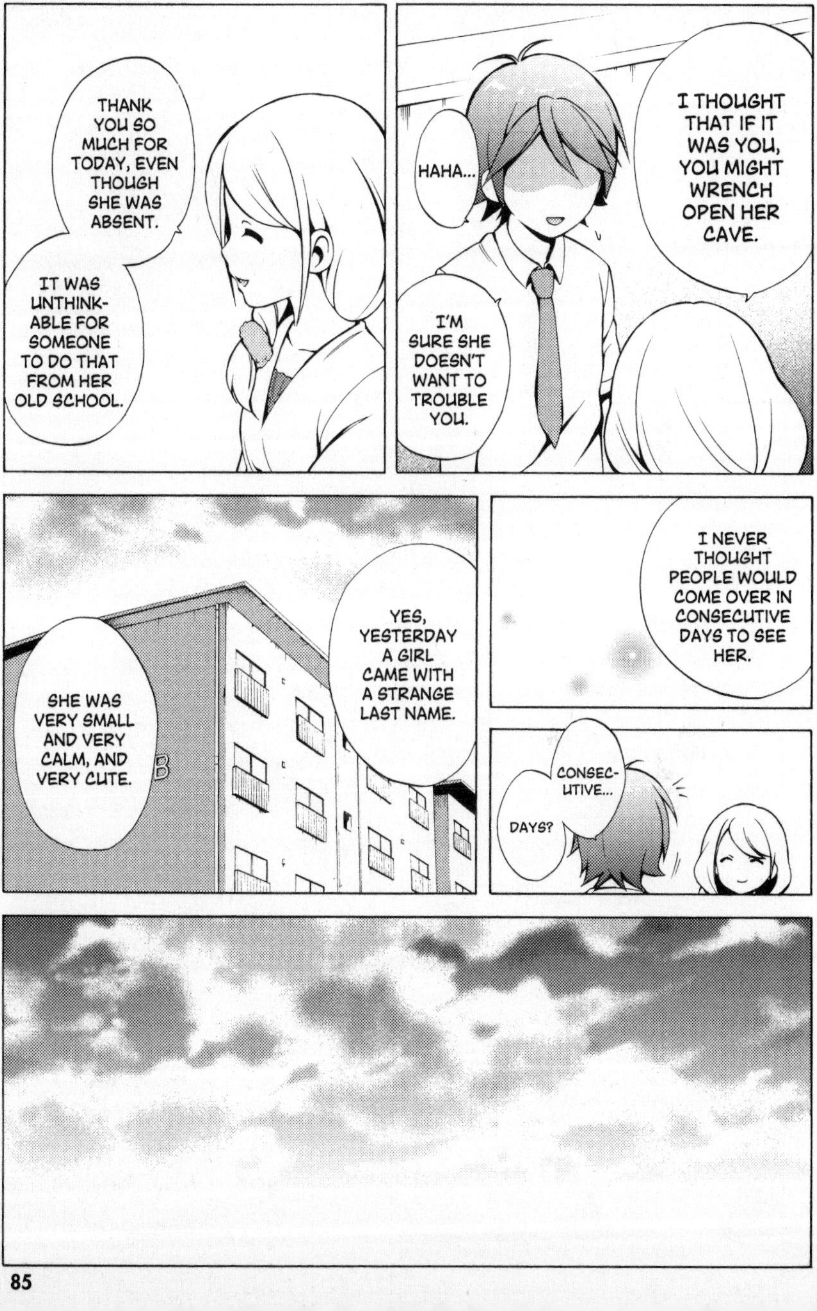
I THOUGHT THAT IF IT WAS YOU, YOU MIGHT WRENCH OPEN HER CAVE.
HAHA...
I'M SURE SHE DOESN'T WANT TO TROUBLE YOU.
THANK YOU SO MUCH FOR TODAY, EVEN THOUGH SHE WAS ABSENT.
IT WAS UNTHINKABLE FOR SOMEONE TO DO THAT FROM HER OLD SCHOOL.
I NEVER THOUGHT PEOPLE WOULD COME OVER IN CONSECUTIVE DAYS TO SEE HER.
CONSEC-UTIVE...
DAYS?
YES, YESTERDAY A GIRL CAME WITH A STRANGE LAST NAME.
SHE WAS VERY SMALL AND VERY CALM, AND VERY CUTE.

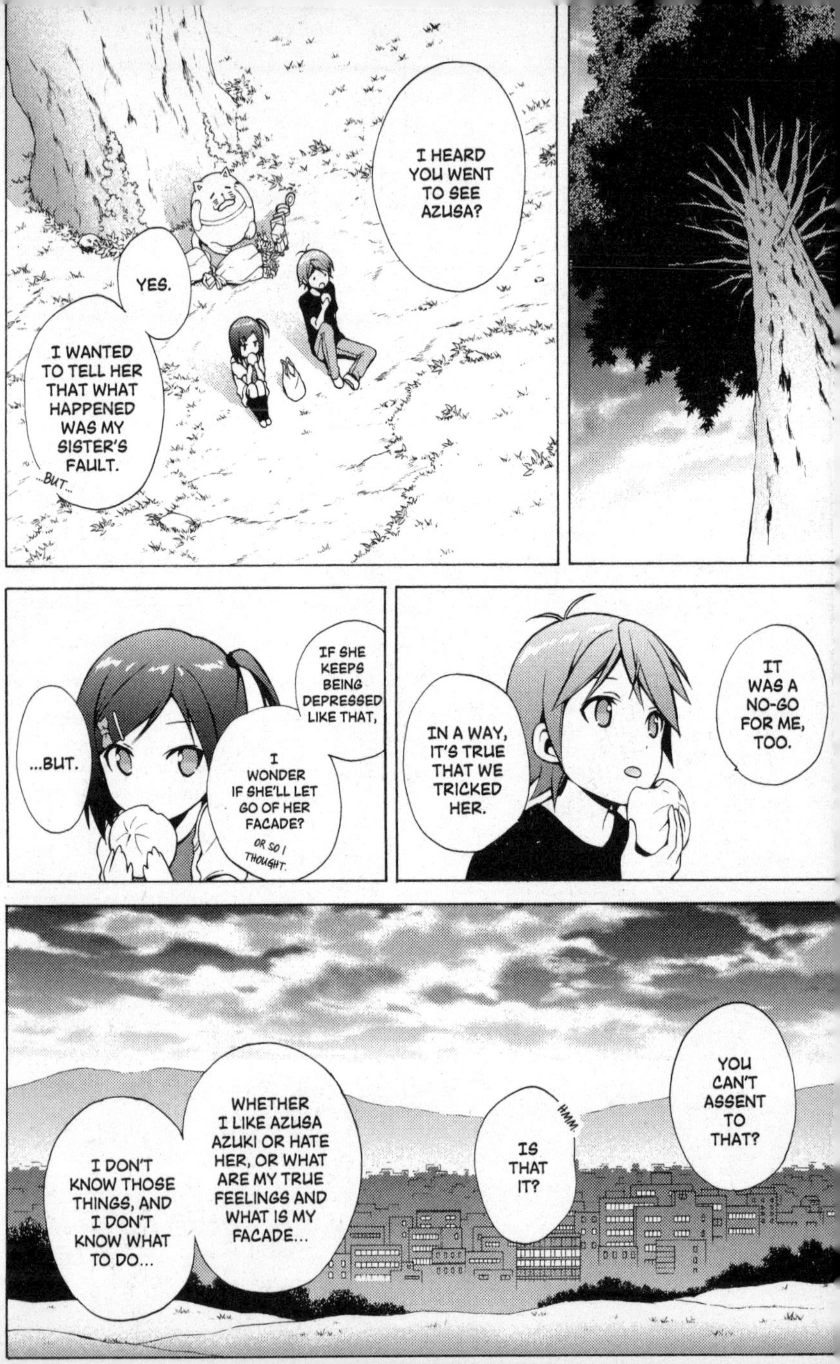
I HEARD YOU WENT TO SEE AZUSA?
YES.
I WANTED TO TELL HER THAT WHAT HAPPENED WAS MY SISTER'S FAULT.
...BUT...
IT WAS A NO-GO FOR ME, TOO.
IN A WAY, IT'S TRUE THAT WE TRICKED HER.
IF SHE KEEPS BEING DEPRESSED LIKE THAT,
I WONDER IF SHE'LL LET GO OF HER FACADE?
OR SO I THOUGHT.
...BUT.
YOU CAN'T ASSENT TO THAT?
HMM.
IS THAT IT?
WHETHER I LIKE AZUSA AZUKI OR HATE HER, OR WHAT ARE MY TRUE FEELINGS AND WHAT IS MY FACADE...
I DON'T KNOW THOSE THINGS, AND I DON'T KNOW WHAT TO DO...

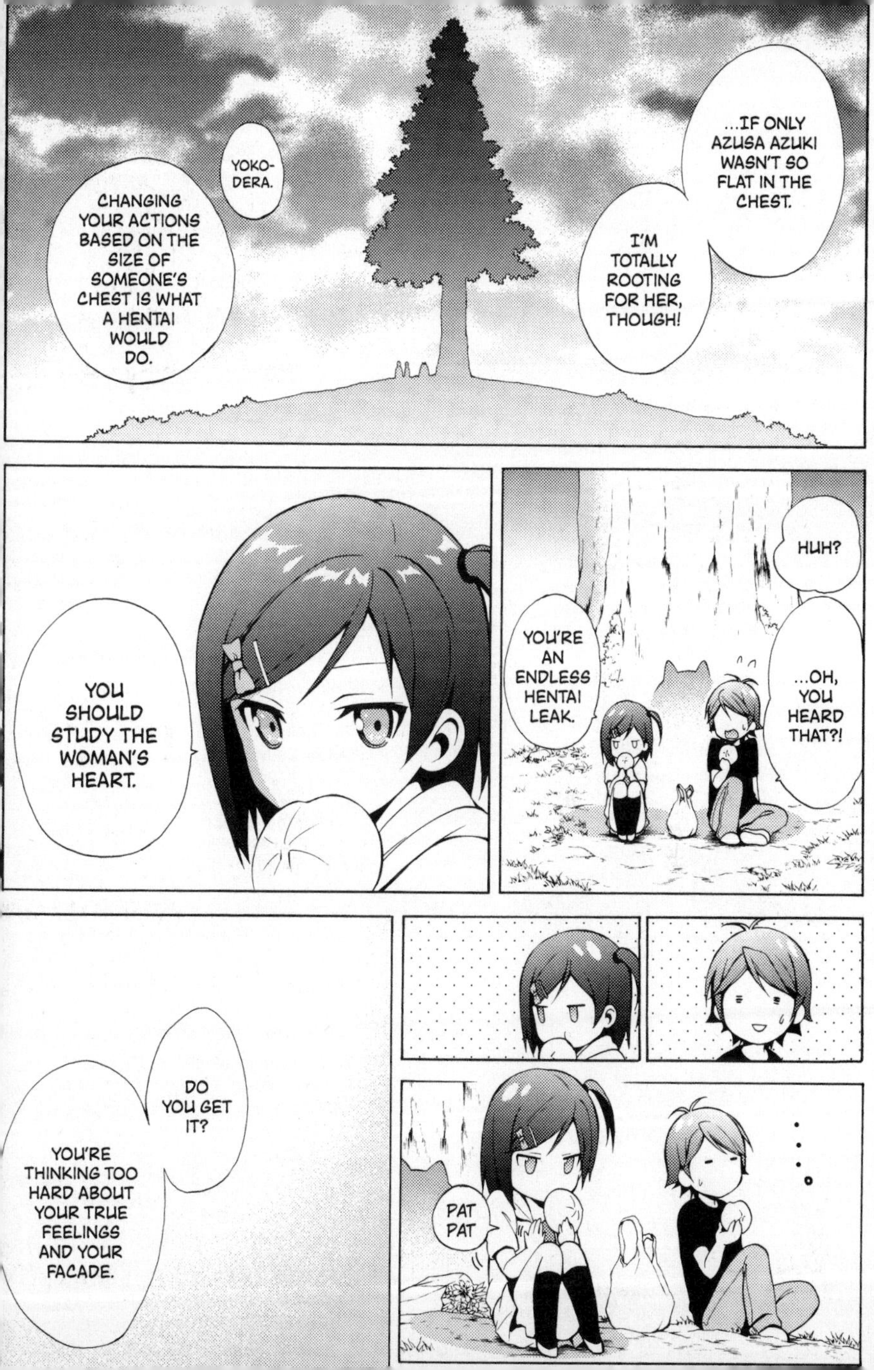
...IF ONLY AZUSA AZUKI WASN'T SO FLAT IN THE CHEST.
I'M TOTALLY ROOTING FOR HER, THOUGH!
YOKO-DERA.
CHANGING YOUR ACTIONS BASED ON THE SIZE OF SOMEONE'S CHEST IS WHAT A HENTAI WOULD DO.
HUH?
...OH, YOU HEARD THAT?!
YOU'RE AN ENDLESS HENTAI LEAK.
YOU SHOULD STUDY THE WOMAN'S HEART.
...
PAT PAT
DO YOU GET IT?
YOU'RE THINKING TOO HARD ABOUT YOUR TRUE FEELINGS AND YOUR FACADE.

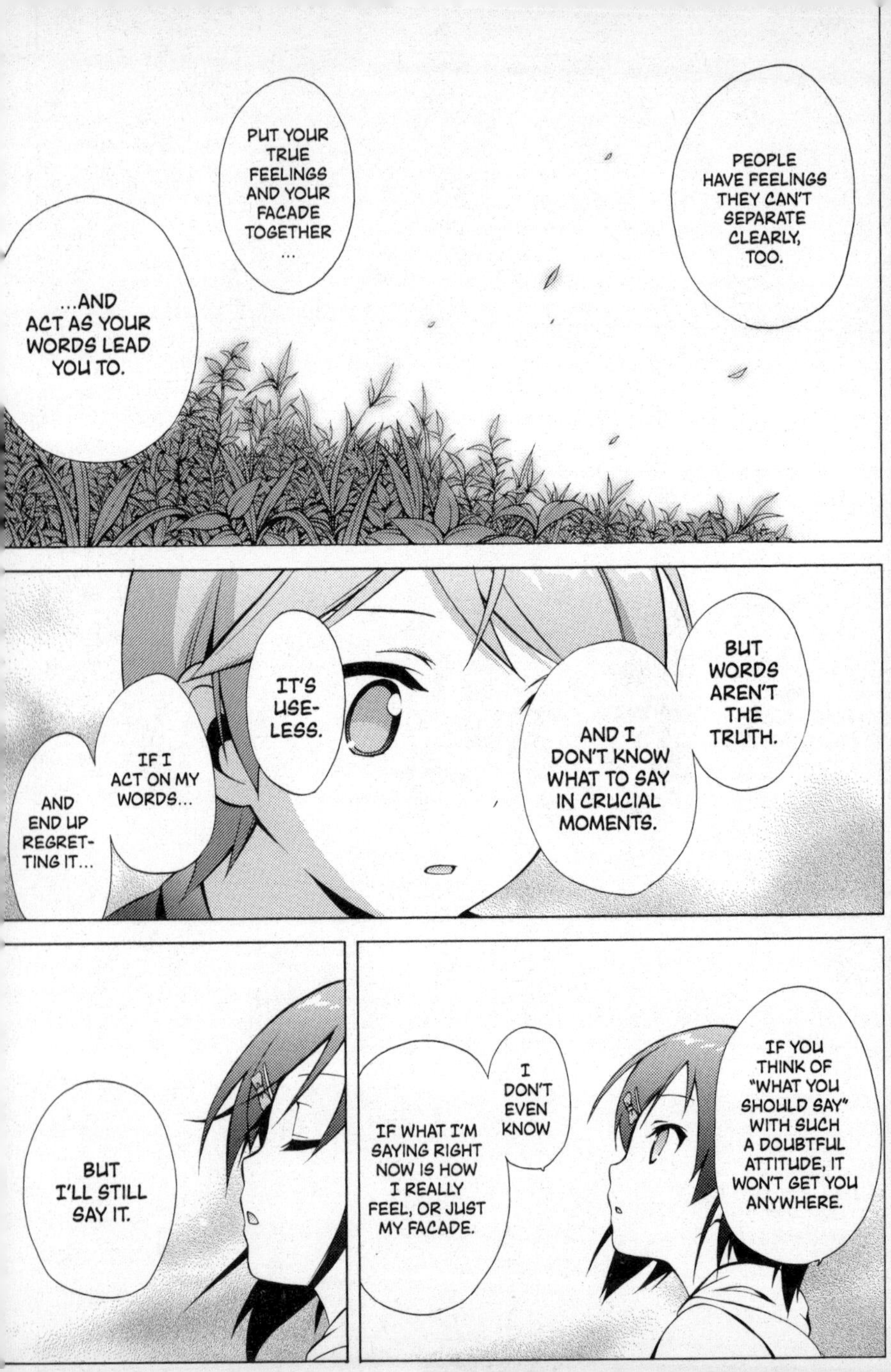
PEOPLE HAVE FEELINGS THEY CAN'T SEPARATE CLEARLY, TOO.
PUT YOUR TRUE FEELINGS AND YOUR FACADE TOGETHER ...
...AND ACT AS YOUR WORDS LEAD YOU TO.
BUT WORDS AREN'T THE TRUTH.
AND I DON'T KNOW WHAT TO SAY IN CRUCIAL MOMENTS.
IT'S USE-LESS.
IF I ACT ON MY WORDS...
AND END UP REGRET-TING IT...
IF YOU THINK OF "WHAT YOU SHOULD SAY" WITH SUCH A DOUBTFUL ATTITUDE, IT WON'T GET YOU ANYWHERE.
I DON'T EVEN KNOW
IF WHAT I'M SAYING RIGHT NOW IS HOW I REALLY FEEL, OR JUST MY FACADE.
BUT I'LL STILL SAY IT.

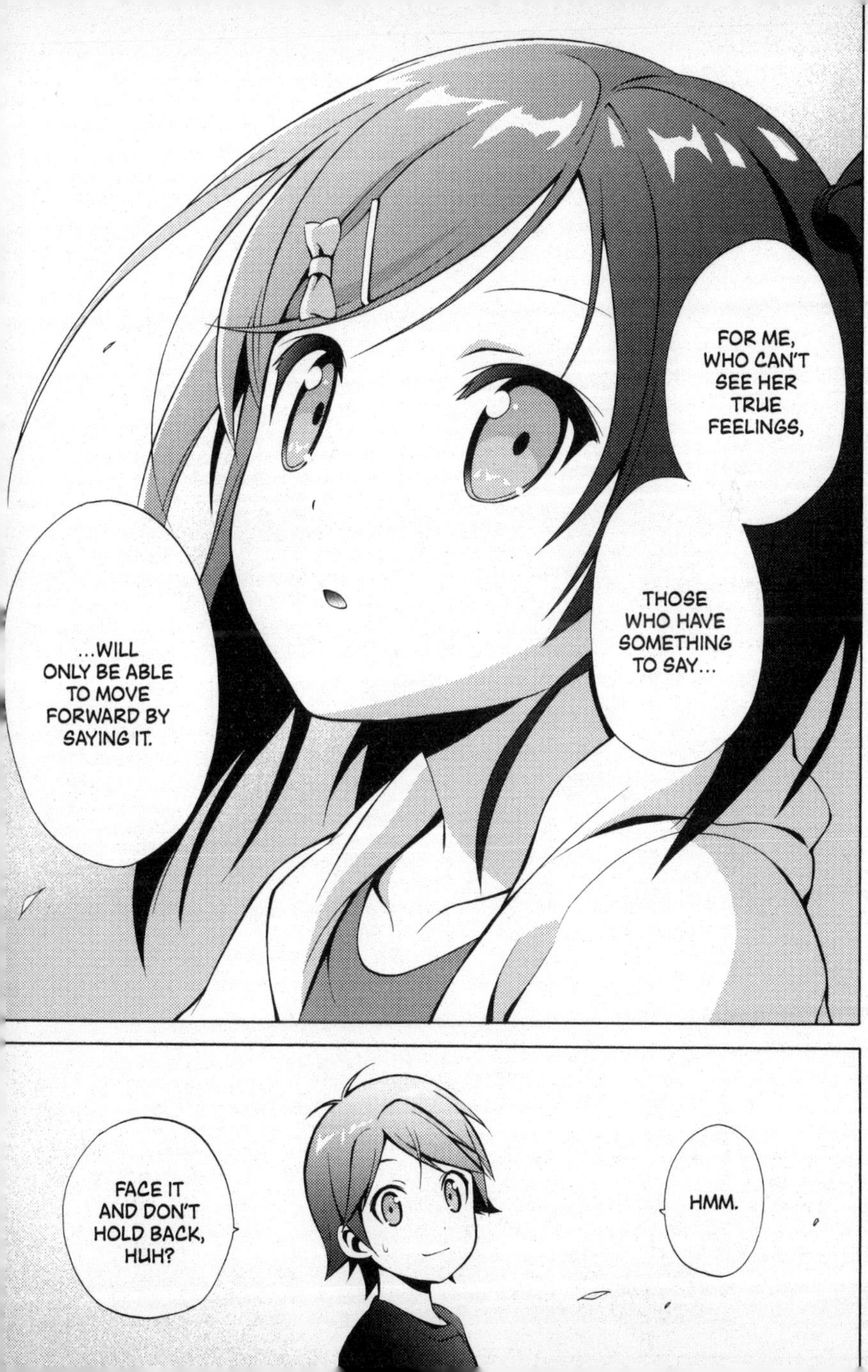
FOR ME, WHO CAN'T SEE HER TRUE FEELINGS,
THOSE WHO HAVE SOMETHING TO SAY...
...WILL ONLY BE ABLE TO MOVE FORWARD BY SAYING IT.
HMM.
FACE IT AND DON'T HOLD BACK, HUH?

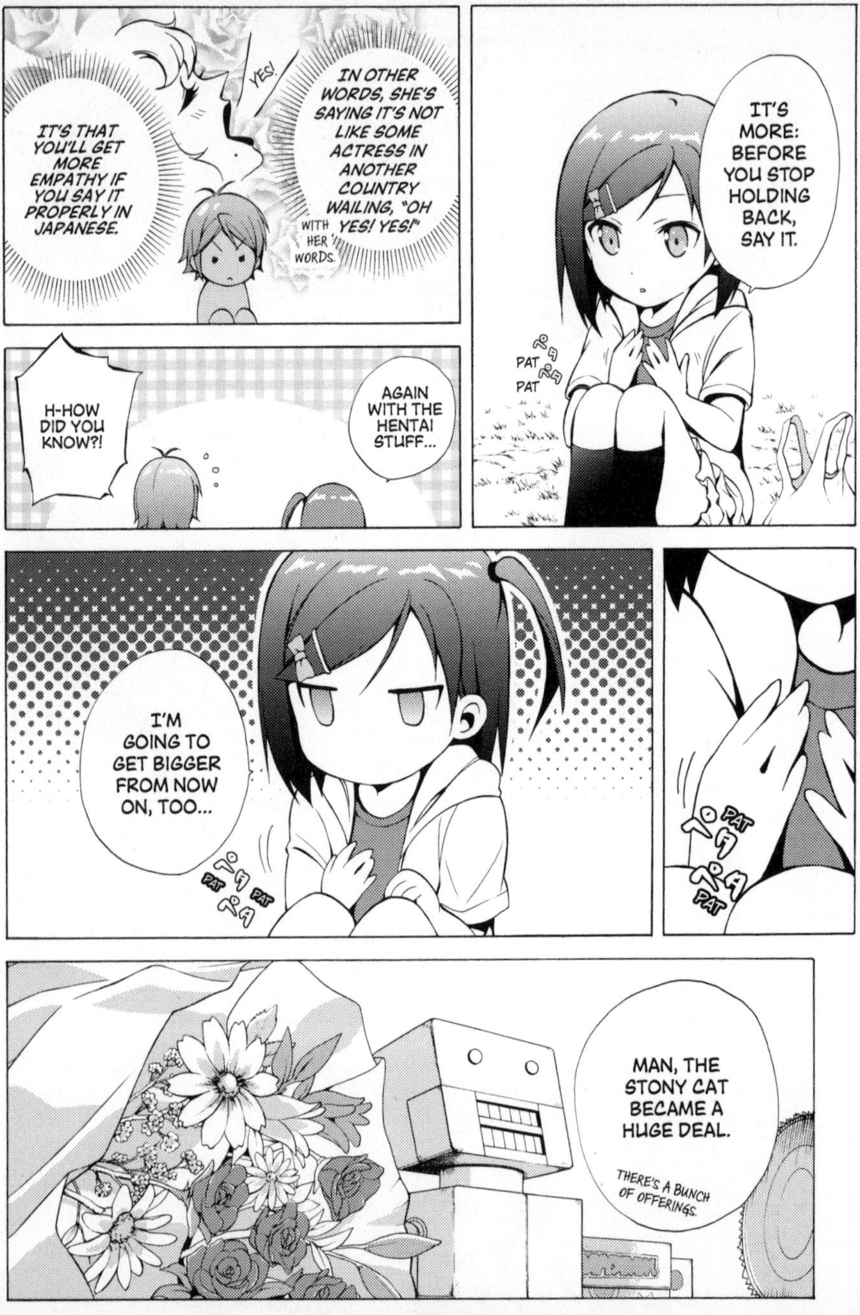
IT'S MORE: BEFORE YOU STOP HOLDING BACK, SAY IT.
ペタ PAT ペタ PAT
IN OTHER WORDS, SHE'S SAYING IT'S NOT LIKE SOME ACTRESS IN ANOTHER COUNTRY WAILING, "OH YES! YES!"
YES!
WITH HER WORDS.
IT'S THAT YOU'LL GET MORE EMPATHY IF YOU SAY IT PROPERLY IN JAPANESE.
AGAIN WITH THE HENTAI STUFF...
H-HOW DID YOU KNOW?!
ペタ PAT ペタ PAT
I'M GOING TO GET BIGGER FROM NOW ON, TOO...
ペタ PAT PAT ペタ
MAN, THE STONY CAT BECAME A HUGE DEAL.
THERE'S A BUNCH OF OFFERINGS.

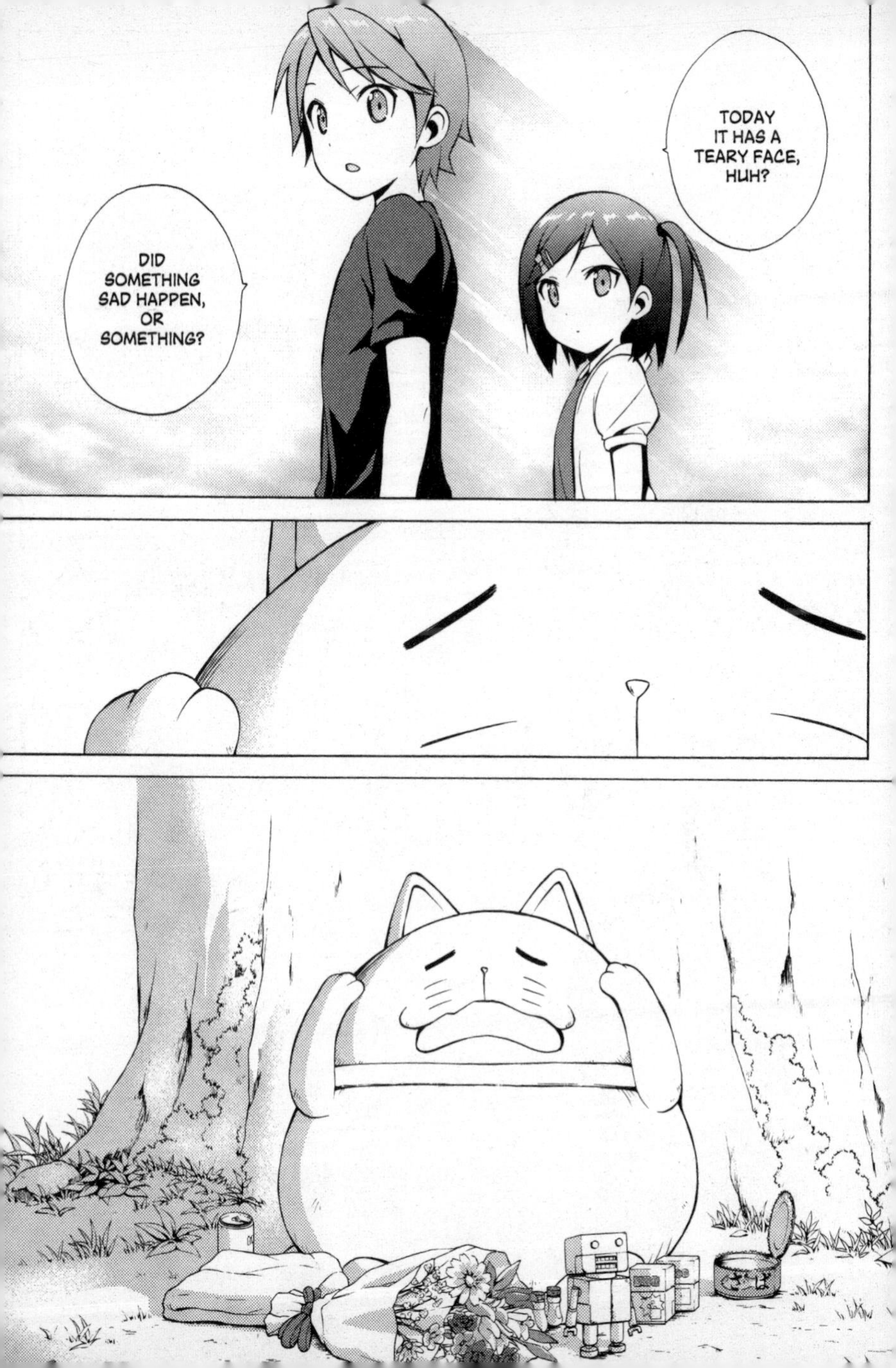
TODAY IT HAS A TEARY FACE, HUH?
DID SOMETHING SAD HAPPEN, OR SOMETHING?

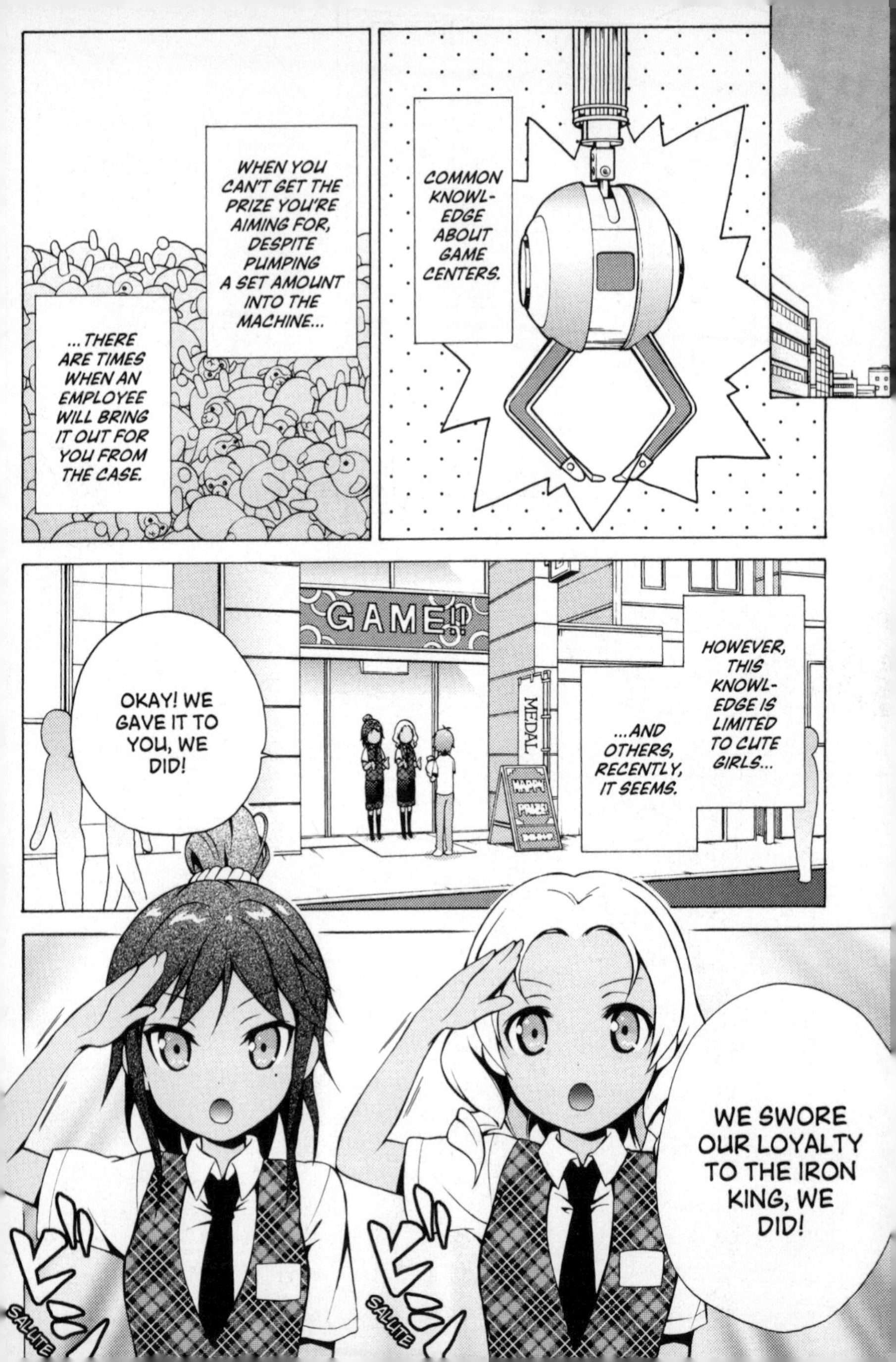
COMMON KNOWLEDGE ABOUT GAME CENTERS.
WHEN YOU CAN'T GET THE PRIZE YOU'RE AIMING FOR, DESPITE PUMPING A SET AMOUNT INTO THE MACHINE...
...THERE ARE TIMES WHEN AN EMPLOYEE WILL BRING IT OUT FOR YOU FROM THE CASE.
GAME!!
MEDAL
HOWEVER, THIS KNOWLEDGE IS LIMITED TO CUTE GIRLS...
...AND OTHERS, RECENTLY, IT SEEMS.
OKAY! WE GAVE IT TO YOU, WE DID!
WE SWORE OUR LOYALTY TO THE IRON KING, WE DID!
SALUTE
SALUTE

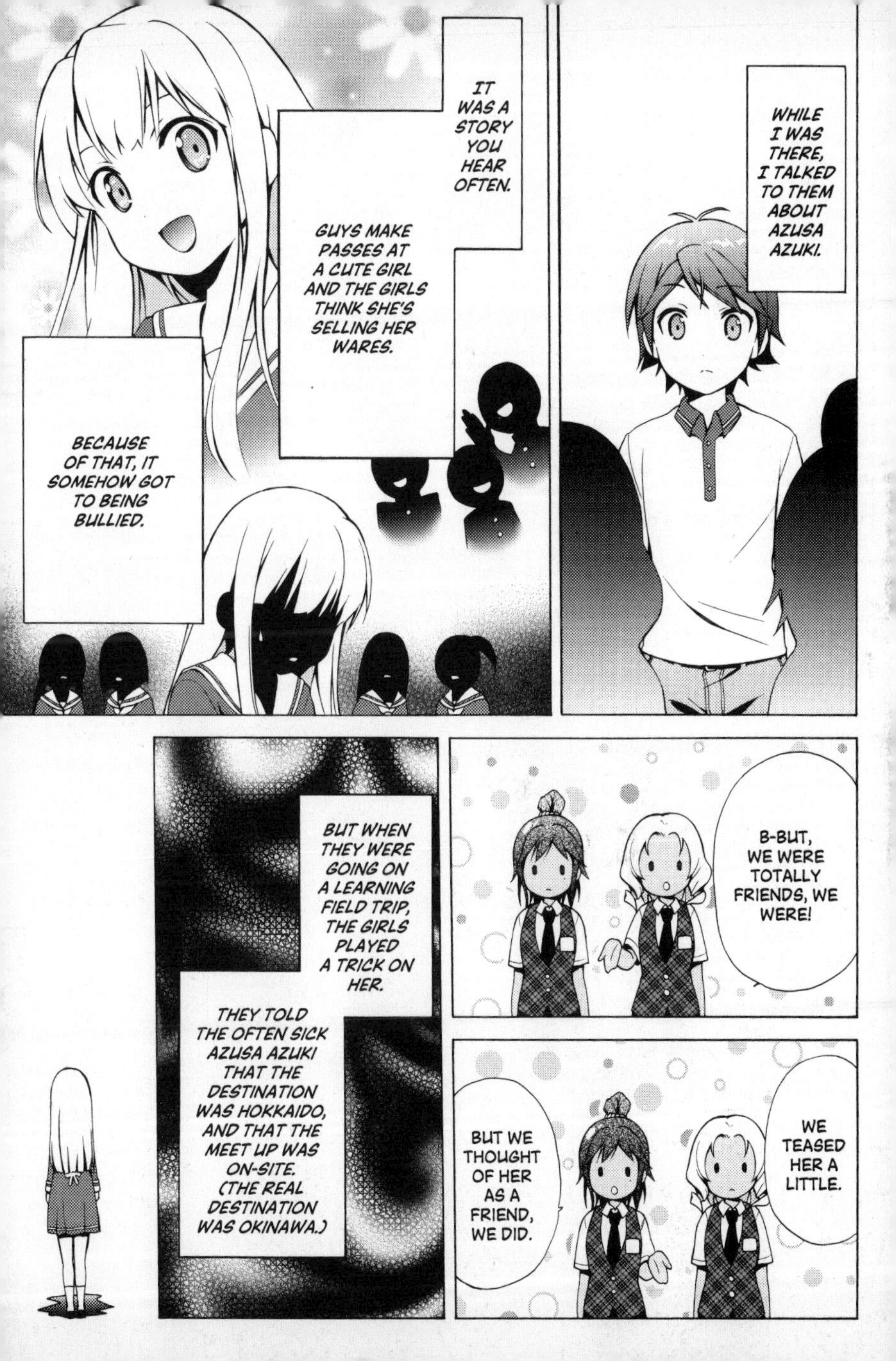
WHILE I WAS THERE, I TALKED TO THEM ABOUT AZUSA AZUKI.
IT WAS A STORY YOU HEAR OFTEN.
GUYS MAKE PASSES AT A CUTE GIRL AND THE GIRLS THINK SHE'S SELLING HER WARES.
BECAUSE OF THAT, IT SOMEHOW GOT TO BEING BULLIED.
B-BUT, WE WERE TOTALLY FRIENDS, WE WERE!
WE TEASED HER A LITTLE.
BUT WE THOUGHT OF HER AS A FRIEND, WE DID.
BUT WHEN THEY WERE GOING ON A LEARNING FIELD TRIP, THE GIRLS PLAYED A TRICK ON HER.
THEY TOLD THE OFTEN SICK AZUSA AZUKI THAT THE DESTINATION WAS HOKKAIDO, AND THAT THE MEET UP WAS ON-SITE. (THE REAL DESTINATION WAS OKINAWA.)

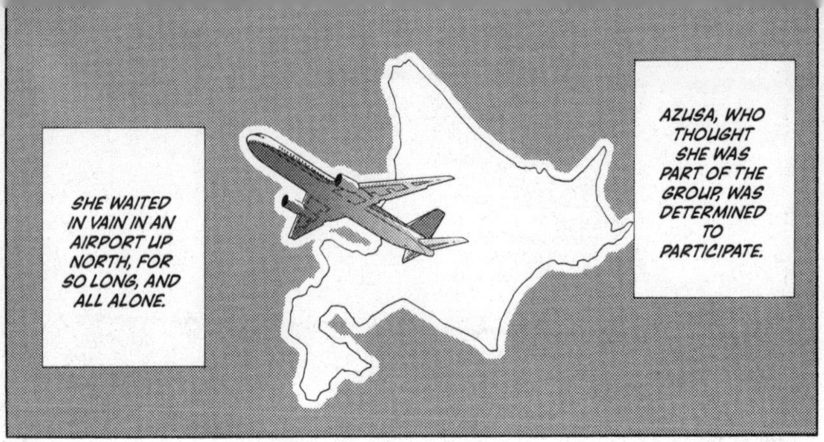
AZUSA, WHO THOUGHT SHE WAS PART OF THE GROUP, WAS DETERMINED TO PARTICIPATE.
SHE WAITED IN VAIN IN AN AIRPORT UP NORTH, FOR SO LONG, AND ALL ALONE.

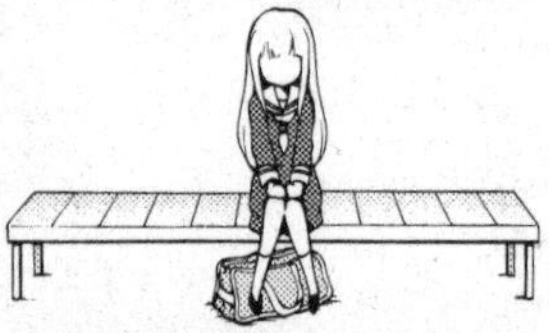

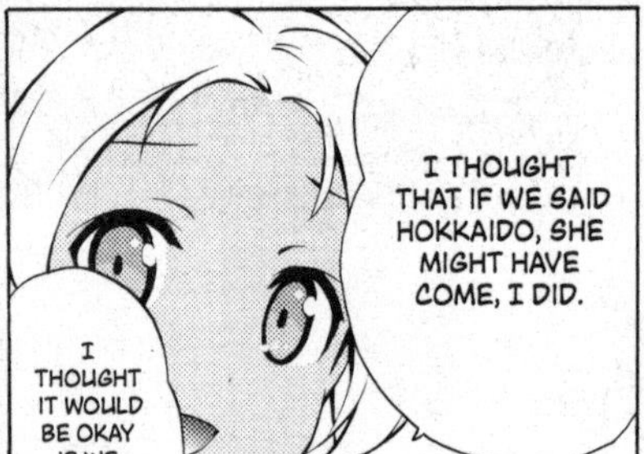
I THOUGHT THAT IF WE SAID HOKKAIDO, SHE MIGHT HAVE COME, I DID.
'CAUSE SHE SAID SHE LIKES EZO RED FOXES.
I THOUGHT IT WOULD BE OKAY IF WE SURPRISED HER AT HANEDA AIRPORT.

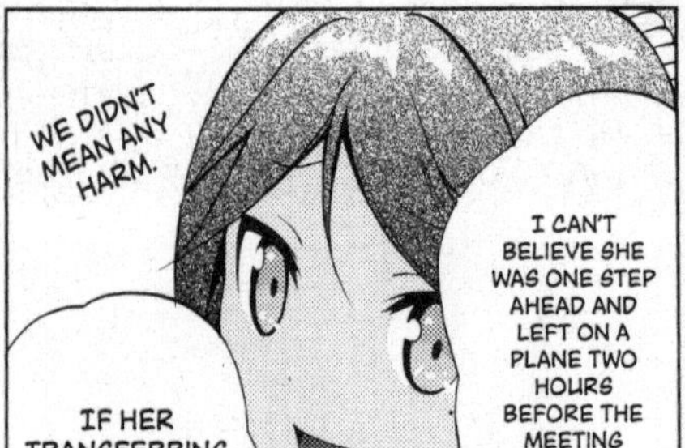
I CAN'T BELIEVE SHE WAS ONE STEP AHEAD AND LEFT ON A PLANE TWO HOURS BEFORE THE MEETING TIME...
WE DIDN'T MEAN ANY HARM.
IF HER TRANSFERRING IS OUR FAULT, WE WANTED TO APOLOGIZE, WE DID.

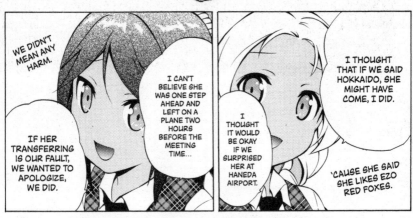

AS OFTEN HAPPENS, THE ONES WHO DO THE BULLYING DON'T THINK OF IT AS THAT SERIOUS. I GET THAT.

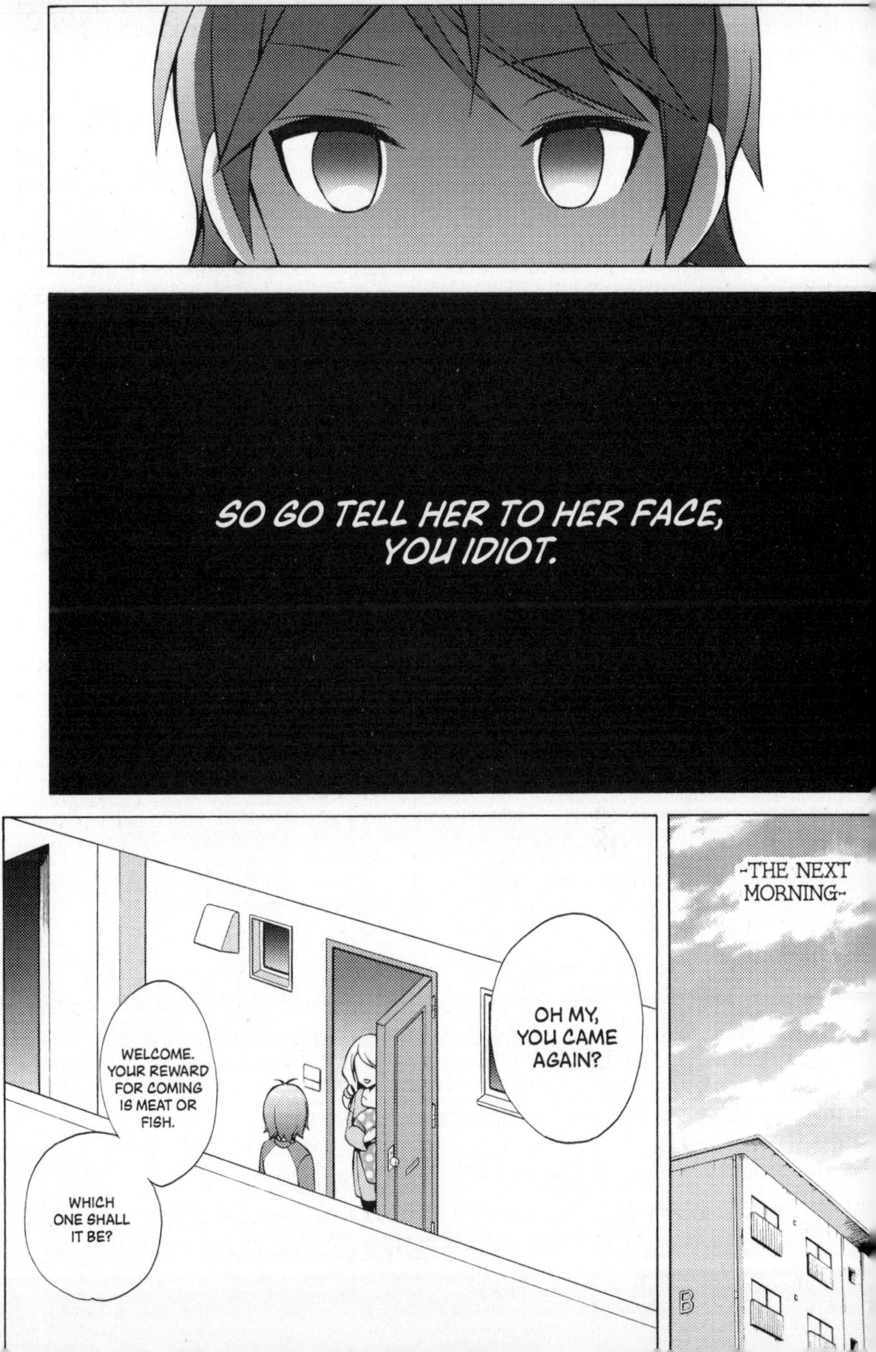
SO GO TELL HER TO HER FACE, YOU IDIOT.
-THE NEXT MORNING-
OH MY, YOU CAME AGAIN?
WELCOME. YOUR REWARD FOR COMING IS MEAT OR FISH.
WHICH ONE SHALL IT BE?

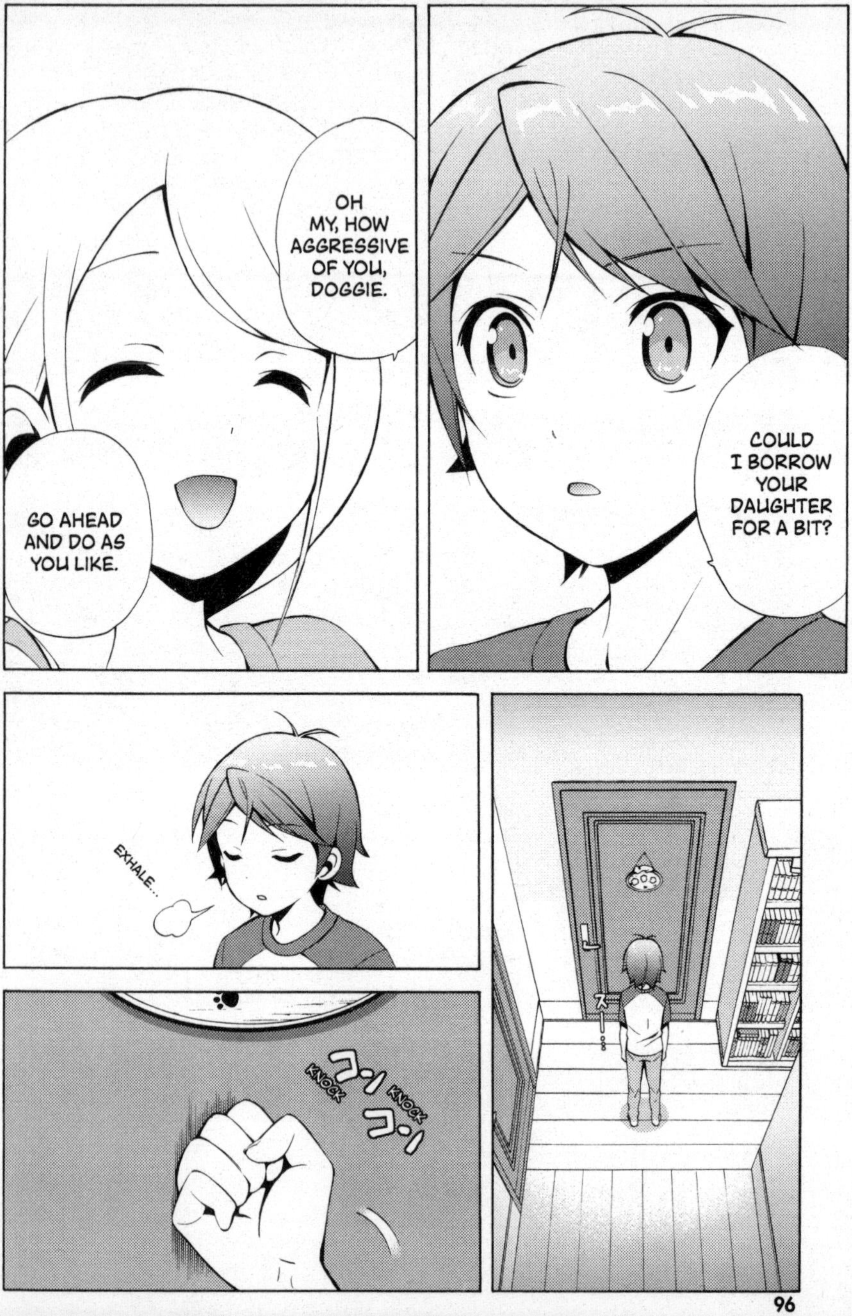
COULD I BORROW YOUR DAUGHTER FOR A BIT?
OH MY, HOW AGGRESSIVE OF YOU, DOGGIE.
GO AHEAD AND DO AS YOU LIKE.
EXHALE...
KNOCK
KNOCK

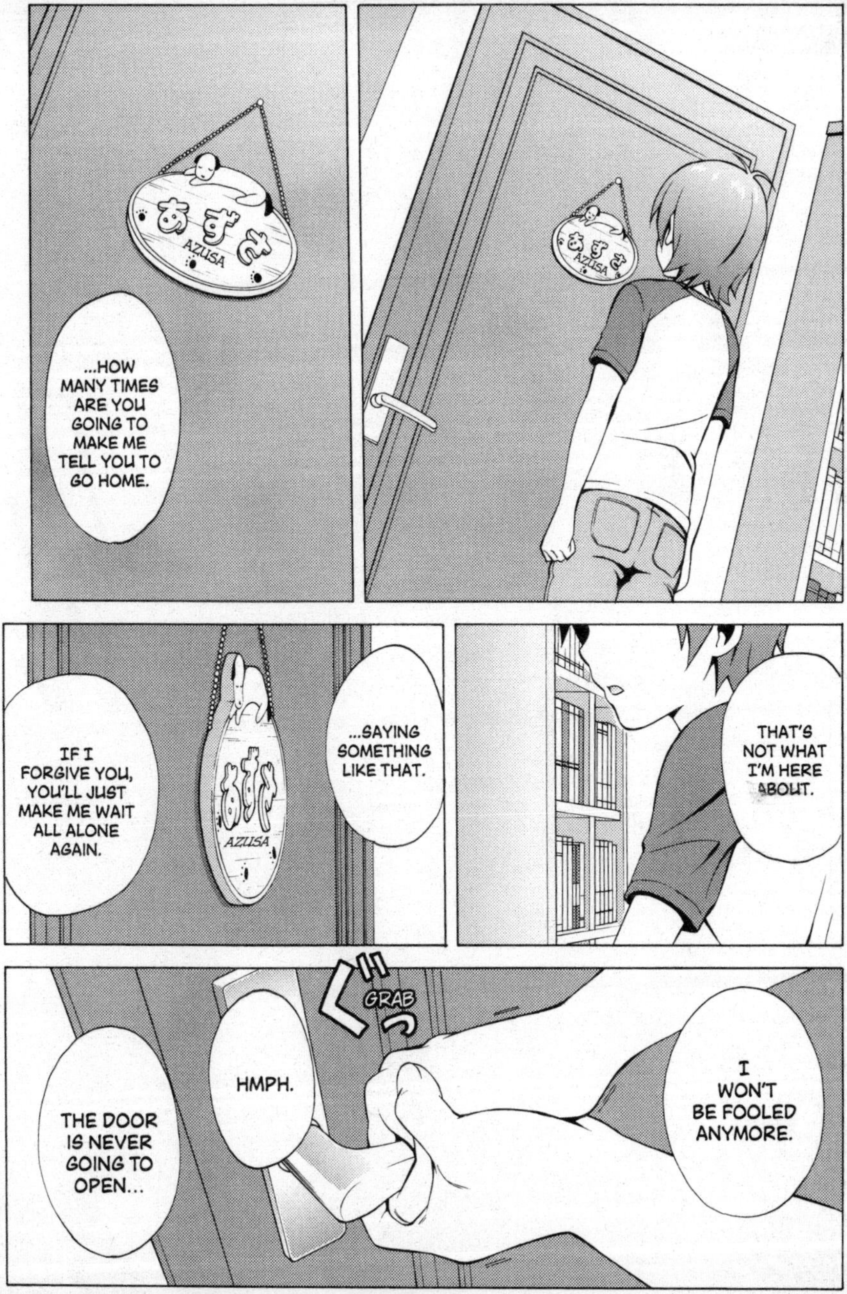
あずさ
AZUSA
...HOW MANY TIMES ARE YOU GOING TO MAKE ME TELL YOU TO GO HOME.
THAT'S NOT WHAT I'M HERE ABOUT.
...SAYING SOMETHING LIKE THAT.
IF I FORGIVE YOU, YOU'LL JUST MAKE ME WAIT ALL ALONE AGAIN.
I WON'T BE FOOLED ANYMORE.
ぐっ
GRAB
HMPH.
THE DOOR IS NEVER GOING TO OPEN...

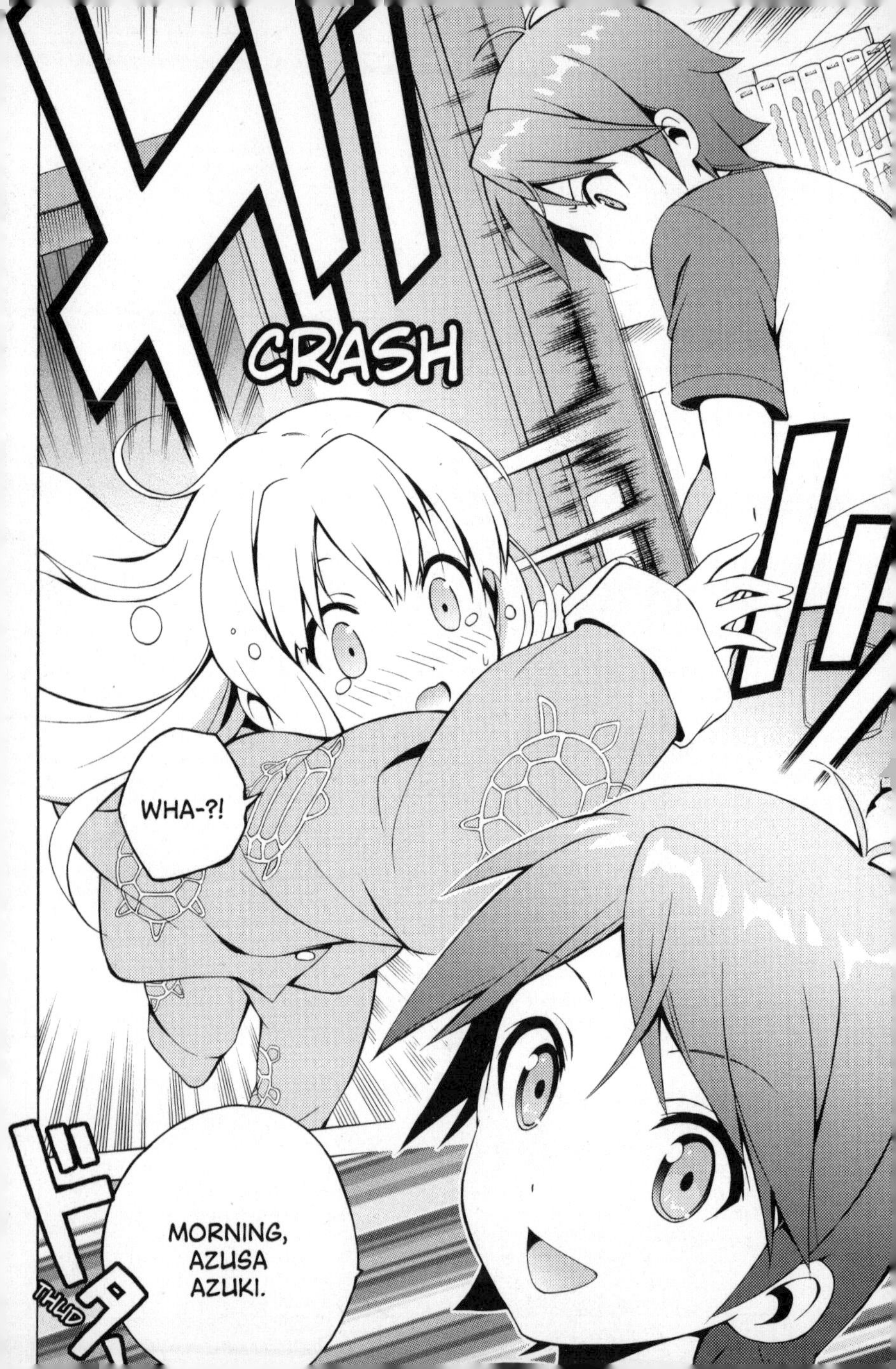
CRASH
WHA-?!
MORNING, AZUSA AZUKI.
THUD

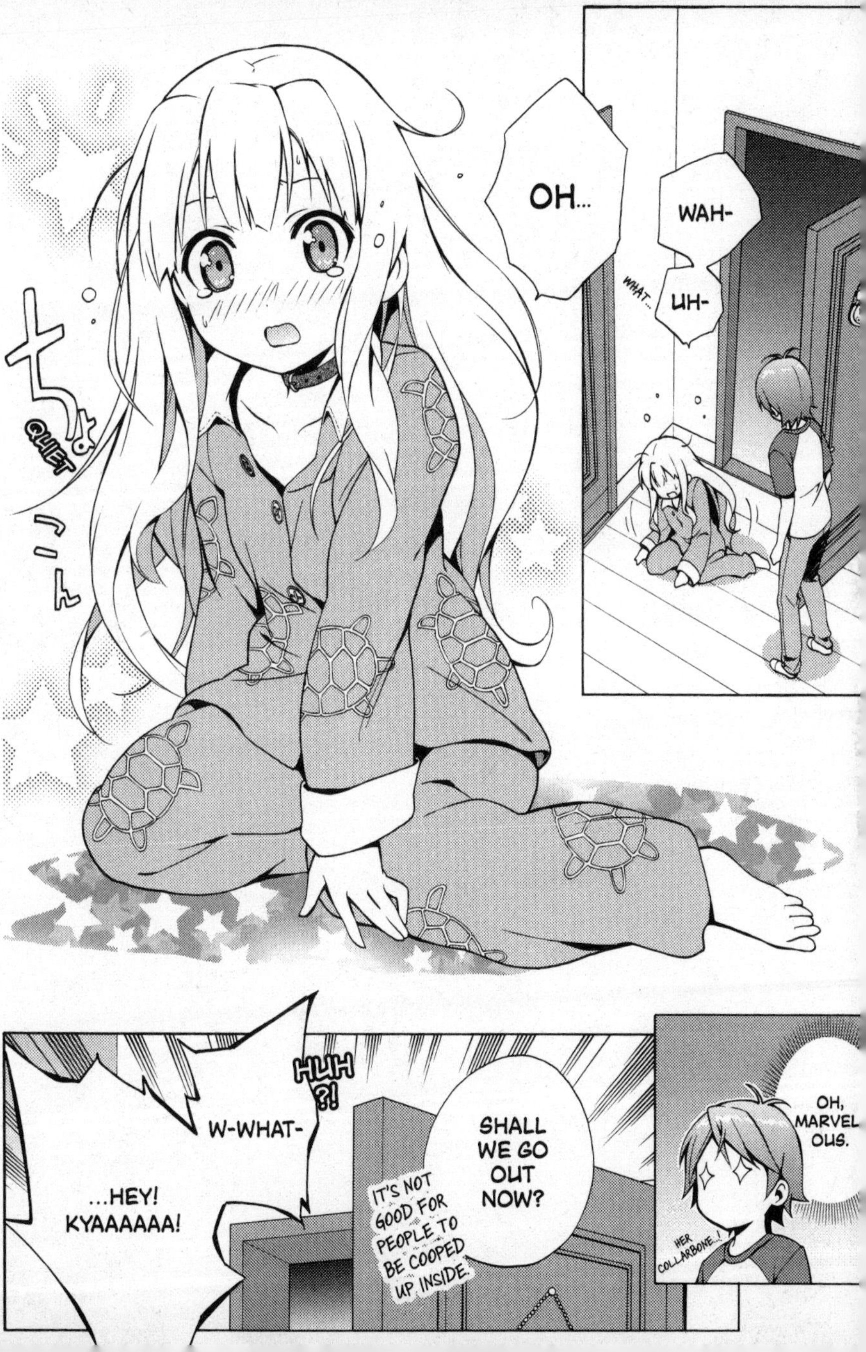
WAH-
WHAT...
UH-
OH...
QUIET
OH, MARVEL OUS.
HER COLLARBONE...!
SHALL WE GO OUT NOW?
IT'S NOT GOOD FOR PEOPLE TO BE COOPED UP INSIDE.
HUH ?!
W-WHAT-
...HEY! KYAAAAAA!

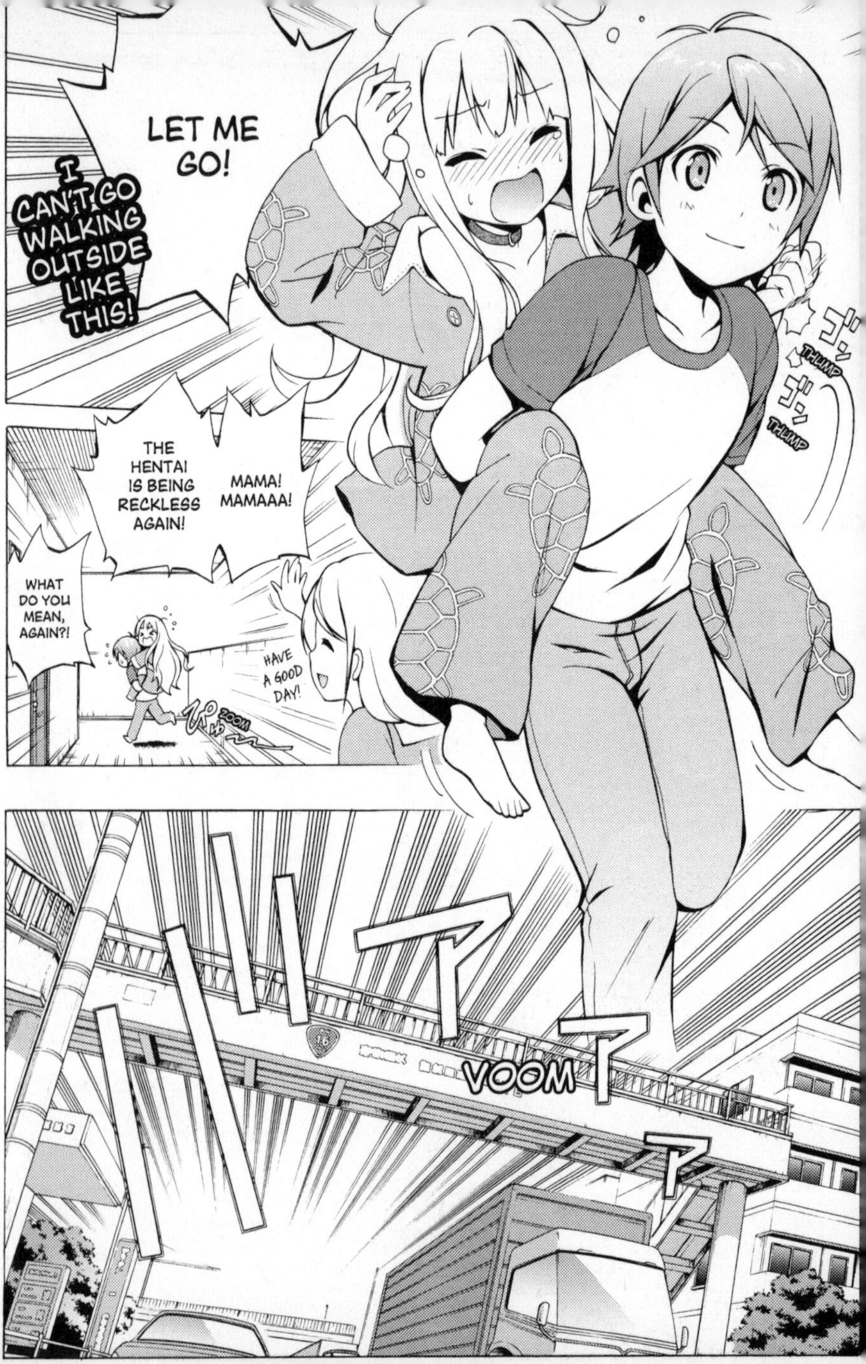
ゴッ
THUMP
ゴッ
THUMP
LET ME GO!
I CAN'T GO WALKING OUTSIDE LIKE THIS!
MAMA! MAMAAA!
THE HENTAI IS BEING RECKLESS AGAIN!
HAVE A GOOD DAY!
WHAT DO YOU MEAN, AGAIN?!
ZOOM
VOOM

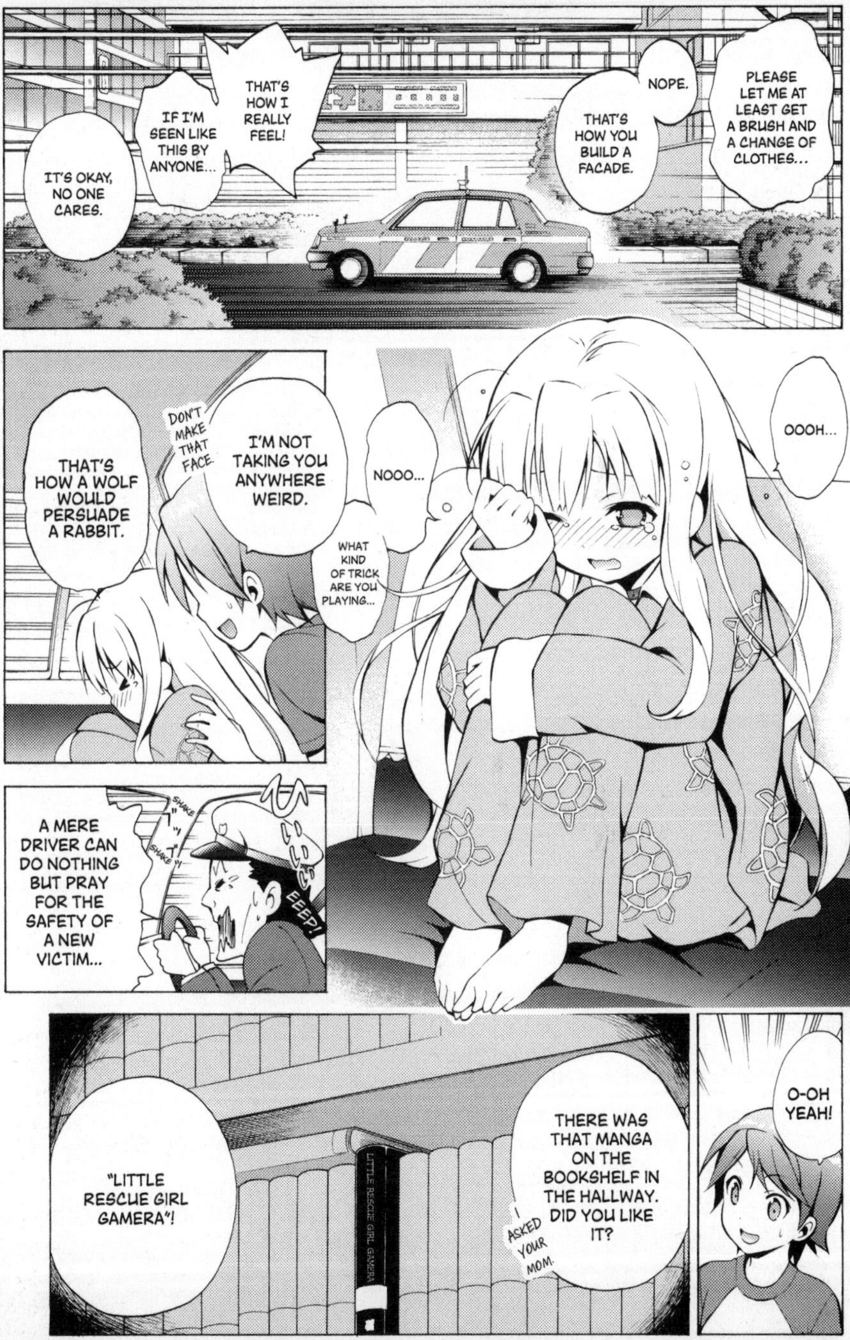
PLEASE LET ME AT LEAST GET A BRUSH AND A CHANGE OF CLOTHES…
NOPE.
THAT'S HOW YOU BUILD A FACADE.
THAT'S HOW I REALLY FEEL!
IF I'M SEEN LIKE THIS BY ANYONE…
IT'S OKAY, NO ONE CARES.
OOOH…
NOOO…
WHAT KIND OF TRICK ARE YOU PLAYING…
I'M NOT TAKING YOU ANYWHERE WEIRD.
DON'T MAKE THAT FACE.
THAT'S HOW A WOLF WOULD PERSUADE A RABBIT.
SHAKE
SHAKE
EEEP!
A MERE DRIVER CAN DO NOTHING BUT PRAY FOR THE SAFETY OF A NEW VICTIM…
O-OH YEAH!
THERE WAS THAT MANGA ON THE BOOKSHELF IN THE HALLWAY. DID YOU LIKE IT?
I ASKED YOUR MOM.
"LITTLE RESCUE GIRL GAMERA"!
LITTLE RESCUE GIRL GAMERA

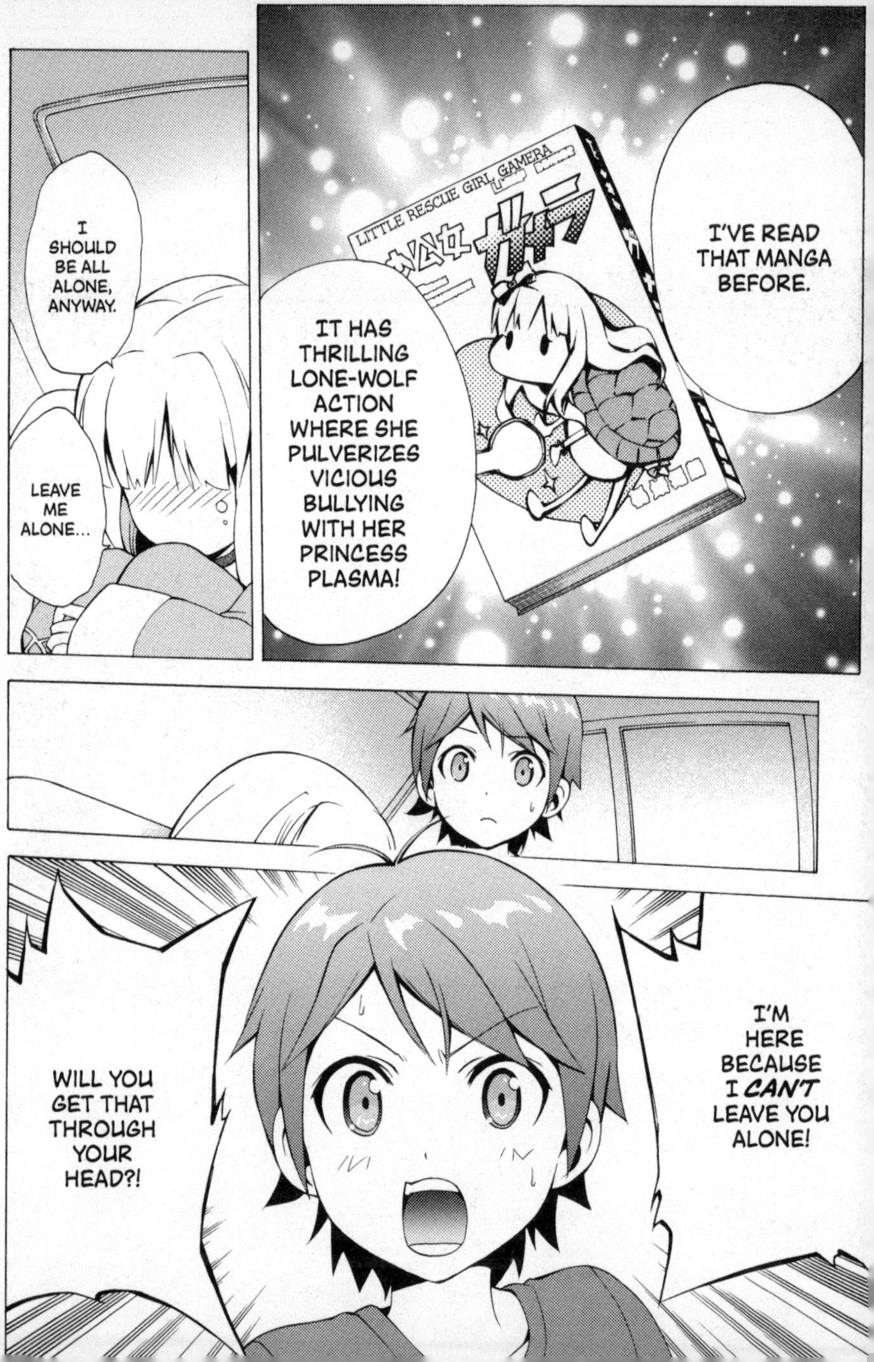
I'VE READ THAT MANGA BEFORE.
LITTLE RESCUE GIRL GAMERA
IT HAS THRILLING LONE-WOLF ACTION WHERE SHE PULVERIZES VICIOUS BULLYING WITH HER PRINCESS PLASMA!
I SHOULD BE ALL ALONE, ANYWAY.
LEAVE ME ALONE...
I'M HERE BECAUSE I *CAN'T* LEAVE YOU ALONE!
WILL YOU GET THAT THROUGH YOUR HEAD?!

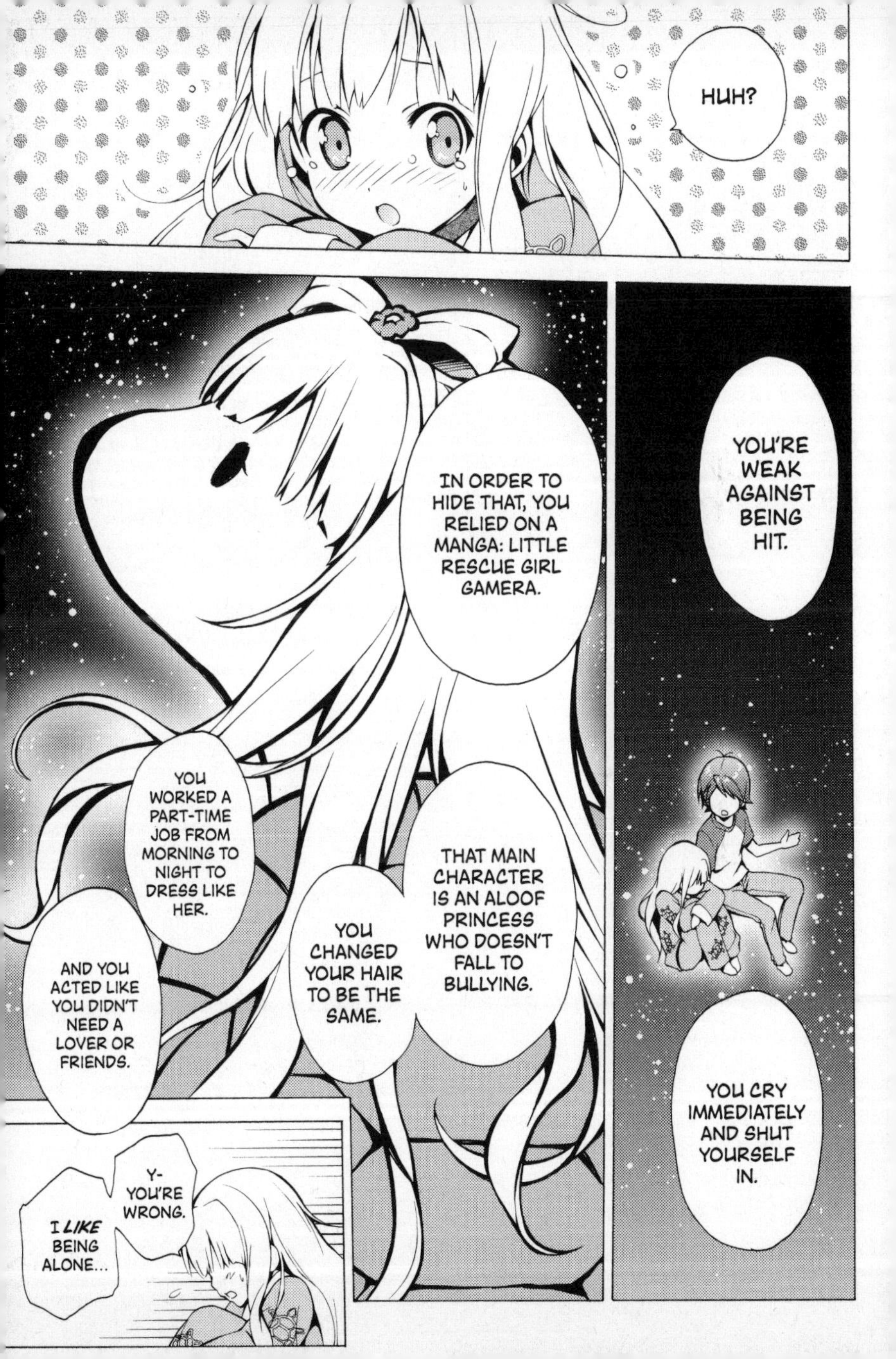
HUH?
YOU'RE WEAK AGAINST BEING HIT.
YOU CRY IMMEDIATELY AND SHUT YOURSELF IN.
IN ORDER TO HIDE THAT, YOU RELIED ON A MANGA: LITTLE RESCUE GIRL GAMERA.
THAT MAIN CHARACTER IS AN ALOOF PRINCESS WHO DOESN'T FALL TO BULLYING.
YOU CHANGED YOUR HAIR TO BE THE SAME.
YOU WORKED A PART-TIME JOB FROM MORNING TO NIGHT TO DRESS LIKE HER.
AND YOU ACTED LIKE YOU DIDN'T NEED A LOVER OR FRIENDS.
Y- YOU'RE WRONG.
I *LIKE* BEING ALONE...

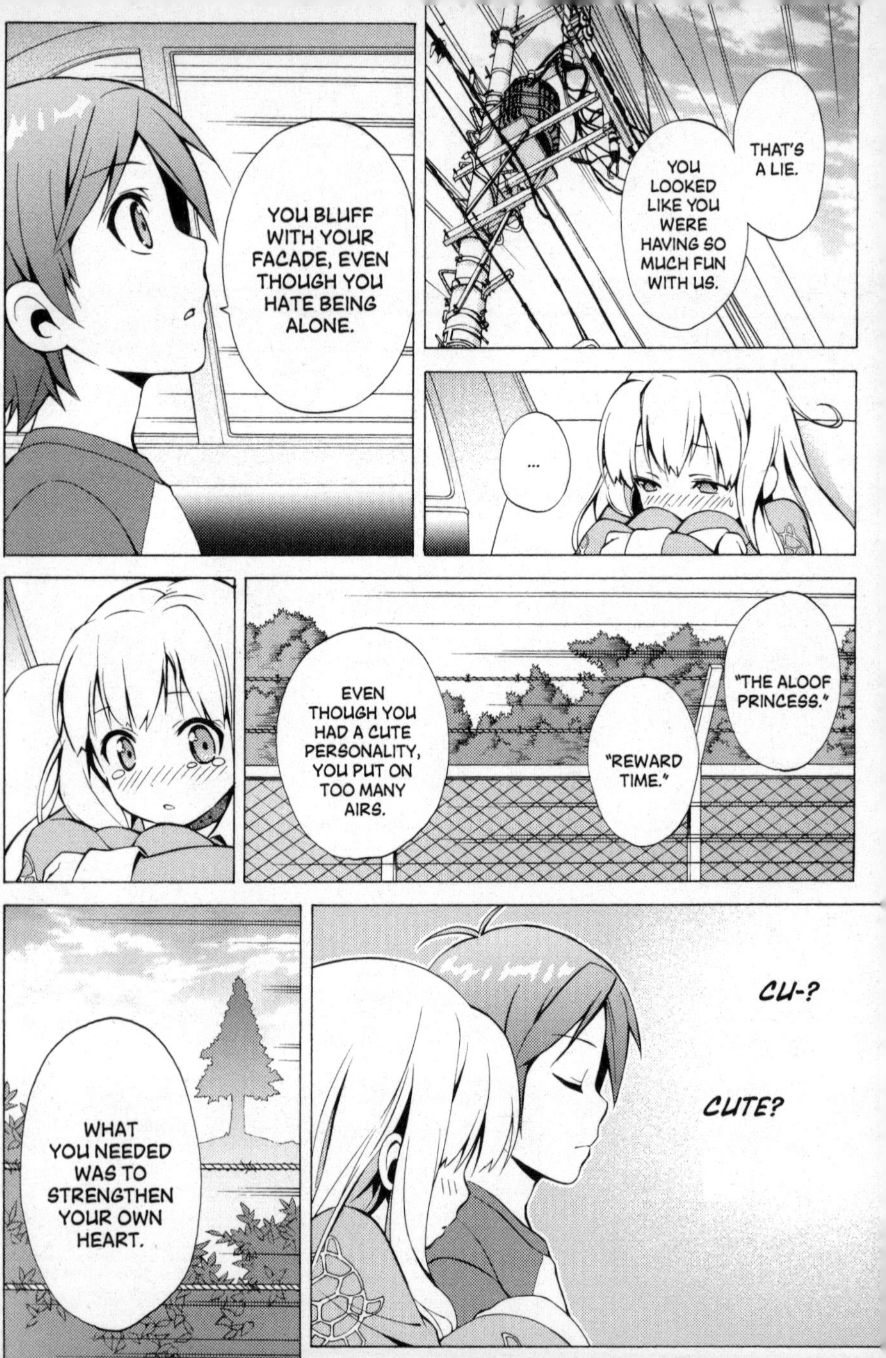
THAT'S A LIE.
YOU LOOKED LIKE YOU WERE HAVING SO MUCH FUN WITH US.
YOU BLUFF WITH YOUR FACADE, EVEN THOUGH YOU HATE BEING ALONE.
...
"THE ALOOF PRINCESS."
"REWARD TIME."
EVEN THOUGH YOU HAD A CUTE PERSONALITY, YOU PUT ON TOO MANY AIRS.
CU-?
CUTE?
WHAT YOU NEEDED WAS TO STRENGTHEN YOUR OWN HEART.

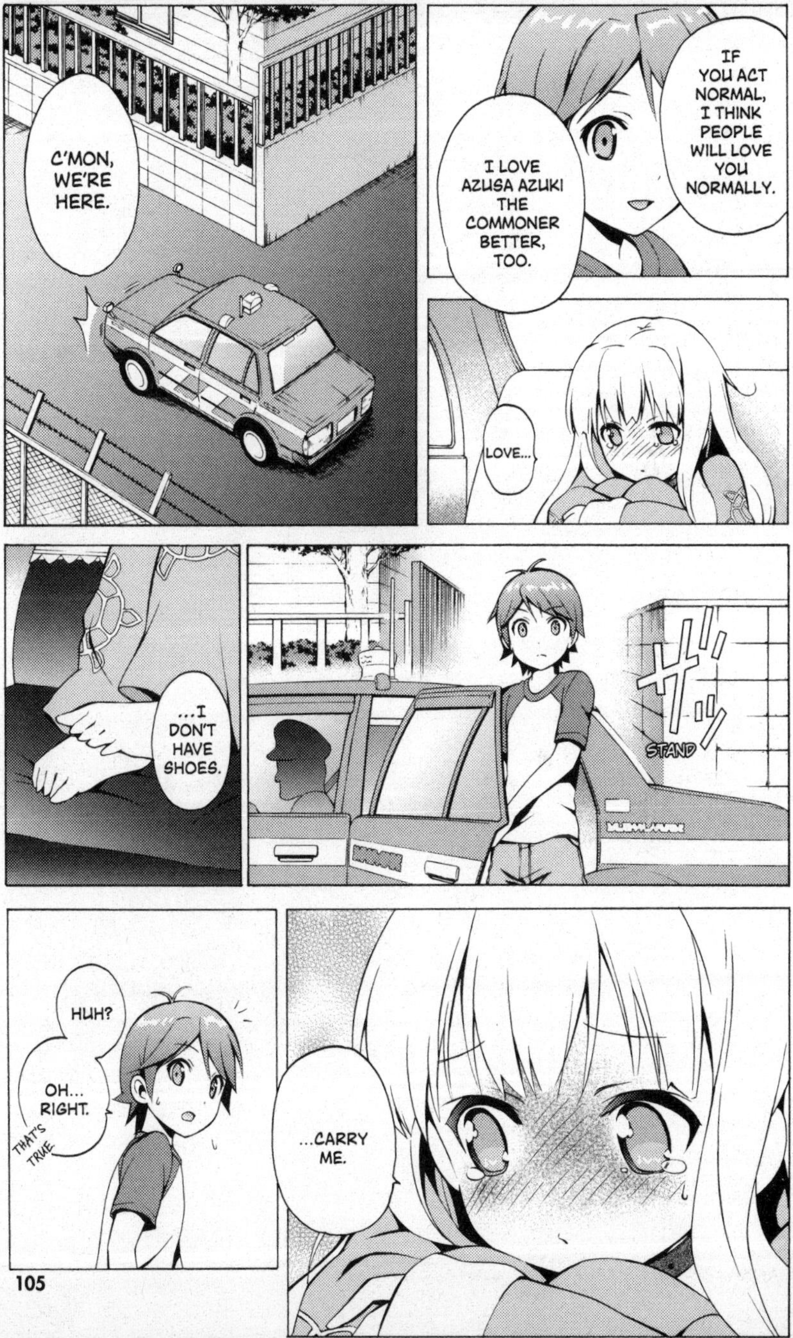
IF YOU ACT NORMAL, I THINK PEOPLE WILL LOVE YOU NORMALLY.
I LOVE AZUSA AZUKI THE COMMONER BETTER, TOO.
LOVE...
C'MON, WE'RE HERE.
STAND
...I DON'T HAVE SHOES.
...CARRY ME.
HUH?
OH... RIGHT.
THAT'S TRUE

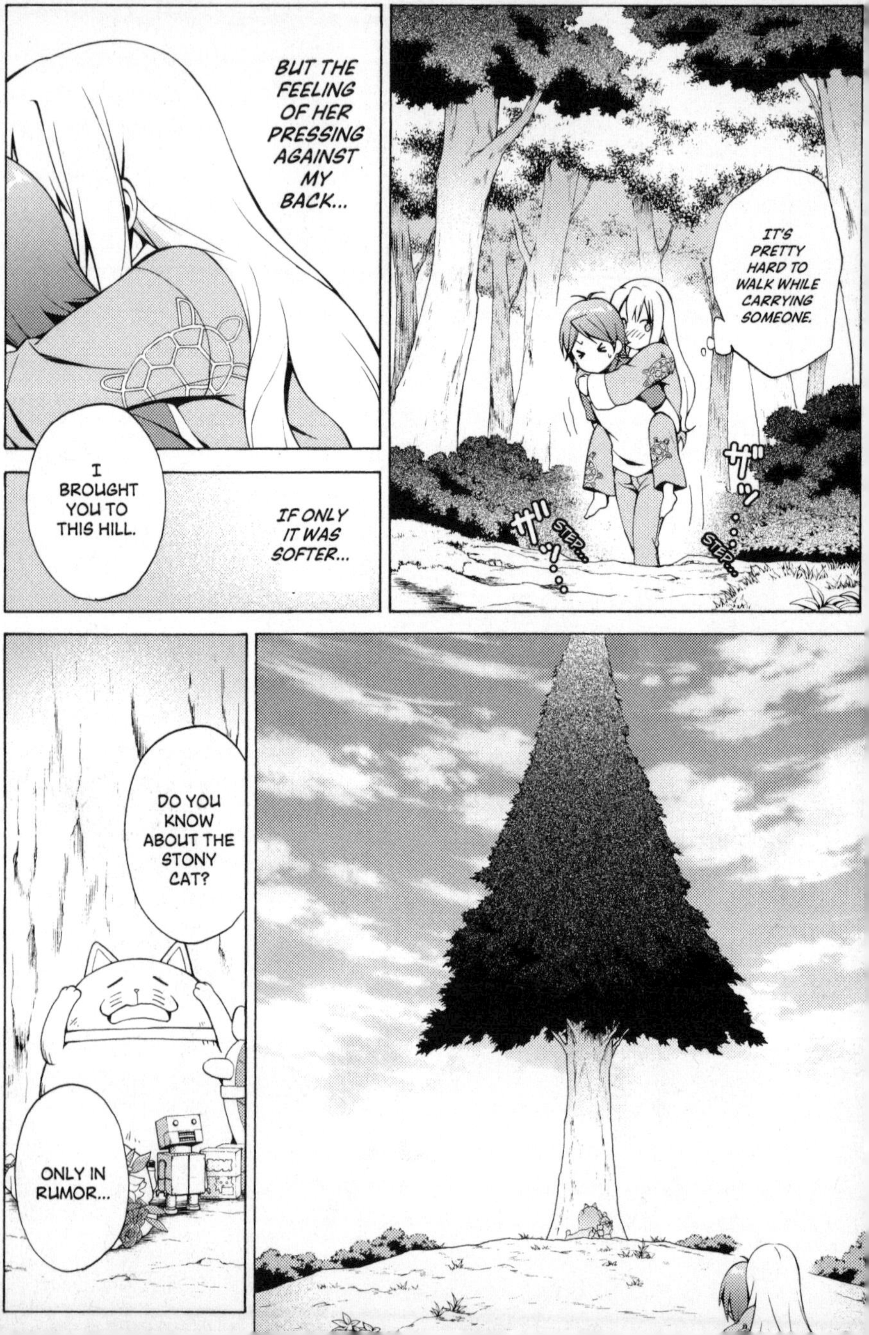
IT'S PRETTY HARD TO WALK WHILE CARRYING SOMEONE.
ザッ
STEP...
ザッ
STEP...
BUT THE FEELING OF HER PRESSING AGAINST MY BACK...
IF ONLY IT WAS SOFTER...
I BROUGHT YOU TO THIS HILL.
DO YOU KNOW ABOUT THE STONY CAT?
ONLY IN RUMOR...

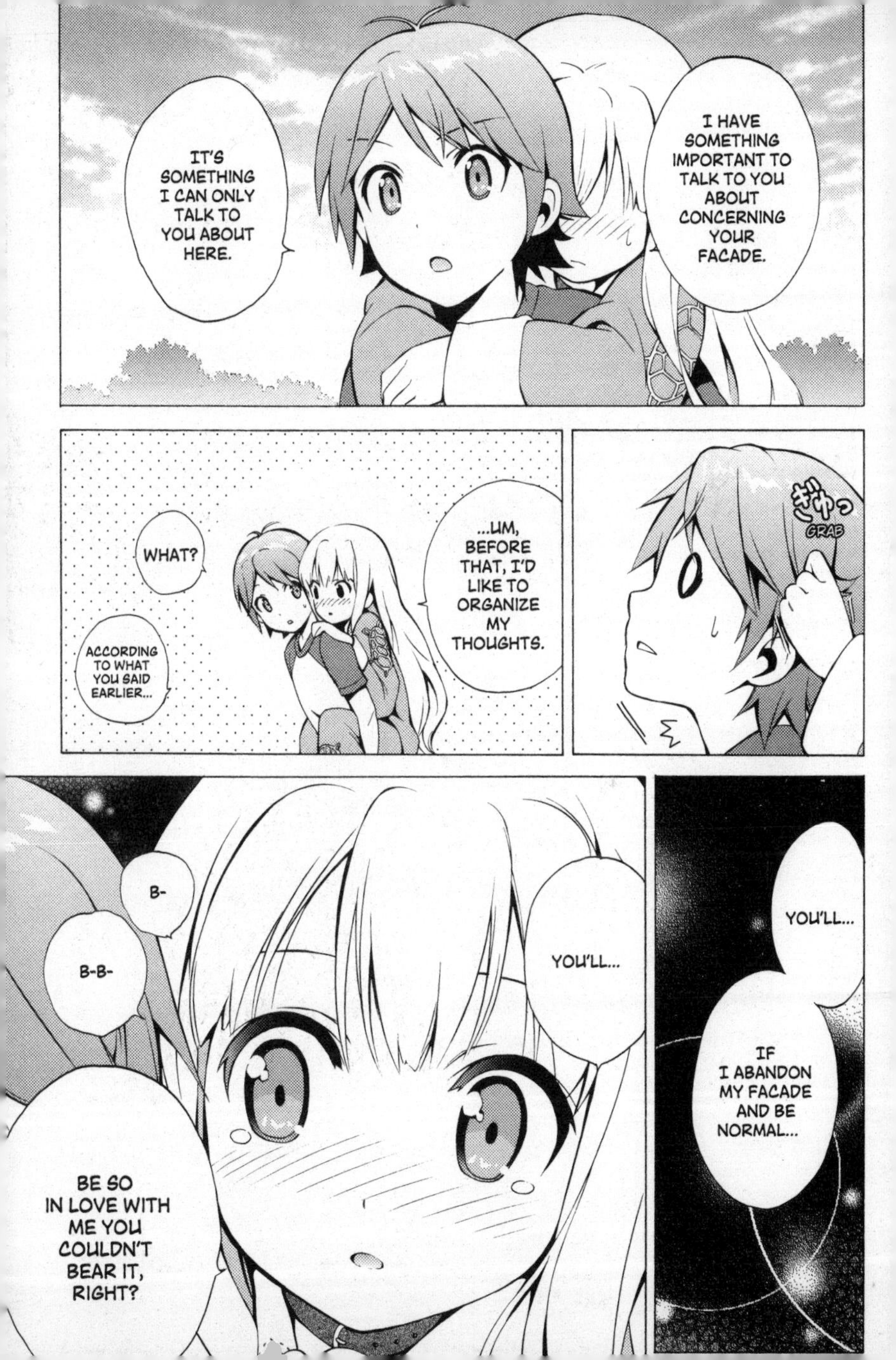
I HAVE SOMETHING IMPORTANT TO TALK TO YOU ABOUT CONCERNING YOUR FACADE.
IT'S SOMETHING I CAN ONLY TALK TO YOU ABOUT HERE.
ぎゅっ
GRAB
...UM, BEFORE THAT, I'D LIKE TO ORGANIZE MY THOUGHTS.
WHAT?
ACCORDING TO WHAT YOU SAID EARLIER...
YOU'LL...
IF I ABANDON MY FACADE AND BE NORMAL...
YOU'LL...
B-
B-B-
BE SO IN LOVE WITH ME YOU COULDN'T BEAR IT, RIGHT?

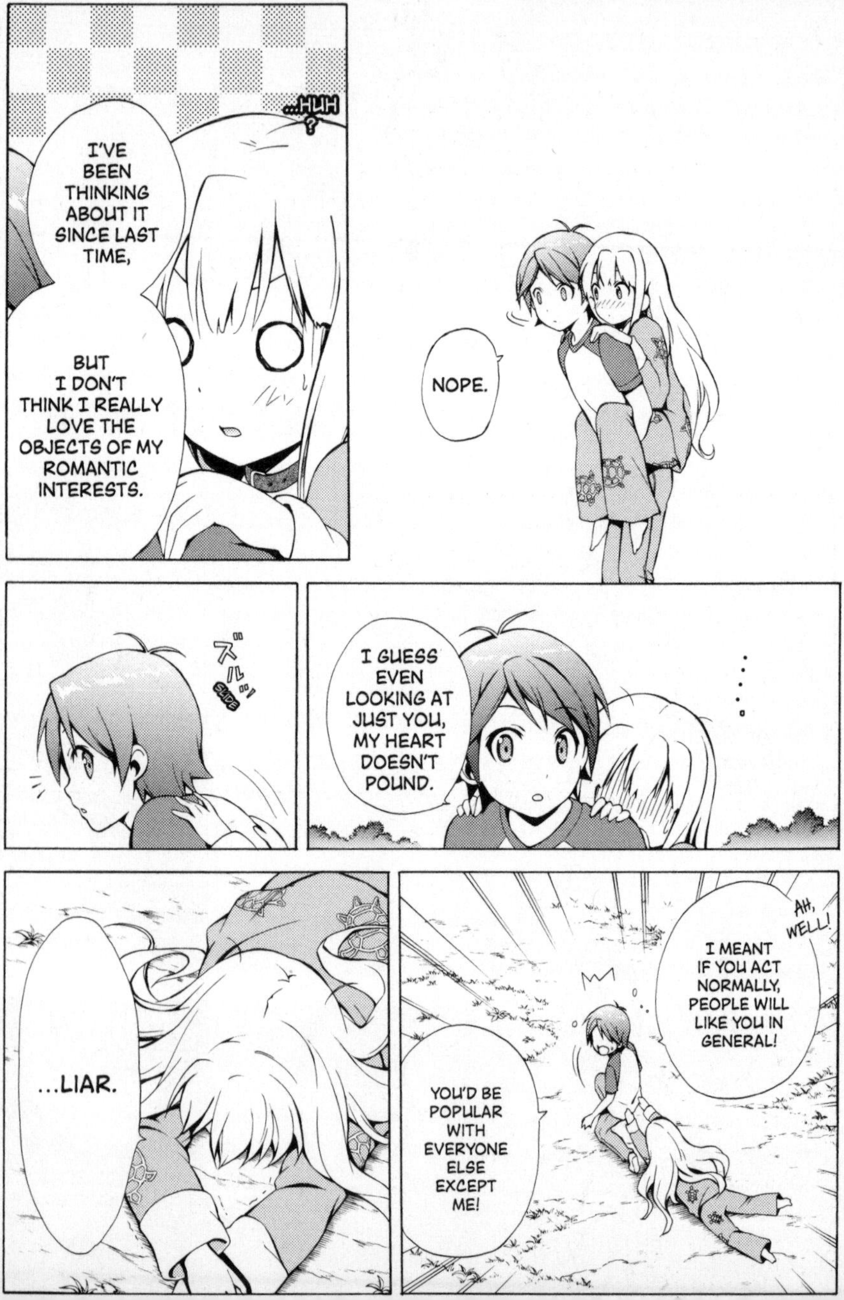
NOPE.
...HUH?
I'VE BEEN THINKING ABOUT IT SINCE LAST TIME,
BUT I DON'T THINK I REALLY LOVE THE OBJECTS OF MY ROMANTIC INTERESTS.
....
I GUESS EVEN LOOKING AT JUST YOU, MY HEART DOESN'T POUND.
ズルッ
SLIDE
AH, WELL!
I MEANT IF YOU ACT NORMALLY, PEOPLE WILL LIKE YOU IN GENERAL!
YOU'D BE POPULAR WITH EVERYONE ELSE EXCEPT ME!
...LIAR.

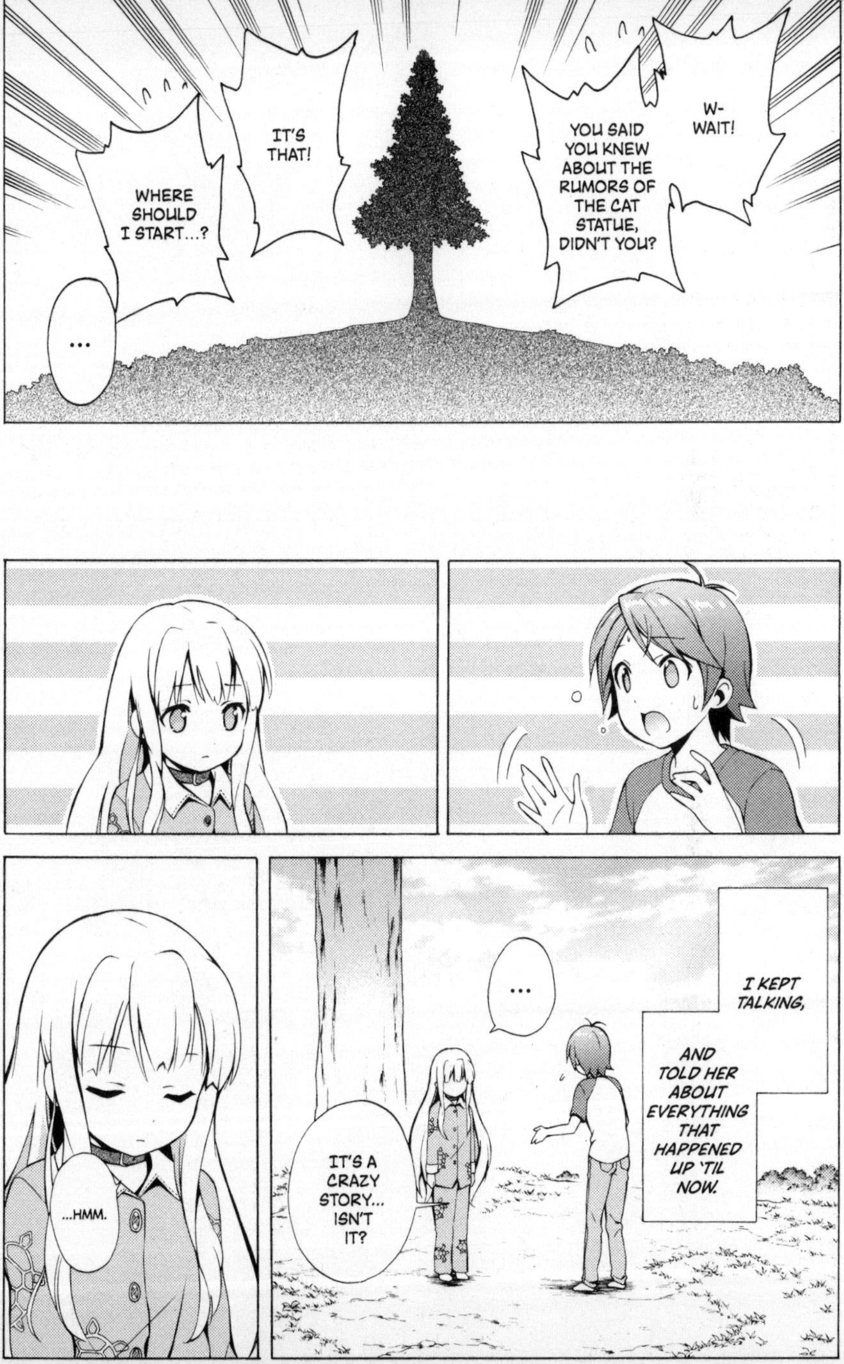
W-WAIT!
YOU SAID YOU KNEW ABOUT THE RUMORS OF THE CAT STATUE, DIDN'T YOU?
IT'S THAT!
WHERE SHOULD I START...?
...
I KEPT TALKING, AND TOLD HER ABOUT EVERYTHING THAT HAPPENED UP 'TIL NOW.
...
IT'S A CRAZY STORY... ISN'T IT?
...HMM.

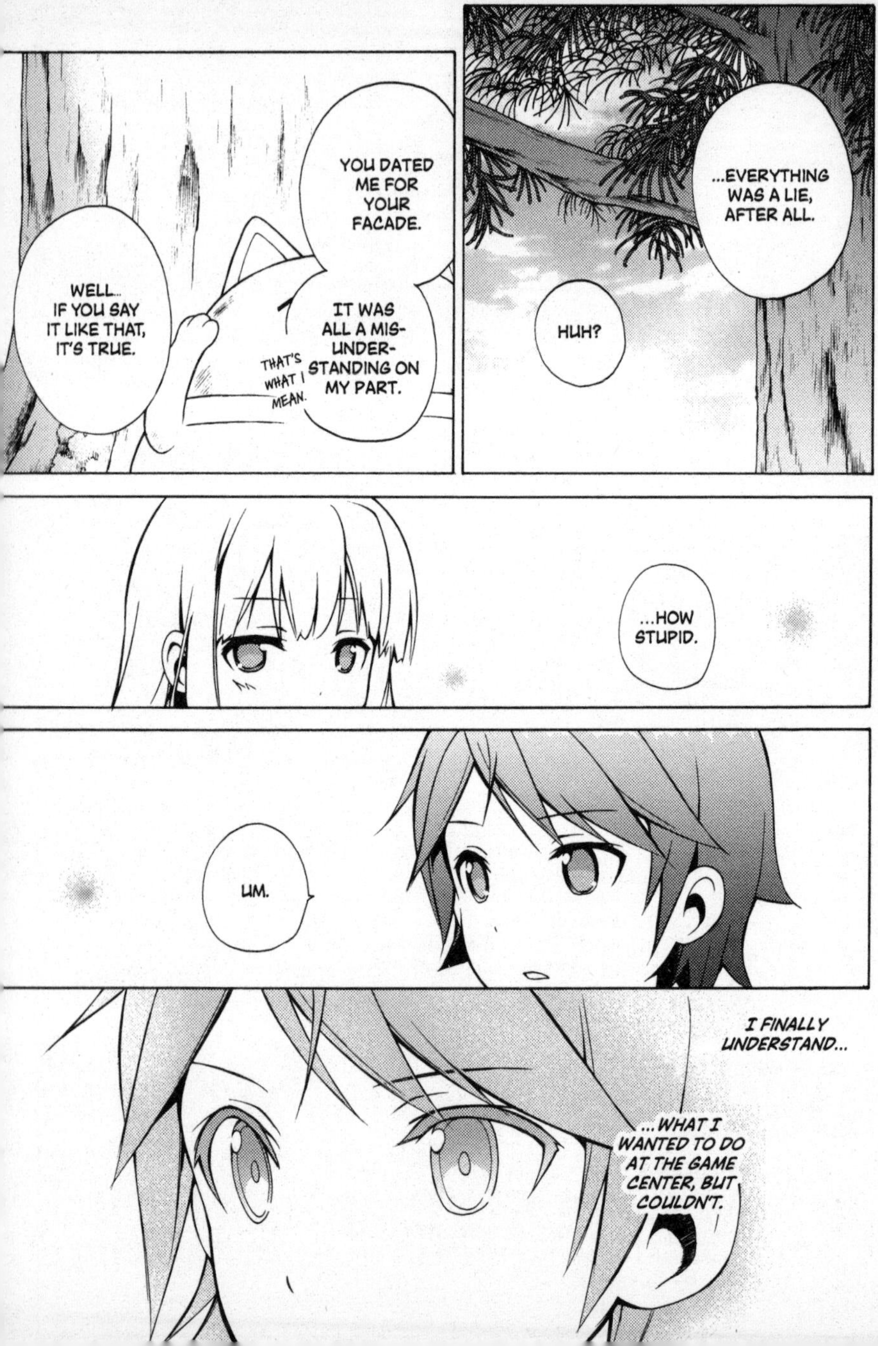
...EVERYTHING WAS A LIE, AFTER ALL.
HUH?
YOU DATED ME FOR YOUR FACADE.
IT WAS ALL A MIS-UNDER-STANDING ON MY PART.
THAT'S WHAT I MEAN.
WELL... IF YOU SAY IT LIKE THAT, IT'S TRUE.
...HOW STUPID.
UM.
I FINALLY UNDERSTAND...
...WHAT I WANTED TO DO AT THE GAME CENTER, BUT COULDN'T.

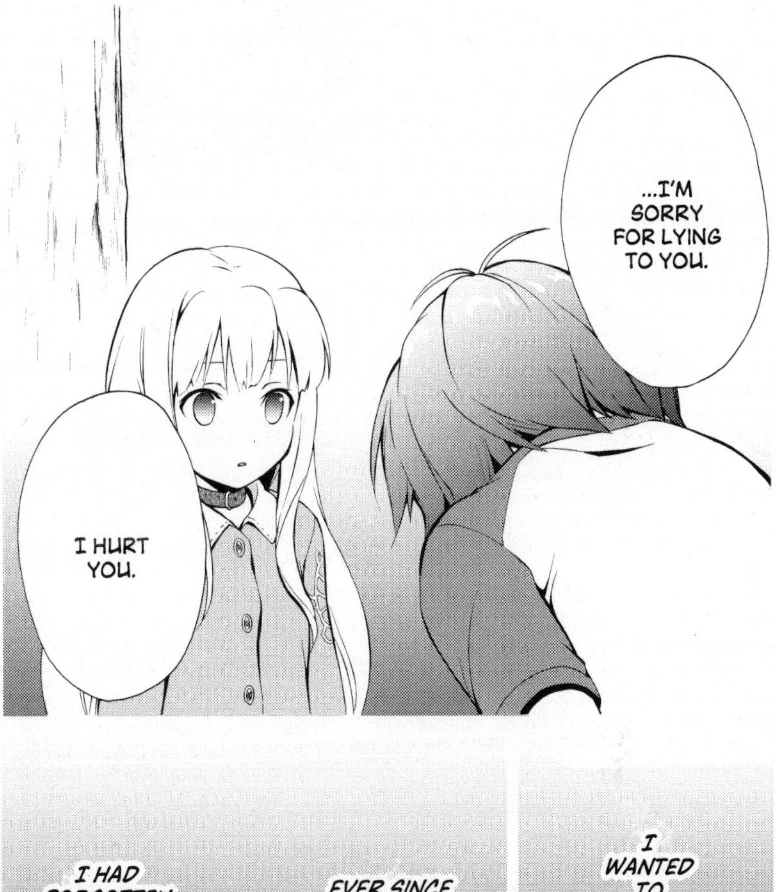
...I'M SORRY FOR LYING TO YOU.
I HURT YOU.
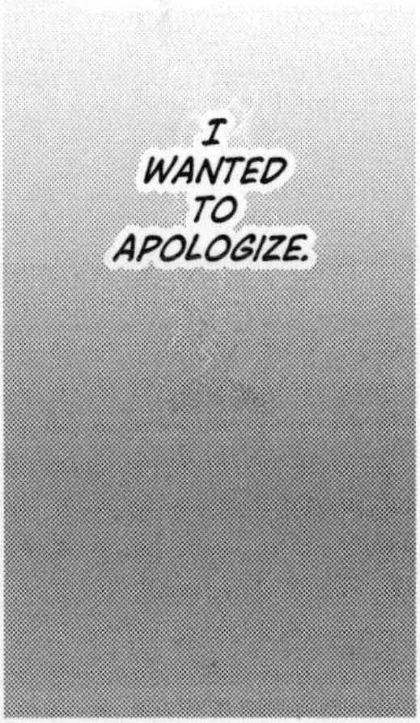
I WANTED TO APOLOGIZE.
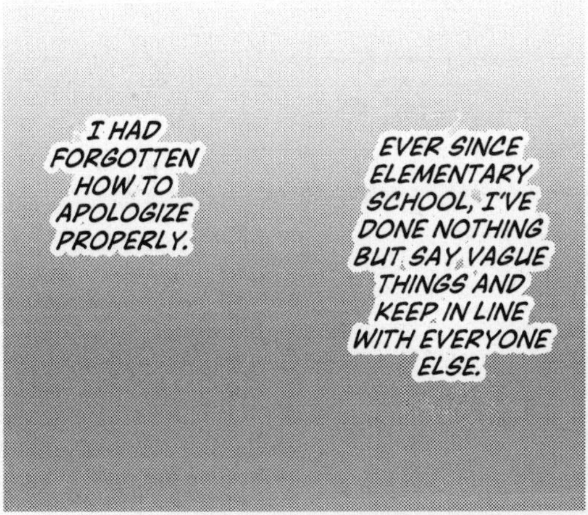
EVER SINCE ELEMENTARY SCHOOL, I'VE DONE NOTHING BUT SAY VAGUE THINGS AND KEEP IN LINE WITH EVERYONE ELSE.
I HAD FORGOTTEN HOW TO APOLOGIZE PROPERLY.

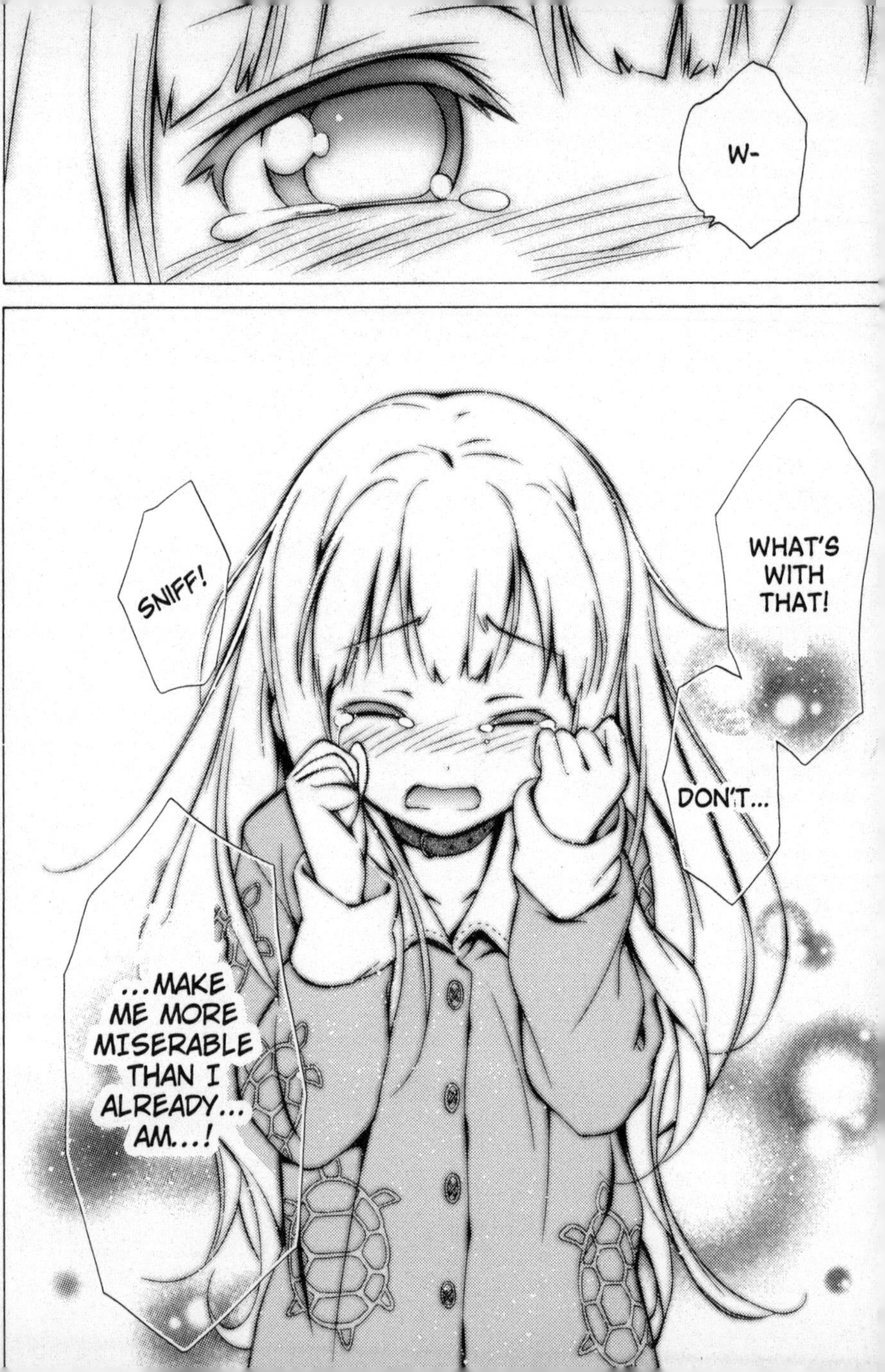
W-
WHAT'S WITH THAT!
SNIFF!
DON'T...
...MAKE ME MORE MISERABLE THAN I ALREADY... AM...!

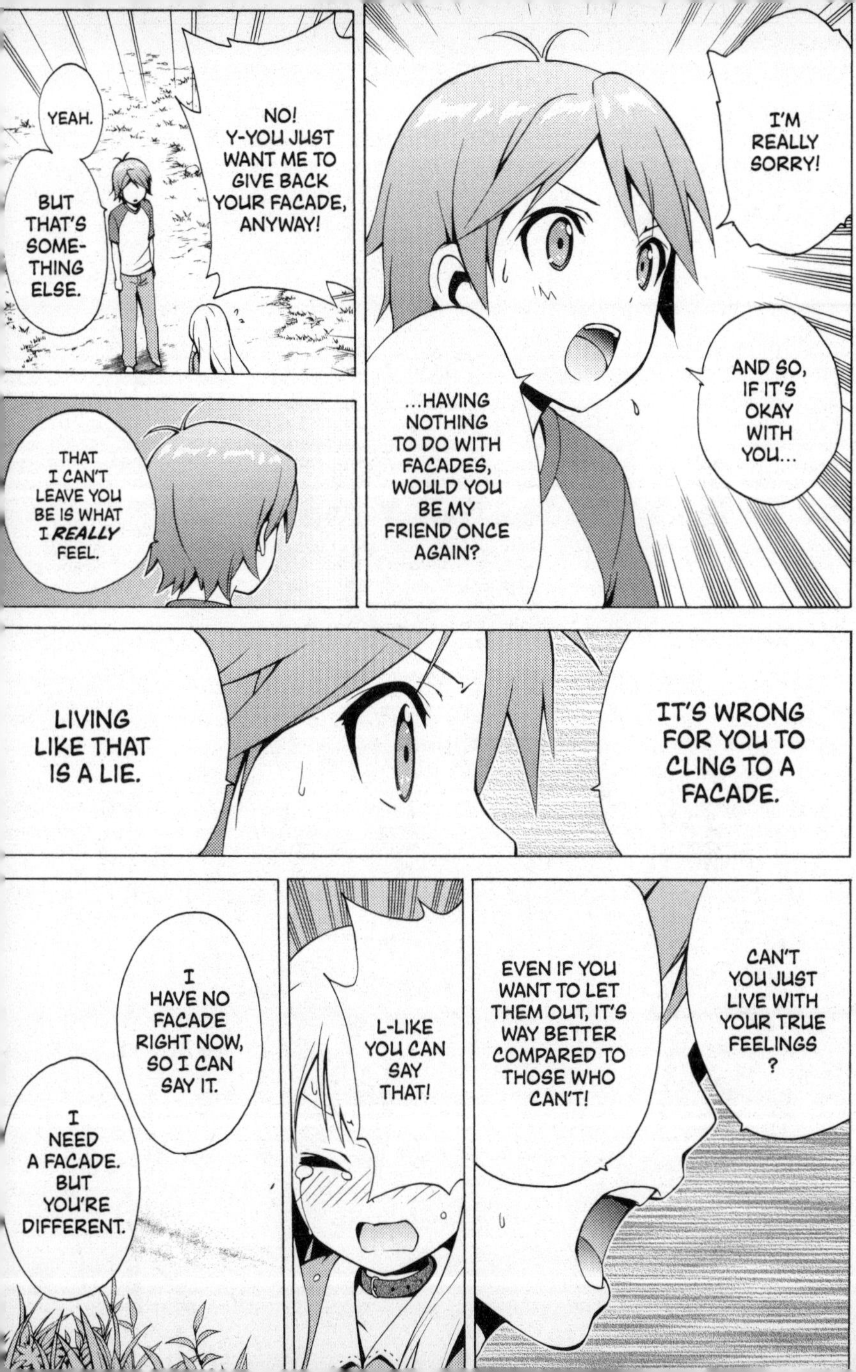
I'M REALLY SORRY!
AND SO, IF IT'S OKAY WITH YOU...
...HAVING NOTHING TO DO WITH FACADES, WOULD YOU BE MY FRIEND ONCE AGAIN?
NO! Y-YOU JUST WANT ME TO GIVE BACK YOUR FACADE, ANYWAY!
YEAH.
BUT THAT'S SOME-THING ELSE.
THAT I CAN'T LEAVE YOU BE IS WHAT I *REALLY* FEEL.
IT'S WRONG FOR YOU TO CLING TO A FACADE.
LIVING LIKE THAT IS A LIE.
CAN'T YOU JUST LIVE WITH YOUR TRUE FEELINGS?
EVEN IF YOU WANT TO LET THEM OUT, IT'S WAY BETTER COMPARED TO THOSE WHO CAN'T!
L-LIKE YOU CAN SAY THAT!
I HAVE NO FACADE RIGHT NOW, SO I CAN SAY IT.
I NEED A FACADE. BUT YOU'RE DIFFERENT.

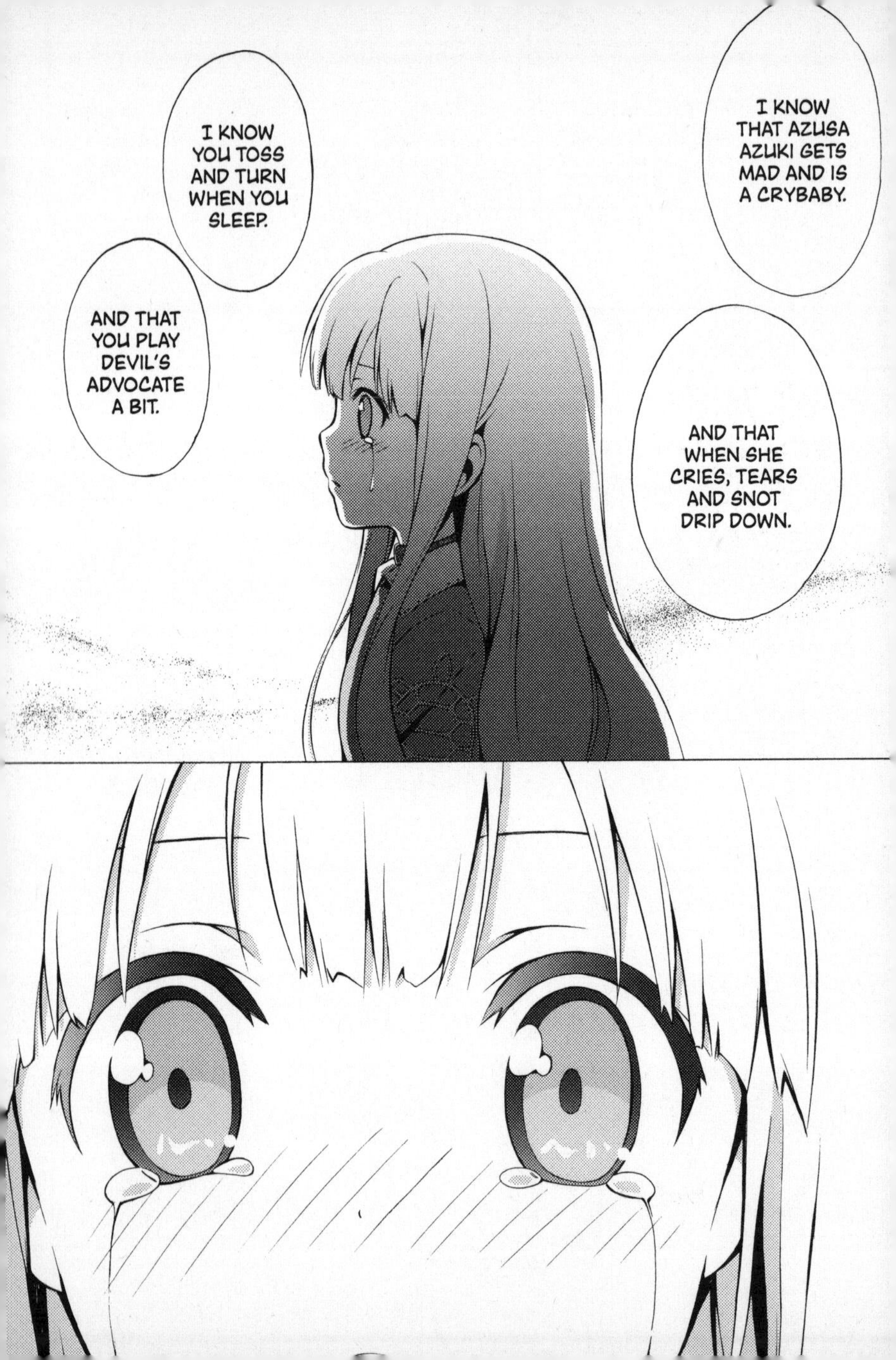
I KNOW THAT AZUSA AZUKI GETS MAD AND IS A CRYBABY.
AND THAT WHEN SHE CRIES, TEARS AND SNOT DRIP DOWN.
I KNOW YOU TOSS AND TURN WHEN YOU SLEEP.
AND THAT YOU PLAY DEVIL'S ADVOCATE A BIT.

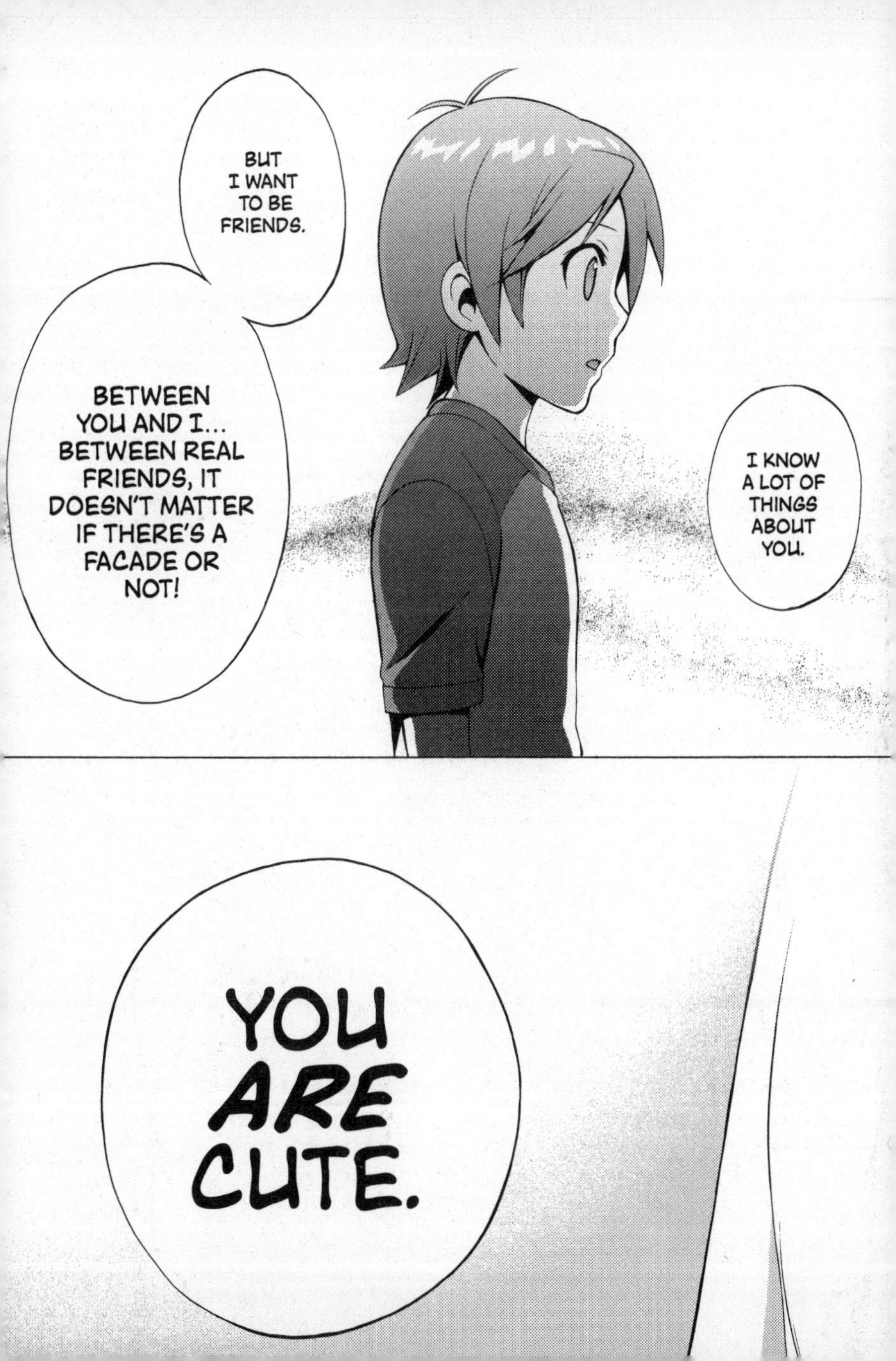
I KNOW A LOT OF THINGS ABOUT YOU.
BUT I WANT TO BE FRIENDS.
BETWEEN YOU AND I... BETWEEN REAL FRIENDS, IT DOESN'T MATTER IF THERE'S A FACADE OR NOT!
YOU *ARE* CUTE.

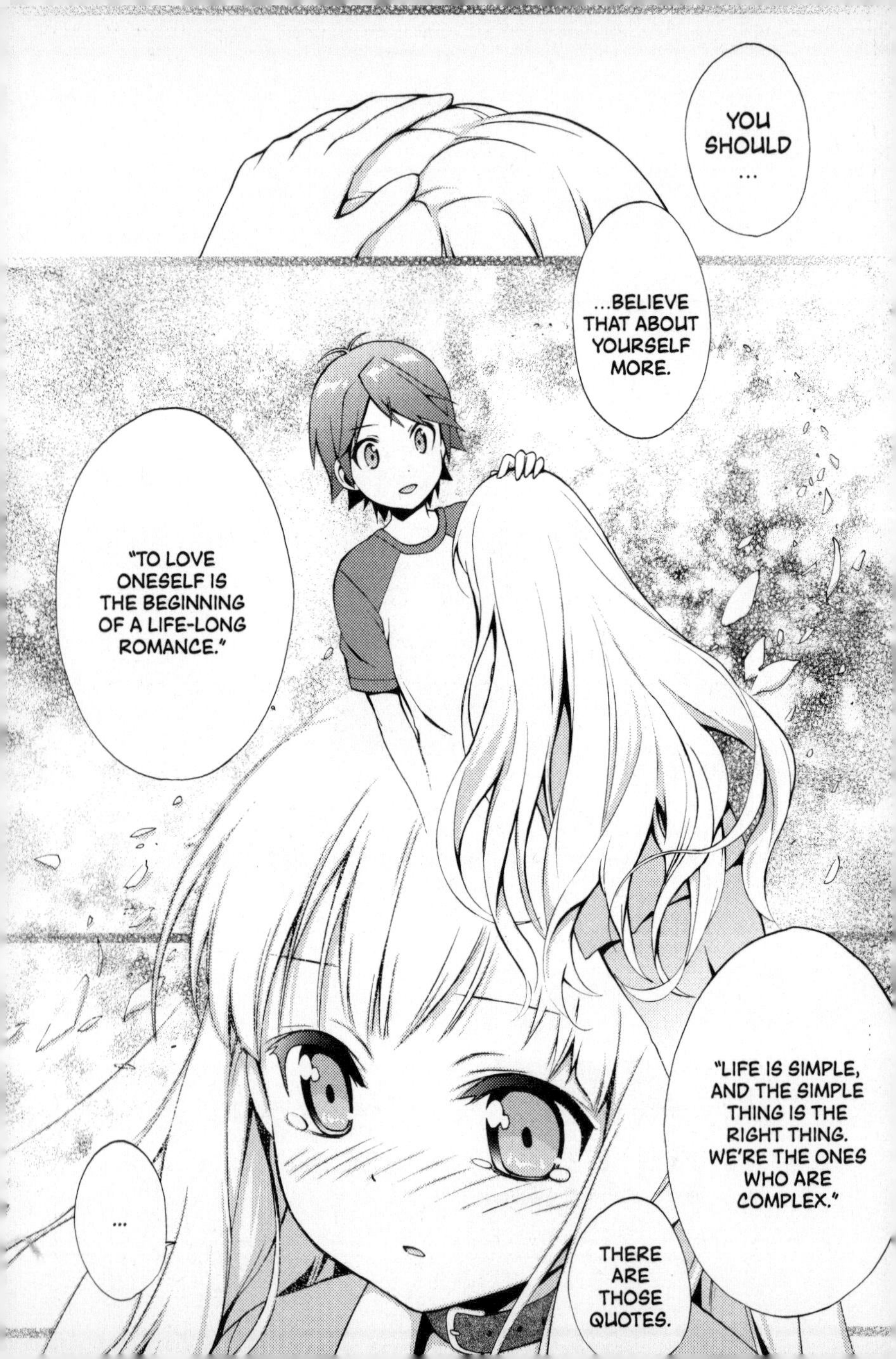
YOU SHOULD ...
...BELIEVE THAT ABOUT YOURSELF MORE.
"TO LOVE ONESELF IS THE BEGINNING OF A LIFE-LONG ROMANCE."
"LIFE IS SIMPLE, AND THE SIMPLE THING IS THE RIGHT THING. WE'RE THE ONES WHO ARE COMPLEX."
THERE ARE THOSE QUOTES.
...

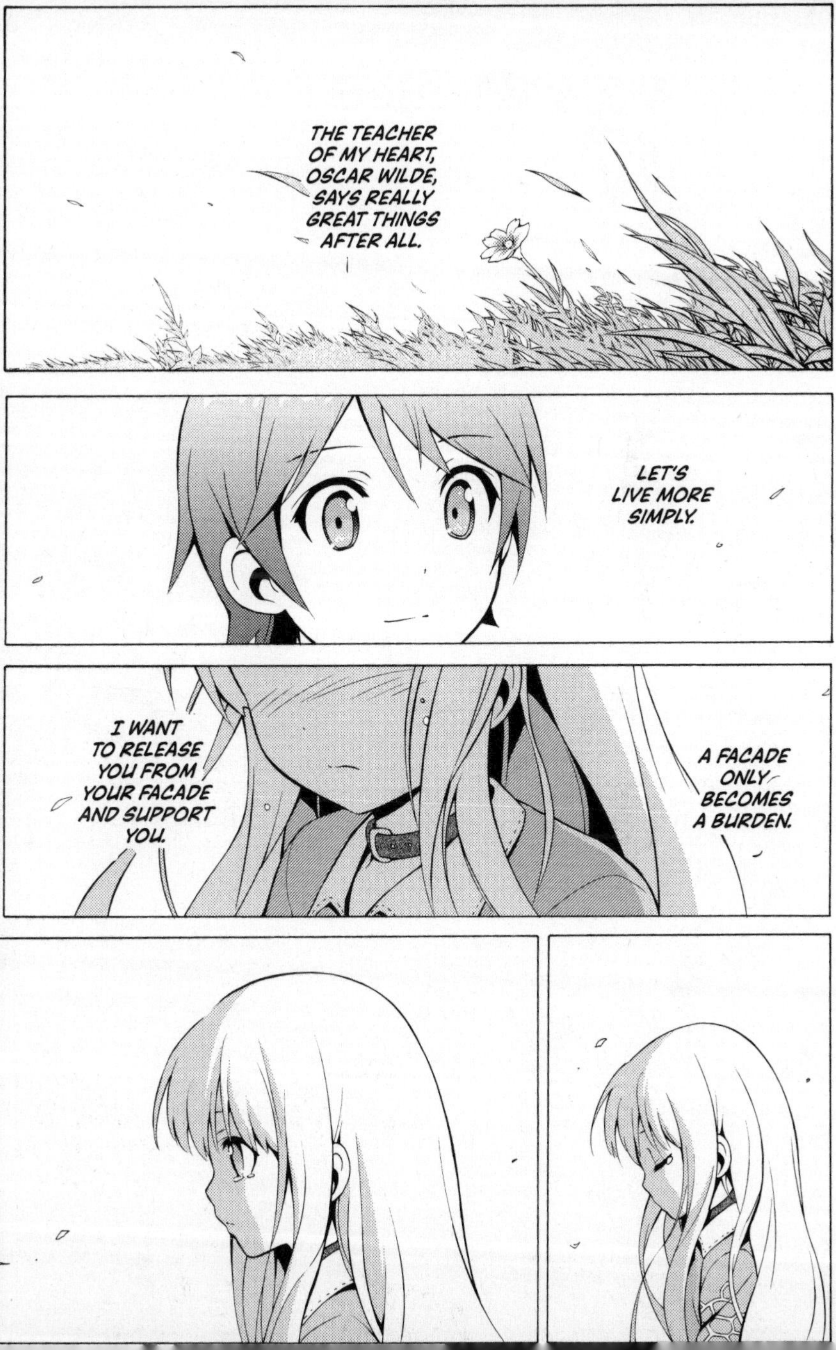
THE TEACHER OF MY HEART, OSCAR WILDE, SAYS REALLY GREAT THINGS AFTER ALL.
LET'S LIVE MORE SIMPLY.
A FACADE ONLY BECOMES A BURDEN.
I WANT TO RELEASE YOU FROM YOUR FACADE AND SUPPORT YOU.

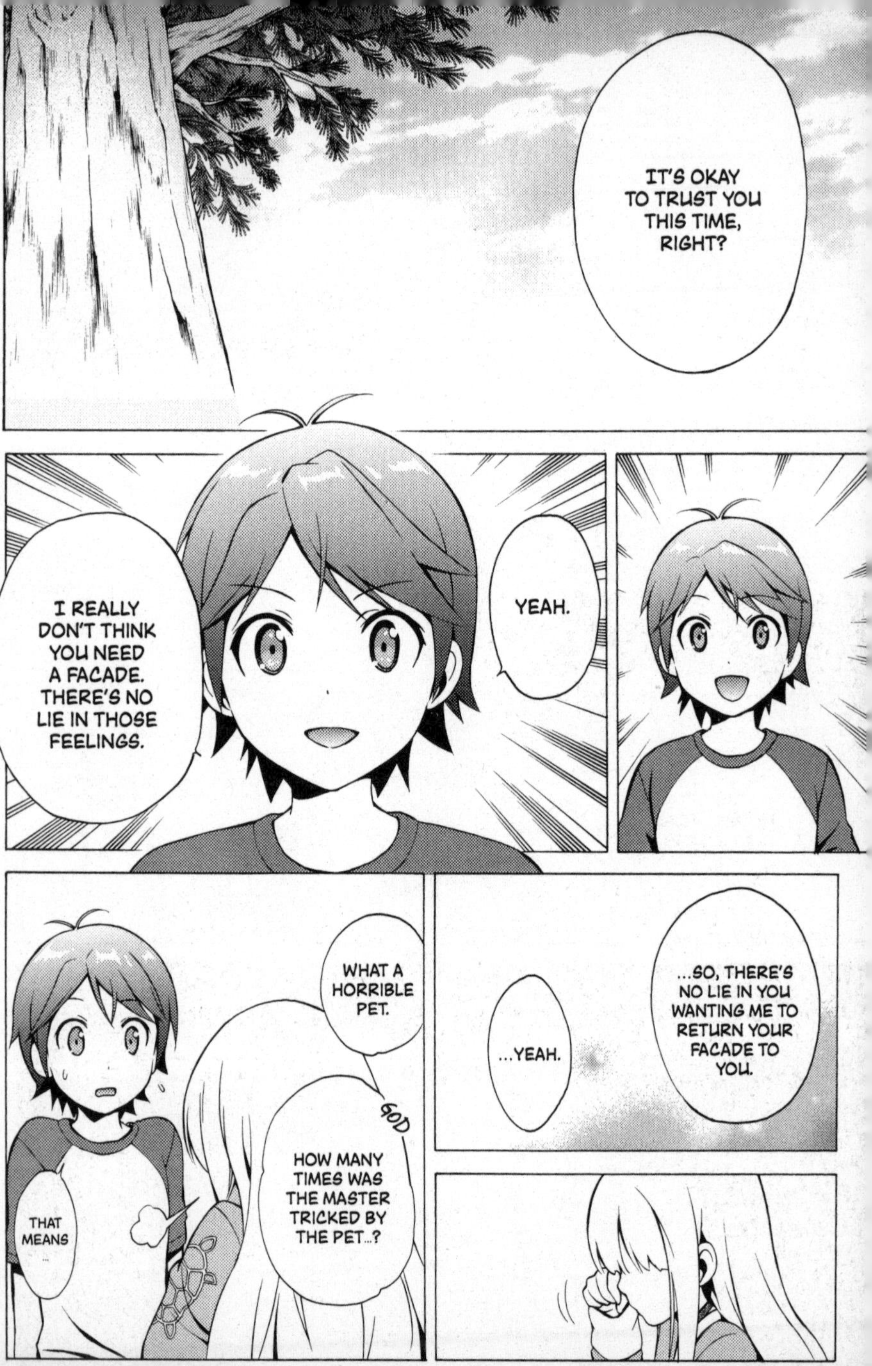
IT'S OKAY TO TRUST YOU THIS TIME, RIGHT?
YEAH.
I REALLY DON'T THINK YOU NEED A FACADE. THERE'S NO LIE IN THOSE FEELINGS.
...SO, THERE'S NO LIE IN YOU WANTING ME TO RETURN YOUR FACADE TO YOU.
...YEAH.
WHAT A HORRIBLE PET.
GOD
HOW MANY TIMES WAS THE MASTER TRICKED BY THE PET...?
THAT MEANS ...

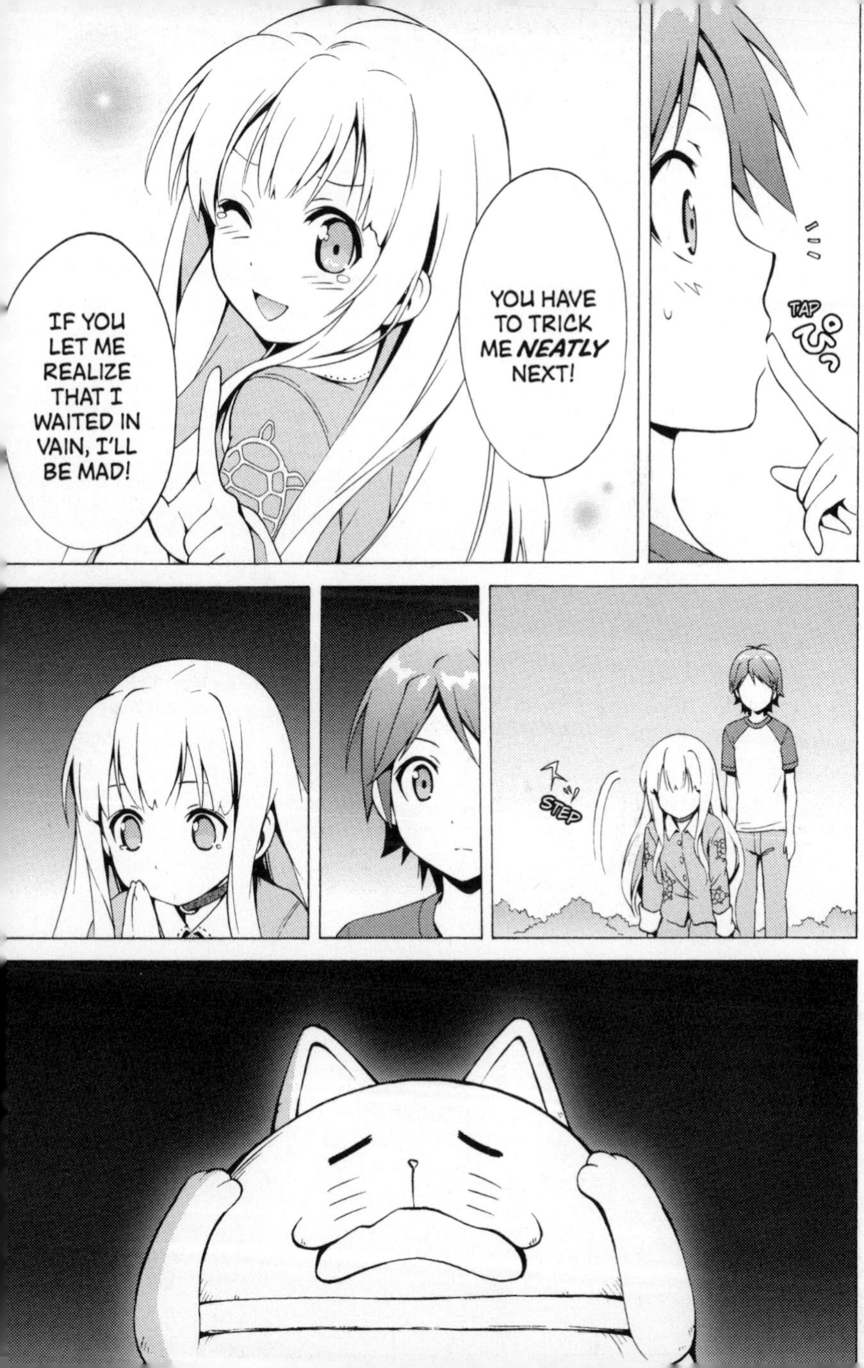
TAP
ぴっ
YOU HAVE TO TRICK ME *NEATLY* NEXT!
IF YOU LET ME REALIZE THAT I WAITED IN VAIN, I'LL BE MAD!
STEP

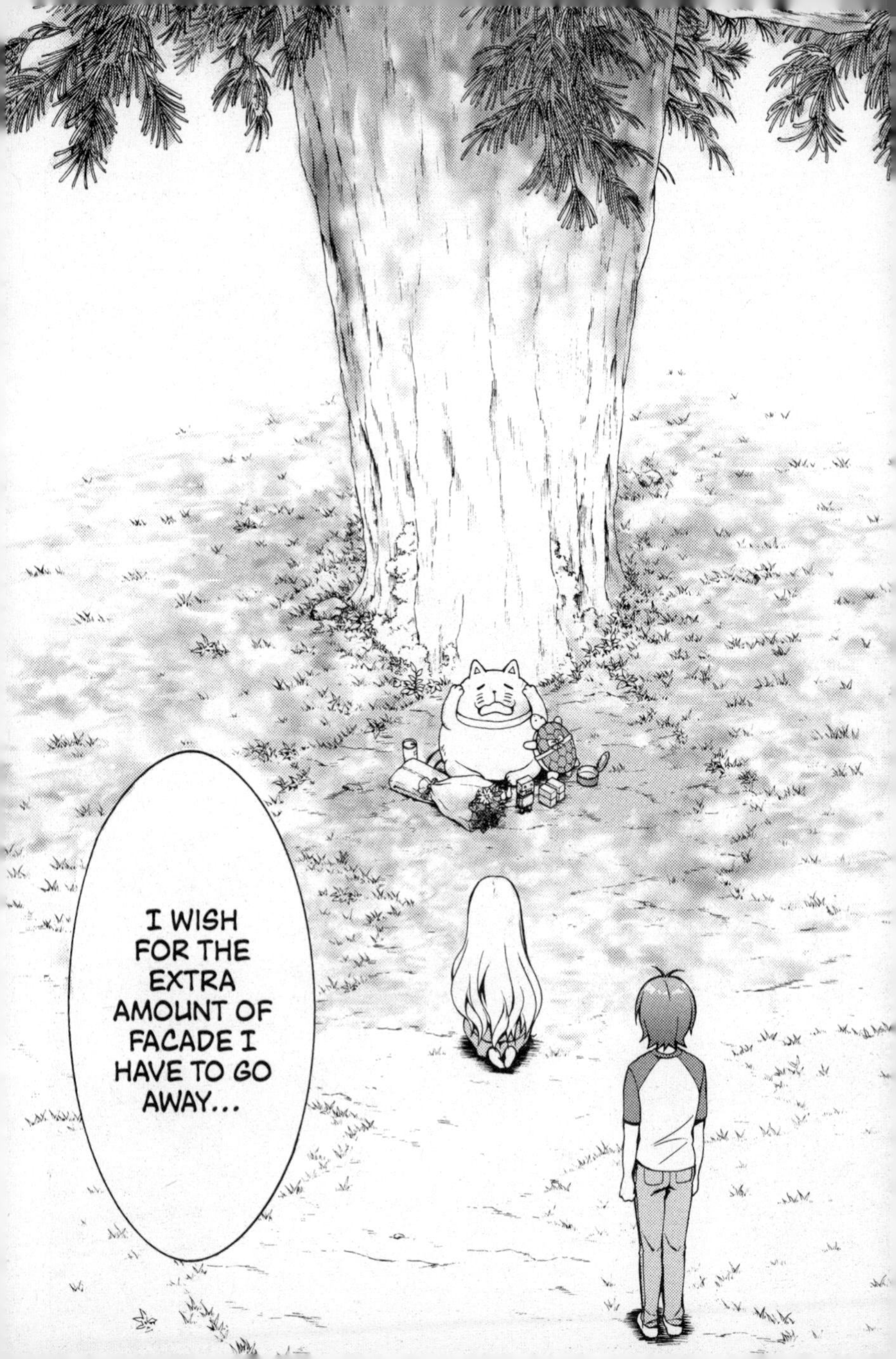
I WISH FOR THE EXTRA AMOUNT OF FACADE I HAVE TO GO AWAY...

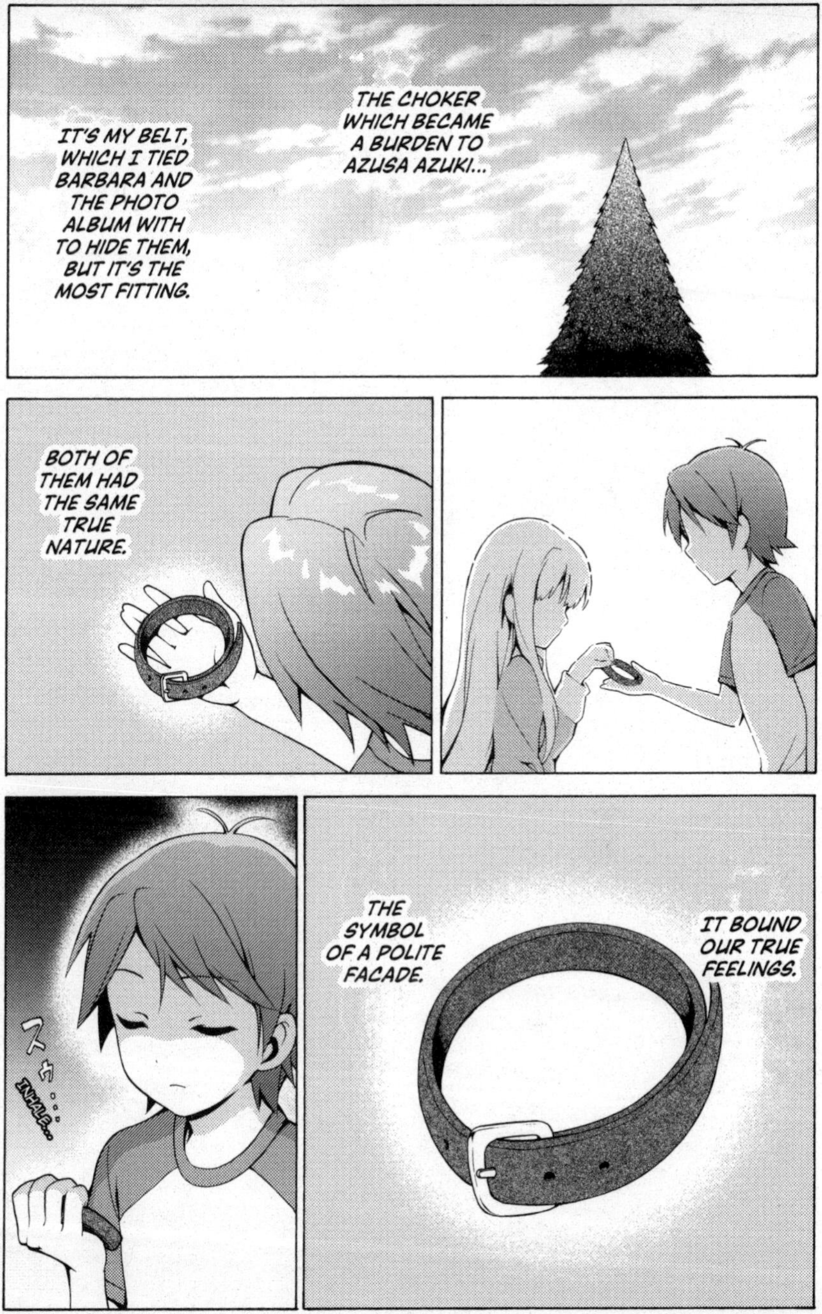
THE CHOKER WHICH BECAME A BURDEN TO AZUSA AZUKI...
IT'S MY BELT, WHICH I TIED BARBARA AND THE PHOTO ALBUM WITH TO HIDE THEM, BUT IT'S THE MOST FITTING.
BOTH OF THEM HAD THE SAME TRUE NATURE.
IT BOUND OUR TRUE FEELINGS.
THE SYMBOL OF A POLITE FACADE.
INHALE...

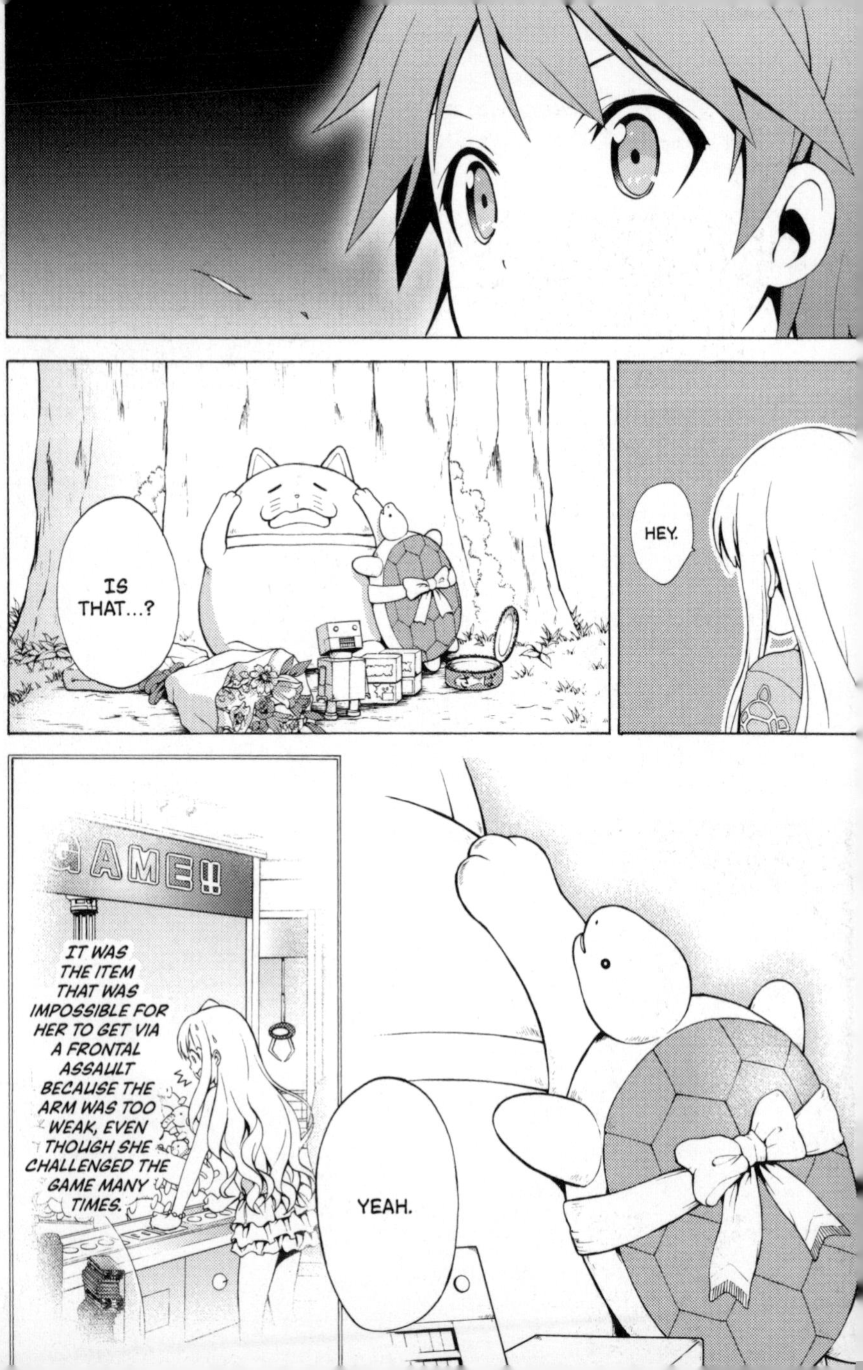
HEY.
IS THAT...?
YEAH.
IT WAS THE ITEM THAT WAS IMPOSSIBLE FOR HER TO GET VIA A FRONTAL ASSAULT BECAUSE THE ARM WAS TOO WEAK, EVEN THOUGH SHE CHALLENGED THE GAME MANY TIMES.
AME!!

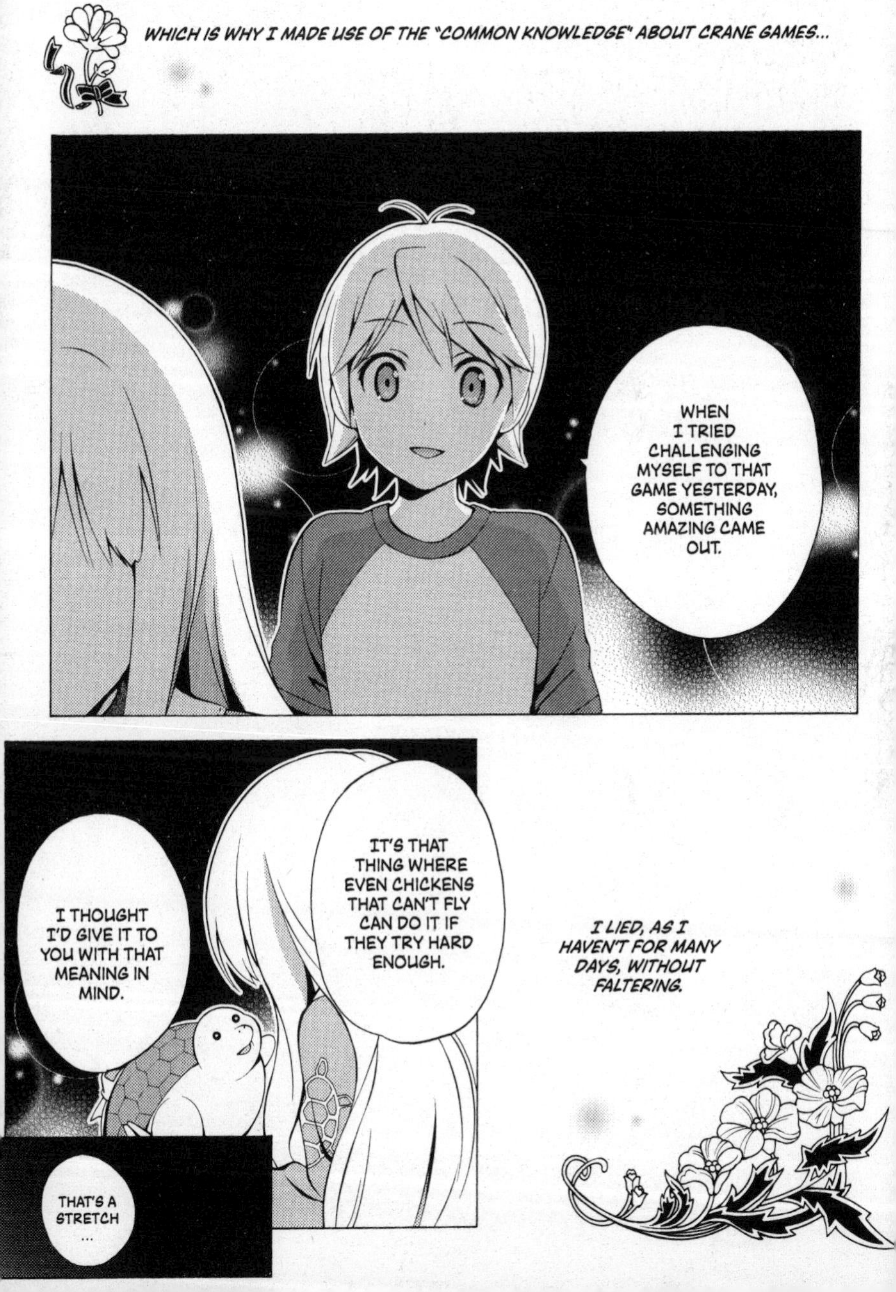
WHICH IS WHY I MADE USE OF THE "COMMON KNOWLEDGE" ABOUT CRANE GAMES...
WHEN I TRIED CHALLENGING MYSELF TO THAT GAME YESTERDAY, SOMETHING AMAZING CAME OUT.
I LIED, AS I HAVEN'T FOR MANY DAYS, WITHOUT FALTERING.
IT'S THAT THING WHERE EVEN CHICKENS THAT CAN'T FLY CAN DO IT IF THEY TRY HARD ENOUGH.
I THOUGHT I'D GIVE IT TO YOU WITH THAT MEANING IN MIND.
THAT'S A STRETCH ...

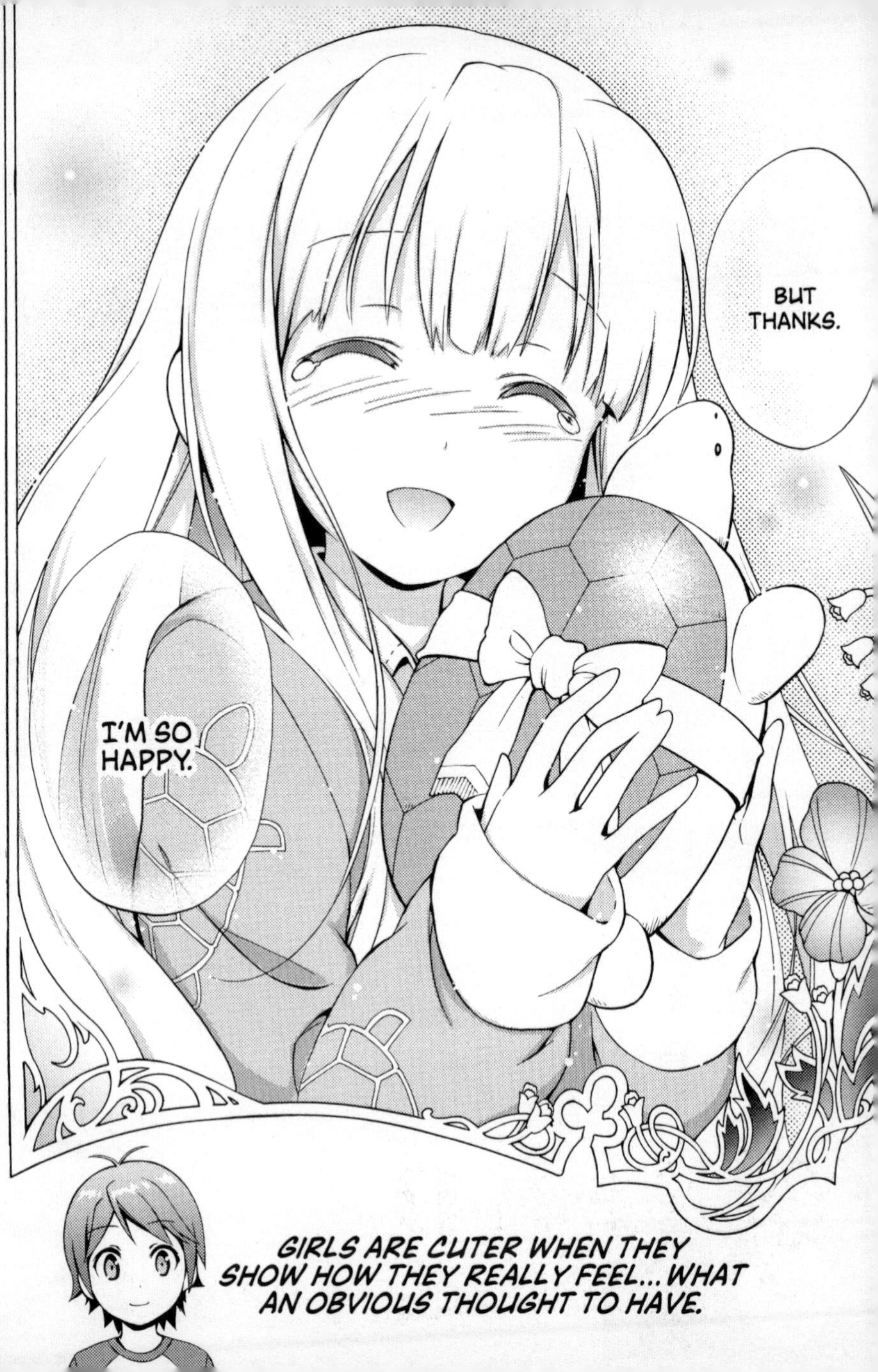
BUT THANKS.
I'M SO HAPPY.
GIRLS ARE CUTER WHEN THEY SHOW HOW THEY REALLY FEEL... WHAT AN OBVIOUS THOUGHT TO HAVE.

The "HENTAI" prince and the stony cat.

変態王子と
笑わない猫。

ILLUSTRATED CATS OF THE WORLD

SPHYNX

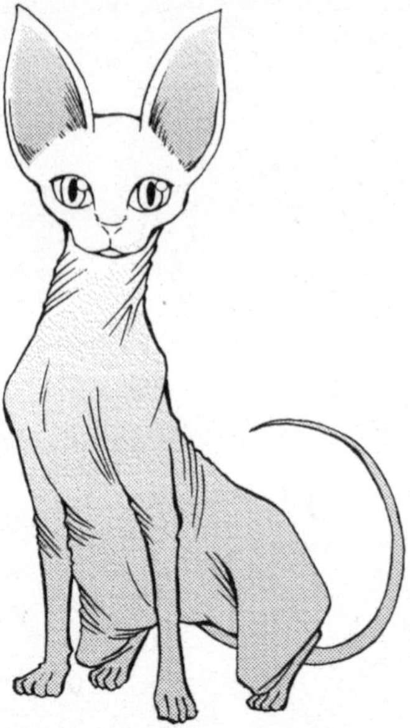

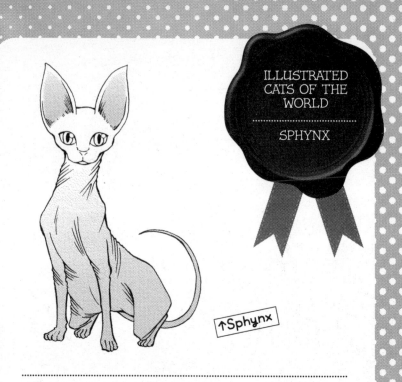

↑Sphynx

THEY WERE CALLED THE CANADIAN HAIRLESS AFTER SUDDENLY BEING BORN A DIFFERENT VARIATION IN CANADA. THEY ARE A HAIRLESS BREED THAT MAKES THEM SEPARATE FROM OTHER CATS, BUT ACTUALLY, DOWNY FUR GROWS, AND A CHARACTERISTIC IS THEIR SKIN FEELING LIKE SUEDE. THE FUR IS THIN WHEN THEY ARE FULLY GROWN, AND BECAUSE A SEBUM SECRETION RISES TO THE SURFACE OF THEIR SKIN DIRECTLY, THERE IS A FREQUENT NEED TO GROOM THEM. ALSO, IT'S A FAMOUS STORY THAT DIRECTOR SPIELBERG USED THEM FOR A REFERENCE MODEL OF ET.

CHAPTER 9 HOW TO OVERTHROW A CAREFREE KING

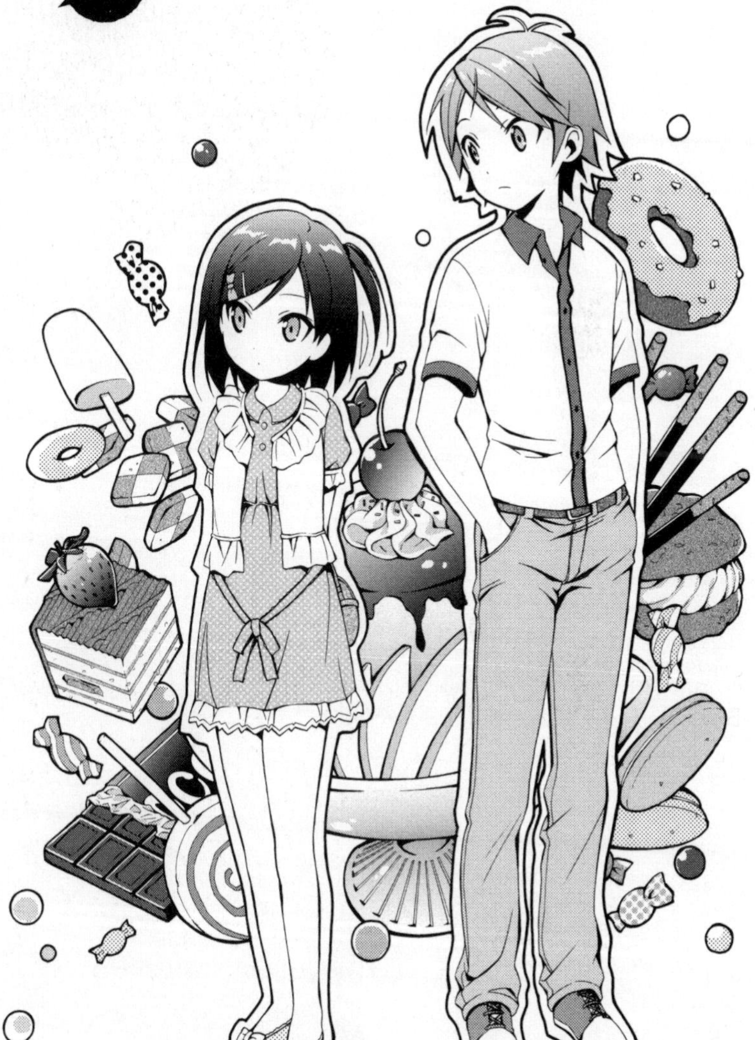

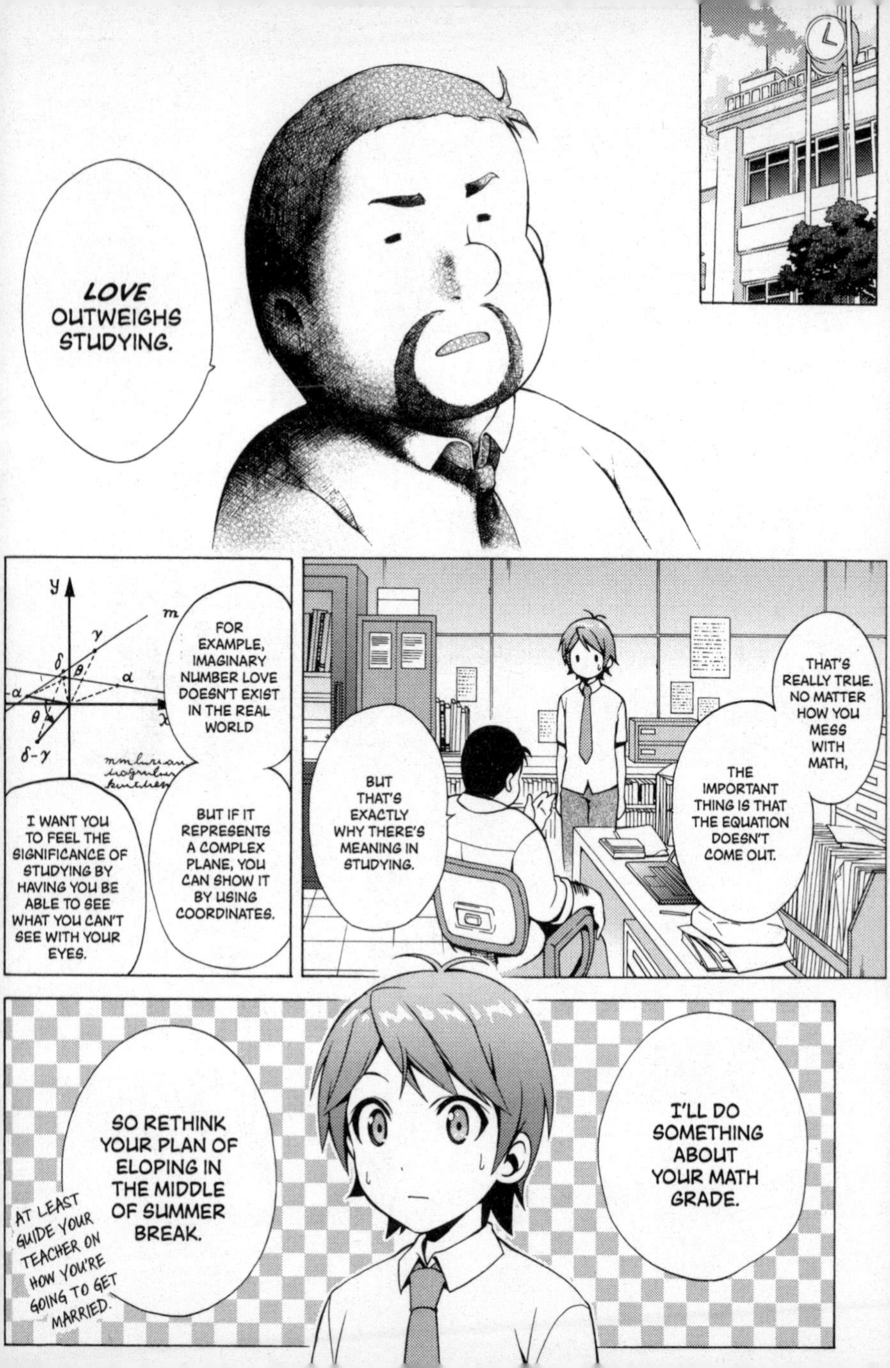
LOVE OUTWEIGHS STUDYING.
THAT'S REALLY TRUE. NO MATTER HOW YOU MESS WITH MATH,
THE IMPORTANT THING IS THAT THE EQUATION DOESN'T COME OUT.
BUT THAT'S EXACTLY WHY THERE'S MEANING IN STUDYING.
FOR EXAMPLE, IMAGINARY NUMBER LOVE DOESN'T EXIST IN THE REAL WORLD
BUT IF IT REPRESENTS A COMPLEX PLANE, YOU CAN SHOW IT BY USING COORDINATES.
I WANT YOU TO FEEL THE SIGNIFICANCE OF STUDYING BY HAVING YOU BE ABLE TO SEE WHAT YOU CAN'T SEE WITH YOUR EYES.
y
m
γ
δ
β
α
-α
θ
x
δ-γ
I'LL DO SOMETHING ABOUT YOUR MATH GRADE.
SO RETHINK YOUR PLAN OF ELOPING IN THE MIDDLE OF SUMMER BREAK.
AT LEAST GUIDE YOUR TEACHER ON HOW YOU'RE GOING TO GET MARRIED.

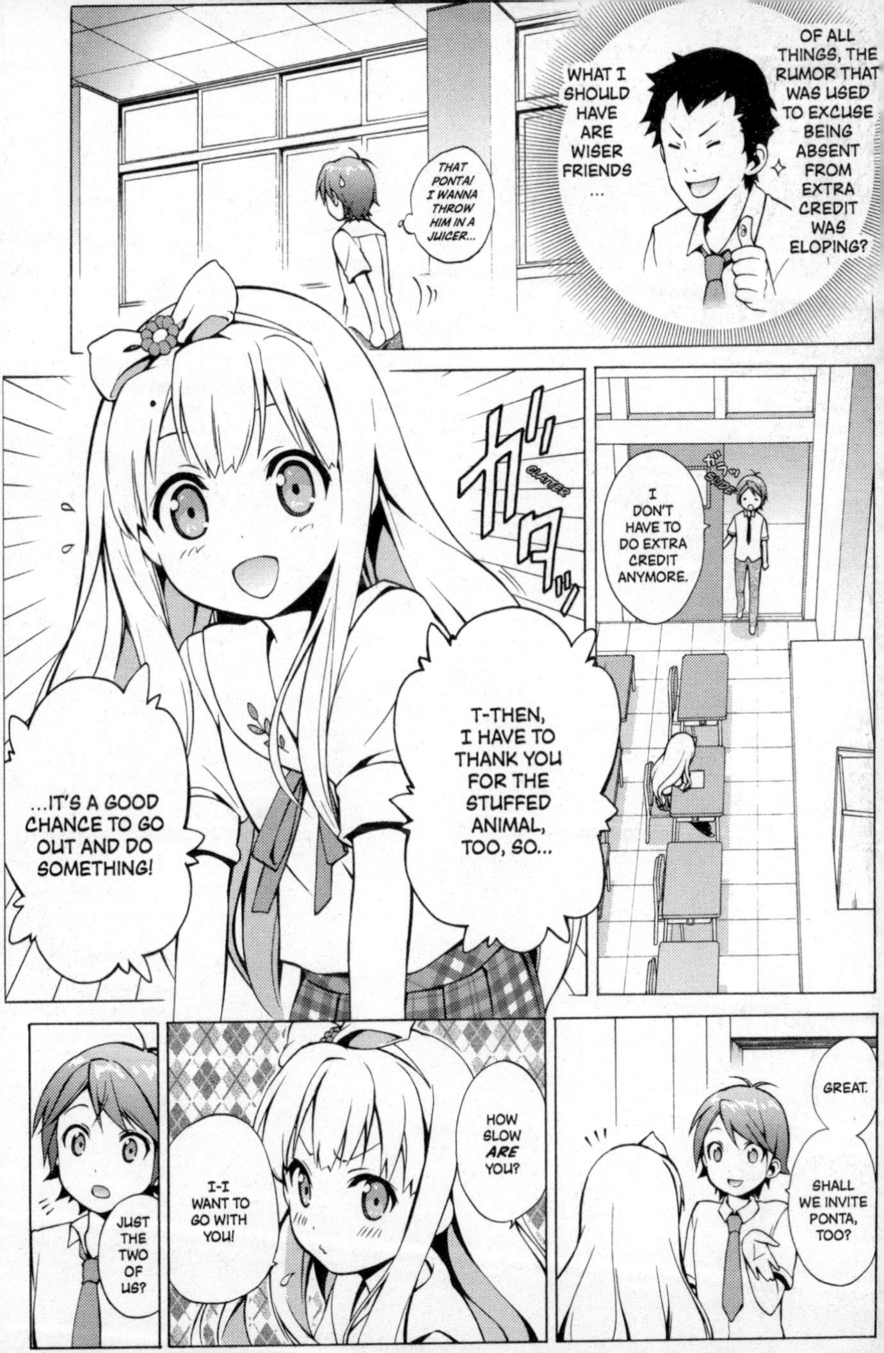

OF ALL THINGS, THE RUMOR THAT WAS USED TO EXCUSE BEING ABSENT FROM EXTRA CREDIT WAS ELOPING?
WHAT I SHOULD HAVE ARE WISER FRIENDS...
THAT PONTA! I WANNA THROW HIM IN A JUICER...
SLIDE
I DON'T HAVE TO DO EXTRA CREDIT ANYMORE.
ガタッ
CLATTER
T-THEN, I HAVE TO THANK YOU FOR THE STUFFED ANIMAL, TOO, SO...
...IT'S A GOOD CHANCE TO GO OUT AND DO SOMETHING!
GREAT.
SHALL WE INVITE PONTA, TOO?
HOW SLOW *ARE* YOU?
I-I WANT TO GO WITH YOU!
JUST THE TWO OF US?

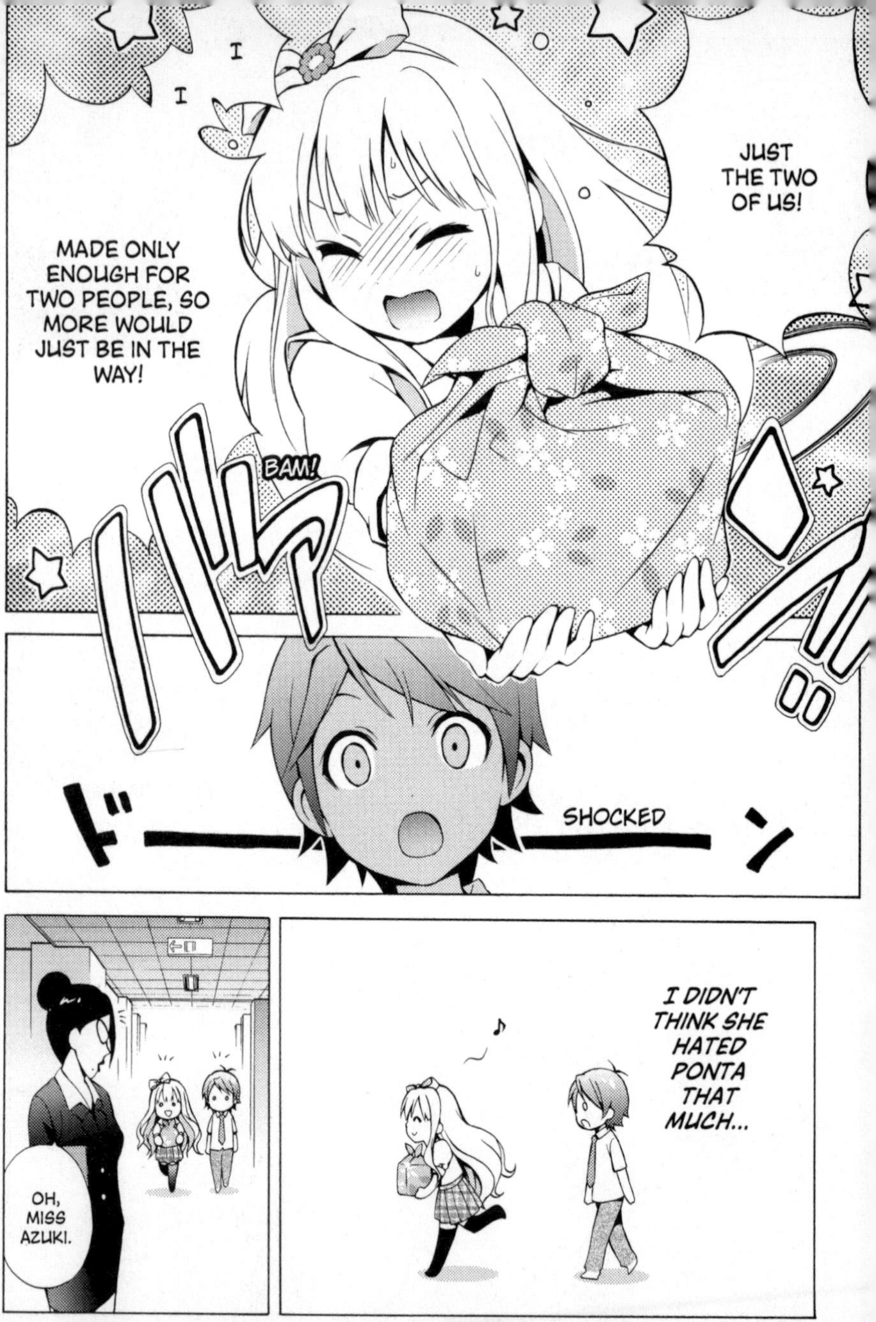

I
I
MADE ONLY ENOUGH FOR TWO PEOPLE, SO MORE WOULD JUST BE IN THE WAY!
JUST THE TWO OF US!
BAM!
SHOCKED
I DIDN'T THINK SHE HATED PONTA THAT MUCH...
OH, MISS AZUKI.

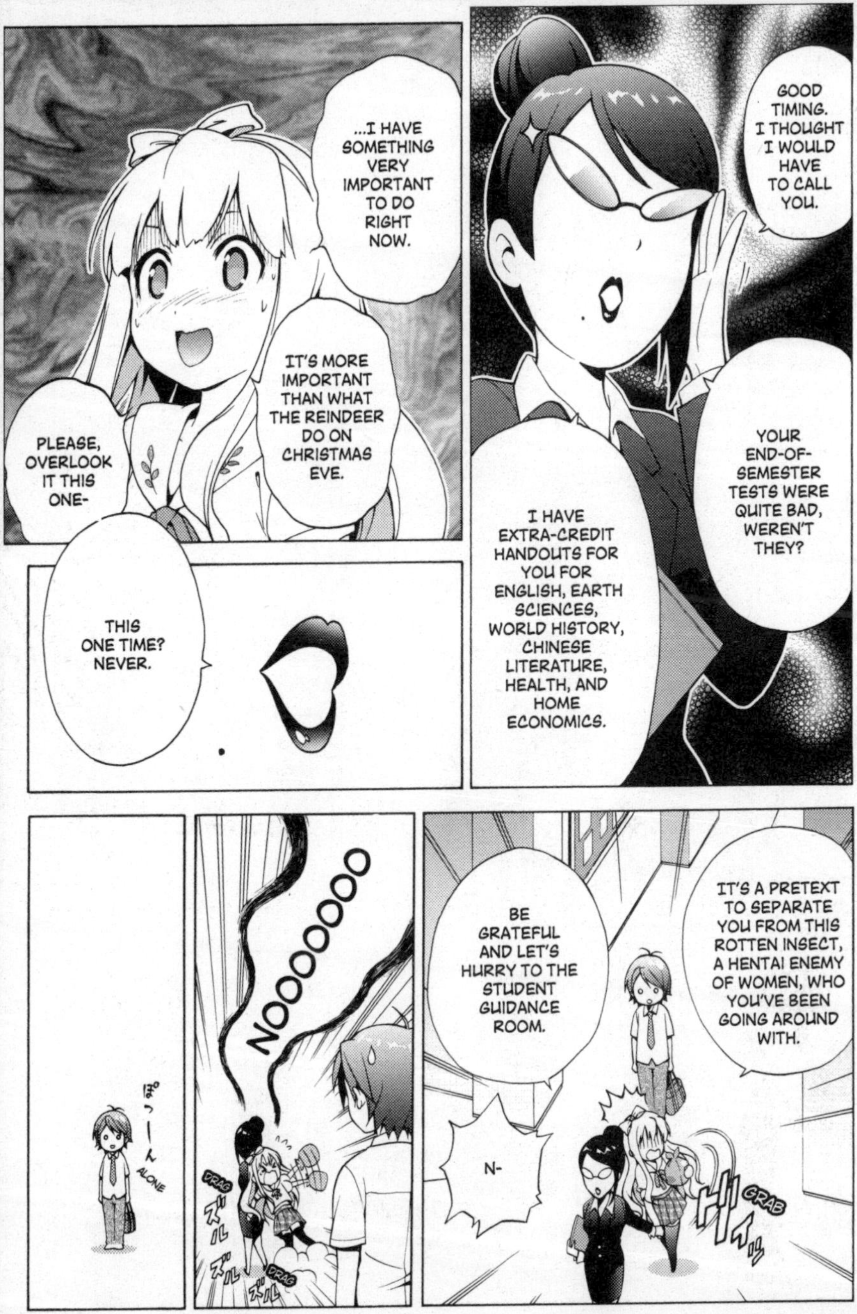
GOOD TIMING. I THOUGHT I WOULD HAVE TO CALL YOU.
YOUR END-OF-SEMESTER TESTS WERE QUITE BAD, WEREN'T THEY?
I HAVE EXTRA-CREDIT HANDOUTS FOR YOU FOR ENGLISH, EARTH SCIENCES, WORLD HISTORY, CHINESE LITERATURE, HEALTH, AND HOME ECONOMICS.
...I HAVE SOMETHING VERY IMPORTANT TO DO RIGHT NOW.
IT'S MORE IMPORTANT THAN WHAT THE REINDEER DO ON CHRISTMAS EVE.
PLEASE, OVERLOOK IT THIS ONE-
THIS ONE TIME? NEVER.
IT'S A PRETEXT TO SEPARATE YOU FROM THIS ROTTEN INSECT, A HENTAI ENEMY OF WOMEN, WHO YOU'VE BEEN GOING AROUND WITH.
BE GRATEFUL AND LET'S HURRY TO THE STUDENT GUIDANCE ROOM.
N-
GRAB
NOOOOOOO
DRAG
DRAG
ALONE

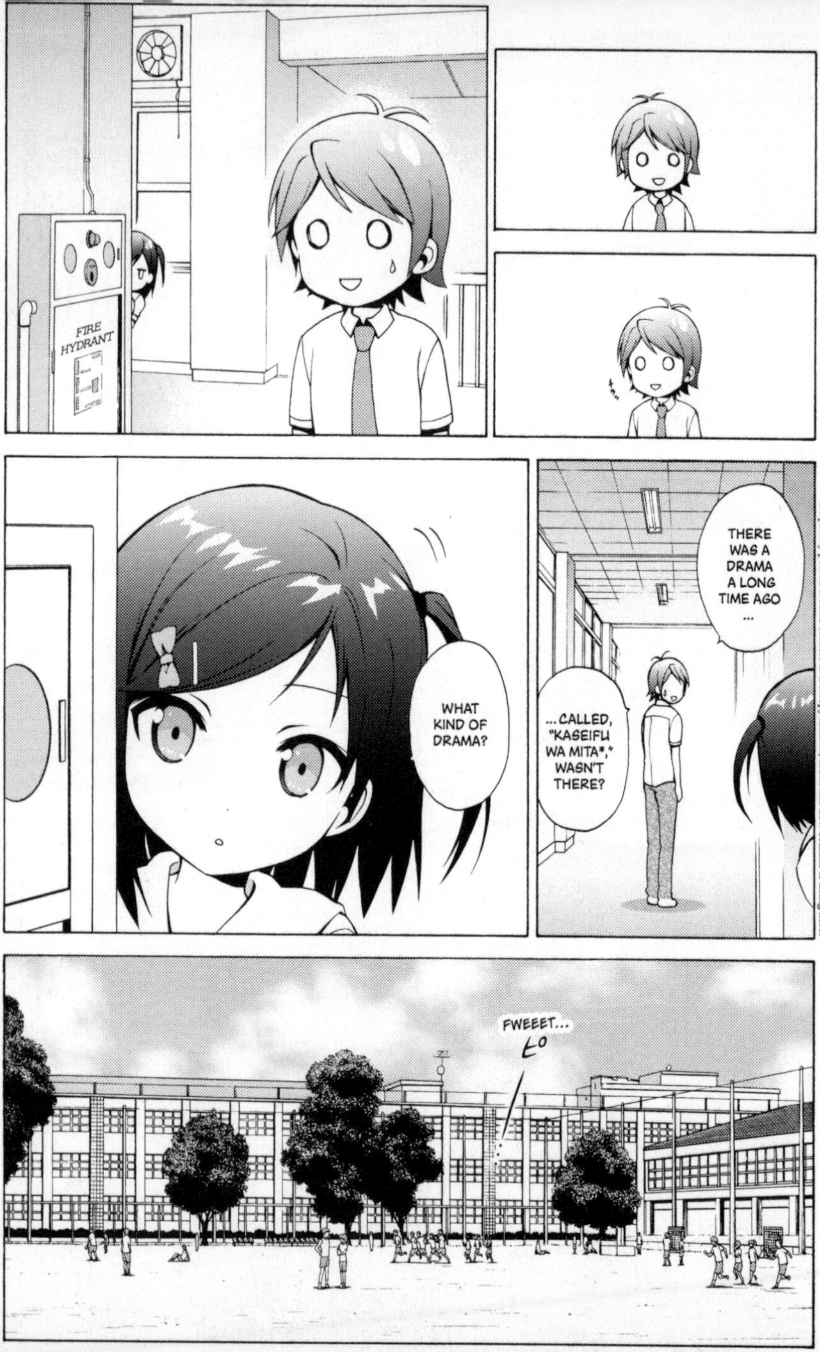
FIRE HYDRANT
THERE WAS A DRAMA A LONG TIME AGO ...
...CALLED, "KASEIFU WA MITA*," WASN'T THERE?
WHAT KIND OF DRAMA?
FWEEET...

*"KASEIFU WA MITA" was a Japanese drama that aired during the 1980s in which one of the characters frequently peered around corners in a creepy fashion, much like how Tsukiko is doing here."

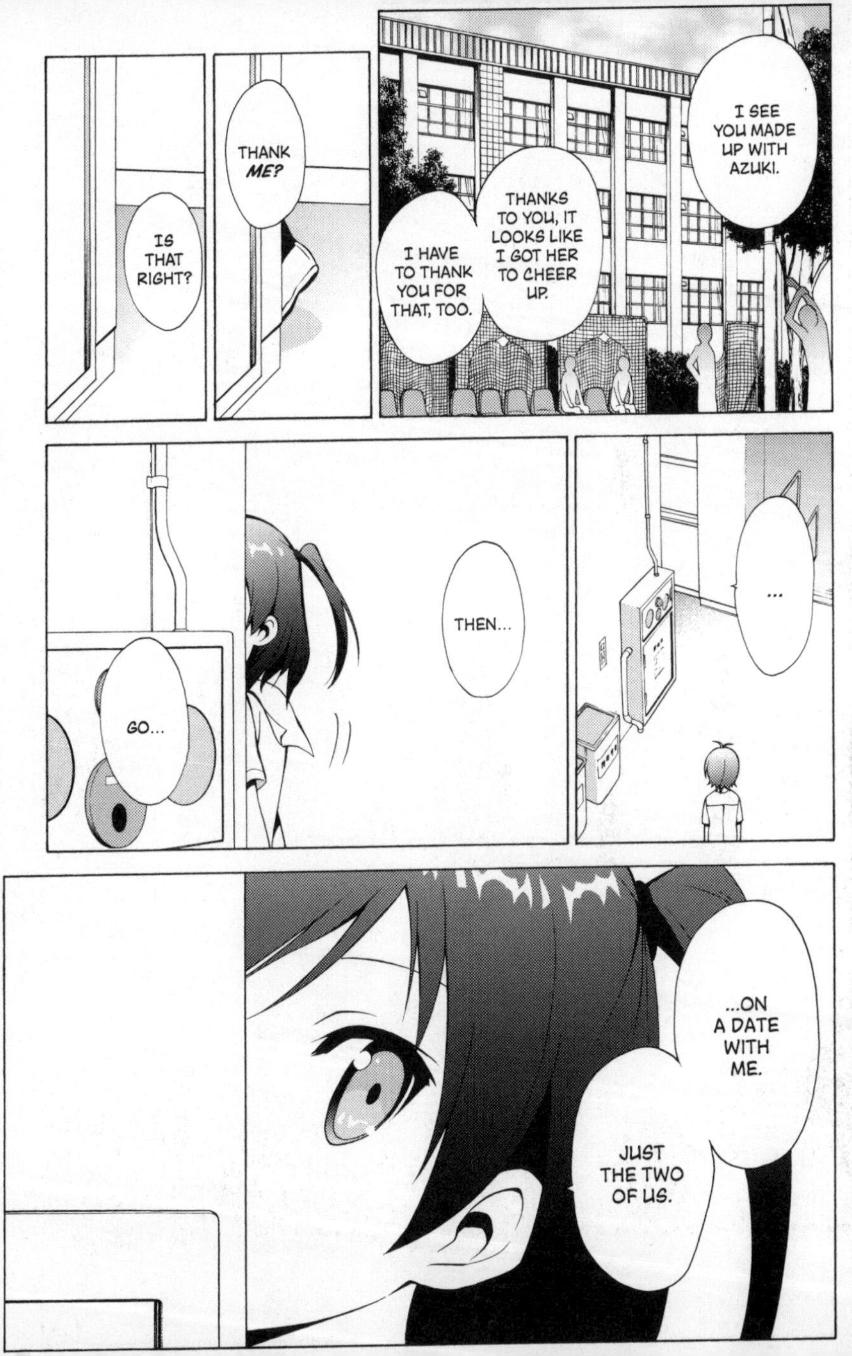
I SEE YOU MADE UP WITH AZUKI.
THANKS TO YOU, IT LOOKS LIKE I GOT HER TO CHEER UP.
I HAVE TO THANK YOU FOR THAT, TOO.
THANK *ME?*
IS THAT RIGHT?
...
THEN...
GO...
...ON A DATE WITH ME.
JUST THE TWO OF US.

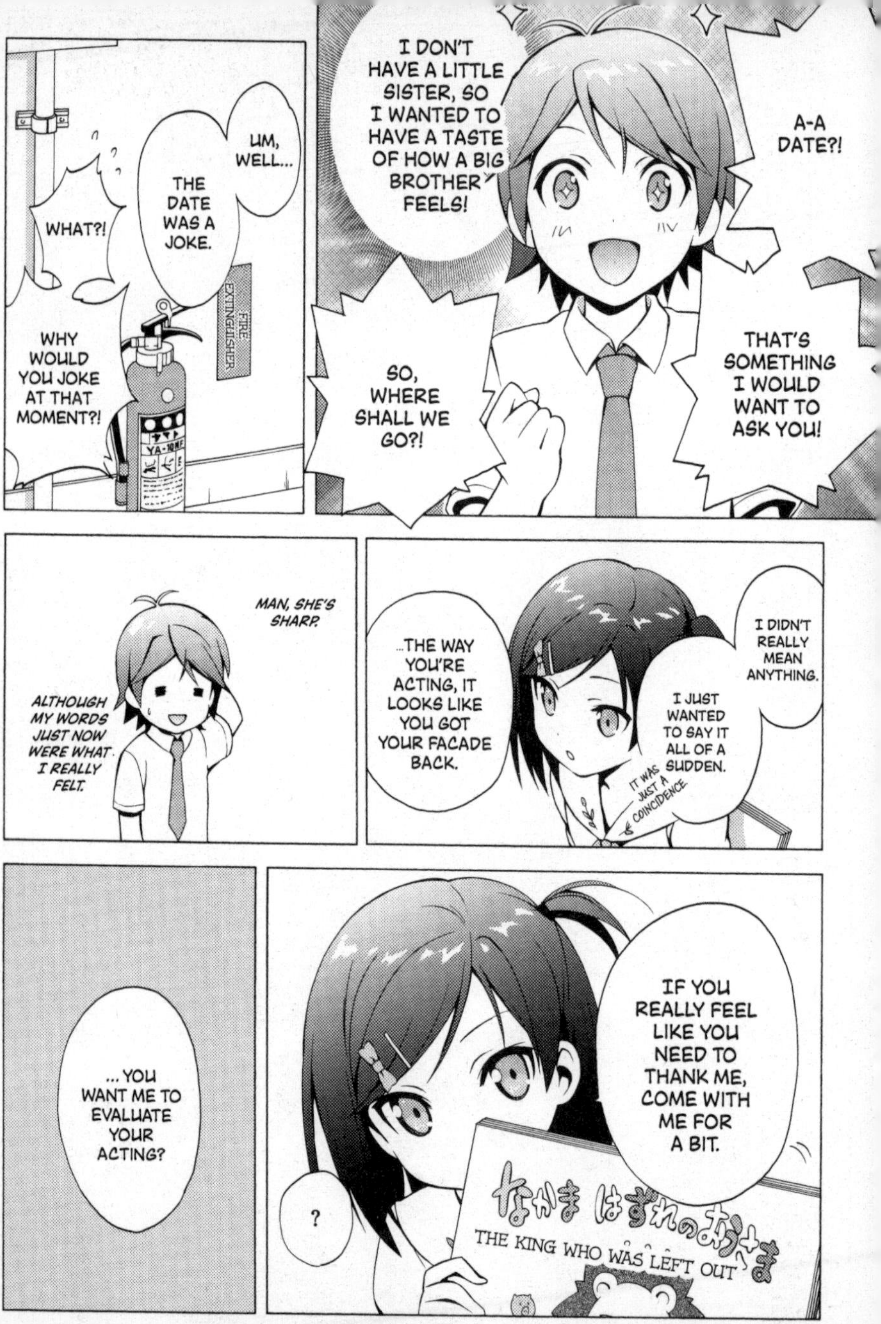
A-A DATE?!
I DON'T HAVE A LITTLE SISTER, SO I WANTED TO HAVE A TASTE OF HOW A BIG BROTHER FEELS!
THAT'S SOMETHING I WOULD WANT TO ASK YOU!
SO, WHERE SHALL WE GO?!
UM, WELL...
THE DATE WAS A JOKE.
WHAT?!
FIRE EXTINGUISHER
WHY WOULD YOU JOKE AT THAT MOMENT?!
I DIDN'T REALLY MEAN ANYTHING.
I JUST WANTED TO SAY IT ALL OF A SUDDEN.
IT WAS JUST A COINCIDENCE.
...THE WAY YOU'RE ACTING, IT LOOKS LIKE YOU GOT YOUR FACADE BACK.
MAN, SHE'S SHARP.
ALTHOUGH MY WORDS JUST NOW WERE WHAT I REALLY FELT.
IF YOU REALLY FEEL LIKE YOU NEED TO THANK ME, COME WITH ME FOR A BIT.
なかま はずれの おうさま
THE KING WHO WAS LEFT OUT
?
... YOU WANT ME TO EVALUATE YOUR ACTING?

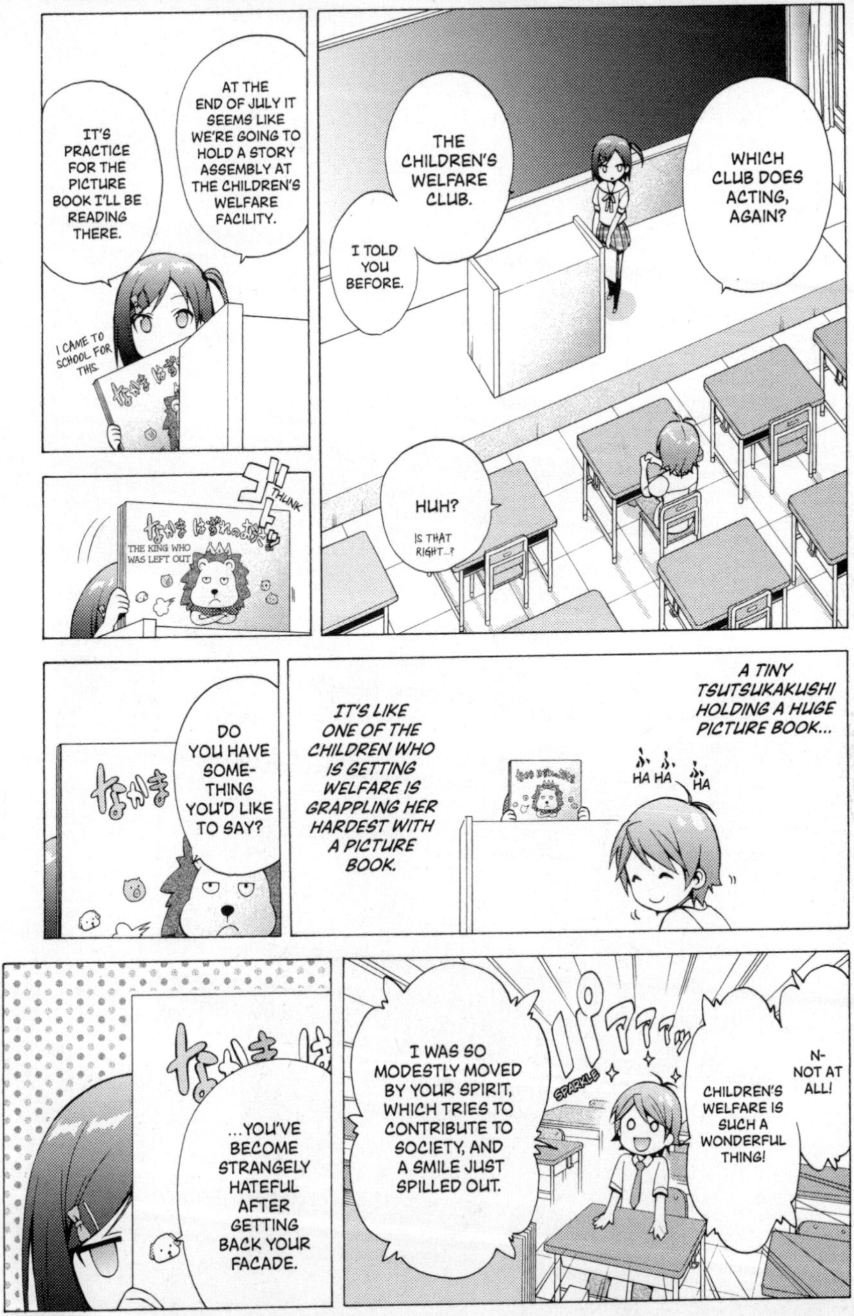
WHICH CLUB DOES ACTING, AGAIN?
THE CHILDREN'S WELFARE CLUB.
I TOLD YOU BEFORE.
HUH?
IS THAT RIGHT...?
AT THE END OF JULY IT SEEMS LIKE WE'RE GOING TO HOLD A STORY ASSEMBLY AT THE CHILDREN'S WELFARE FACILITY.
IT'S PRACTICE FOR THE PICTURE BOOK I'LL BE READING THERE.
I CAME TO SCHOOL FOR THIS.
THUNK
THE KING WHO WAS LEFT OUT
A TINY TSUTSUKAKUSHI HOLDING A HUGE PICTURE BOOK...
IT'S LIKE ONE OF THE CHILDREN WHO IS GETTING WELFARE IS GRAPPLING HER HARDEST WITH A PICTURE BOOK.
HA HA HA
DO YOU HAVE SOME-THING YOU'D LIKE TO SAY?
N-NOT AT ALL!
CHILDREN'S WELFARE IS SUCH A WONDERFUL THING!
SPARKLE
I WAS SO MODESTLY MOVED BY YOUR SPIRIT, WHICH TRIES TO CONTRIBUTE TO SOCIETY, AND A SMILE JUST SPILLED OUT.
...YOU'VE BECOME STRANGELY HATEFUL AFTER GETTING BACK YOUR FACADE.

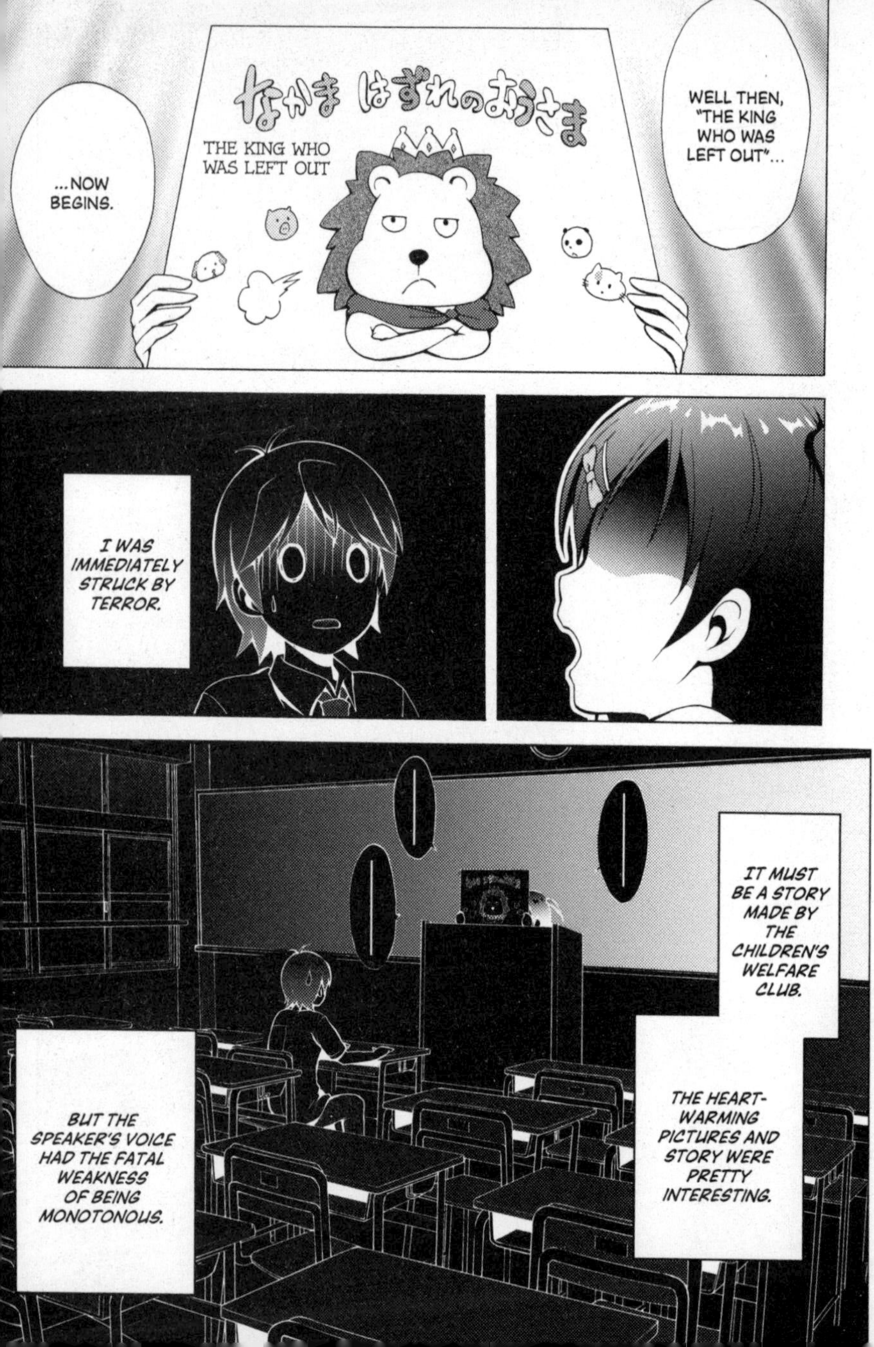
WELL THEN, "THE KING WHO WAS LEFT OUT"...
なかま はずれの おうさま
THE KING WHO WAS LEFT OUT
...NOW BEGINS.
I WAS IMMEDIATELY STRUCK BY TERROR.
IT MUST BE A STORY MADE BY THE CHILDREN'S WELFARE CLUB.
THE HEART-WARMING PICTURES AND STORY WERE PRETTY INTERESTING.
BUT THE SPEAKER'S VOICE HAD THE FATAL WEAKNESS OF BEING MONOTONOUS.

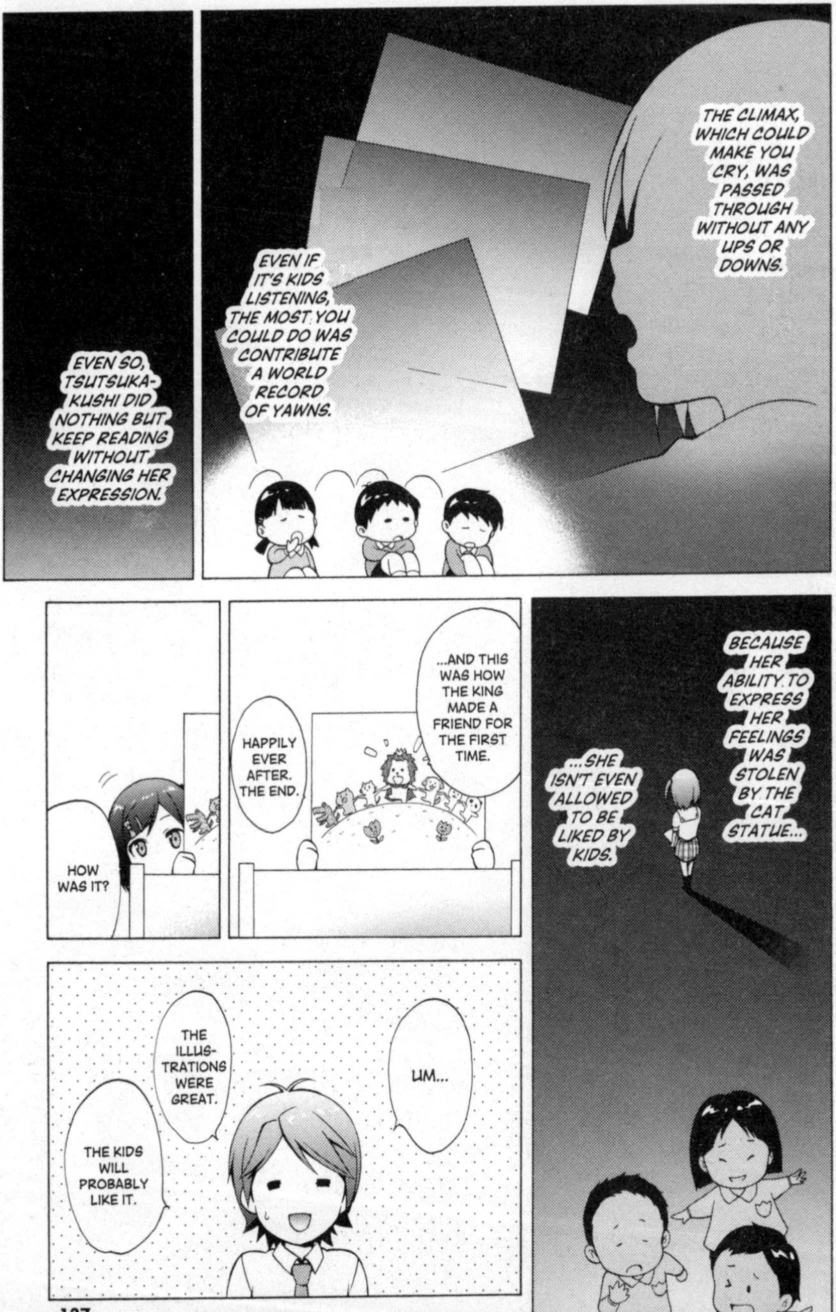
THE CLIMAX, WHICH COULD MAKE YOU CRY, WAS PASSED THROUGH WITHOUT ANY UPS OR DOWNS.
EVEN IF IT'S KIDS LISTENING, THE MOST YOU COULD DO WAS CONTRIBUTE A WORLD RECORD OF YAWNS.
EVEN SO, TSUTSUKA-KUSHI DID NOTHING BUT KEEP READING WITHOUT CHANGING HER EXPRESSION.
BECAUSE HER ABILITY TO EXPRESS HER FEELINGS WAS STOLEN BY THE CAT STATUE...
...SHE ISN'T EVEN ALLOWED TO BE LIKED BY KIDS.
...AND THIS WAS HOW THE KING MADE A FRIEND FOR THE FIRST TIME.
HAPPILY EVER AFTER. THE END.
HOW WAS IT?
UM...
THE ILLUS-TRATIONS WERE GREAT.
THE KIDS WILL PROBABLY LIKE IT.

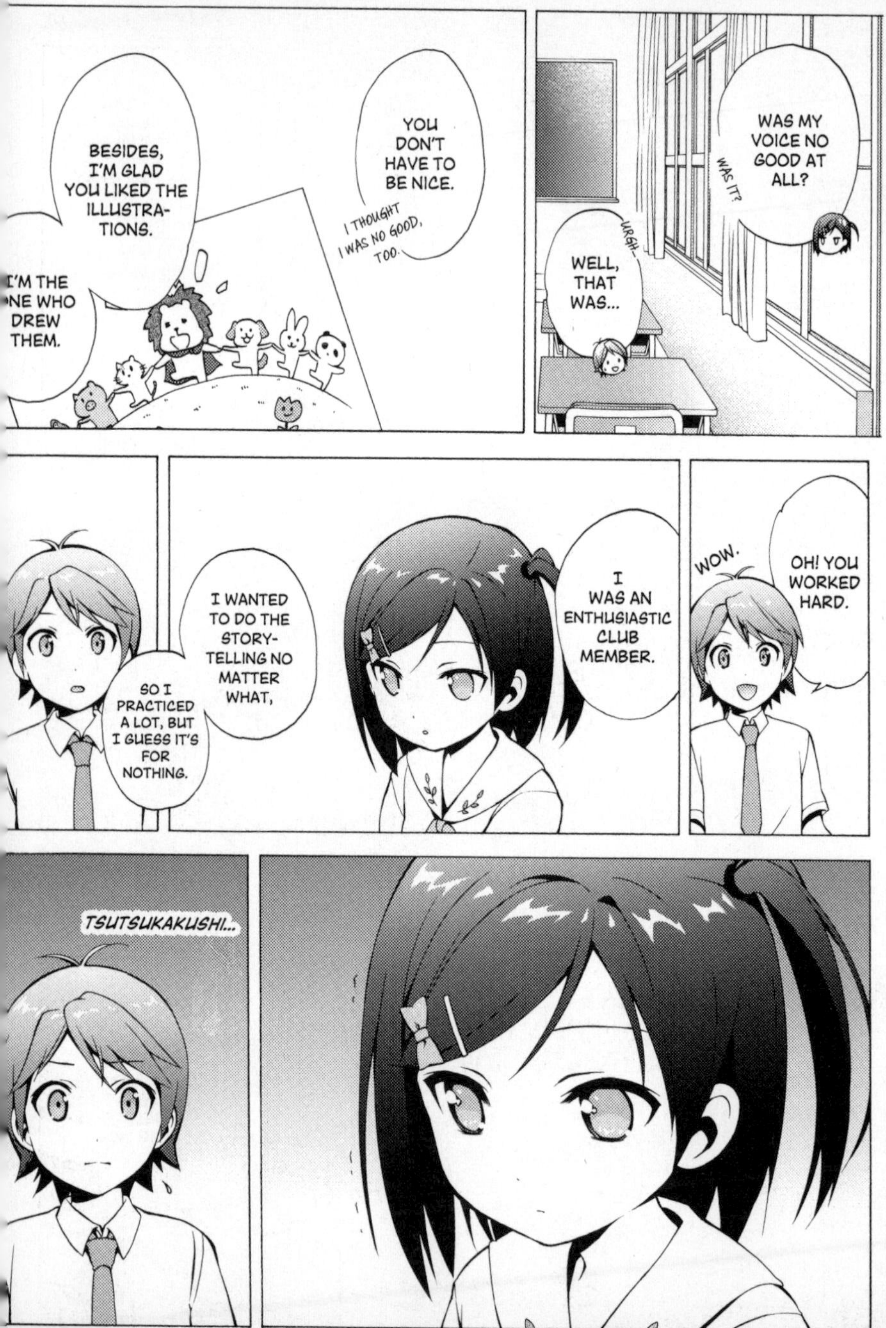

WAS MY VOICE NO GOOD AT ALL?
WAS IT?
URGH—
WELL, THAT WAS...
YOU DON'T HAVE TO BE NICE.
I THOUGHT I WAS NO GOOD, TOO.
BESIDES, I'M GLAD YOU LIKED THE ILLUSTRATIONS.
I'M THE ONE WHO DREW THEM.
WOW.
OH! YOU WORKED HARD.
I WAS AN ENTHUSIASTIC CLUB MEMBER.
I WANTED TO DO THE STORY-TELLING NO MATTER WHAT,
SO I PRACTICED A LOT, BUT I GUESS IT'S FOR NOTHING.
TSUTSUKAKUSHI...

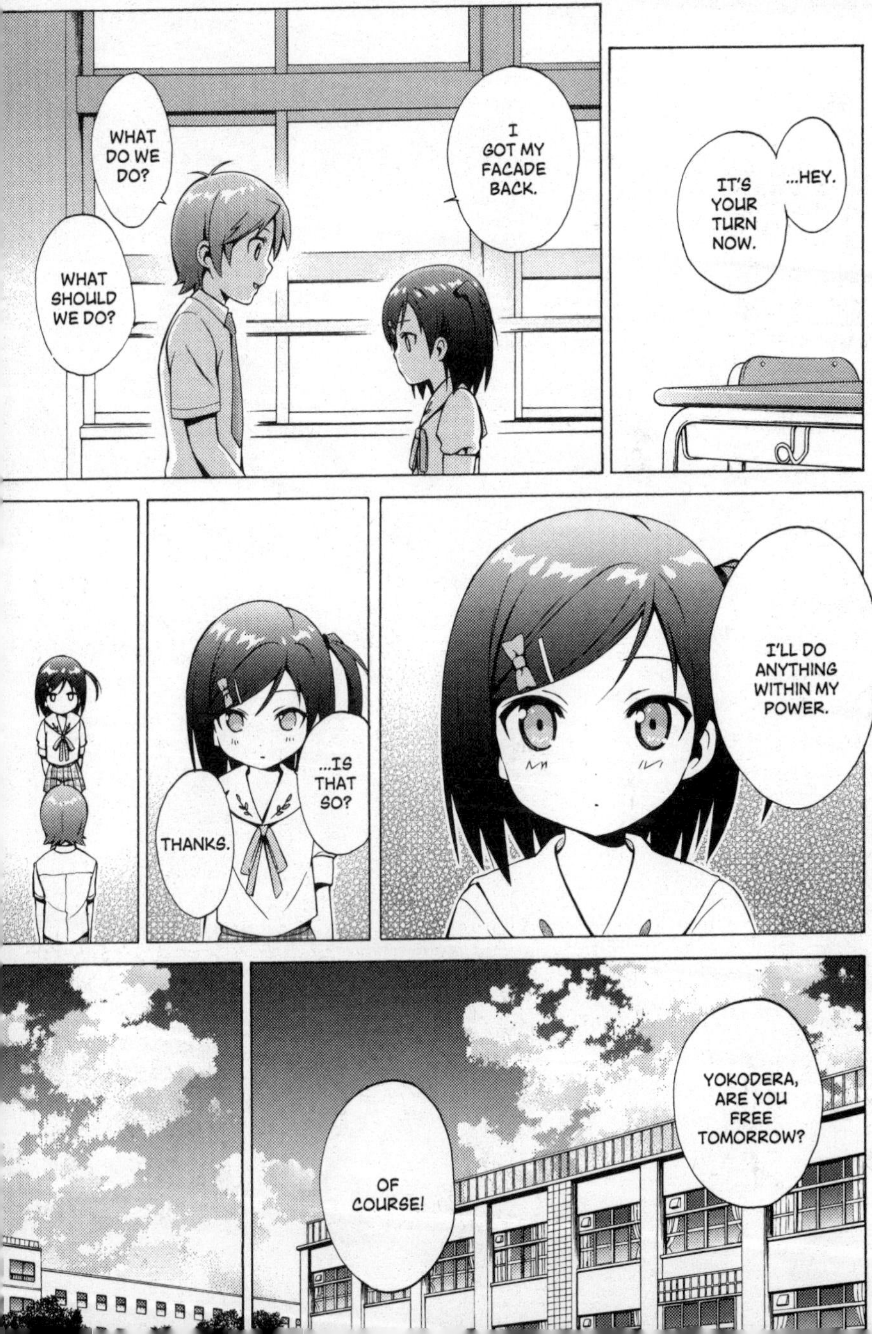
...HEY.
IT'S YOUR TURN NOW.
I GOT MY FACADE BACK.
WHAT DO WE DO?
WHAT SHOULD WE DO?
I'LL DO ANYTHING WITHIN MY POWER.
...IS THAT SO?
THANKS.
YOKODERA, ARE YOU FREE TOMORROW?
OF COURSE!

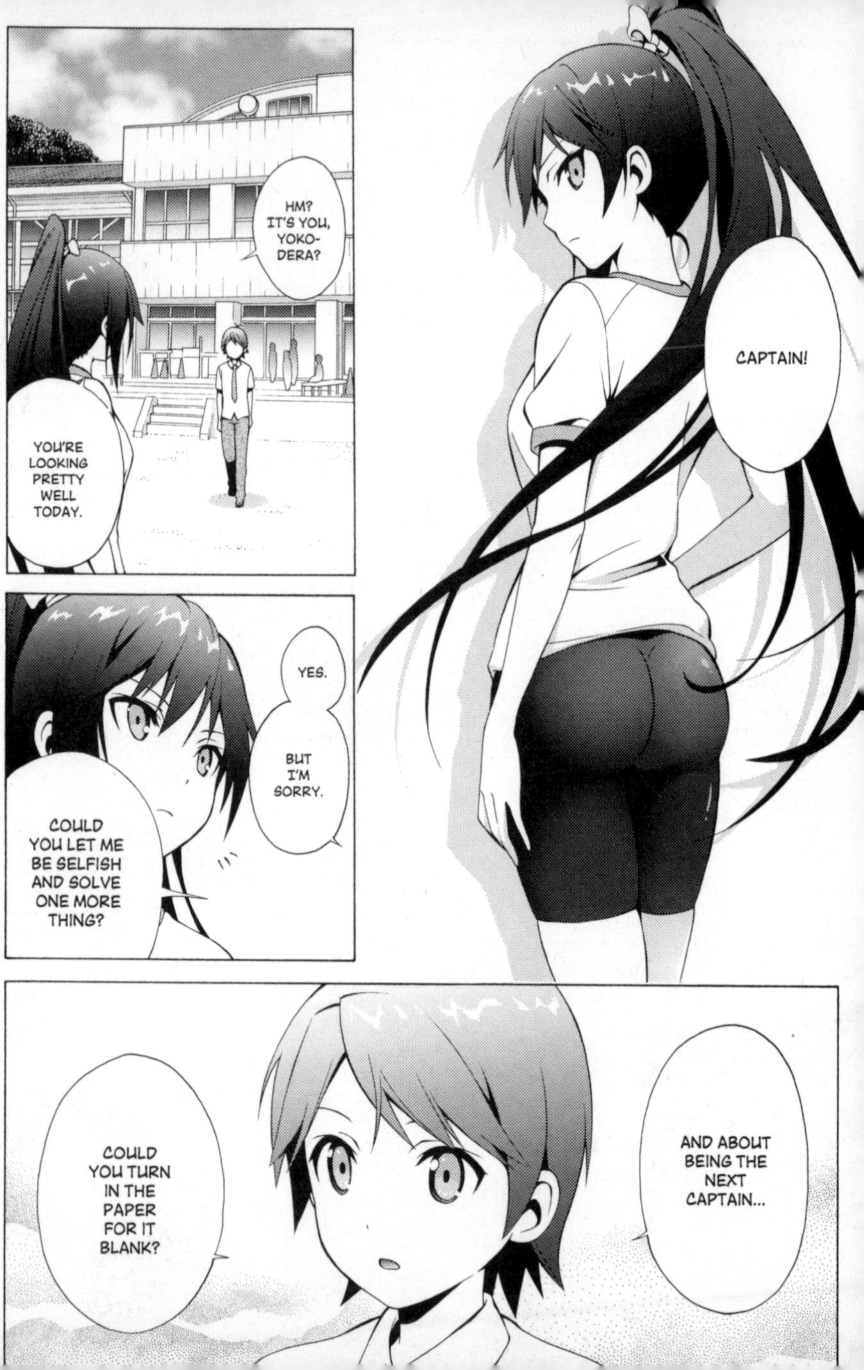
CAPTAIN!
HM? IT'S YOU, YOKO-DERA?
YOU'RE LOOKING PRETTY WELL TODAY.
YES.
BUT I'M SORRY.
COULD YOU LET ME BE SELFISH AND SOLVE ONE MORE THING?
AND ABOUT BEING THE NEXT CAPTAIN...
COULD YOU TURN IN THE PAPER FOR IT BLANK?

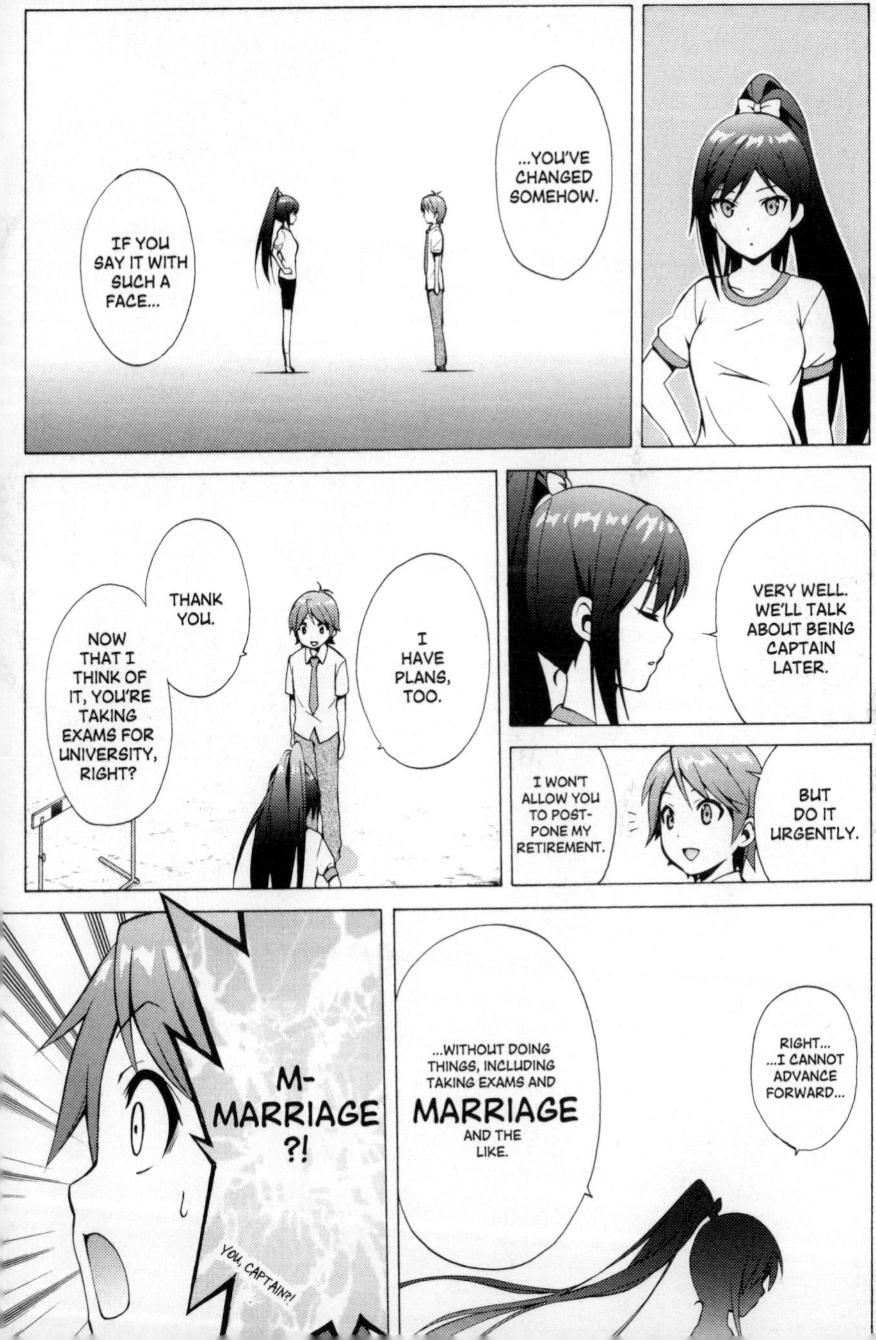
...YOU'VE CHANGED SOMEHOW.
IF YOU SAY IT WITH SUCH A FACE...
VERY WELL. WE'LL TALK ABOUT BEING CAPTAIN LATER.
BUT DO IT URGENTLY.
I WON'T ALLOW YOU TO POST-PONE MY RETIREMENT.
I HAVE PLANS, TOO.
THANK YOU.
NOW THAT I THINK OF IT, YOU'RE TAKING EXAMS FOR UNIVERSITY, RIGHT?
RIGHT... ...I CANNOT ADVANCE FORWARD...
...WITHOUT DOING THINGS, INCLUDING TAKING EXAMS AND MARRIAGE AND THE LIKE.
M-MARRIAGE ?!
YOU, CAPTAIN?!

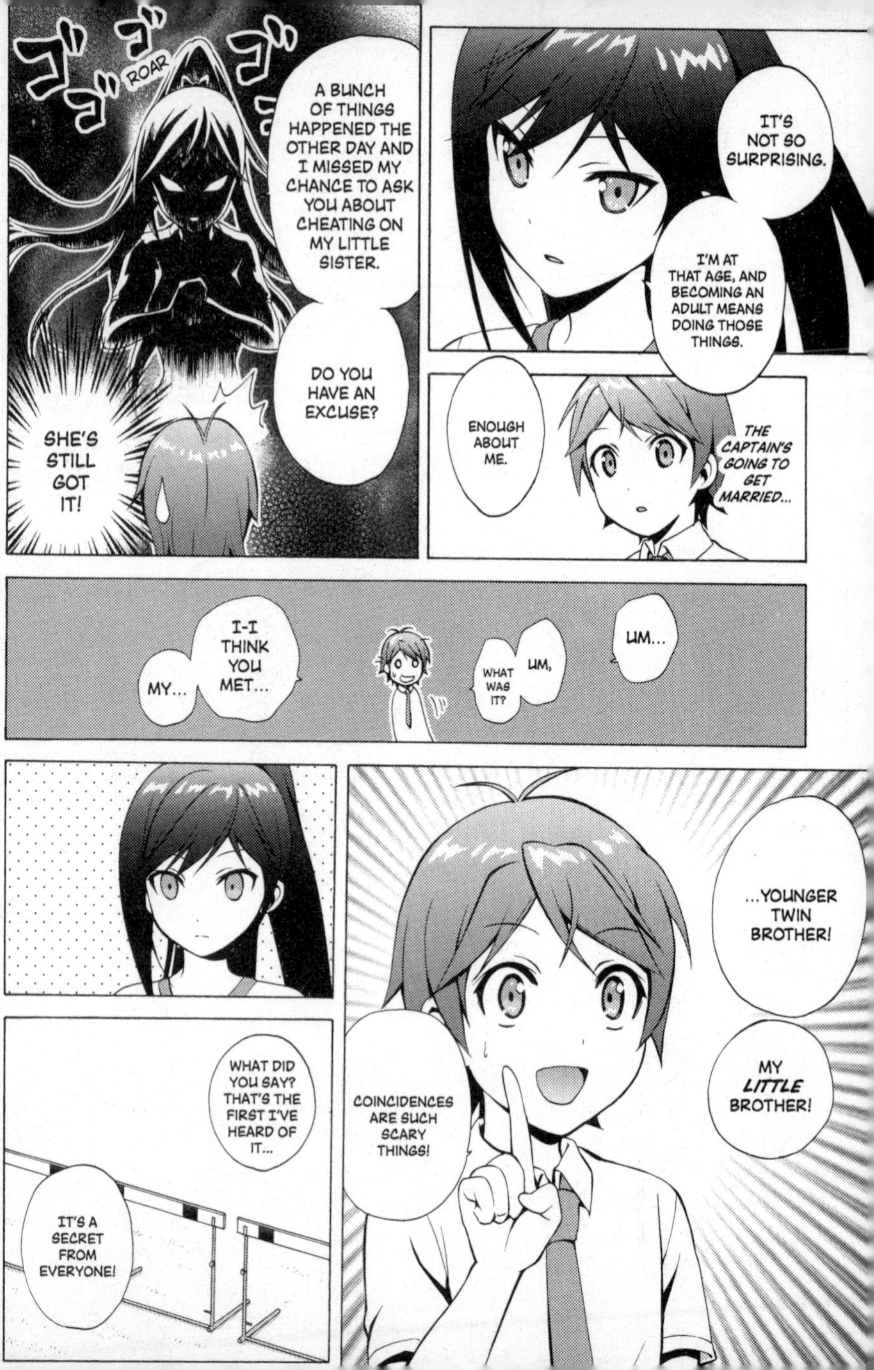
IT'S NOT SO SURPRISING.
I'M AT THAT AGE, AND BECOMING AN ADULT MEANS DOING THOSE THINGS.
THE CAPTAIN'S GOING TO GET MARRIED...
ENOUGH ABOUT ME.
ROAR
A BUNCH OF THINGS HAPPENED THE OTHER DAY AND I MISSED MY CHANCE TO ASK YOU ABOUT CHEATING ON MY LITTLE SISTER.
DO YOU HAVE AN EXCUSE?
SHE'S STILL GOT IT!
UM...
UM,
WHAT WAS IT?
I-I THINK YOU MET...
MY...
...YOUNGER TWIN BROTHER!
MY *LITTLE* BROTHER!
COINCIDENCES ARE SUCH SCARY THINGS!
WHAT DID YOU SAY? THAT'S THE FIRST I'VE HEARD OF IT...
IT'S A SECRET FROM EVERYONE!

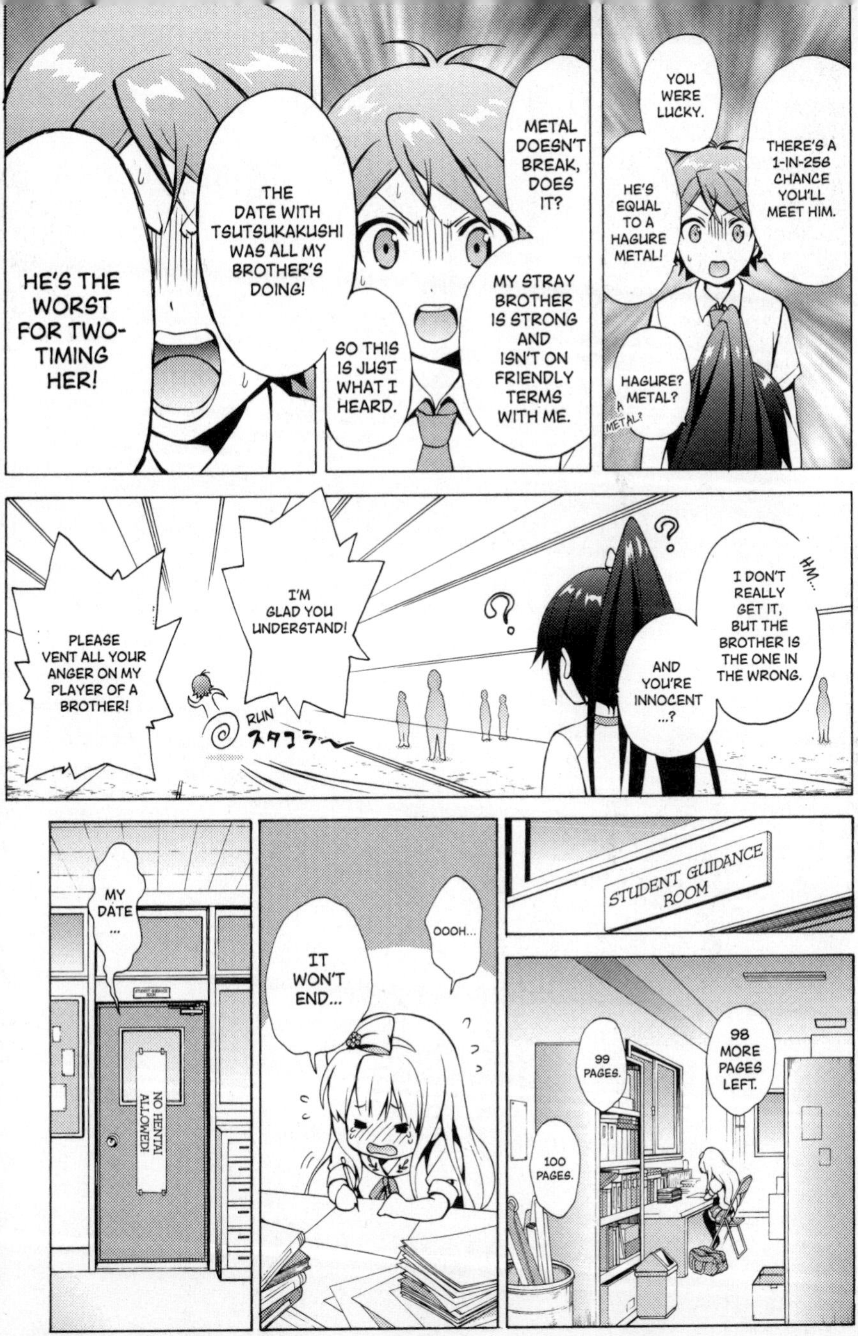
YOU WERE LUCKY.
THERE'S A 1-IN-256 CHANCE YOU'LL MEET HIM.
HE'S EQUAL TO A HAGURE METAL!
HAGURE? METAL?
A METAL?
METAL DOESN'T BREAK, DOES IT?
MY STRAY BROTHER IS STRONG AND ISN'T ON FRIENDLY TERMS WITH ME.
SO THIS IS JUST WHAT I HEARD.
THE DATE WITH TSUTSUKAKUSHI WAS ALL MY BROTHER'S DOING!
HE'S THE WORST FOR TWO-TIMING HER!
HM...
I DON'T REALLY GET IT, BUT THE BROTHER IS THE ONE IN THE WRONG.
AND YOU'RE INNOCENT ...?
I'M GLAD YOU UNDERSTAND!
PLEASE VENT ALL YOUR ANGER ON MY PLAYER OF A BROTHER!
RUN
スタコラ〜
STUDENT GUIDANCE ROOM
98 MORE PAGES LEFT.
99 PAGES.
100 PAGES.
OOOH...
IT WON'T END...
MY DATE ...
NO HENTAI ALLOWED!

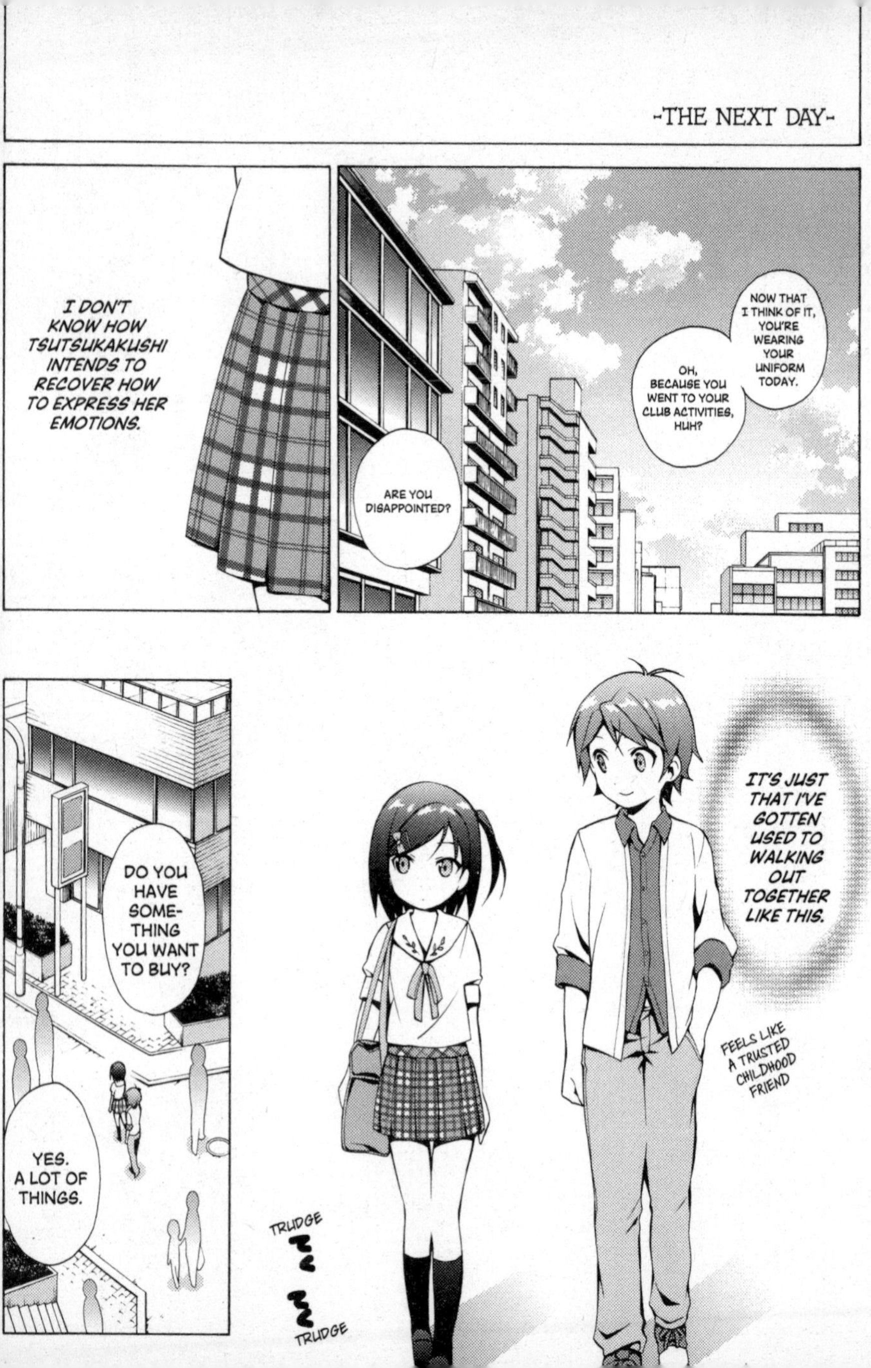
-THE NEXT DAY-
NOW THAT I THINK OF IT, YOU'RE WEARING YOUR UNIFORM TODAY.
OH, BECAUSE YOU WENT TO YOUR CLUB ACTIVITIES, HUH?
ARE YOU DISAPPOINTED?
I DON'T KNOW HOW TSUTSUKAKUSHI INTENDS TO RECOVER HOW TO EXPRESS HER EMOTIONS.
IT'S JUST THAT I'VE GOTTEN USED TO WALKING OUT TOGETHER LIKE THIS.
FEELS LIKE A TRUSTED CHILDHOOD FRIEND
TRUDGE
TRUDGE
DO YOU HAVE SOME-THING YOU WANT TO BUY?
YES. A LOT OF THINGS.

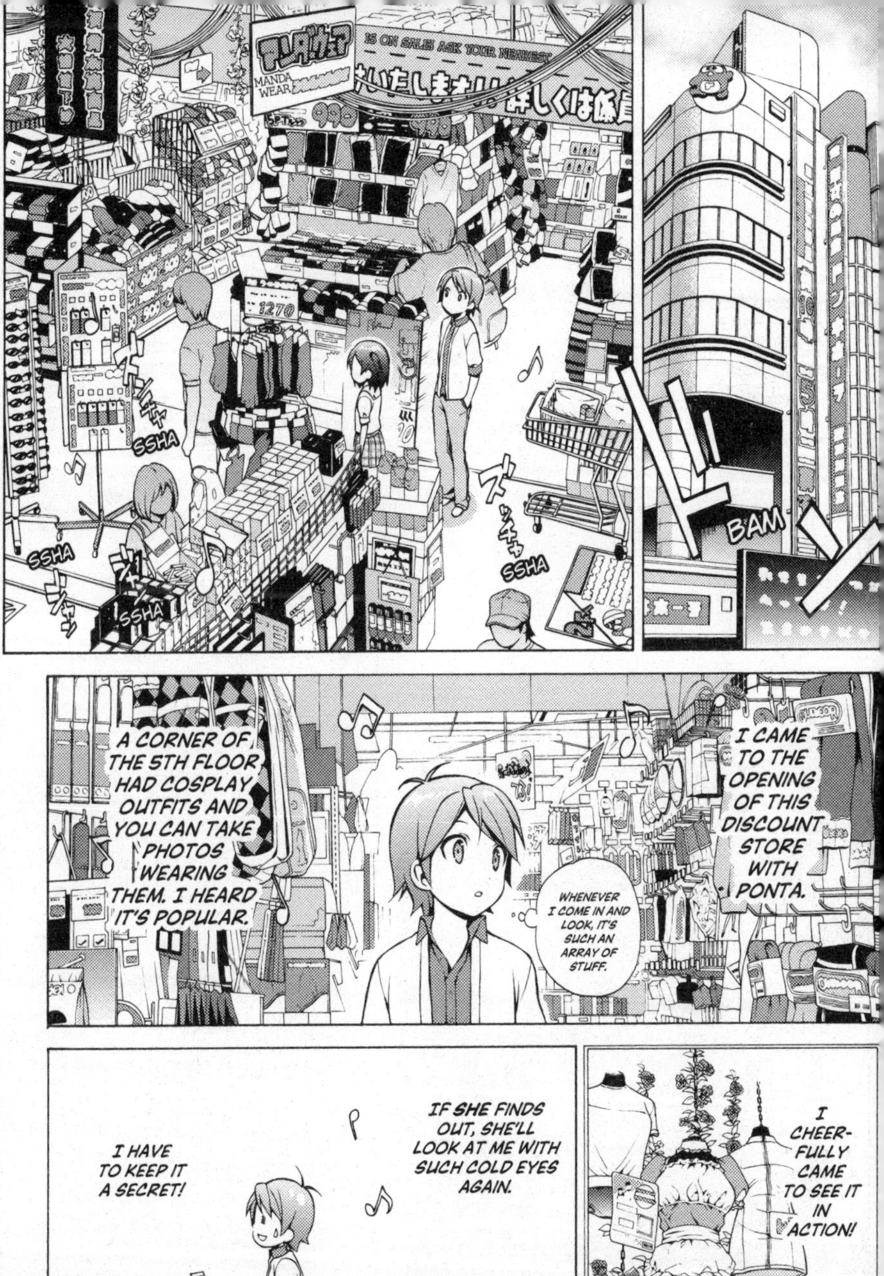
BAM
IS ON SALE! ASK YOUR NEAREST
MANDA WEAR
SSHA
SSHA
SSHA
SSHA
I CAME TO THE OPENING OF THIS DISCOUNT STORE WITH PONTA.
A CORNER OF THE 5TH FLOOR HAD COSPLAY OUTFITS AND YOU CAN TAKE PHOTOS WEARING THEM. I HEARD IT'S POPULAR.
WHENEVER I COME IN AND LOOK, IT'S SUCH AN ARRAY OF STUFF.
I CHEERFULLY CAME TO SEE IT IN ACTION!
IF SHE FINDS OUT, SHE'LL LOOK AT ME WITH SUCH COLD EYES AGAIN.
I HAVE TO KEEP IT A SECRET!

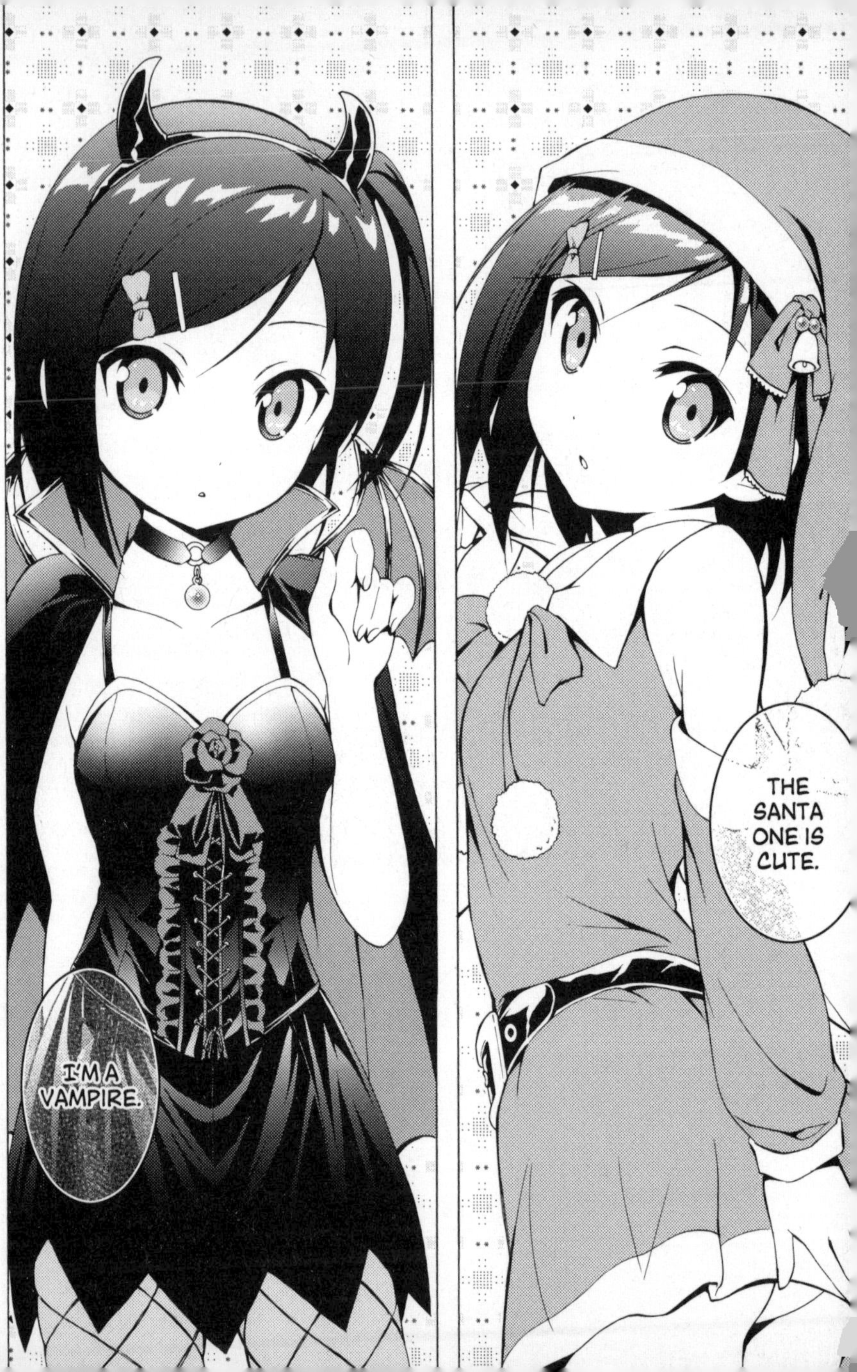
THE SANTA ONE IS CUTE.
I'M A VAMPIRE.

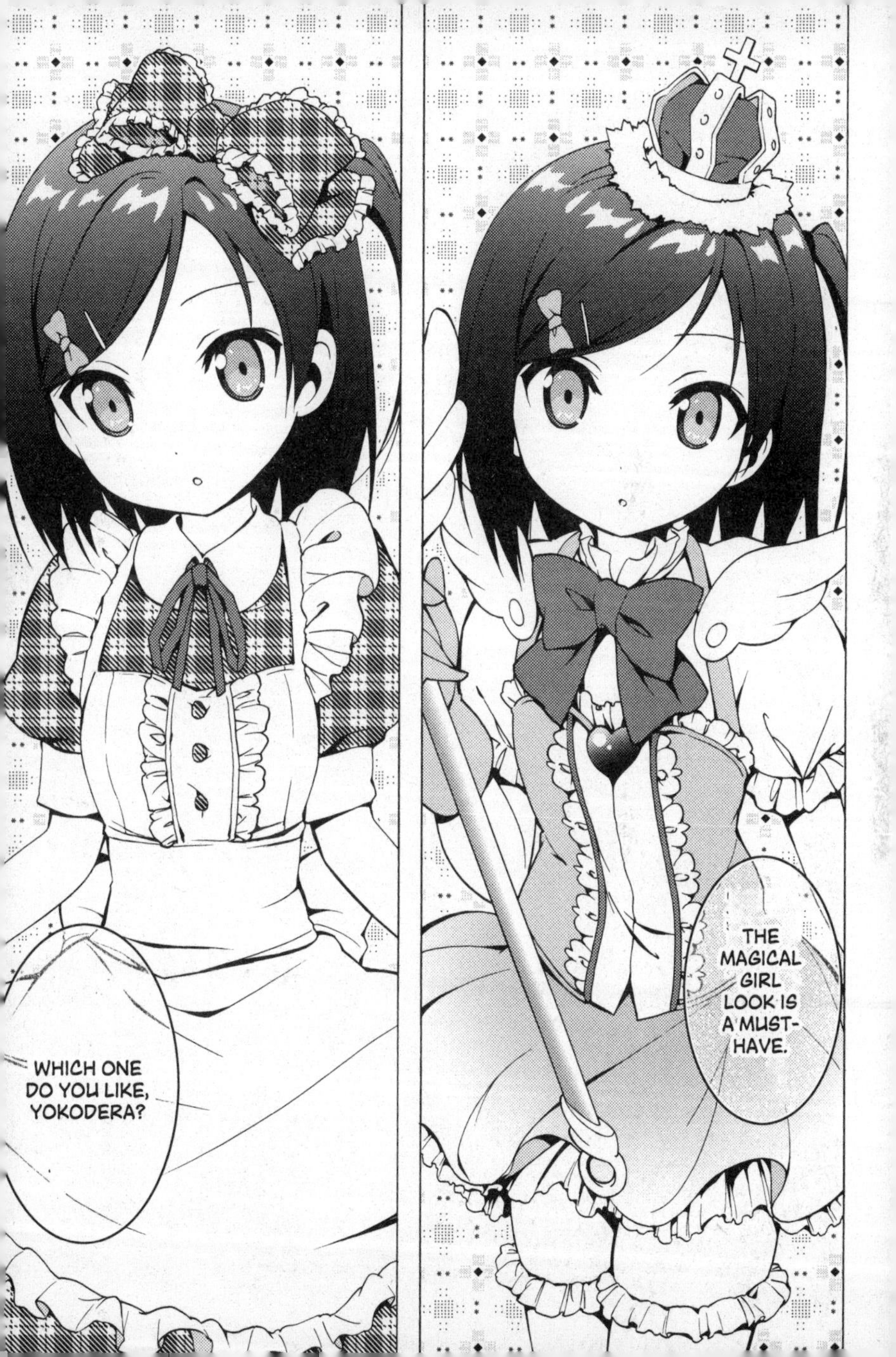
THE MAGICAL GIRL LOOK IS A MUST-HAVE.
WHICH ONE DO YOU LIKE, YOKODERA?

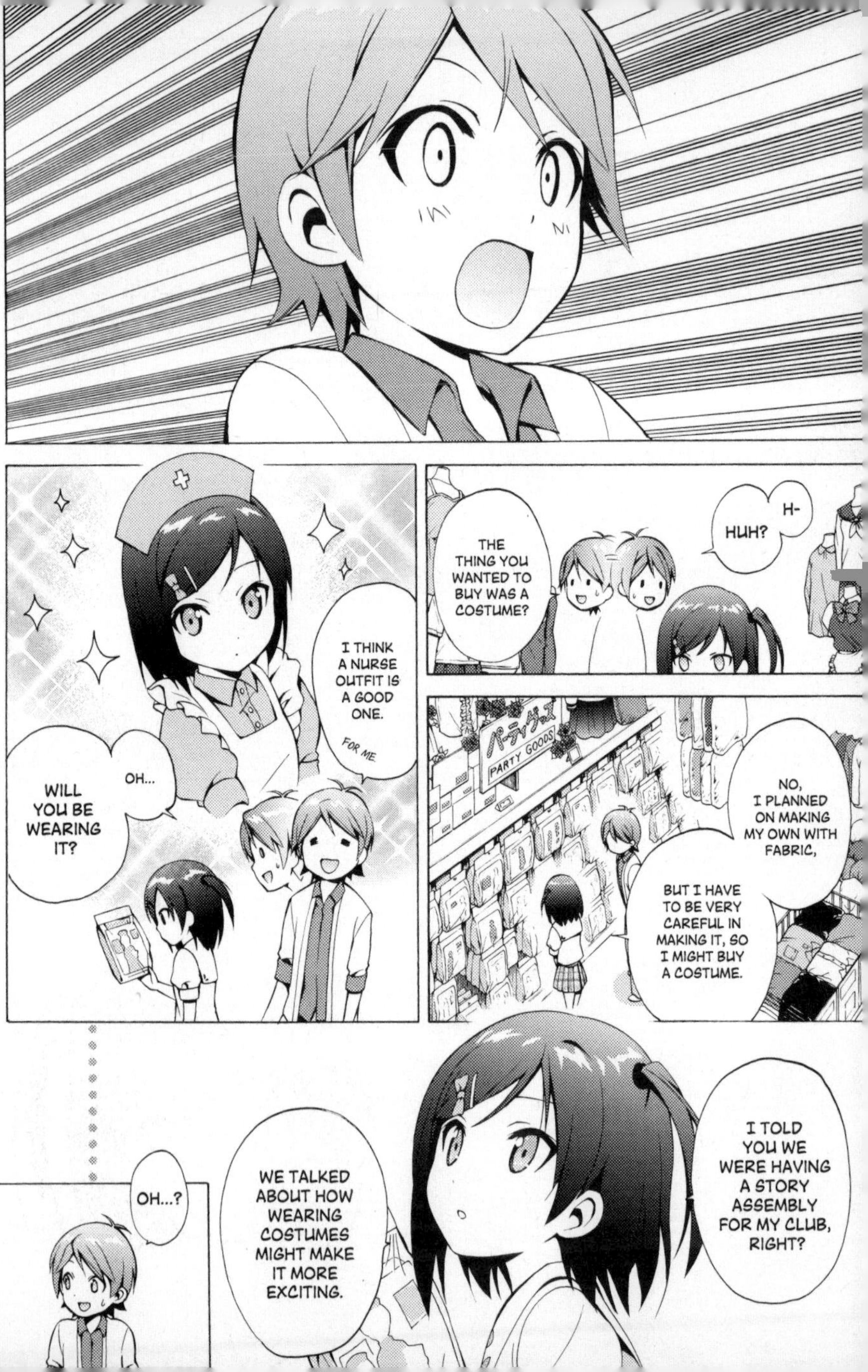
H- HUH?
THE THING YOU WANTED TO BUY WAS A COSTUME?
NO, I PLANNED ON MAKING MY OWN WITH FABRIC,
BUT I HAVE TO BE VERY CAREFUL IN MAKING IT, SO I MIGHT BUY A COSTUME.
PARTY GOODS
I THINK A NURSE OUTFIT IS A GOOD ONE.
FOR ME
OH...
WILL YOU BE WEARING IT?
I TOLD YOU WE WERE HAVING A STORY ASSEMBLY FOR MY CLUB, RIGHT?
WE TALKED ABOUT HOW WEARING COSTUMES MIGHT MAKE IT MORE EXCITING.
OH...?

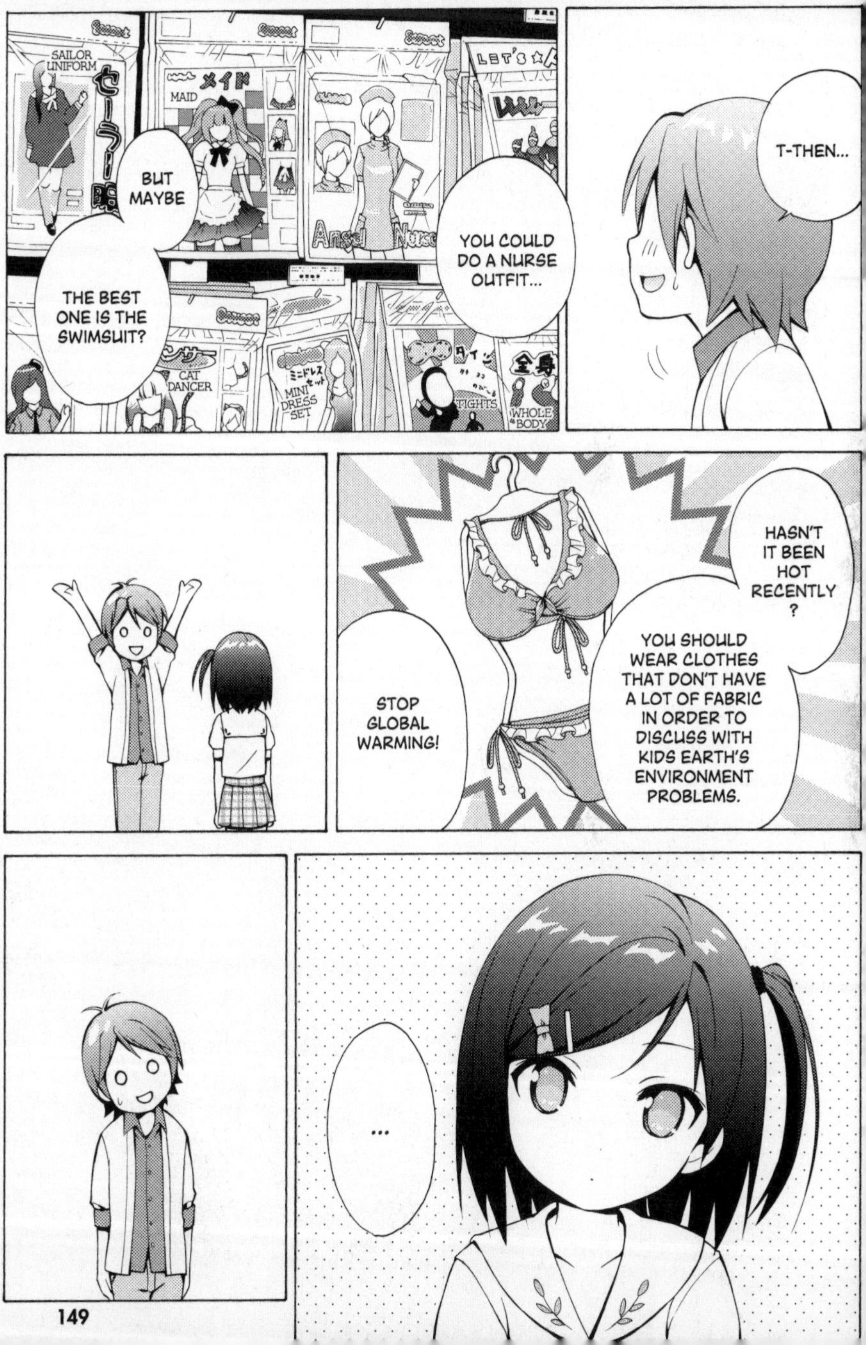
T-THEN...
YOU COULD DO A NURSE OUTFIT...
BUT MAYBE
THE BEST ONE IS THE SWIMSUIT?
SAILOR UNIFORM
MAID
CAT DANCER
MINI DRESS SET
TIGHTS
WHOLE BODY
HASN'T IT BEEN HOT RECENTLY?
YOU SHOULD WEAR CLOTHES THAT DON'T HAVE A LOT OF FABRIC IN ORDER TO DISCUSS WITH KIDS EARTH'S ENVIRONMENT PROBLEMS.
STOP GLOBAL WARMING!
...

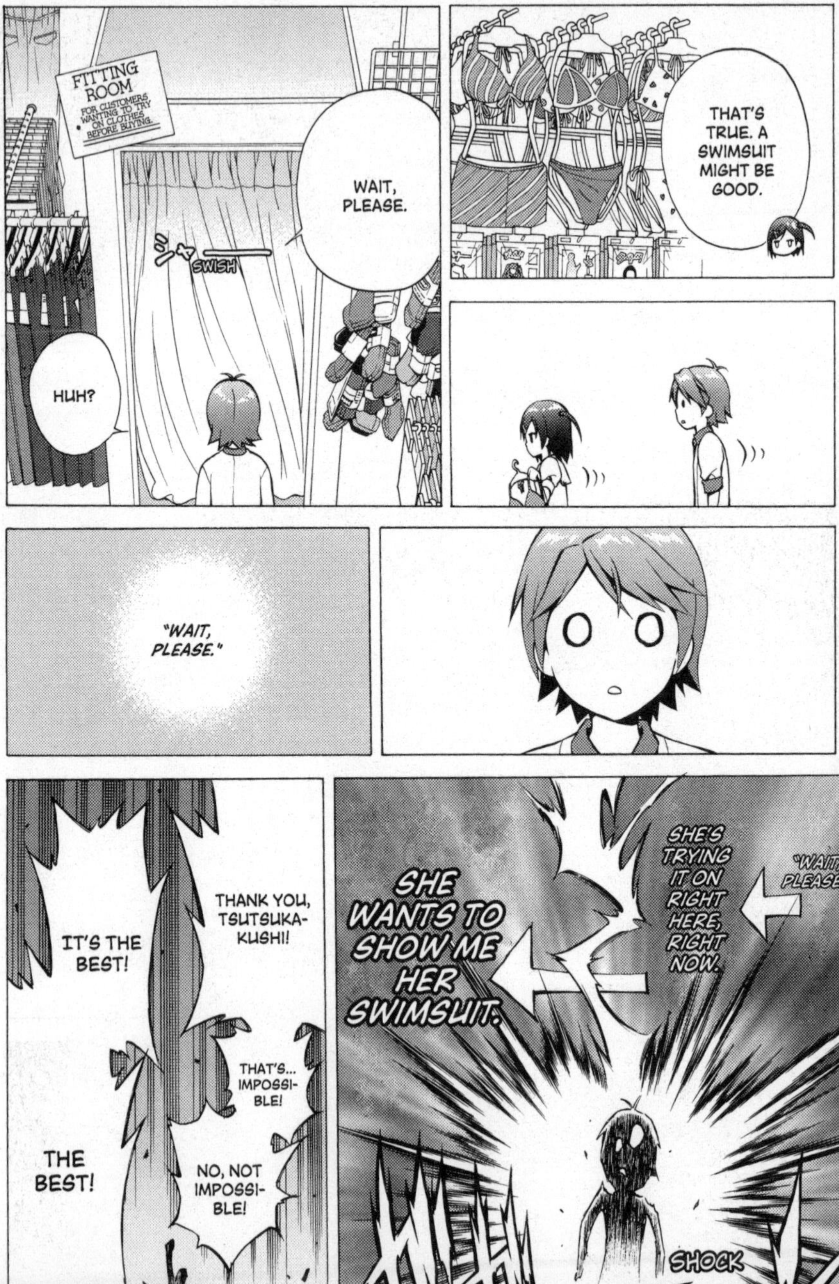
THAT'S TRUE. A SWIMSUIT MIGHT BE GOOD.
WAIT, PLEASE.
FITTING ROOM
FOR CUSTOMERS WANTING TO TRY ON CLOTHES BEFORE BUYING.
SWISH
HUH?
"WAIT, PLEASE."
"WAIT, PLEASE."
SHE'S TRYING IT ON RIGHT HERE, RIGHT NOW.
SHE WANTS TO SHOW ME HER SWIMSUIT.
SHOCK
THANK YOU, TSUTSUKAKUSHI!
IT'S THE BEST!
THAT'S... IMPOSSIBLE!
NO, NOT IMPOSSIBLE!
THE BEST!

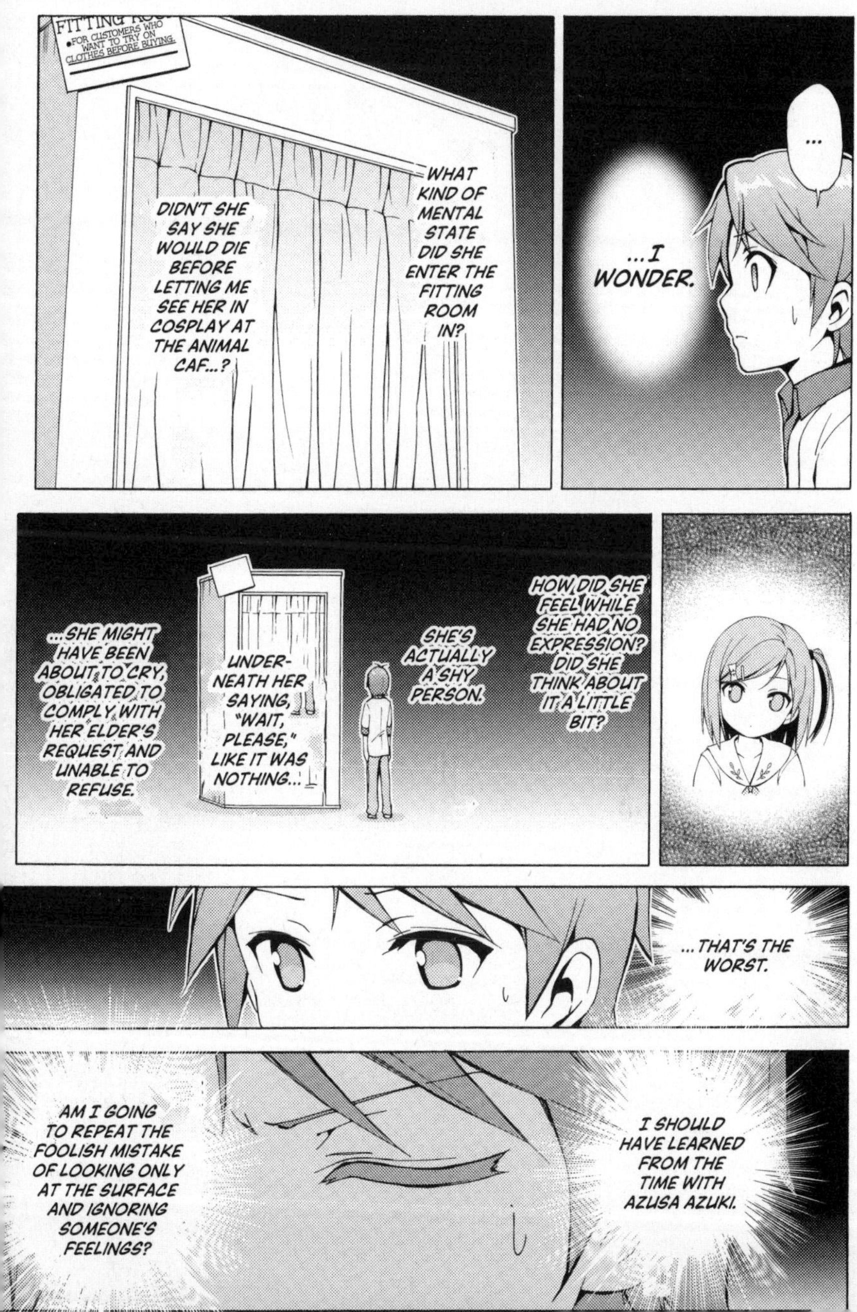
...
...I WONDER.
FITTING ROO
●FOR CUSTOMERS WHO WANT TO TRY ON CLOTHES BEFORE BUYING.
WHAT KIND OF MENTAL STATE DID SHE ENTER THE FITTING ROOM IN?
DIDN'T SHE SAY SHE WOULD DIE BEFORE LETTING ME SEE HER IN COSPLAY AT THE ANIMAL CAF...?
HOW DID SHE FEEL WHILE SHE HAD NO EXPRESSION? DID SHE THINK ABOUT IT A LITTLE BIT?
SHE'S ACTUALLY A SHY PERSON.
UNDER-NEATH HER SAYING, "WAIT, PLEASE," LIKE IT WAS NOTHING...
...SHE MIGHT HAVE BEEN ABOUT TO CRY, OBLIGATED TO COMPLY WITH HER ELDER'S REQUEST AND UNABLE TO REFUSE.
...THAT'S THE WORST.
I SHOULD HAVE LEARNED FROM THE TIME WITH AZUSA AZUKI.
AM I GOING TO REPEAT THE FOOLISH MISTAKE OF LOOKING ONLY AT THE SURFACE AND IGNORING SOMEONE'S FEELINGS?

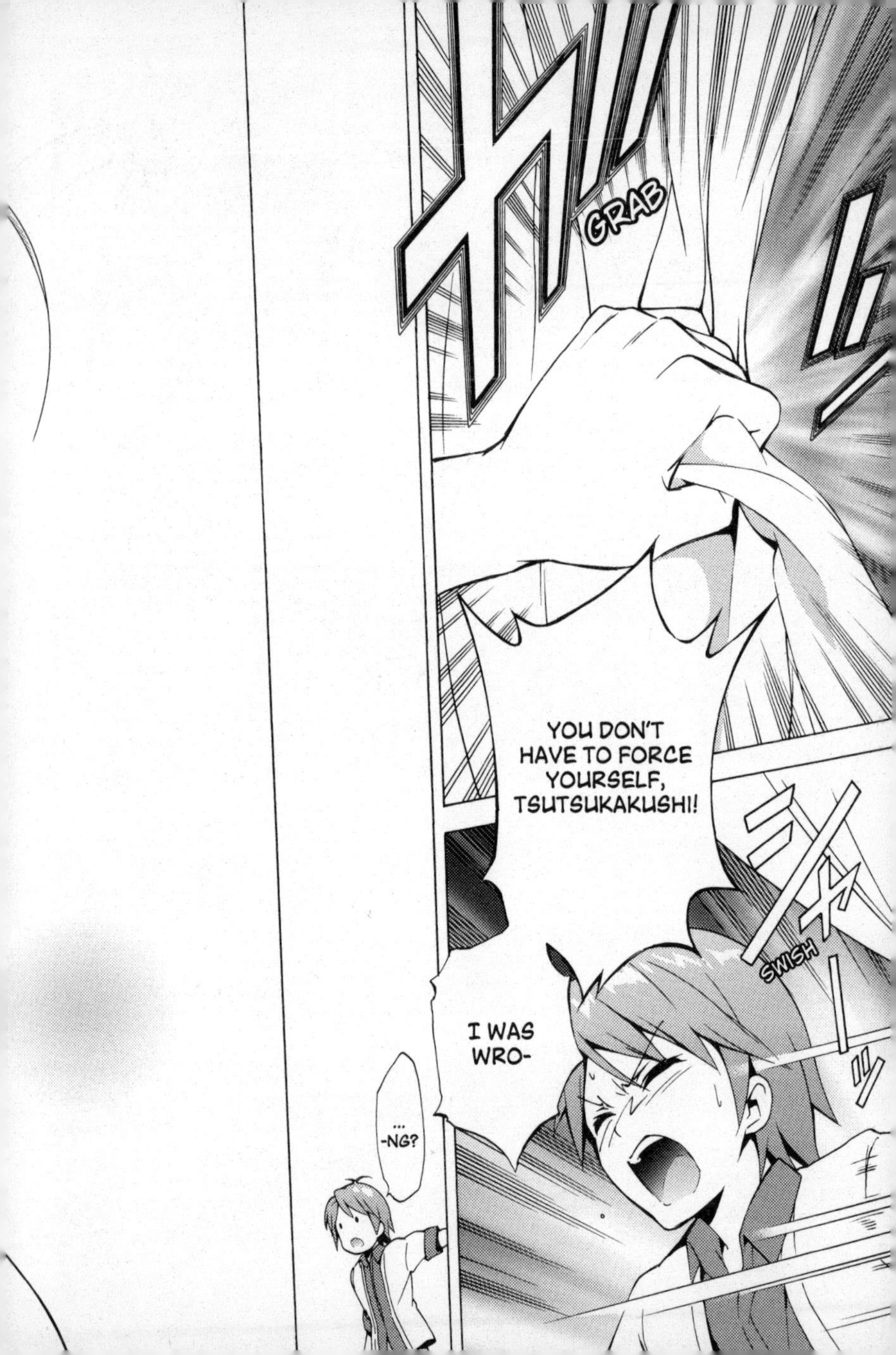
GRAB
YOU DON'T HAVE TO FORCE YOURSELF, TSUTSUKAKUSHI!
SWISH
I WAS WRO-
... -NG?

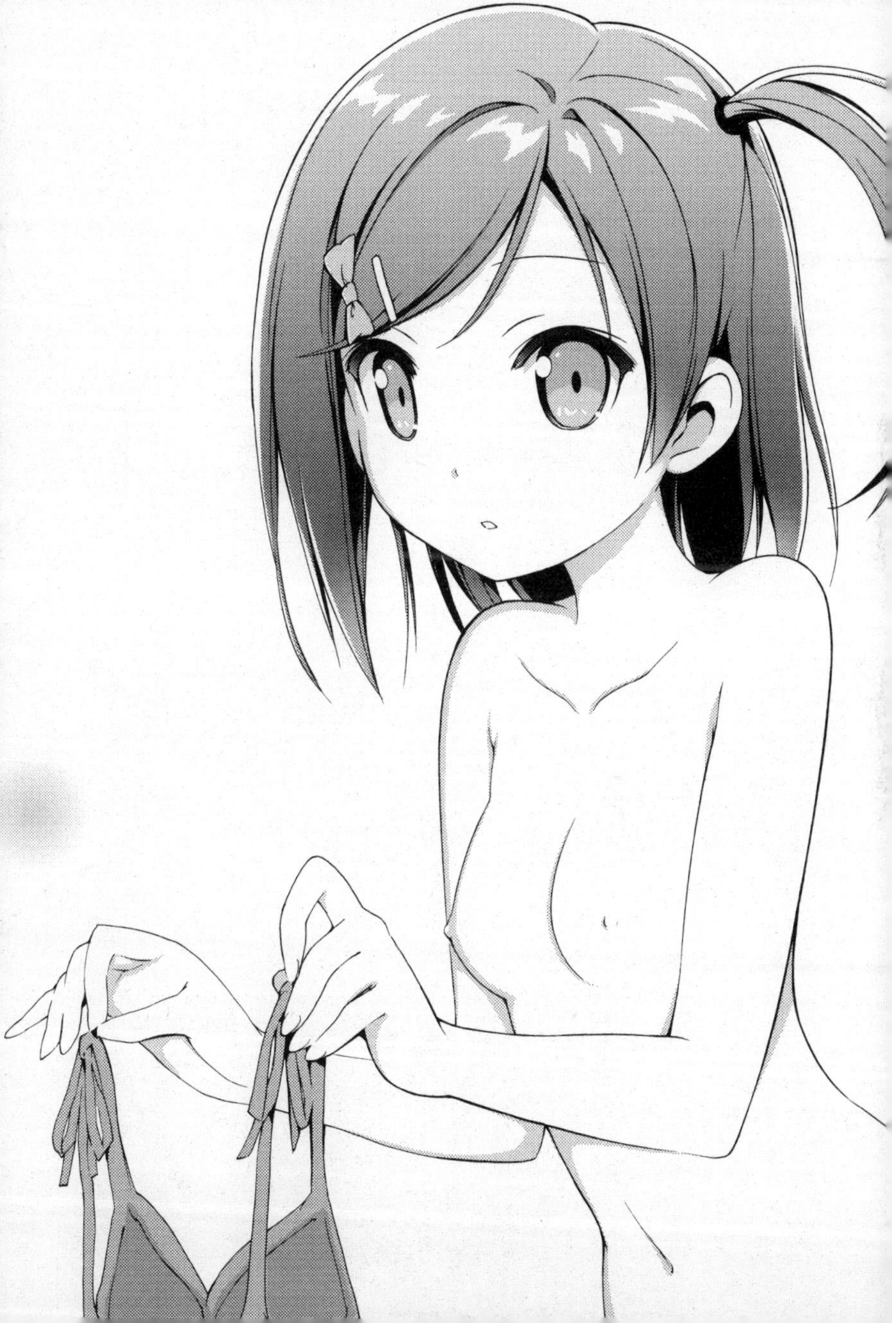

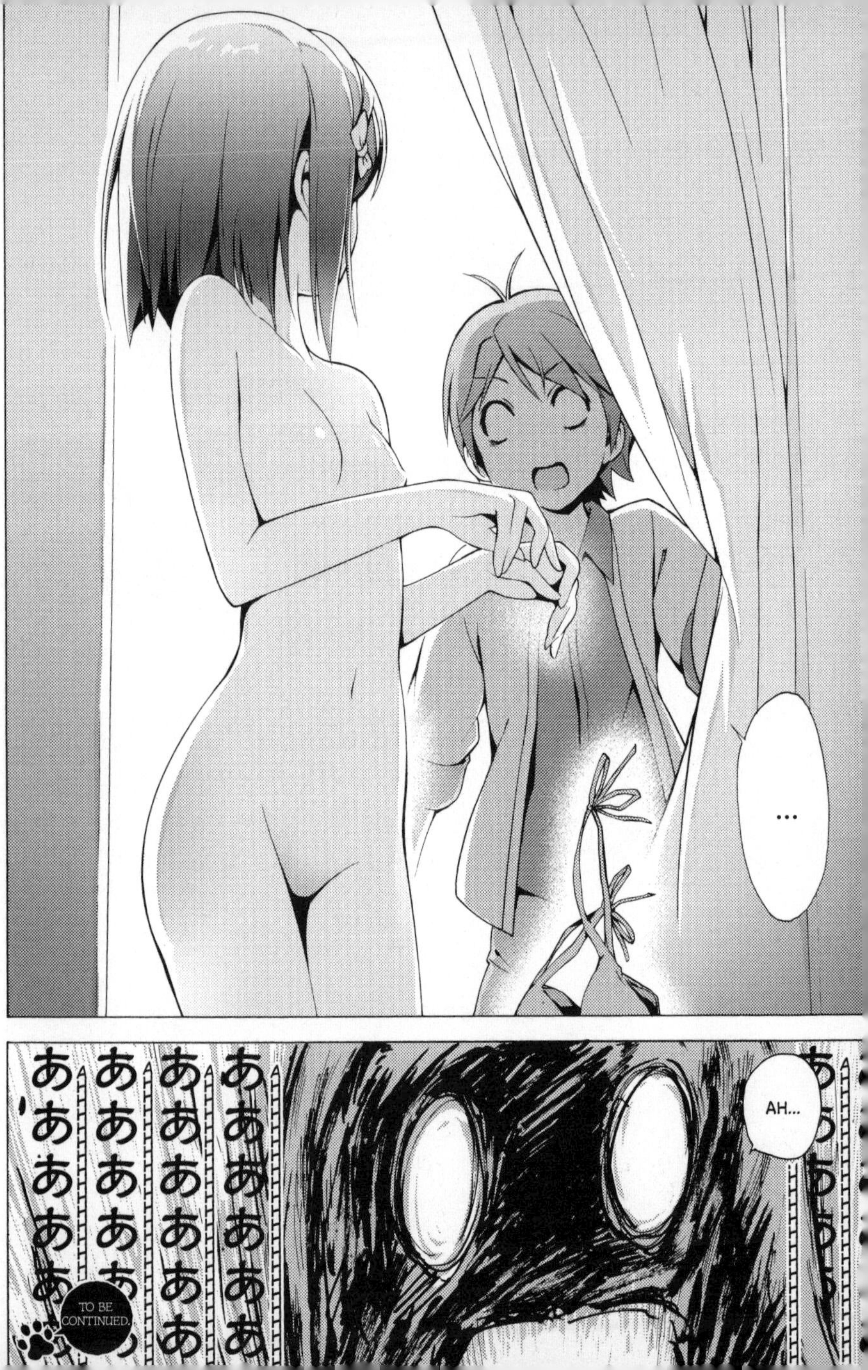
...
AH...
ああああああ
ああああああ
ああああああ
あああああ
TO BE CONTINUED.

The "HENTAI" prince and the stony cat.

変態王子と笑わない猫。

AFTERWORD

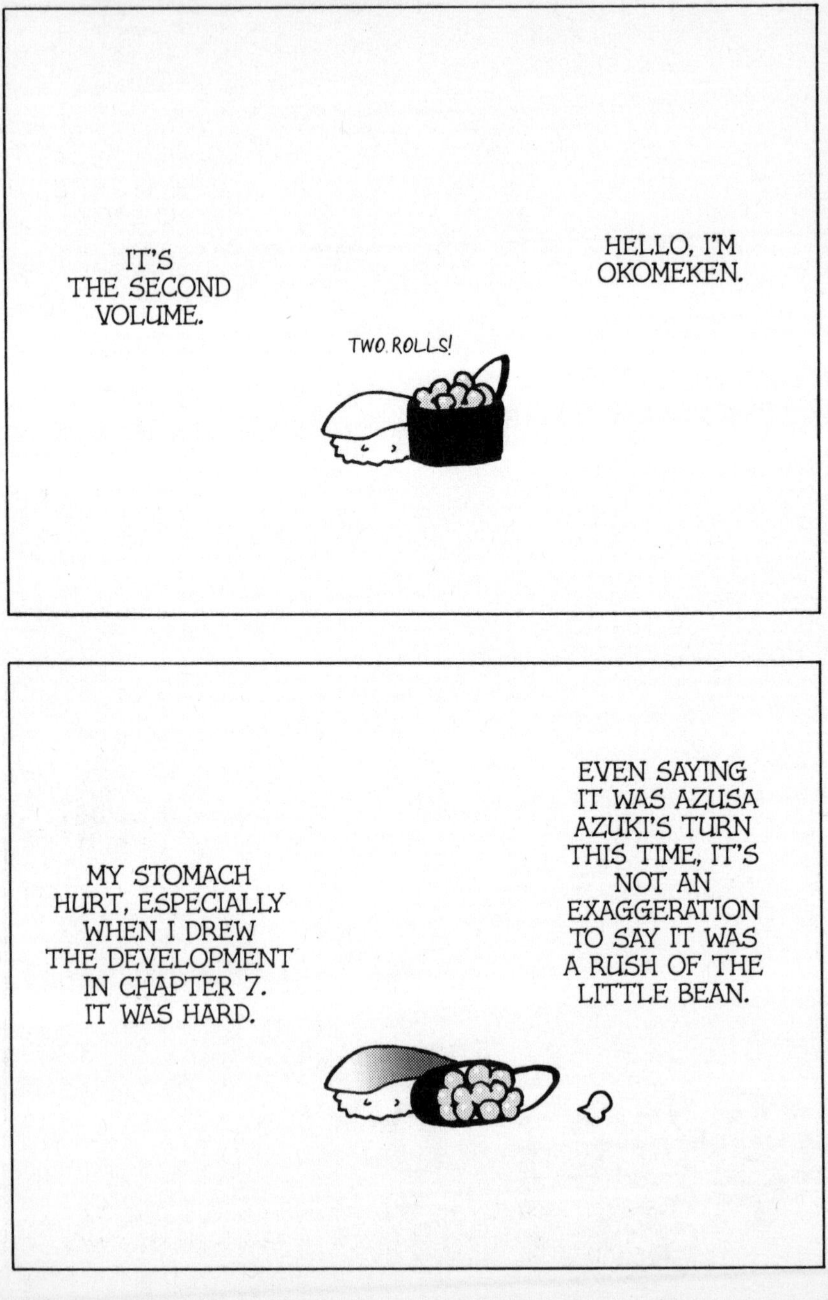
HELLO, I'M OKOMEKEN.
IT'S THE SECOND VOLUME.
TWO ROLLS!
EVEN SAYING IT WAS AZUSA AZUKI'S TURN THIS TIME, IT'S NOT AN EXAGGERATION TO SAY IT WAS A RUSH OF THE LITTLE BEAN.
MY STOMACH HURT, ESPECIALLY WHEN I DREW THE DEVELOPMENT IN CHAPTER 7. IT WAS HARD.

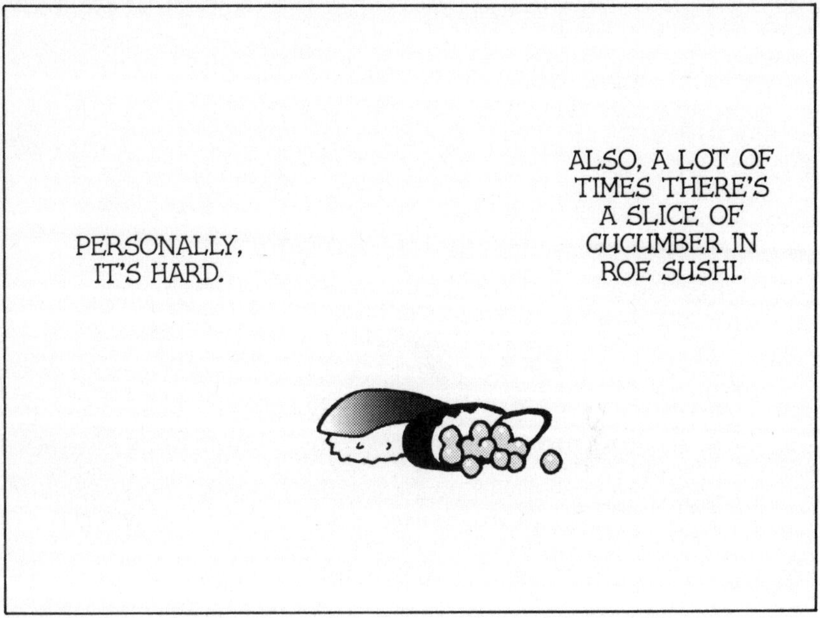
ALSO, A LOT OF TIMES THERE'S A SLICE OF CUCUMBER IN ROE SUSHI.
PERSONALLY, IT'S HARD.

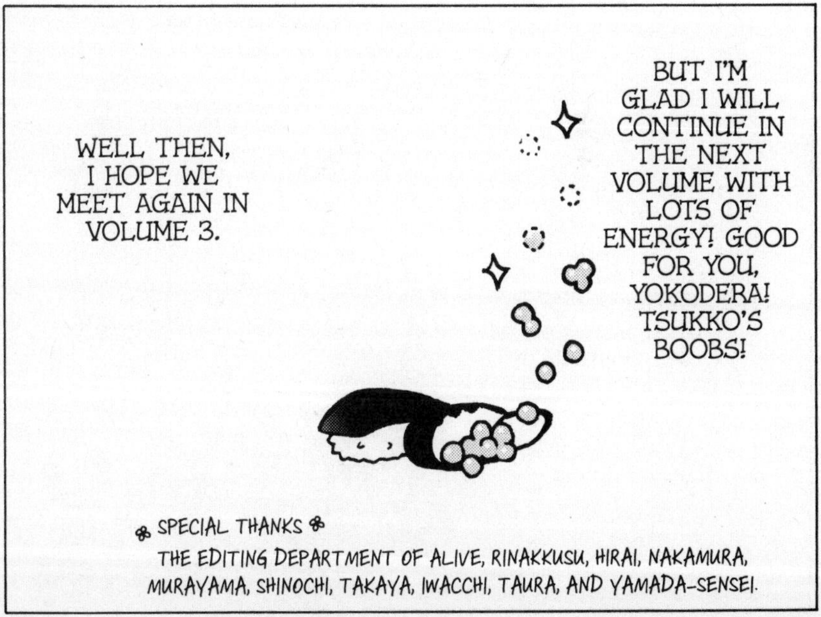
BUT I'M GLAD I WILL CONTINUE IN THE NEXT VOLUME WITH LOTS OF ENERGY! GOOD FOR YOU, YOKODERA! TSUKKO'S BOOBS!
WELL THEN, I HOPE WE MEET AGAIN IN VOLUME 3.
SPECIAL THANKS
THE EDITING DEPARTMENT OF ALIVE, RINAKKUSU, HIRAI, NAKAMURA, MURAYAMA, SHINOCHI, TAKAYA, IWACCHI, TAURA, AND YAMADA-SENSEI.

The "HENTAI" prince and the stony cat.

変態王子と笑わない猫。

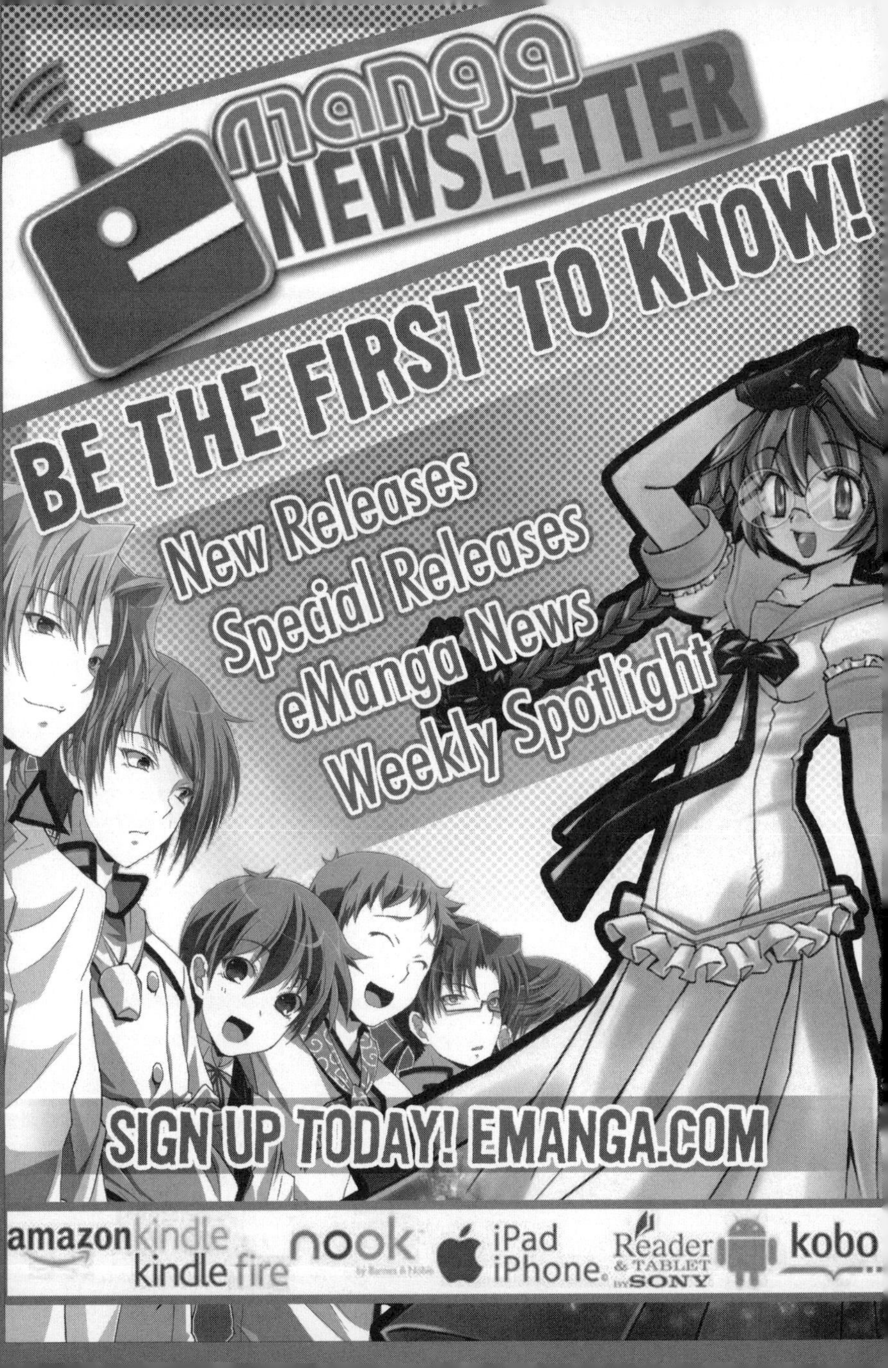
eManga NEWSLETTER
BE THE FIRST TO KNOW!
New Releases
Special Releases
eManga News
Weekly Spotlight
SIGN UP TODAY! EMANGA.COM
amazon kindle
kindle fire
nook
iPad
iPhone
Reader & TABLET BY SONY
kobo

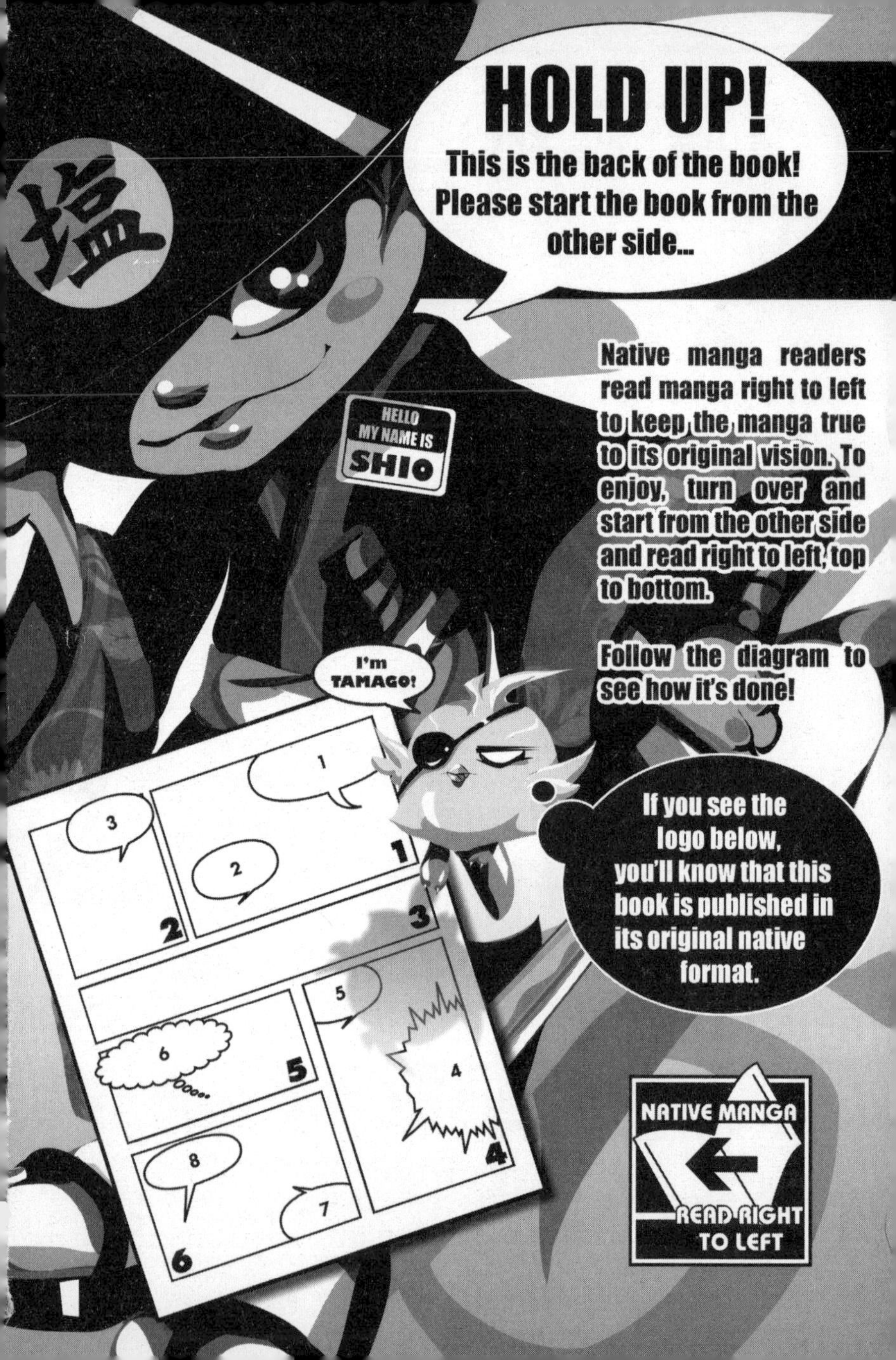
HOLD UP!
This is the back of the book! Please start the book from the other side...
HELLO MY NAME IS SHIO
Native manga readers read manga right to left to keep the manga true to its original vision. To enjoy, turn over and start from the other side and read right to left, top to bottom.
Follow the diagram to see how it's done!
I'm TAMAGO!
1
2
3
4
5
6
7
8
oooo
If you see the logo below, you'll know that this book is published in its original native format.
NATIVE MANGA
READ RIGHT TO LEFT